Haynes
Restoration
Manual

Ford Escort & Cortina MkI & MkII

Kim Henson

First published by G. T. Foulis & Co as
Ford Escort & Cortina Purchase and
Restoration Guide in 1987
Reprinted 1990, 1993 and 1996
Reprinted by Haynes Publishing as
Ford Escort & Cortina MkI & MkII
Restoration Manual in 2003

© Kim Henson 1987

A catalogue record for this book is
available from the British Library

ISBN 1 85960 978 3

Library of Congress catalog card
number 86-83369

Haynes Publishing, Sparkford, Yeovil,
Somerset BA22 7JJ, UK

Tel: 01963 442030
Fax: 01963 440001
Int. tel: +44 1963 442030
Int. fax: +44 1963 440001

E-mail: sales@haynes-manuals.co.uk
Website: www.haynes.co.uk

Haynes Publications Inc.
861 Lawrence Drive, Newbury Park,
California 91320, USA

Printed in USA

Jurisdictions which have strict
emission control laws may consider
any modifications to a vehicle to be an
infringement of those laws. You are
advised to check with the appropriate
body or authority whether your
proposed modification complies fully
with the law. The publishers can
accept no liability in this regard.

While every effort is taken to ensure
the accuracy of all information given in
this book, no liability can be accepted
by the author or publishers for any
loss, damage or injury caused by
errors in or, omissions from, the
information given.

Contents

Foreword by Rodney Jacques

Fords have always been cars beloved of enthusiasts – and particularly 'do it yourself' enthusiasts. The Cortinas and Escort Mark I and II are no exception. Their basic simplicity of design and inherent ruggedness means of course that they are ideal for restoration at home.

However, there has never – until now – been a book which explains in detail the history of the cars, what to look for when buying one (and in particular a restoration project vehicle) and step by step instructions on how to tackle the various aspects of restoring these vehicles.

In producing this book, Kim has tackled the restoration jobs at first hand. In doing so, he has met – and overcome – the same problems that someone working at home would encounter, and described these in graphic detail in the book.

Wherever possible Kim has used 'standard' tools, and has described how several jobs which 'officially' need special tools can be tackled by improvisation, and also how many of the common pitfalls can be avoided.

The book is, of course, essentially practical, and within its covers can be found a multitude of hints, tips and down to earth advice for any would-be restorer, whether a beginner or an 'old hand'. As well as detailed information on the individual histories of the Cortina and Escort models, and a full chapter on what to look for when buying a car, there is specific and detailed advice on restoring the bodywork, mechanical components, electrical systems and interiors of each model. There is also an extremely useful chapter on 'Modifications', covering many of the ways in which the cars can be improved.

One of the many good aspects of the book is that it takes the reader through stages in restoration ranging from 'easy first steps' to major rebuild operations. For example, in the bodywork chapter, the operations covered range from simply removing items of trim, to minor bodywork jobs *(not* requiring specialist tools or welding gear) to panel, sill and floor replacement! This approach is continued through the book, so that *all* aspects of restoration are covered. In addition, where it is perhaps prudent to call upon professional help – to save time and money – Kim has not been afraid to say so.

Rodney Jacques
(Technical Editor,
'Practical Motorist' Magazine).

Using this book

The layout of this book has been designed to be both attractive and easy to follow. However, to obtain the maximum benefit from the book, it is important to note the following points;

1) Apart from the introductory pages, this book is split into two sections; chapters 1 to 8 dealing with history, buying and practical procedures; appendices 1 to 7 providing supplementary information. Each chapter/appendix may be sub-divided into sections and even sub sections. Section headings are in italic type between horizontal lines and sub-section headings are similar, but without horizontal lines.

2) Step-by-step photograph captions, and line drawing captions are an integral part of the text (except those in chapters 1, 2 and 3) – therefore the photographs/drawings and their captions are arranged to "read" in exactly the same way as the normal text. In other words they run down each column and the columns run from left to right of the page.

Each photograph and diagram carries an alpha-numeric identity, relating it to a specific section. The letters before the caption number are simply the initial letters of key words in the relevant section heading, whilst the caption number shows the position of the particular photograph in the section's picture sequence. Thus photograph caption 'DR22' is the 22nd photograph in the section headed "Door Repairs", for example.

3) All references to the left or right of the vehicle are from the point of view of somebody standing behind the car, looking forwards.

4) The bodywork repair chapter deals with problems particular to the Ford Cortina and Escort, Mark I and II models. In concentrating on these aspects, the depth of treatment of general body repair techniques is necessarily limited. For more detailed information covering all aspects of body repair it is recommended that reference be made to the Haynes book 'The Car Bodywork Repair Manual', by Lindsay Porter.

5) Because this book concentrates upon restoration, regular maintenance procedures and normal mechanical repairs of all the car's components are beyond its scope. It is therefore strongly recommended that the *Haynes Owners' Workshop Manual* relevant to your particular model should be used as a companion volume.

6) We know it's a boring subject, especially when you really want to get on with a job – but your safety, through the use of correct workshop procedures, must ALWAYS be your foremost consideration. It is essential that you read, and UNDERSTAND appendix 1 before undertaking any of the practical tasks detailed in this book.

7) Before starting any particular job it is important that you read the introduction to the relevant Chapter or Section, taking particular note of 'safety' notes, and 'special' tool requirements. It is recommended that you read through the section from start to finish before getting into the job.

8) Whilst great care is taken to ensure that the information in this book is as accurate as possible, the author, editor or publisher cannot accept any liability for loss, damage or injury caused by errors in, or omissions from, the information given.

Introduction
and Acknowledgements

Old Fords Never Die . . .' was the slogan adorning the back of a very tidy Mark I Cortina I was following on the way home from a rally some time ago. How true it is. The Ford Cortina and Escort Mark I and II models have brought family motoring to millions of people since the early 1960s, when the first Cortina was produced. Like the famous Ford Model Y of the 1930s, these Fords were straightforward, easy to drive and easy to maintain vehicles, and their popularity has been maintained largely because of this.

Of course the cars developed, with regular model changes and updating, but the basic design concept remained the same throughout. Uncomplicated, 'traditional' front engine/rear wheel drive, plus room for the family and all the luggage, meant that Ford's slogan of the 1980s, 'Simple is Efficient' in fact applied long before it was officially introduced, with the Mark III (front wheel drive) Escort.

Not that Fords didn't give choice in their models; with a range of trim levels and engine sizes for both Cortina and Escort, there was a car to suit everyone's needs. The fast versions of both cars were well ahead of their time in terms of performance and roadholding. The Cortina Lotus, when introduced, was looked

upon as a yardstick by which others could be judged, for acceleration and top speed. The story continued with Escort models such as the Twin Cam, RS 1600, Mexico, RS 2000, RS 1800 – the list is formidable.

Success in motor sport helped promote the Ford name throughout the 1960s and 1970s, and indeed many of the Escorts, in particular, are still used in competition today.

Of course a car doesn't need to be fast for it to be worth restoring. One of the interesting aspects of these models is that there is such a range to choose from, from the 1200cc Cortinas and 1100cc Escorts to Lotus Cortinas and much modified RS 2000s – there are cars to suit all tastes.

As the variety of cars is wide, so is the range of uses to which they are put. There are many Mark I Cortinas still in everyday use, for example, while others are kept just for occasional outings to 'old' car rallies and 'concours' competitions, and there is a similar diversity of use applicable to all the models, from the earliest 1962 cars to the late, 1980 vehicles.

One of the nice things about restoring one of these Fords is, of course, that it can be put to practical use, whether this is occasional or 'everyday'. Many restorers are therefore getting

double the pleasure from their cars – they have enjoyed restoring them from scratch, and then derive great satisfaction from driving and looking after the 'finished product', the result of their hard work.

Mark I and Mark II Ford Cortinas and Escorts can be restored by anyone with enthusiasm, a reasonable tool kit and a little ingenuity. The signs are that enthusiasts will be reviving and caring for these models for many years to come.

Do it yourself

In the course of writing this book, I have attempted to carry out as much of the practical work on the vehicles covered, as possible, in order to experience and relate the problems that can be encountered during restoration of these cars, and how they can be overcome. Therefore the book is the result of restoring two complete vehicles – one Cortina and one Escort – from 'literally falling apart' stage to 'completely rebuilt' and in addition various jobs have been carried out and photographed on many other cars, specifically for the book.

This is obviously not a job I could have carried out alone, and my sincere thanks are due to a

number of people and organisations for their help.

For technical guidance on tools and components I should like to thank Sykes-Pickavant Ltd., Automec Equipment and Parts Ltd., LMC Hadrian Ltd., and Cortina Parts (U.K.) Ltd., Piston Rings and Components (Parkstone) Ltd., and a dozen other organisations who have assisted in various ways; I hope they will forgive me for not listing their names in full. Their enthusiastic assistance has been very welcome.

To my ex colleagues on 'Practical Motorist' magazine, I am extremely grateful for being allowed the use of some of their photographs in the 'Mechanical Components' and 'Modifications' chapters. I appreciate the extensive research which Rod Jacques, their Technical Editor, went to in digging out 'long lost' negatives.

Thanks must also go to another 'ex PM' man, Kevin Slater, who helped me out by drawing diagrams, often at short notice.

I should like to express my gratitude to the staff of the BP Motoring Library, at Beaulieu, for their help in my initial researches for this book.

I must also express my gratitude to the various owners' club officials and individual owners of Cortinas and Escorts who have so readily assisted with information, tips and so on, about their cars, and who, in many cases, have allowed me to 'borrow' their cars for photography, and to carry out work on! Specifically, my thanks in this respect go to Robert Watt and Laurence Clark, (both of the Escort 1300E Owners' Club), Roger Raisey, (of the Mark I Cortina Owners' Club), Mr. Dibben, Margaret Smith, Carl Scammel, Jan Morgan, Dave Mudd, and all the others who helped in this way. If I must single out one person for his particular help, it must be Dave Ashenden, of Wimborne. Always enthusiastic and willing to help, Dave, who is also a member of the Mark I Cortina Owners' Club, is a mine of information on matters Cortina.

For his enthusiastic help and the loan of many parts for photography. I must also thank Bob Dick, of Specialised Motor Components, Parkstone – a Ford devotee himself, and always willing to assist with the project.

I am grateful to all the personnel at Ford Motor Company Limited who have helped with my researches, notably David Burgess Wise, Derek Sansom, G.M. Townsend, and Mr. S.T. Clark, supervisor of the Photographic Services Department. In addition, Ford dealers around the country have assisted in the tracking down of various information, and in particular I must thank Malcolm Sharp, Parts Director of New English Ltd., of Poole, for his efforts in tracking down 'obsolete' information on my behalf.

I am greatly indebted to the many friends and relations who have helped me in the various stages of vehicle reconstruction and photography for the book. These include Paul Davis, David Lovering, Rob Flockton, and my brother Clive, among others, and Andrew Kayes who kindly supplied one dilapidated Cortina!

However, for their extraordinary efforts in helping to finish the vehicles, which involved 'round the clock' work at times, I have to express my deep gratitude to Ian Curly, Richard Smith, Peter Exley, my father and my father-in-law, all of whom worked like Trojans, against the clock (and often in garages at temperatures of minus 8 degrees!) to help me.

For their assistance in proof-reading, labelling photographs, and so on, my appreciation and thanks go to my mother and mother-in-law, while for her support and help in every way during this project, and for putting up with a garage and driveway full of old Fords, I must thank Elaine, my wife.

**Kim Henson,
Poole, Dorset.**

1 Heritage - Cortina

In order to establish the background against which Ford introduced their first famous Cortina, it is necessary to look at the state of the British motor industry, and the Ford range of cars in particular, as it stood in the late 1950s and early 1960s.

Ford's market share had been increasing through the 1950s, with a gradual change in design from the pre-war style 'perpendicular' Anglia, Prefect and Popular to cars with modern lines – the attractive 100E models and the larger Consuls, Zephyrs and Zodiacs. Cars of modern character were demanded by an increasingly aware motoring public. In line with these requirements, Ford's planning policy changed from a 'piecemeal', one model at a time approach to a co-ordinated attack on the various market sectors, by introducing a new generation of Fords, while updating the existing model range.

The man who was largely responsible for introducing these new cars was Terence Beckett, who was appointed manager of Ford's product planning team, in 1955, under the chairmanship of Sir Patrick Henessy.

The first vehicle to emerge with the full benefit of Ford's new product planning arrangements was the Anglia (105E), announced in October, 1959.

This small car, with its radically new styling, including the famous 'swept back' rear window, and its new overhead valve, 'over-square' engine, allied to a four-speed gearbox, was a major step forward for Ford. Their previous small cars, however good, had long been showing their age in terms of design, with sidevalve engines and three-speed gearboxes, and the opposition in the market place had been moving steadily ahead. Until 1959, the Ford range consisted of the 'perpendicular' Popular 103E, of pre-War design, the more modern styled 100E models (two door Anglia, four door Prefect and Escort estate car), all with 1172cc side-valve engines and three-speed gearboxes, and the large, overhead valve engined 'Mk II' Consul (four-cylinder), Zephyr and Zodiac (both six-cylinder). The gap in the range, in the 'medium size' sector, was to have been filled by the Classic, originally due to have been introduced in 1960. However, with the immediate and huge success of the Anglia, Ford delayed the launch of the Classic until May, 1961.

The new model was a stylish car, designed by Colin Neal, who also took responsibility for the Anglia's looks. The Classic inherited the angular look of the smaller car, when it appeared,

and, like the Anglia, had a sharply 'cut in' rear window line.

The Classic (109E in Ford's numbering system) was an attempt by Ford to provide an 'upmarket' vehicle, with a higher price tag to match, compared with their previous models.

Therefore the Classic, and its two door fastback brother, the Capri, were good, if expensive cars. By the time these models were eventually launched, Ford had already looked closely at them and decided that they were over-engineered in many ways, and consequently heavy, and costly to build. This made them difficult to sell competitively in an increasingly price-conscious market, especially in view of the introduction by BMC, in 1959, of their technically advanced Mini, at a very low price, and with their equally significant front wheel drive 1100 model already 'in the pipeline'.

So the Ford team were already aware that perhaps another model could be introduced, to give the public the benefits of a medium-sized family car, yet selling for a small car price.

At the same time, Ford in Germany were also working on a family car, to be sold in Europe and the United States.

The German car was codenamed 'Cardinal' (after a small American bird), and took

9

the form of a V4 engined, front wheel drive saloon, to be marketed as the Taunus 12M, following on from earlier 12M models. The engine was to be of 1.2 (or 1.5) litres capacity.

It was initially on the cards that Ford of Britain might get involved with the German project, but, in the event, each country developed their own, entirely separate, family model.

Through time and cost factors, the British vehicle was destined to be strictly 'conventional' in layout; that is, front engine, rear wheel drive, and with a traditional approach to the steering and suspension layouts.

This was, of course, a diametrically opposite path of attack on the family car market to that adopted by BMC. Their 1100 model, introduced in 1962, had a transversely mounted engine, driving the front wheels through an 'integral' gearbox, rack and pinion steering and 'Hydrolastic' syspension – in fact, at the time, it was a very advanced vehicle in its layout and concept.

However, Ford felt it would be better (and cheaper to produce) for their new model to stick to tried and tested engine, transmission and suspension components.

Therefore, the new car was to emerge as a concept very similar to the already proven and very popular Anglia 105E, with an overhead valve engine, four-speed gearbox, recirculating ball steering, MacPherson strut front suspension, and leaf springs at the rear, supporting a live axle.

The Cortina is born

The 'Archbishop', as the British Ford was termed initially, was given a design objective aiming to achieve space, brisk performance and good fuel consumption. This dictated a

weight reduction of around 15 per cent, compared with the existing Classic model, of similar size.

Therefore lightweight box sections were to form part of the new body, and the number of components used in the structure were to be reduced considerably – in fact by about one fifth, compared with the Classic.

By keeping production costs as low as possible, Ford aimed to hold the selling price to a minimum – thereby returning to their traditional 'maximum value for money' policy.

The new car was later named 'Cortina', after Cortina d'Ampezzo, in Italy, which had been the venue for the 1960 Winter Olympics, and which helped to impart a modern, 'sporty' image.

The body style for the new model, finalised in late 1960, was neat, up to date and functional. With a distinctive, angular look, complemented by tapering strengthener 'flutes' along each side, the car differed from the Anglia and Classic in having a conventionally angled rear window.

From the rear, the Cortina was immediately identifiable by its circular rear light clusters, incorporating a 'Y' frame between the lenses.

Drive train

The choice of engine was relatively straightforward. Ford were already working on the theory of a 'family' of engines, based around a common cylinder block. The idea, originated under Lawrence Martland, was followed through by Alan Worters, the Executive Engineer responsible for power units.

The first of these engines to see the light of day in a production car was the Anglia 105E's 997cc motor, followed by the 1340cc version, used in the

Classic. This family 'group' of engines later became known as the 'Kent' range, and they were to become the mainstay power units for family Fords over the next two decades. With a common bore size of 80.96mm, many components (including pistons) were interchangeable, and even the cylinder heads (with minor differences) were basically similar. The different capacities were achieved by varying the throw of the crankshaft, and the connecting rods. The cylinder block heights naturally varied a little from model to model, according to the capacity.

Inherent in the design, the new, small 'Kent' engines were 'oversquare' units, with the bore dimension exceeding the stroke. This meant that piston travel could be reduced, and hence piston, piston ring and cylinder bore wear. As an example, the old sidevalve 100E engines produced a piston speed of some 2,730 feet per minute (which is in fact 31 miles per hour!) at 4,500 rpm, while that of the 997 Anglia was only 1,588 feet per minute at 5,000 rpm.

Apart from this wear factor, however, the oversquare engines could also be made smaller and lighter, for a given capacity.

In line with this policy, it was decided that the new Cortina should receive an engine from the new series, with a capacity between that of the Anglia and the Classic.

Therefore, a stroke of 58.17mm gave the unit a capacity of 1198cc, and the only new components needed to produce it were the crankshaft, connecting rods, and cylinder head of the correct combustion chamber volume. This engine was also used in the 1200 Anglia, announced at the same time as the introduction of the Cortina to the public.

The power output was 48.5 bhp at 4,800 rpm, promising to give reasonable performance – the body shell was, after all, relatively light, and the new car

also had the benefit of a four-speed, all-synchromesh gearbox. This was developed from the Classic's unit, and was available with floor or column change.

The control cables employed on the column change units were easy to adapt to either left or right hand drive cars – an advantage on a car destined for foreign markets as well as for home sales.

The column change option went hand in hand with a bench type front seat, and dashboard mounted handbrake, compared with the floor mounted parking brake and individual front seats fitted to floor gearchange equipped cars.

The Cortina's suspension was based on proven principles too. The front wheels were suspended by MacPherson struts with integral coil springs and shock absorbers, as fitted to the earlier Consuls, Zephyrs, Zodiacs, 105E Anglia and Classic. However, the bearings and shock absorbers were improved for the new car.

At the rear, conventional semi-elliptical springs were fitted, after initial thoughts of using independent suspension. Telescopic hydraulic shock absorbers were used to control the springs, on which the driving axle was mounted well forward of their centre line, to reduce excessive dipping of the propeller shaft sliding joint.

Into production

Cortina production began in June, 1962, and early tests of the car gave impressive results. The official announcement to the public took place in September, 1962, and the 'Consul Cortina' as it was now known (linking the theme of family motoring to the car through the already well known 'Consul' name) appeared at the Earls Court Motor Show, in October, 1962.

Another family car on show for the first time was BMC's Morris 1100 – a complete contrast in approach by the manufacturer, but both cars, of course, aimed at the same market.

The Cortina attracted a great deal of interest, not least because of the car's deceptive interior and luggage space. The Morris 1100 also had a roomy interior, but the boot was far smaller than the Cortina's 20 cubic feet luggage compartment. On the other hand, BMC's technical innovation with the 1100 also drew a great deal of attention.

Press and public reaction to the Cortina was nevertheless favourable. Performance was reasonable for the time, with a top speed of nearly 80 mph and up to 40 mpg being claimed. A standstill to 60 mph acceleration time of around 25 seconds is not electrifying today, but it was creditable in the early 1960s.

With a price tag of just £639 (in 'basic' two door form; it was also available as a four door saloon), the Cortina represented a lot of motor car for anyone's money, and compared with £675 for an equivalent Morris 1100, and £723 for the Classic.

Improvements

Ford decided to produce a 1498cc version of the 'Kent' engine for use in the Classic. With a five bearing crankshaft, this new motor was stronger, more powerful, and also quieter than the three main bearing engine on which it was based. A longer stroke of 72.75mm was employed, comparing with 48.41, 58.17, and 65.07mm for the 997, 1198 and 1340cc units respectively.

The new power unit was announced for the Classic and Capri in August 1962, and was introduced to the Cortina in January 1963, as an option on 'De Luxe' models, and as a standard fitting for the new 'Super' version.

Models

The differences between the three Cortina models now available were unmistakable.

The 'Standard' version had a painted radiator grille, and very little bright trim, with a rubber floor covering inside.

The 'De Luxe' featured opening rear side windows (on two door cars), a bright plated grille and other fittings, two tone interior trim, a passenger side sun visor, 'Hi-tone' PVC/rubber floor covering, twin ashtrays in the back, a door operated courtesy light, temperature and oil pressure warning lights, aluminium scuff plates on the sills, and a padded facia cowl.

The 'Super', in addition to the 59.5 bhp, 1498cc engine and more powerful brakes, had larger section tyres (5.60 x 13 instead of 5.20,) bright metal wheel trims and (wider) side flashes, a carpeted interior, 'lustre' finish trim, a vanity mirror, a heater/demister (this was only available as an extra cost option on Standard and De Luxe cars), screenwasher, cigarette lighter and (optional) cloth upholstery.

For these 'extra' features over the Standard model, one paid a premium of £24 for the De Luxe, and £97 for the Super.

Extra cost Ford 'factory' options included white sidewall tyres, hide/PVC upholstery, two tone paint schemes (De Luxe versions only), and a bench seat with column gearchange and dash-mounted handbrake. On cars so equipped, it was theoretically possible to seat three people abreast in the front seat, without impairing driving control. This option could also be specified on two door cars, thanks to the ingenious

arrangement of the individual folding seat backs employed on the front bench seat, to give access to the rear seats.

Cortina Lotus

In January, 1963, one of the most significant Cortina models made its debut.

It was the highly potent Cortina Lotus. This used a strengthened Cortina body shell (two door only), allied to the Lotus/Cosworth developed, Ford based 1558cc twin overhead camshaft Lotus Elan engine, fitted with twin Weber DCOE carburettors.

This power unit developed 105 bhp, and gave the car a top speed generally acknowledged to be 107/108mph, and a nought to sixty mph acceleration time of around eight seconds – good by today's standards, and revolutionary in the early 1960s.

To help give good performance, considerable weight savings were achieved by the use of aluminium in place of steel, in a number of areas. The doors, bonnet, bootlid, clutch casing, gearbox extension housing and differential carrier were all of aluminium on the Lotus model.

Other major differences between this model and its more ordinary brothers started with the bodywork.

The distinctive white paintwork, with contrasting green body side flashes, the front quarter bumpers, wide wheels and 'Lotus' badges all gave the game away. Less noticeable but still vital were the 'under the skin' changes. For example, the use of the Lotus Elan close ratio gearbox, the lowered front suspension, the coil/trailing link and 'A' bracket rear springing, and the front disc brakes (servo-assisted), together with a sporty interior and remote control gearchange, emphasized that this was no ordinary Cortina.

With this car, Ford had a vehicle with the same sort of image as the Mini-Cooper, and with which they could make serious strides in motor sport over the following years.

Meanwhile. the name and reputation of the Cortina was becoming more widely known, and in the same month as the Lotus version was announced, Eric Jackson and Ken Chambers drove a Cortina Super nearly 12,000 miles, from London to Capetown, South Africa, in 13 days, 8 hours and 48 minutes, changing only the fanbelt on the way!

Estate cars

In March, 1963, Ford added estate cars to the Cortina line-up. Mechanically similar to the saloons (with the exception of stronger rear suspension), the new estates offered 65 cubic feet of load capacity, with the rear seat folded down, or 33 cubic feet, with it in use. The galvanised steel floor was 6ft 5½ins long, with the rear seat folded, giving plenty of room for long, bulky loads, or for occasional use as a double bed.

The estates were available in De Luxe form, with the 1200cc engine (1500 optional), or in Super guise, with the 1498cc engine as standard, together with 'Di-Noc' imitation wood trim on the body sides and tailgate. There was no charge for the column change/bench seat option on the Super version, but buyers requiring this facility on the De Luxe model had to pay extra!

To cope with the extra weight normally associated with estate car use, larger section (6.00 x 13) tyres were fitted, and the rear springs comprised six leaves, compared with the saloon's four, with each leaf being far thicker than the saloon items. Lever arm rear shock

absorbers were used on the estate cars, in place of the telescopic variety employed on the saloons.

A modified exhaust system was used, to provide 'clean' access to the tailgate.

Cortina GT

In April, 1963, another version of the Cortina was announced – the GT. Originally derived from demands for a Cortina with a tougher body and uprated suspension, to cope with the terrain in Australia, the vehicle, with its strengthened body shell, emerged in Britain as the GT, in two or four door form.

Externally, the car was the same as the De Luxe, apart from discreet 'GT' badges on the rear wings, but there were major mechanical changes, in addition to the 'heavy duty' body shell.

The 1498cc engine was used as a starting point, and 'breathed on' by Cosworth, who had established a reputation for successful tuning of the 997cc Anglia engine, in the past. So, by fitting a special exhaust manifold, larger inlet valves, a twin choke carburettor (Weber), a high lift camshaft, better pistons and copper-lead bearing shells, and with a higher compression ratio (9.0:1 instead of 8.3:1), the power output was raised by over 30 per cent, from 59.5bhp to 78bhp!

To help cope with the considerable extra power, a stronger clutch and propeller shaft were fitted, along with stiffer suspension, disc brakes at the front and larger drums at the rear, and a front anti-roll bar.

The interior was similar to that used in the Cortina De Luxe, except that the GT had a remote control gearchange, centre console and extra instruments. With a tachometer, ammeter and oil pressure gauge, in addition to the normal fuel and water

temperature instruments, the GT was well equipped in terms of 'driver information'.

Performance was good, too, with a maximum speed of around 95 mph, and nought to sixty mph taking only 13.2 seconds. This compares with top speeds of around 78 mph and 85 mph respectively for the 1200 and 1500 models in standard tune, and corresponding times to 60 mph of 25 and 21 seconds.

GT estate cars were produced in small numbers, while the GT version of the fastback Capri used the same engine, suspension and brake modifications, and gave similar performance.

Success Story

The Cortina was an instant, profitable success for Ford – the gratifying sales figures reinforcing the fact that the 'recipe' was right. In July, 1963, Ford announced that in the first ten months of production, 90,000 Cortinas had been sold in the U.K., and a further 120,000 abroad, earning Britain £50 million in foreign currency.

At the end of the first full year in production, total sales had risen to 300,000!

To keep the Cortina 'up to date', Ford made many revisions to the car during its production life, helping to keep it attractive to buyers.

For example, in September, 1963, the original strip type speedometer was replaced by the dial variety. A small change, perhaps, but significant for a potential purchaser. Childproof rear door locks were fitted to the four door cars at the same time, and the GT gained twin radius arms to help locate the rear axle. Subtle, but important, changes such as these did a lot to uphold Ford's image as an innovative and go-ahead company, making the purchase of 'this year's

model' seem more important to the car buying public.

In December, 1963, another landmark was achieved, when 1498cc versions (but not the GT) were made available with the Borg Warner 35 automatic three-speed gearbox. This made the Cortina two door, when so equipped, the cheapest British car available with fully automatic transmission.

Due to the extensive use of light alloys, the automatic gearbox weighed only 30lbs more than the conventional clutch and gearbox assembly, and performance loss was minimal.

With a lock-up available for 'low' and 'intermediate' gears, and with a 'kickdown' switch, beyond the normal accelerator pedal travel, effective engine braking was possible, and fast changedown for overtaking or hill-climbing. This made the Cortina a particularly easy car to drive in its (optional) automatic form.

The main Cortina range then continued unchanged for another nine months before the most significant improvements were made in the history of the 'Mark I' . . . more of these later.

However, in the meantime, the Lotus version was considerably altered in July, 1964, when the aluminium body panels were replaced by steel ones, and the conventional propeller shaft was dropped in favour of a split unit. At the same time, the close ratio Lotus Elan gearbox was replaced by a Ford item, with a more useful second gear ratio.

Two months later, the whole Cortina range was radically revised. Using the same basic body shell and power train, alterations were made to the facia, grille, brakes and ventilation system.

The dashboard now featured recessed and shrouded instruments, and simpler heater controls, while a new, deeply dished steering wheel was also fitted. The front body grille was

now full-width, and 9½ inch disc brakes were standard at the front.

One of the most innovative alterations to the range concerned the heating/ventilation system. The new models had "Aeroflow" ventilation, which employed fresh air vents and extractors, and had face level dashboard outlets. The interior comfort was also improved by the use of more thickly padded seats, and by the use of revised, colour keyed, interior trim.

Mechanically, the compression ratio of the 1.2 litre engine was raised to 9.0:1 giving a 1½ bhp power increase! Not a lot, perhaps, but it all helps, and to give an idea of the sort of performance available from the new Cortina, it had a top speed of 78 mph, a zero to 60 mph acceleration time of 22.5 seconds, and a touring fuel consumption of around 38 mpg. These figures compare almost exactly with the rather heavier BMC 1100 of the same period.

The GT was also modified at this time; radius arms were fitted at the rear, to control spring 'wind-up', and the facia now featured a neat cluster of four auxiliary instruments, mounted in the centre. They comprised rev counter, ammeter, temperature gauge and oil pressure gauge.

All Cortinas now featured screenwashers as standard.

Further changes were made in September, 1965, when the 'Standard' model was dropped, as was the column gear change option, and the wood panelling on the 'Super' estate cars. The quarter light vents were now fixed on all Cortinas.

On Lotus versions, a number of changes were made, the most obvious being the reversion to conventional leaf rear springing from the coil springs previously employed. It had been found that with the coil spring set-up, leaking oil from the rear axle could soften the 'A' bracket bushes, and also that the coil spring system was more prone to

damage on rough roads.

In October, 1965, the gear ratios on the Lotus model were revised to match those of the close-ratio Corsair 2000E gearbox, giving higher first, second and third gears. Modified front disc calipers, self-adjusting rear brakes, and GT seats were fitted at the same time. The Cortina GT also received the benefit of braking system modifications, with larger diameter front discs and calipers, and with self-adjusting brakes at the rear, this fitting being introduced on the new V4 engined Corsairs at the same time.

The 'Mark I' Cortinas were produced for another year, but in September, 1966, the saloons were discontinued, followed by the estate car, in November, to make way for the new Mark II models. However, a staggering 1,010,000 'Mark I' Cortinas had been built – a record for a British car.

The Mark II arrives

Successful though the Mark I was in world terms, on the home market it was being beaten by the BMC 1100, which refused to be budged from its position as Britain's top selling car.

The Mark II Cortina was therefore an important vehicle to Ford, in showing that constant development and improvement would help make their cars attractive to an increasingly discerning motor public.

Introduced in the autumn of 1966, the Mark II was built around the same floor pan as its predecessor, but with new, 'boxy' bodywork, having more angular styling and flatter panels than were seen on the Mk I.

The new car was available in De Luxe, Super and GT guises.

A new, five bearing

crankshaft, 1297cc engine powered the De Luxe, with the proven $1\frac{1}{2}$ litre unit (by now having a marginally longer stroke, of 72.82 mm, giving it a capacity of 1499.9cc) being fitted to the Super and GT versions, and being an option on the De Luxe; all models were available with two or four doors. The new cars had diaphragm clutches, and, as with the late Mark I models, there were no 'chassis' lubrication points.

Interior comfort was improved, with more leg room than in the earlier model. There was, in addition, an extra two inches available width at shoulder height, front and rear, this being made possible by the use of curved side windows.

Standard features now included a heater, and childproof locks on the rear doors of four door cars. White sidewall tyres were optional.

Super models sported exterior embellishments, wheel trims, looped pile carpet, a cigarette lighter, coat hooks and a padded facia, with the option of reclining seats on four door versions.

The 'high flying' GT, with its 1500cc engine and Weber twin choke carburettor, would reach 60 mph from standstill in 13.8 seconds – good for 1966 – and continue to accelerate to a top speed in the mid-nineties. The car's inherent good handling was helped by the use of twin radius arms to locate the rear axle, as on the Mark I version. Its sporty character was complemented by the fitting of temperature, oil pressure, ammeter and tachometer gauges, a console behind the gear lever, and bucket front seats. The rather novel option of reclining front seats on four door models only was also available on the GT, as were wider rimmed wheels and radial ply tyres. The old steering column gearchange/bench seat option reappeared with the advent of the Mk II, having been phased out in late 1965 for the Mk I.

Mechanical changes

Under the new bodywork, Ford engineers had been at work to improve upon the original Cortina concept. As a result, the track widths were increased over the first model, giving more stability, and the brakes on all Cortinas were now disc type at the front, with self-adjusting drums at the rear. Under the bonnet, all engines now had five bearing crankshafts, and the smallest engine size was increased from 1198cc to 1297cc, by lengthening the stroke. The increased power (now 53.5 bhp) enabled automatic transmission to be offered as an option on the 1300 – it had never been available with the old 1198cc engine. This meant that auto transmission could be specified on any Cortina but the GT.

1967 dawned with minor alterations to the GT specification, giving improved gear ratios. The effect of these, combined with the remote control gearchange now used on the GT, gave the car a more sporting feel.

In February the same year, estate car versions were announced; in 1300cc form, with manual gearbox only, or with the 1500cc engine, allied to manual or (optional) automatic transmission.

An interesting, and now rare machine, was the 1500 GT estate car, which was not listed in generally available Ford literature, but which was nevertheless available to special order, and which was a potent load carrier.

The main asset of any estate car is, of course, its capacity for cargo, and the Cortinas were no exception. With heavy duty rear springs, and a flat load area some 6ft $4\frac{1}{2}$in long (giving a massive 70.5 cubic feet of luggage capacity), the new Cortina estate was a useful vehicle. Even with the rear seats in their passenger carrying mode, there was 36

cubic feet of luggage space, and a usable cargo compartment width of 4ft 5ins. The high-lifting, single tailgate, and the sharply angled corners of the loading aperture, combined with a relatively low sill and flat floor, all added up to a vehicle that was easy to load and unload. As the estate cars also had two side-opening rear passenger doors, the loading of long or bulky items was easy.

In March, 1967, the sportiest version of the Mark II appeared. Unveiled at the Geneva Motor Show, the Cortina Lotus, with the 1558cc overhead camshaft engine which had made the Mark I version so potent, was a welcome derivative, and entirely appropriate. During the first four years of production, the Cortina had notched up over 500 victories in international rallies and races, gaining valuable experience to build into production vehicles. By early 1967, one in five Cortinas produced were GT or Lotus models, so there was certainly a strong demand for these sporting versions. It is interesting to note, too, that of the growing number of cars exported to the United States (Cortina shipments for the first three months of 1967 were 40 per cent up on the same period in 1966), one in three were GTs.

The new Lotus model was based around the same formula as the earlier car, but, using the rakish bodywork of the Mark II Cortina, it had a positively aggressive 'get up and go' look about it.

Available in two door form only, the car looked the part, with lowered, beefed up suspension, 5$\frac{1}{2}$J wheels and radial tyres, and with the famous Lotus 'green flash' adorning both sides of the bodywork, when in white. However, any of the standard Cortina body colour/trim combinations could be specified.

The top speed was around 107 mph, and nought to sixty took under 10 seconds – a

respectable figure today, and extremely quick in the late 1960s.

Using many parts which were common to the GT model, including the twin trailing link rear suspension, the Mark II Cortina Lotus could be constructed almost entirely on the Dagenham production lines, and was subject to the same quality checks as 'mainstream' production Fords.

Engine changes

The most significant changes to the mechanical specification of the Mark II came in August, 1967, when the engines were radically redesigned. The new units to be used in the Cortinas were 1300 and 1600cc 'bowl in piston' designs, as used in Formula 1 racing. With the combustion chamber formed by the bowl in the piston top, these engines were more efficient than their predecessors, with the inlet manifolds along one side of the motor, and the exhaust pipework on the other, providing a smooth flow of gases through and ACROSS the engine. Hence the term, 'cross-flow', which has applied to the Ford engines of recent years.

The range therefore now consisted of the De Luxe, in 1298cc or 1599cc form, the Super, 1599cc only, the 1600GT, and the Lotus. The De Luxe saloon now had carpets instead of rubber floor mats, with reclining front seats optional on the four door version. The Super now featured the GT style remote control gearchange and electric centre console clock, and the GT had improved brakes and radial tyres with other specifications remaining as before.

The Super estate cars featured foam rubber matting in the load area, 'exclusive' seat trim and the polished aluminium wheel trims, and stainless steel window and bodywork

mouldings of the saloon.

The Lotus model gained twin tone horns, a leather-trimmed steering wheel, a new centre console with electric clock, and the famous 'Twin Cam' badge on the bootlid.

Performance

Performance was improved with the more powerful engines, of course, and the 57 bhp, 1298cc cars would now reach 60 mph in about 19 seconds from rest (compared with 21$\frac{1}{2}$ seconds for the non-cross-flow 1300), and continue accelerating to a top speed of 84 mph (80 mph for the previous model).

Comparative figures for the new, 71 bhp 1600cc engines, over the 1500cc units they replaced, show similar gains, with the new model reaching 60 mph in 16 seconds, and having a maximum speed of around 90 mph. The 1600GT would attain the magical 60 mph in 12$\frac{1}{2}$ seconds, and top 95 mph, with its 88 bhp output.

Fuel consumption figures were almost identical to the previous models, averaging around 30 mpg for the 'standard' 1300 and 1600 engines, and about 26-28 mpg for the more potent GT.

1600E is born

In September, 1967, what was to become one of the most sought after Cortinas arrived on the scene.

Based on the four door version of the GT, the 1600E (for 'Executive') was packed with luxury exras and trimmings, which made it a very attractive package at its 'under £1,000' price tag of £982.2s.1d!

With the same drivetrain components as the GT,

performance was good, with a top speed of 95 mph, a nought to sixty capability of 12¹/₂ seconds. However, handling was better still, due to the fitting of the suspension from the Lotus Cortina.

From the outside, the car looked very neat, with 'Ro style' road wheels, lowered suspension and extra twin driving lamps. Inside, too, the car was well-appointed, with reclining front seats, polished wood door cappings and facia, leather-covered, aluminium steering wheel, cut pile carpets, special acoustic insulation, and full GT type instrumentation. It was indeed a luxurious and fast Ford, and the package was well received by the motoring public.

Indeed, even before these latest improvements to the range, the Mark II models had been selling well, with 100,000 going in the first four months, and more than a quarter of a million being sold in the first ten months of availability. During this same period, Cortina sales in Europe had increased by 25 per cent, and in the U.S.A. by a staggering 112¹/₂ per cent!

However, despite its success, the Mark II Cortina lost its briefly held supremacy in the home sales league again to the BMC 1100, in 1968, having taken over the 'number one' position during 1967, following good initial public reaction to the 'new' Cortina.

Variations

During the following two years, only minor changes were made to the Cortina. These included, in October, 1967, interior changes to the Lotus model, with revisions to the Aeroflow ventilation system, and the mounting of the clock on the centre console.

A year later, all models received the remote control type gearchange, first introduced on the GT, and reclining seats became optional. The letters F O R D appeared on the bonnet and bootlid from this time, too.

The range then continued without material alterations, until production ceased.

An interesting conversion which was offered by the Crayford Company, of Kent, meant that open-air Cortina motoring was available to those who wanted it. Crayford's car was a convertible version of the Cortina, based on the two door bodyshell, reinforced along the lower sections of the bodywork. It gave full weather protection when required, and a quick change to open top driving when the sun came out!

End of the Mark II road

In late 1969, following continued success in the American market, it was announced that the Cortina had become the best selling British car in the U.S. market. In 1970, however, to make way for the introduction of the 'Coke bottle' shaped Mark III Cortina, the Mark II was phased out, starting in July, when the Lotus version was discontinued, and continuing in August, when the 1600E disappeared, and September, when the end of the Mk II line came.

Ironically, the demise of the Mk II was due to the Cortina's success, as a model, and to Ford's policy of bringing in a completely new version every four years, with a facelift each two years, to maintain the buying public's interest in their cars.

Total production of the Mk II was just a few hundred units more than that of the Mk I, at nearly 1,010,600.

It is interesting to note that the Mk II Cortina never did regain its top selling position in Britain between 1968 and 1970; the BMC 1100 was on top of the British sales chart until ousted again by the Mark III Cortina, in 1971!

HC1. The original Ford Cortina, with its distinctive, angular styling, and 'nose to tail' body fluting, which gave the car a graceful look.

HC2. The first Cortina GT introduced in April, 1963, features the early, strip type speedometer, with the ammeter and oil pressure gauge mounted on the centre console, and the tachometer mounted in a separate pod in front of the driver.

HC3. Mark I Cortinas for the 1965 model year onwards are identifiable by the wider, close mesh grille, 'Cortina' scripting on bonnet and boot, and the 'Aeroflow' extractor vents on the rear quarter panel. This one is a GT model, and has discreet badges on the rear wings, to announce the fact.

HC4. Cortina estate cars are useful vehicles. This one, a rare automatic version, is in everyday use all year round, and is meticulously cared for by its owner, Dave Ashenden. This is a 'De Luxe'; 'Super' models featured exterior wood panelling, until September, 1965.

HC5.   Even with the rear seat in use, the load platform is sufficiently large to carry bulky items; with the seat back folded forward, the volume of available carrying space is enormous!

HC6.   The engines used on the Mark I Cortinas look very much like those found in the Anglias, not surprisingly, in view of their heritage! Accessibility is extremely good for maintenance.

HC7.   The facia on later Mark I cars is simple and uncluttered, the twin dials replacing the strip layout previously employed. This car has the column change/bench seat option fitted.

HC8.   The fastest production Mark I was the Cortina Lotus. With its contrasting body stripe, 'Lotus' badges, low suspension and wide wheels, it is a neat, sleek car which looks the part.

HC9.   Sheer muscle! Under the bonnet of a Cortina Lotus there is little room for anything other than engine. With the distinctive, twin cam covers, and side-mounted carburettors, this Lotus engine strongly suggests hidden power.

HC10.   The facia in Lotus models is neat and functional, with tachometer close to the speedo, and auxiliary gauges mounted in the centre of the dashboard. Note the wood-rimmed steering wheel.

HC11. The Mark II models arrived in 1966, and this is an early example. The much squarer styling was well received by the public, and gave the car a compact, practical look.

HC12. The 1600E was – and still is – considered by many to be the finest Cortina model built. This immaculate example retains the chunky, purposeful look which captured the 'Executive' image of the late 1960s.

HC13. The 1600E interior was enhanced by the use of walnut for the dashboard and door top trims, and was comfortable, with 'wall to wall' carpeting. The facia is similar in layout to GT models.

HC14. The tubular exhaust manifold and '1600GT' label on the rocker cover help identify this 1600E's engine bay. One of the attractive features of the car was the relative ease of servicing for a 'sports' saloon.

HC15. Get up and go! The very appearance of the Mark II Cortina Lotus has an air of power and speed about it – and with good reason. This model was, and remains, one of the most desirable Cortinas.

HC16. The huge air cleaner box dominates the top of the engine, obscuring the motor from view. Yet beneath it is 105 bhp waiting to go!

2 Heritage - Escort

Heritage – Escort

By the mid 1960s, Ford's small and medium size family models were the Anglia and Cortina respectively, with both cars doing extremely well in terms of sales, both at home and abroad. In fact 1.3 million Anglias were sold between 1959 and 1967, when it was phased out of production.

However, from 1965 Ford had been considering an 'Anglia replacement', to keep up to date in the public's imagination, and to change their model range in line with a rapidly changing market. At this time there was a wide choice of new small and medium size cars, with an equally diverse range of mechanical layouts.

BMC had their front wheel drive Mini, with its luxury Wolseley Hornet and Riley Elf derivatives, and the sporty Cooper variants, all with the legendary fuel economy and limpet-like roadholding. The Rootes approach, with rear engine and rear wheel drive, was also unconventional, but the Imp, with its advanced (and initially temperamental) all alloy, overhead camshaft engine, was lively, frugal and modern, and a competitor for Anglia sales.

Vauxhall's boxy 'HA' model Viva, introduced in 1963, was nearing the end of its short production life, to be replaced for 1966 by the mechanically conventional and elegantly designed 'HB' Viva. This new Vauxhall was longer, wider and more comfortable than its predecessor, while losing little in performance and fuel consumption, from its 1159cc overhead valve engine, over the 1057cc unit used previously.

These facts were significant, for Ford's thinking for their new model was also running along similar lines – that is, to increase the passenger space available, and to modernise the styling. The Anglia had always been hailed as a pretty car, but the sharply cut back rear window of this model (and the Classic) did rob the vehicle of rear seat and parcel shelf room, and was to disappear in favour of a conventionally angled rear screen for the new car.

Once again Ford based the new car's design framework on tried and tested components and principles, rather than branching out into relatively costly and occasionally unreliable areas such as front wheel drive, for example. As history shows, this was probably wise, with the first front wheel drive Ford – the Fiesta – not appearing until 1977.

This policy meant that swift development could take place, using existing components, suitably modified and developed for the new application.

Therefore the new 'Anglia' (the name was originally intended to be continued with the new car, but changed to 'Escort' at a late stage in development) was destined to be a front-engined, rear wheel drive vehicle.

Mechanical layout

The heart of the car was to be a cross-flow overhead valve engine from the 'Kent' family, originally developed from the 997cc Anglia non-crossflow power unit, and used in the Cortina. For the Escort, the engine sizes chosen were 1098cc (53.29mm stroke), and 1298cc (62.99mm stroke); the common Ford bore size of 80.98mm being retained. These five bearing crankshaft engines were strictly conventional in design, and produced 45 bhp and 52 bhp respectively for the 'standard' high compression 1100 and 1300cc units. Lower compression versions produced 3 bhp less, for either engine size. A 'GT' version of the 1300 engine produced 64 bhp, the extra power being obtained from similar modifications as used in the make-up of the Cortina 1600GT. These included a high

lift camshaft, larger valves, twin choke Weber carburettor, and fabricated steel exhaust manifold in place of the cast iron item used on 'standard' engines.

The power was fed to the rear wheels via a 7^{1}/$_{2}$in diameter clutch (6^{1}/$_{2}$in on 1100 models) and a new, fully synchromesh, four speed, single rail gearbox. This was, incidentally, the first Metric gearbox to be used in a 'British' Ford, and was hailed at the time as being one of the slickest units available.

The front suspension was by MacPherson struts, with integral shock absorbers, as per the Cortina, and the previous Anglia models, with track control arms locating the lower end of each suspension unit. Each track control arm was connected by a compression strut to strengthened mountings on the car's side members.

The rear axle was located by conventional leaf springs, 'hung' below the axle tube, and inclined telescopic shock absorbers completed the set-up.

Of particular interest on the Escort was the steering system chosen, for this car was the first mass produced British Ford to be fitted with rack and pinion steering; the Mk II Cortina, for example, was still running with a recirculating ball steering box system. Therefore the Escort's steering was rather more positive, and the excellent turning circle available – 29 feet – while not quite down to London Taxi or Triumph Herald proportions, certainly made the car easy to manoeuvre in tight corners.

The original standard Escorts had drum brakes all round, with discs and servo-assistance standard on the GT. However, one had the option of specifying the useful discs/servo assistance on the less powerful cars, if desired, adding around £16 to the price.

The two door saloon bodywork was of unitary, all steel construction, with unusual, rather bulbous styling for the late 'sixties, and in contrast, for example, with the rather smoother lines of the HB Viva of the same era. Many at the time thought that the Anglia was a much better looker . . . it all depends on your point of view!

Into production

Production of the new Ford began at Halewood, near Liverpool, in November, 1967, with the official announcement of the new range following in January, 1968.

By the time the cars were available to the public, extensive testing had taken place, in a wide range of climatic and road conditions. With test mileage approaching a quarter of a million in total, cars were put through their paces in climates as extreme as South Africa, Belgium and Finland, with extensive 'home ground' assessment as well.

The cars unveiled initially were the basic 1100 and 1300, De Luxe and Super versions in each engine capacity, the 1300GT and the Escort Twin Cam, more about which later.

The Escort's fittings and trim were originally rather basic when compared with the opposition – for instance the front door quarter windows were fixed, a cost-cutting move later followed by other makers. The basic Escort was, as most basic models are, rather spartan in terms of interior furnishings too, with rubber floor matting, and 'knitweave' vinyl trim. The De Luxe version had bodywork trims and bright metal wheel embellishers, while the Super cars had, in addition, loop pile carpets, embossed vinyl seats and a simulated walnut facia panel.

Apart from the servo/disc brake option already mentioned (which was in any case standard on the GT and Twin Cam), the would-be Escort owner could also specify 4^{1}/$_{2}$ inch wide wheel rims, shod with radial tyres, inertia seat belts, manual radio, a sports steering wheel, a higher ratio rear axle (3.777 to 1 in place of the standard 3.900 to 1), and metallic finish paintwork.

GTs already had many useful 'extras' built into the specification. These included extra instrumentation, in the form of a tachometer, oil pressure gauge, coolant temperature gauge and battery condition indicator (voltmeter!), close ratio gearbox, radial tyres, loop pile carpet and contoured pvc seats, in addition to the servo/discs braking alterations.

As an aid to identification, when 'Escort spotting', the early basic and De Luxe cars had round headlamps, while the Super and GT were fitted with the neater looking (and more difficult to obtain today) rectangular units.

In early 1968, when the Escort was announced, prices (including purchase tax and delivery, but exclusive of front seat belts!) started at £605 for the basic 1100 saloon, moving up to £635 for the De Luxe, and £666 for the Super, while the 1300 Super, for example, cost £691, and the 1300GT a hefty £765.

Incidentally, 1968 was not the first time that the name Escort had appeared on Ford's price lists, for back in the 1950s this was the name given to one of the two 100E estate car derivatives, the other being the Squire. These cars, with the 1172cc sidevalve engine, had a horizontally split rear tailgate arrangement and folding rear seats, giving very versatile luggage carrying facilities. Introduced in late 1955, the Escort was the cheaper of the two, at £587, and was based on the Ford Anglia 100E and 300E van bodywork. The Squire, at £631, had wooden body side adornments, and the same standard of interior finish as the 100E Prefect De Luxe. The later Squire lost its wooden trims, and was not produced after 1959, but

the Escort, with its revised 'Popular' grille and fittings, continued until April, 1961, just over a year ahead of the Popular – the last sidevalve Ford – which finished production in June, 1962.

It is interesting that the technically much more advanced 'new' Escort was conceived just three years later, and appeared on sale to the general public less than six years after production of the 100E ceased. The drivetrain design of this model, of course, dated back to 1932, and the famous Ford Model Y – but that's another story!

Good reception

The new Escort received an enthusiastic response from the motoring press and the public, following its launch. Ford began selling the car on the slogan "The new Ford Escort. The small car that isn't", which seemed to sum up the feelings of most people towards it. It was hailed as a practical vehicle, with the emphasis on family motoring, which of course is right where it was aimed.

The introduction of any new rear wheel drive model in the 1980s is viewed with a certain amount of scepticism, particularly by motoring correspondents. In these days when front wheel drive is the norm, a 'conventional' rear drive car like the Sierra naturally arouses a great deal of comment. In contrast, when the Escort was announced, in early 1968, most drivers accepted rear wheel drive as the norm. For example, when the Escort was conceived, its market opposition at that time, as well as the 'new' designs already mentioned (like the BMC 1100/1300), included popular 'old favourites' such as the 1098cc Austin A40 Mk II, the revised version of the Morris 1000 (also now 1100cc) and the independently sprung Triumph

Herald – all three, of course, were rear wheel drive cars. So the strictly traditional design of the new Ford was accepted quietly by press and public alike.

Twin cam

The Escort Twin Cam (TC) was announced at the same time as the other saloons, but was introduced primarily as a rally car – indeed it did achieve success in many rallies, including the Acropolis and Tulip events, as well as making an enviable name for itself in the British Saloon Car Championships of the time.

Developed at Ford's Competitions Department, at Boreham, the now rare production TCs were built at Halewood, Liverpool, as of course were the other Escorts.

Externally the TC was identifiable by its round headlights, 'quarter' front bumpers, flared wheel arches, Ermine White paintwork and contrasting matt black grille, plus wide (5^1/$_2$J) 13 inch wheels ('normal' Escorts had 12 inch rims) bearing radial tyres. It also bore a 'TC' badge on its bootlid. The interior of the TC was similar to the GT, but was all in black, and lacked the simulated wood trim on the facia, instrument binnacle and rear quarter mouldings.

It was under the TC's skin that the changes really showed, however. With reinforced 'chassis' sections and suspension mounting points, it was obviously a car built with competition work in mind. The front suspension was, like all Escorts, of the MacPherson strut variety, but stronger, and with a stabiliser bar added, while the rear suspension consisted of leaf springs, with twin trailing links. Further 'chassis' modifications included the use of large (Corsair), servo-assisted disc and drum brakes.

The engine was a modified version of the Cortina Lotus unit, of 1558cc capacity (82.55mm bore, 72.75mm stroke), and producing a hefty 110 bhp at 6000 rpm. To achieve this, two twin choke Weber 40DCOE carburettors were employed, and a free-flow, four branch exhaust set-up, mounted on the alloy, twin camshaft Lotus cylinder head. The power was fed via a four-speed gearbox ('borrowed' from the Corsair 2000E) to a two-piece propeller shaft and into a Cortina Lotus rear axle. Owing to lack of room under the bonnet, hydraulic clutch operation was employed, and the brake master cylinder was mounted remotely, with a separate supply tank.

Performance was scintillating, even by today's standards, with 60 mph appearing from standstill in around 8^1/$_2$ seconds, 100 mph in under half a minute, then continuing to a top speed in excess of 110 mph . . . pretty good in 1968! Average fuel consumption for the TC would normally be between 20 and 25 miles per gallon.

What about the others?

So the fastest of the original Escorts was the TC, but what performance could be expected of the less powerful models?

Well, the 1100 Escort was no ball of fire. In fact, it was positively sluggish, even when lightly laden. With a full load, even main road gradients necessitated changing down a cog or two. While this in itself was not difficult, courtesy of the light and positive gearchange, it could make long journeys rather laborious. Once rolling, steady progress could be made at today's legal motorway limit; it just took a long time to reach it! For the same reason, overtaking needed careful planning in the

lowest powered Escort.

From a standing start, an 1100 Escort would reach 60 mph in around 20 seconds, and eventually clock an uninspiring 78 mph top speed, unless there happened to be a headwind . . .

The 1300 Escort was a much better bet in terms of driving enjoyment. While not a sports car, it provided reasonable performance, helped by a flexibility not encountered in the 1100. As a comparison, a 1300 would reach 60 mph in around $16^1/2$ seconds, and had a true maximum speed of about 85 mph. While maximum intermediate gear speeds were similar to those of the 1100, at approximately 25, 40 and 60 mph for first, second and third gears respectively, the 1300 would reach these speeds more quickly, and would be far happier about pulling away at relatively low engine speeds. This obviously reduced the amount of gear changing needed, especially around town and on main road hills. The fuel consumption of the 1300 was about the same as that for the 1100, turning in over 40 mpg on a run, and around 35 mpg around town. This may appear to be slightly surprising, but the extra capacity of the 1300 engine allowed the engine to work less hard than the poor little 1100, which had to be flogged to maintain reasonable progress in traffic.

Some years ago I used an Escort 1100 for several months, and spent a lot of this time wishing that it had been a 1300 – those friends of mine who had the 'luxury' of owning 1300cc models at that time took great delight in proving the point!

The 1300GT was a different kettle of fish again. With its performance modifications, it was a spritely vehicle, capable of reaching 60 mph in under 13 seconds, and had maximum gear speeds of just under 50 mph in second, a little under 70 mph in third, and about 93 mph in top. The breathing mods made to the

1298cc engine gave the GT a power advantage of more than 15 per cent over the standard 1300, and this was well worth having. The improved efficiency of this modified engine again meant that fuel consumption would not suffer below the standard car's figures – unless the extra power was used up ALL the time!

Performance tuning firms such as Allard, of Richmond, Surrey, had long been uprating Ford Anglias, and continued their good work with the Escort. For example, they could provide an Escort 'GT+', giving 92 bhp, by employing the Cortina 1600GT engine, and they also offered a 1300 GT+. Indeed, many other tuning firms did (and still do) provide performance parts for the Escort, and there is much scope for uprating even the smallest engined cars.

More models

In March, 1968, an estate car version of the Escort was announced. In 1100 or 1300 form, the new vehicle was fitted with a $7^1/2$ inch clutch, to cope with the anticipated extra loads to be carried, and for the same reason had wider ($4^1/2$ inch) wheel rims, and 6.00, six-ply tyres as standard, plus uprated rear springs and shock absorbers.

The estates were four inches longer than the saloons, giving a load compartment over five feet long, and a luggage capacity of some $53^1/3$ cubic feet, with the rear seats folded forward, or 31 cubic feet with them in use.

There was also marginally more rear legroom than in the saloons.

To aid loading, the sill height was just over 20 inches from ground level, and the rear tailgate opening was a useful 47 inches wide at floor level. Even between the rear wheel arches, there was a handy 39 inch gap!

In April, van versions of the Escort were announced, in 6 cwt (1100cc) and 8 cwt (1300 cc) forms. The previous small Ford vans, based on the Anglia, had been popular vehicles, but the new Escort versions were nine inches longer, and four inches wider. They could therefore offer a payload some 112 lb up on the Anglia van, and accommodate another nine cubic feet of goods on their load platform, which was some three inches longer than their predecessors.

In May, 1968, automatic transmission became an option on all Escorts except the 1100cc estate cars and vans, the 1300GT and the TC. The Borg Warner 35 gearbox worked well, but the 1100 engine really didn't have enough power to cope with the automatic gearchange (having enough difficulty hauling itself along with a manual gearbox!), and the option was withdrawn from the 1100 saloon in August, 1969.

Revisions to the interior of the Escort were made in October, 1968, by which time 200,000 examples had been sold around the world. Safety 'break-off' door and window winder handles were fitted, and extra use was made of 'colour coded' trim, with new body colours also being made available.

Super and GT models gained 'wood grain' facias, and chrome beading around the door and rear windows, while at the same time losing the bright trim from the drip rail.

In May the following year, a Super version of the estate car was introduced. This had rectangular headlights, a two speed heater fan, pile carpeting, and padded rear armrests, giving a more luxurious option to what had become a popular load carrying vehicle.

On 30th May it was announced that the millionth vehicle had been produced at the Halewood plant since its opening, in 1963. The car was, of course, an Escort, and almost a

quarter of a million of them had been produced there. Anglias had also been built at Halewood (as well as at Dagenham) – some 487,000 of them!

Escort production was not confined to Britain, however, with Ford of Germany building the cars in earnest from 1969 onwards, in their Saarlouis plant, close to the French border.

'Our' small Ford (in left hand drive form) found favour with continental drivers as it did here, and the cars were to be produced in large quantities in Germany as here in Britain, over the next few years.

Demand from Germany for a four door Escort bore fruit in October, 1969, and also benefited British customers, giving still wider appeal to the range. A buyer could specify the extra two doors on 1100 or 1300 De Luxe or Super models, and on the GT.

In the same month, Ford uprated the suspension on all Escorts, to provide better ride comfort. Earlier cars had been prone to 'bottom' on their suspension, when heavily loaded.

RS arrives

January, 1970 heralded the announcement of the first 'RS' ('Rallye Sport') Escort, to be available from May, although 'full scale' production did not begin until November! A product of the Ford Advanced Vehicle Operations centre (FAVO) at Aveley, in Essex, the RS 1600 was a combination of 'Twin Cam', heavy duty Escort bodywork received from Halewood, mated with potent running gear at Aveley. This was based on a 1601cc version of the 1600GT Ford cylinder block (and employing Ford crankshaft, connecting rods, bearings and oil pump), but with a 16 valve, Cosworth designed cylinder head. This featured twin overhead

camshafts, driven by a fibre-glass reinforced, rubber belt, four branch exhaust system, and fuel supply by twin DCOE Weber carburettors. This 1.6 litre 'BDA' engine ('Belt Drive "A" Series – "A" denoting Anglia, from which the engine was originally developed) in fact represented a de-tuned (by about 100 bhp!) version of the Formula 2 engine developed by Ford and Cosworth in 1966. Its capacity of 1601cc, compared to the standard 1599cc, allowed it to compete in larger engine classes in competition, and the healthy 115 bhp output at 6,000 rpm gave it good performance. With a nought to sixty miles per hour time of around 8.3 seconds, a top speed of over 110 mph, and fuel consumption varying between 22 and 28 mpg, according to use, it gave very similar performance to the Lotus engined Twin Cam.

To handle the considerable performance, the car had stiff suspension, with the rear axle located for track and camber by additional longitudinal swinging arms, dual circuit brakes, 5^1/2J wheels, and uprated transmission, as also fitted to the TC model. External identification was easy, for the RS had flared wheel arches and quarter bumpers, like the TC, but, unlike the TC, it also had 'RS' badges on the front wings and the bootlid.

The RS also featured inset reversing lamps, a leather-rimmed steering wheel, an alternator, a dipping mirror, front and rear grab handles, two-speed wipers, quartz-iodine headlights, and laminated windscreen.

For the new model, customers had to find around 12 per cent more money than for the Twin Cam model, for a car that was marginally better equipped (the interior was still rather spartan), but which ultimately had much greater performance potential for competition work.

Although the two cars were initially sold 'side by side', the Twin Cam was discontinued just a few months later, in June,

1970, leaving the field clear for the RS 1600.

A less potent, but still spritely, and very useful Escort, was the 1300GT estate car, announced in April, 1970. With the 64 bhp version of the 1300cc pushrod engine, this car had a combination of trim, with elements from the Super and GT models.

Range changes

Of course the majority of Escort buyers did not want or need specifically sporty models, and of perhaps more relevance to them would be the changes made to the Escort range in September, 1970.

'Across the board' alterations included new, centrally mounted heater and windscreen wiper controls, with provision below for a radio, and the inclusion of better front seat anti-tip locks, and the fitting of a steering column lock as standard.

Gone were the 'De Luxe' and 'Super' specifications, to be replaced with a new system of designations.

The new 'basic' Escort replaced the De Luxe, and was available with the 1100cc engine, although the 1300cc engine was optional on the new estate, and standard if automatic transmission was specified. A new, full-width parcel shelf was standard, as was 'wood effect' facia trim.

The Escort 'L' boasted a carpeted interior, a map pocket, two-speed wipers, over-riders, reversing lamps, and grab handles, plus a useful boot mat and light.

The 'XL' versions, available only with the 1300 engine, also had a vanity mirror, cigarette lighter, opening rear side windows on two door models, and better interior trim, plus rectangular headlights and extra

brightwork. The XL estate car was also endowed with loop pile carpeting for the load area.

The GT models were given matt black grilles and rear panels, and most of the interior fittings of the XL, plus simulated leather seats, front armrests and a centre console, while the Twin Cam received the features of the new 'basic' saloon.

A new range of colours and trim materials was offered at the same time.

However, of more significance to most drivers were the improvements made to the valve timing, porting and combustion chambers, plus revised jet sizes, for the 1100cc and 1300cc engines. These resulted in useful power gains, starting with an extra 3 bhp (to a total of 48 bhp) from the standard 1100cc engine – an increase of 6.7 per cent, to another 5 bhp (now 57 bhp) from the 1300cc unit – an extra 9.6 per cent, and an additional 8 bhp from the 1300GT motor, this extra 12^1/$_2$ per cent giving a total output of 72 bhp from this unit.

On the road, this meant better performance all round, of course, and, for example, knocked around one second off the 1100's zero to sixty mph time, and increased its top speed by around 2 mph. The standard 1300 models were also a second or so faster to 60 mph, with an improvement of about 4 mph in top speed, while the GT gained approximately half a second during its nought to sixty dash, and now had a maximum speed of around 95 mph.

The extra 3 bhp for the 1100 was particularly welcome, for, while not making it a potent vehicle, it certainly helped it to keep up with the traffic rather better than it had done previously.

Low compression versions of the uprated 1100 and 1300 engines were available, offering economies of running on lower octane fuel, with power outputs of 44 bhp and 54 bhp respectively.

High performers

1970 was the year of the London to Mexico World Cup Rally, which Ford dominated with a team of 140 bhp, 1800cc, overhead valve Escorts, and Ford made much of this when they introduced their 'road going' Escort Mexico, in November of that year.

The new Escort was built at Aveley, and was based around the reinforced bodyshell and running gear of the RS 1600. The engine, however, was the 86 bhp, 1599cc, overhead valve 'Kent' engine, as fitted to the Cortina GT. The result was, to a certain extent, a 'sheep in wolf's clothing', when compared to the TC and RS 1600 models. On the other hand, the engine was easier to maintain and keep 'on song', and still gave good performance for the time, with a respectable nought to sixty mph time of around 10^1/$_2$ seconds, and a true top speed of just over 100 mph. At £1,150, it was also considerably cheaper – by about 25 per cent – than the RS.

The Mexico was normally sold with distinctive side stripes and 'Mexico' wording along each side.

In July, 1971. 'Clubman' packs were offered for the Mexico and RS 1600. They consisted of fog lights, long range driving lights, competition seats, a roll-over bar, and a map-reading light. The suspension was modified by using gas shock absorbers, front and rear, and by fitting stiffer front suspension.

The next 'hot' model to be announced, in October, 1971, was the two door Escort Sport, based on the mechanical components of the GT, but with a more basic specification, and bodywork closely resembling that of the RS 1600, complete with flared wheel arches, round headlights, quarter bumpers, and matt black grille, as fitted to all the 'sporty' Escorts. Again, in common with the faster Escorts, the Sport had 13 inch wheels, compared with the 12 inch items fitted to the standard production models up to GT level.

From the rear, the Sport could be identified by its black-painted rear panel.

Inside the car were GT type instruments, including a separately mounted tachometer, a sports steering wheel, and dipping rear view mirror, but none of the additional 'luxury' touches found in the more expensive GT, which was trimmed to a level approximating with the XL models. As a comparison, the two door GT cost around six per cent more than the Sport.

The more extrovert Escort Sport ran on stiff suspension, had servo-assisted disc brakes, and its cross-flow power was fed through a close ratio gearbox, all characteristics shared with the RS 1600. However the body shell, although visually resembling that of its more powerful, BDA engined stable mate, was not the heavy duty, reinforced item as fitted to the RS and Mexico.

Custom Packs for the RS and Mexico models were also announced in October, 1971, comprising additional sound-proofing, deep pile carpet, and cloth trim, plus a centre console, map reading light, and heated rear screen.

One million made

October, 1971 saw another landmark in Escort production, with the news that the millionth Escort had been produced, just three years and nine months since its introduction. This set a new production record for Ford, and made the Escort the fastest

selling Ford ever produced in Europe, even surpassing the pace set by the very popular Anglia.

The Halewood plant had contributed 555,000 cars and 110,000 vans to these total (European) Escort production figures.

The cars continued unchanged for 1972, but 1973 models, announced in late 1972, were given two-speed wipers, hazard warning lights, and a temperature gauge as standard. The same range designations were continued, with the XL specifications remaining highest. With the GT style instruments (tachometer, oil pressure and battery condition gauges), extra trim and other 'luxury' fittings, the XL was a well-equipped small car, in 1973.

The only other change for 1973 was the fitting of an aluminium cylinder block to the RS 1600. The weight was obviously reduced, but performance remained the same. Meanwhile, many specialist firms continued to provide fast versions of the Escort by various means. For example, Jeff Uren Ltd. were offering a conversion involving the fitting of the two litre overhead camshaft Cortina (Mk III) engine, giving 106 mph and nought to sixty mph in 8$^{1}/_{2}$ seconds, for £297, and their 'Navajo' conversion was just one of many available at this time.

The 1300E is born

March, 1973 saw the introduction of probably the most under-rated of all the Escorts – the 1300E. This model was the result of the same kind of thinking that had brought about the famous – almost legendary – Cortina 1600E, of which around 60,000 had been sold. That was, to provide an unusual level of refinement in a semi-sports saloon. Therefore, the 1300E (for 'Executive') was built on the

running gear of the Sport, with wide 13 inch wheels, coupled with bodywork features and trimmings showing more of a luxury than a sporting character. Therefore, apart from the flared wheel arches, the 1300E was recognisable by its rectangular headlamps and auxiliary lights, bright chrome wheel trims on spoked wheels (with radial tyres), extra side indicators on the front wings, pin striping, door-mounted mirror, badges on the rear pillars, black vinyl roof, and special metallic paintwork – purple, Amber Gold, or Venetian Gold.

Inside the car, there was extra sound insulation, cut pile carpet, wooden (walnut) facia and door top cappings, centre console, cloth seats, padded facia and sun visors, GT/Sport instrumentation, and three spoke steering wheel.

Under the bonnet was the 1300GT Kent engine, giving 72 bhp, and mated to the GT's close ratio gearbox. An alternator was standard equipment, as were the servo-assisted front disc brakes and the Escort Sport 4.125:1 differential.

The 1300E was one of the most pleasant Escorts, and it is a pity that in many ways its virtues have been overshadowed by those of the more powerful models. Yet despite this, there is a strong following for the car today, even if not on the same scale (yet) as for the Cortina 1600E.

RS 2000

June, 1973 saw the introduction of the RS 2000. Produced at FAVO, the new car was again based around the heavy duty, strengthened body shell of the RS 1600 and Mexico models, and started life in left hand drive form only, as the result of a £2 million order from Rallye Sport dealers in Germany. Right hand drive versions were available from

October, 1973, to satisfy the British market. The RS 2000 was powered by the two litre 'Pinto' engine, originating in the United States, and of course powering the two litre Cortina in Britain, in which model it was rated at 98 bhp. For the RS 2000, it was fitted with an electric fan, which gave it back another 2 bhp, and in this form it propelled the new Escort to 60 mph in around nine seconds, and gave the car a true top speed of 110 mph. When it is considered that there are still relatively few cars even today which can match this performance, it can be seen how revolutionary the RS 2000 was considered at the time of its introduction.

Power was fed via an adapted, close ratio Cortina 2000 gearbox and rubber insulated propeller shaft, to a high ratio (3.54:1) rear axle, giving relaxed engine revs at high speeds, and an impressive overall fuel consumption of between 26 and 28 mpg.

De-cambered rear springs allowed a lower ride height at the rear, with reduced shock absorber settings, compared with the Mexico and RS 1600, while the front springs were uprated by 30 per cent. The result was a fairly firm ride (and that's being kind!), but with excellent, neutral handling, which again set standards for its day. Inside the car were reclining, cloth trimmed front seats, loop pile carpet, and comprehensive instrumentation, in line with the other fast Escorts. Quartz halogen headlights were standard.

Changes

In October, 1973, suspension modifications were carried out across the main Escort range. The shock absorbers at the rear were now mounted vertically, instead of being inclined, and a rear anti-roll bar, designed to help

locate the axle as well as cut down body roll, was fitted.

At the front, a larger diameter anti-roll bar was employed. The combined effect of these changes gave the car a far better ride than previously.

One month later, the GT Escort was discontinued, although of course the GT's engine continued to power the Sport and 1300E models.

A four door version of the 1300E was introduced in April, 1974, giving a welcome option to this well appointed model.

Meanwhile, for the RS 2000, one could now specify Rallye Sport packs to uprate the engine (to 163 bhp), the transmission, the suspension, steering and brakes, and safety protection, to bring the car up to Group 1 competition standard, if required.

Rallye packs could also be bought for the Mexico, now consisting of a map reading light, fireproof bulkhead, roll cage, full harness, sump shield, battery isolator switch, oil cooler and so on.

There was also, of course, the Custom pack, with interior improvements including reclining seats, fabric trim, vinyl roof, centre console, and body stripes, plus a wide range of paint and other options.

The end of the Mark I

1974 was to provide a number of production landmarks for the Escort, with the two millionth example being built in June; 60 per cent had been produced in Britain, with around 1,187,700 coming from Halewood (including over 375,000 complete Escorts for export), and over 13,000 fast models originating from FAVO at Aveley – this plant being closed at the end of 1974, incidentally.

Escorts built in Germany had totalled just over 799,000, by comparison.

By the end of November, production of the Escort in Britain overtook that of the Anglia, at 1,288,957 units, the model to achieve this honour being a 1300E. At the same time, in Germany, production of the Escort Mk I was being phased out, with their final tally being just under 848,400 vehicles.

By January, 1975, U.K. sales of the original Escort were just over 649,000, out of worldwide sales totalling over two million. By comparison, total Anglia production just exceeded 1,829,600.

Hail the Mark II

The Mark II Escort was announced in January, 1975. The basic concept and layout remained the same as the original car, but the bodywork had been re-styled, and a host of detail changes were made, to update the Escort range, to take it into the 1980s.

The mechanical layout was identical to that of the previous model, with front engine driving the rear wheels through a four-speed, all synchromesh gearbox. There was also the option of a new, Bordeaux built, three-speed automatic gearbox.

The suspension had been considerably modified, to improve ride comfort, and to give better stability in side winds. At the front, the shock absorbers had been uprated, and the anti-roll bar diameter increased, while at the back the springs, previously having four leaves, had been replaced with wider, three leaf items.

The main part of these revisions were applied to the very late Mark I Escorts, but were refined in detail for the new model, and the car gained much praise for the quality of its ride comfort.

Ford took the opportunity of offering potential Escort

customers the 1599cc Kent engine, in 84 bhp form, as an alternative to the continuing 1.1 and 1.3 litre power units, and this was a welcome option, since the 1600 motor had previously only been available in the Mexico.

The most immediately striking difference between the Mark I and Mark II Escorts was the bodywork. For the new model, which was virtually the same size as the car it replaced, although fractionally narrower, more angular styling was applied, with fewer curves and flatter panels. While some people preferred the earlier car's lines, the general reaction to the new Escort was favourable, and the car had a neat, uncluttered look about it.

The stylish bodywork was slightly less wind-cheating than that of its predecessor, but there were other beneifts. To start with, the glass area had been increased by some 23 per cent, giving better all-round vision for the driver, and making the interior of the car seem considerably lighter, and more spacious. In fact, this was not just an illusion, for rear seat legroom, for example, had increased by two inches, over the earlier car. Luggage space, too, had increased, by some 10 per cent, to 10.3 cubic feet, while the boot sill height had been dropped by two inches, which helped when loading heavy items.

Inside the car there was much improved soundproofing, better front seats, and new instrumentation. This was neat and functional, winning praise and design awards for the layout and clarity of the gauges.

The facia of the Mark II Escort also saw the re-appearance of the Cortina type 'eyeball' air vents, which greatly improved ventilation and demisting.

There were 19 variations on the new theme, starting with the base 1100 and 1300, then 'L' and 'GL' versions, 1300 and 1600 Sport variants, and two 'luxury' models, the 1300 and 1600

Ghias. As before, there was a choice of two or four doors on most models (but not the Sport), and three door estate cars were available up to GL trim level.

The 'base' models were pretty basic, although they did now have radial tyres, electric windscreen washers, and two-speed wipers. The 'L' cars, however, featured many useful items such as halogen headlights, reversing lamps, heated rear window, hazard warning lights, dipping rear view mirror, grab handles/coat hooks, and (loop pile) carpeted passenger compartment, while the 'GL' (roughly equating with the previous 'XL') was also fitted with reclining front seats, a vanity mirror, a console (incorporating a clock), a chrome plated gear lever, armrests, a cigarette lighter, and a luggage compartment light.

The Sport models had quarter bumpers at the front, with black rear bumpers and body sills, two door-mounted rear view mirrors, over-riders, sports wheels and wider (175 SR 13) tyres, and auxiliary long-range driving lamps, plus unusual pin stripes along the body sides. Inside the car there was a sports steering wheel, extra instrumentation and a mileage trip recorder.

The plush Ghia Escorts were additionally endowed with rubber bumper inserts, tinted glass, bright exterior trim, protective body side mouldings, rectangular halogen driving lamps, black sills, a vinyl roof, sports wheels with bright rim embellishers, and tasteful 'Ghia' badging. The interior was refined, and incorporated cloth seats, high quality carpet (including the luggage compartment), a 'soft feel' steering wheel, head restraints and a rev counter in its high specification. In fact Ford's association with Ghia (a Ford-owned styling subsidiary company), in Turin, was to bear fruit in the form of consistent demand for more luxurious versions of their high volume models, like the Escort, Cortina,

Granada, Capri and, more recently, the Sierra.

Another useful feature of the Ghia models, shared with the Sport, was the fitting of a Weber twin choke carburettor. The two cars also both had new manifolding, a sporty camshaft, and stronger, close ratio gearboxes.

An interesting aspect of the new estate car models was that the bodywork was the same as that used for the Mark I versions, rear of the front doors.

The 53.3 cubic feet of luggage capacity in the estates was extremely useful, while the van models were more spacious still, with 62 cubic feet capacity, and they too shared the new front end/original rear and amalgum, which worked equally well.

As with the Mark I models, those in the Mark II range could be identified, to a certain extent, by the shape of their lights – the headlights of the GL and Ghia were large, square units, while those on all other models, including the Sport, were round. Both Sport and Ghia versions were fitted with additional, long-range driving lamps, which dominated the frontal appearance.

The new models, although announced in January, did not go on sale until March.

Another RS!

The 16 valve, BDA engined RS 1800 was also announced in January, 1975 (but did not become available until June). A very rare model, the RS 1800 had 115 bhp under its bonnet, supplied by the 1840cc (86.75mm bore, 77.62mm stroke) 'breathed on' twin overhead camshaft motor. Carburation was via a Weber 32/36 DGAV twin choke unit.

Transmission components

used on the RS 1800 owed a lot to the earlier RS 2000, but, for example, the gearbox was uprated.

The body looked very little changed from the less powerful Escort II models, but had subtle 'hints' at performance, courtesy of the front (black) quarter bumpers, neat front airdam and rear, bootlid-mounted spoiler. Acceleration was vivid, and the car reached 60 mph in under 9 seconds, going on to clock a top speed of around 115 mph. Equally impressive was the flexibility of the engine – perhaps not surprising with 120 lb.ft. of torque to play with! Fuel consumption varied between 24 and 30 mpg, depending on how much of a hurry the driver was in!

Only two months after the introduction of the RS 1800, the Mark II version of the RS 2000 was introduced. This model still featured the two litre Pinto engine, now developing 110 bhp (having a new exhaust system), and giving smooth, powerful acceleration to 60 mph in little over 8 seconds, and with a top speed of about 112 mph.

Fuel consumption was reasonable, and figures in the upper twenties could normally be expected.

Handling was excellent, with the car going exactly where it was pointed, even at high speed. To aid an enthusiastic driver, instrumentation was comparable with the earlier sporting Escorts.

It is no surprise, therefore, that the RS 2000 made a lot of friends, due to its impressive capabilities.

Against this, the interior of the car was quite spartan (despite the sports seats), and almost overpowering in its blackness, while the suspension was extremely firm, giving a very restless ride for passengers. However most RS 2000s were bought for their driving qualities, rather than for comfort. Having said that, four seats and a large luggage boot were always

provided on even the fastest production Escorts.

The 'ahead of its time' new RS featured unusual styling, with a wedge shaped front section made from deformable polyurethane, and with a flexible spoiler on the bootlid lip. It also had four round quartz halogen headlights adorning the black front panel, which, together with the extended section, had a rather 'stuck on' appearance. The nose reduced air drag by 16 per cent over the standard Escort bodywork, however, and Ford obviously felt that aerodynamics were more important than styling – a philosophy which is more prevalent among motor manufacturers today, of course.

Looks apart, the RS 2000 will always be remembered for its smooth, torquey power and superb handling.

Success story

That the Escort was well received by the public is evidenced by the fact that, in May, 1975, it was declared the best selling car in Europe.

However, it was becoming more expensive, when compared with the opposition. In addition, new cars such as the Vauxhall Chevette were providing challenges to the Escort's position in Britain, for example.

To make the Escort more competitive on price, Ford announced 'Popular' versions in July, 1975. The Populars were available as two door 1100 and 1300 models, and as two or four door 'Popular Plus' designations, again with the same choice of engine sizes.

In line with these changes, the 'base' Escort saloon model was dropped from the range, and the Popular became the starting point of the Escort line-up. To a great extent, Ford were repeating their move of the 1950s, when the 103E Popular was introduced

as a de-chromed and de-trimmed version of the Anglia, at a low price.

Similarly the Popular of 1975 was a very basic car, with black finish bumpers, door handles and window surrounds, and gone were the parcel shelf and body floor sound insulation, for example. It also had rubber floor mats, and ran on cross ply tyres, at a time when radials were very much in vogue. On the other hand, the two door 1300 version sold for around £200 less than the 'L' model, representing a saving of about 15 per cent.

The Popular Plus cars had equipment levels intermediate between the Popular and the 'L' models, and featured sound insulating underfelt, carpet, cloth seats, a parcel shelf, reversing lamps, a dipping interior mirror, and radial tyres.

One of the less desirable features of the Popular models was the fitting of 'economy' engines. These, based on the standard 1100 and 1300 Kent units, featured leaner mixtures and throttle limiters, resulting in less power, and, more often than not, INCREASED fuel consumption, since the cars had to be driven a lot harder to maintain progress! As an example, the 1100cc version of the 'economy' engine produced just 41 bhp – less even than the original 1100 Escort's far from generous 45 bhp!

At the same time as the Popular was introduced, minor improvements were made to the other Escorts. The 'L' cars received 13 inch wheels and front disc brakes, bright window trims, black painted sills, twin coachlines and reclining seats, 13 inch wheels, and body side mouldings.

Another Mexico

In January, 1976, the new RS 2000, announced the previous

March, and the latest Escort Mexico, were officially launched. I have already outlined the main aspects of the RS 2000, but the new RS Mexico (often referred to as the 'Mk II' Mexico) was a rather different vehicle, in many ways.

It was based around a strengthened version of the standard Mk II body shell, but without the plastic front end of the RS 2000. It featured a deep airdam at the front, and a bootlid mounted rear spoiler, and was identifiable by its black bumpers and window trims, and by its subtle coach lines.

Under the bonnet was a 95 bhp version of Ford's 1.6 litre, overhead camshaft 'Pinto' engine, featuring a Weber twin choke carburettor, and a special exhaust system.

In comparison with the pushrod-engined Escort Sport, in 1.6 litre form, the Mexico produced another 11 bhp, giving it a nought to sixty time of around 10 seconds, and a top speed of almost exactly 100 mph.

To handle this capability, the Mexico had the same transmission, brakes, steering, suspension and wheels as the RS 2000, and had identical driving qualities, but without quite so much 'go' as the larger engined car.

The Mexico's interior was similar to that of the RS 2000, but with more modest seats.

Changes

In February, 1976, all 1100 Escorts were fitted with the dreaded 'economy' engine from the Popular, but a more important landmark for Ford came in the summer. At this time, the Escort became Britain's best selling car, taking over this position for a short while from the Cortina, and helping to give Ford their biggest market share in this country since the early 1960s.

The following year saw the discontinuation of the RS 1800, in January, and major changes to the suspension on the main Escort range, in the autumn. These included the fitting of single leaf springs at the rear, accompanied by altered shock absorbers settings, and the reduction of the size of the anti-roll bars used. Improved ride and handling resulted.

At the same time, the Escort was now endowed with the traditional oval 'Ford' badge, and the engine size was scripted onto the bootlid. The estate cars were given rear wash/wipe systems as standard equipment (optional on models below GL level).

It is interesting to note that, at this time, more than nine out of ten 'home' sales Escorts were built in Britain, at Halewood, with only the Ghia and RS models being built in Germany.

Towards the 'Eighties

September, 1978 saw the last major revamp of the rear wheel drive Escort range. To start with, all cars except the Ghia were fitted with black front grilles, and a new 'soft feel' steering wheel became a standard fitting on all except Sport and RS models.

The track width increased by $1\frac{1}{4}$ inches, as a result of using wider-offset wheels, and handling was further improved on the Popular and basic estate cars, by the fitting of radial tyres.

Interior trim levels were also uprated, with the more lowly designations gaining carpet instead of matting, and the passenger side parcel shelf re-appeared. The Popular Plus cars also had a heated rear screen as standard equipment now, in addition to a body coachline.

'L' models were considerably enhanced by gaining square (tungsten) headlights, protective body side mouldings, and sports steel road wheels, plus extra sound deadening, an intermittent windscreen wipe facility, and 'houndstooth' trim.

A radio became a standard fitting on the GL, along with a new headlining, and 'Diamond' fabric trim, while the Sport models also gained a radio, and had extra soundproofing. They were also trimmed in a new 'Chevron' material.

Ghias had a new steering wheel, but were otherwise unchanged.

Revised fast Escorts

The 'hot' Escorts did not escape the range alterations, with the discontinuation of the short-lived Mk II Mexico, and with the RS 2000 now being available in two forms. The standard RS 2000 now had the basic trim from the discontinued Mexico, while the new RS 2000 Custom model had six inch alloy road wheels, sports seats and bronze tinted windows. It also gained a remote-control (driver's) door mirror, and had a centre console and better door panels, as well as carpeting and a light in the luggage compartment.

The performance of the two versions was identical, but the basic RS cost just over £3,900, while the Custom's price was some £500 higher.

The last years

1979 saw minor alterations to the Escort's specifications, with, for example, the addition of viscous couplings for the cooling fan, and the fitting of carpets and a brake fluid warning light to the basic estate cars. They, together with the Populars, also gained hazard warning lights and inertia reel seat belts, later in the year, while, in the autumn, the Sport featured a centre console and a cigarette lighter.

October saw the introduction of the 'Linnet' – a 'Special Edition' model based on the 1300 Popular Plus, but with GL seats, head restraints, a push-button radio, side stripes, a passenger door mirror and a sports steering wheel.

In December, the Escort Harrier appeared. This had the running gear of the 1.6 litre Sport, but had sports seats, tinted glass and black interior, with a push-button radio, a rear spoiler, and a remote control (driver's) door mirror.

The last of the Limited Edition rear wheel drive Escorts, which typified the final years of the car's production, was the Goldcrest, announced in May, 1980. This was built around 1.3 and 1.6 'L' models, with colour-coded wheels, seats from the GL, a centre console with radio and clock, side stripes, passenger door mirror and sports steering wheel.

End of the road

By the time the Mk III, front wheel drive Escort became available, in October, 1980, more than 960,000 Mk II models had been built at Halewood, while comparable production in Germany totalled over 647,000, giving the total figure for this model of around 1,607,000 units. With production figures for the Mark I standing at approximately 1,076,000 and 848,000 for Halewood and Germany respectively, the total for all rear wheel drive Escorts (Mk I and II form) from 1968 to 1980, amounts to well over three and a half million cars!

The success of the car in sales terms speaks for itself, and is reflected in the enormity of these numbers. Most Escorts

represented by these figures were used as daily transport for families and for enthusiasts, depending on the model.

However, while this book is primarily concerned with 'everyday' road use and restoration, it should not be forgotten that the Escort earned itself a formidable reputation in the field of motor sport, just as did the Cortina Mks I and II.

With victory after victory being notched up in International rallying, in particular, the Escort proved its versatility and popularity as a sports machine, and indeed there are still many rear wheel drive cars used today,

and competing successfully in all kinds of motor sport, around the world.

The new front wheel drive Escorts, with their modern design and hatchback bodywork, proved popular from their introduction, some 12 years after the first rear wheel drive cars appeared.

However, there are still many who mourn the passing of the old, 'traditional design' Escorts, from the hard working 1100cc family versions to the Twin Cam and RS road burners, and preservationists are around in numbers to make sure that many of these vehicles will survive for a long time to come.

HE1. An early Escort Twin Cam at speed. The car looks very similar to the less powerful models, but the front quarter-bumpers and wider wheels do hint at the potential performance, which is considerable.

HE2. The BDA engined RS 1600 is an extremely potent machine, and very similar in looks to the Twin Cam. Under the bonnet, however, the scene is rather different, with the Ford/Cosworth developed engine providing the power, instead of the Lotus unit.

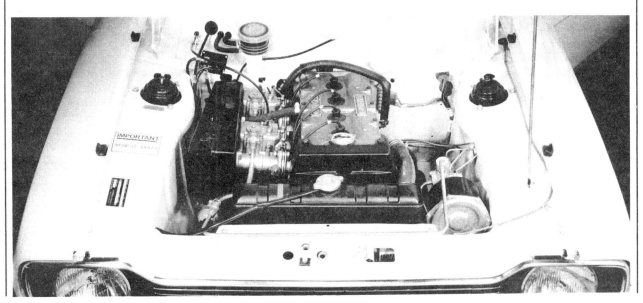

HE3. The car which many owners will be familiar with is the smallest engined of the Escorts – the 1100. This is an 'L' model, dating from 1972. Pre-1970 cars have plain hub caps.

HE4. Interior fittings on the cheaper Escort models are rather sparse, with rubber floor mats and lots of plastic in evidence. The padded, three spoke steering wheel identifies this car as a post 1970 model.

HE5. Escort estate cars are roomy vehicles, with 31 cubic feet of luggage space with the rear seats in use, and 53⅓ cubic feet with them folded down. This 1971 'L' model has carpet throughout.

HE6. The Mexico, announced in late 1970, is extrovert in character, with sports wheels, broad stripes and unashamed 'Mexico' lettering along the vehicle sides. The quarter bumpers of the other 'hot' Escorts were perpetuated with the Mexico.

HE7. It looks docile enough, but the engine of the Mexico – an 86 bhp 1600GT unit, mated with the Escort TC and RS running gear, has won the car a lot of friends for its willing performance. This pushrod, overhead valve engine also makes the Mexico easier to look after than earlier fast Escorts.

HE8. The 1300E was to the Escort what the 1600E was to the Cortina, although, until recently, it has not attracted the same interest. This example, in pristine condition, is just one of many looked after today by enthusiastic owners.

HE9. The interior of the 1300E is a far cry from that of the basic Escorts. With better seats, carpets and wood trims, it is a sought-after model today.

HE10. The Mark I Escort RS 2000s featured striking paint design, sports wheels and (still) quarter front bumpers. The model was introduced in June, 1973, and has built up a strong following.

HE11. The underbonnet view of the RS 2000 is very similar to that of a two litre overhead cam Cortina, with what is basically the same engine installed in the Escort. The performance from the RS 2000 is extremely quick, and on par with much of today's sporting machinery.

HE12. The cockpit of the RS 2000 was designed with performance driving in mind, and features comprehensive instrumentation, sports seats and centre console.

HE13. The advent of the Mark II Escort brought cleaned up body lines and a new, attractive grille. This 1.1 litre Escort Popular is a neat car, although it looks very basic, with its lack of bright trim.

HE14. The facia of the cheaper Mark II models is rather austere, but the instruments are easy to read. The stalk controls are less easy to comprehend, compared with the switchgear used on the Mark Is . . .

HE15.   The 'Ghia' versions of the
Mark II are smart cars, and
tastefuly furnished within. The
large, square headlights were also
fitted to GL models.

HE16.   Pin-stripes identify the
Mark II Sport, as do the rather
vulnerable driving lamps. It
shared its 1.6 litre pushrod
engine with the 1.6 Ghias.

HE17.   Interior fittings on the
Sport are less luxurious than on
Ghia models, and the facia still
looks a little spartan, with the
exphasis more on performance
than comfort.

HE18. With similar pin-striping to that used on the Sport, the Mark II Mexico features a front airdam, and has no over-riders on its quarter bumpers. Its high performance and neat looks made it a car which was, and still is, much in demand.

HE19. The Mark II RS 2000 was acclaimed for its taut handling and breathtaking performance, still not rivalled by many of today's high performance saloons. The 'add-on' front end helps the aerodynamics.

3 Buying

Which vehicle?

If you are looking for a second-hand vehicle of any sort, it is helpful to have a good idea in your mind of the kind of car you are looking for. The same applies when contemplating buying a Cortina or Escort.

There are several important factors to take into account, and these usually include, to start with, the amount of money you have to spend on the vehicle, and the amount of time and effort you intend to apply to it, having bought it. For example, you could set out with the intention of buying a complete wreck of an early Cortina or Escort, with the express thought of stripping and rebuilding the car to 'as new' condition. On the other hand, you may prefer to buy a later car in roadworthy condition, with the intention of carrying out just 'running repairs', and gradually improving it while using the car for everyday transport.

Then again there are those cars which are bought in anticipation of them being put into use fairly quickly, but which in the event turn out to be major rebuild projects.

So it is good to be aware of how much money, time, effort and skill you are likely to have to expend on your chosen vehicle,

before you actually buy it.

However, even before you get to this stage, you will need to know roughly which model you are going to aim for – whether this is to be an 'original' Mark I Cortina, for example, or a late sporting Escort?

If you have already read the 'Heritage' chapters in this book, you should now have a reasonable idea of the character and performance potential of each Cortina and Escort, and you will probably know whether you want a car strictly for family use, or whether a fast road vehicle is your aim. Fortunately one of the advantages of choosing the Escort/Cortina ranges as a starting point is that there are so many different models, with widely differing characteristics, to choose from.

While on this subject, it is also worth considering very seriously the insurance costs of your car, even if it is going to be some time before it is restored and actually used. For insurance groupings vary from very low (Group 2) for the smallest engined cars, to Group 7 for the Cortina Lotus and Escort RS2000, for example. If you are a young driver, or pay high premiums anyway, this will obviously be important.

It may in any case be worth taking out an 'agreed value' collector's car policy on older or

rare models. Such policies normally specify the car's value, agreed between yourself and the insurance company (often subject to the report of an independent valuer or engineer), and may carry low premiums in return for a limit on the mileage covered each year. While these policies are fine if you use the car, say, just at weekends, or only for high days, holidays and old vehicle rallies, they may not be of much use if you intend to use your car for daily transport, and cover, say 10,000 miles a year. Your best bet is to talk to a member of the British Insurance Brokers' Association for expert specific advice, when you know which model you are looking for.

Wreck or unmarked example?

Presumably, if you are reading this book, you are interested in carrying out at least some restoration work on the car you eventually buy. However, it is often easy to be led into believing that a restoration project will soon be accomplished, and that a total wreck can be transformed into a

gleaming concours winner in a matter of weeks. Such hopes can soon be dashed by a few horrific discoveries made when you start work on the vehicle (guess how I know?).

Make no mistake, restoring a car from 'the ground up' is hard work. It is also, almost inevitably, expensive, at times very frustrating (especially when you cannot obtain a vital part, for example), and extremely time-consuming. As a general rule, make an estimate of the time and money you reckon you will need to complete a major rebuild, and the figures obtained can almost certainly be at least doubled. There will also be times when you really wish you had never started the project, and, sadly, many people do give up halfway through, and often after much of the hard work has already been done.

Other serious problems can arise when rebuilding a total wreck, simply through lack of skills or facilities. For instance, for any structural bodywork repairs, welding is essential, not just desirable. Unless you know someone who is willing to do the work for you, or you are able to weld yourself, you may end up with terrific bills for structural restoration – often sufficient to drain funds originally put aside to complete the mechanical jobs, for example.

I don't wish to put anyone off, but it is a good idea to be aware of the potential problems before you start; that way, it is easier to overcome them!

Therefore, it is wise to take into account – and be honest about – your own affinity for d-i-y work, when viewing your would-be project vehicle. It may be more sensible (and cheaper in the long run) to spend a little more on a car in better basic condition, and carefully restore the paintwork and mechanical parts, for instance, than to take on a 'jigsaw puzzle' back to basics restoration.

There are sufficient Escorts and Cortinas being restored these days to come across 'half done' cars, often at bargain prices. In many cases the owner will part with the car at less than cost price, just to see it go to a good home, although this doesn't always apply, of course.

Such cars usually give plenty of scope for work, but, if the basic structure has already been tackled properly, they can save a lot of your money and time.

If you are not sure what you are looking for, it pays to take someone with you who at least understands cars, and preferably who is also particularly at home with Fords. In any event two heads are better than one for spotting dodgy areas, and for balancing your own view of the vehicle. This applies equally to buying a wreck, a restored vehicle, or an original example.

Of course "All that glistens is not gold" is a saying which is especially true when applied to second-hand cars. You may find a Ford that positively glows from a distance, and which may be advertised as "fully restored", or "much bodywork carried out", etc. Unfortunately not everyone is honest, and what appears to be shiny bodywork in excellent condition just could be harbouring large areas of quickly disguised rust and old body filler. It therefore pays to treat everything the vendor says as possibly doubtful, at least until you have satisfied yourself. The old trick of running a magnet over any 'suspect' areas of bodywork still applies today; a magnet will stick to steel, but never to filler! Tapping the surface can also tell you a lot about what lies beneath the paintwork – a dull thud is a possible indication of the presence of glass fibre and filler, compared with the more hollow ring of sound metal, but this isn't a conclusive test, unless you are absolutely sure what filler sounds like!

It is much more difficult to tell if a car is a hastily prepared 'rogue' vehicle when the paintwork is new – at this stage it will look very much like the superbly restored car you think you are looking at! Far better, if possible, to look at a car several months after its restoration, when, if it has been a job done properly, it will still look in first class condition. If, on the other hand, the bodywork rectification has been hastily carried out, without proper attention to rust killing, and with areas quickly filled, you will find evidence of this, with rusty bubbles emerging, and with filler cracking in places due to weathering. Filler applied on top of rust soon lifts off again.

Is it sound?

If you are confident that you can tackle any aspect of bodywork repair, you may not be concerned so much if the floor, 'chassis' sections and suspension mountings are in imminent danger of collapse.

If, on the other hand, you are looking for a sound vehicle as a basis for a less 'in depth' restoration, you really need to be sure that these areas on your Ford are in good condition, and the most important aspect of inspecting the vehicle is therefore its underside. Whether Escort or Cortina, try to view the whole of the underbody of the car by putting it on ramps, and with the aid of a strong light; take a torch with you.

Whatever you do, NEVER crawl under a car supported only by a jack – it may collapse. ALWAYS use axle stands or ramps.

Cortinas and Escorts are similar in many respects. Therefore, the following sections apply equally to either car, except where the text highlights specific checks for each model.

Front suspension mountings

All Mark I and II Escorts and Cortinas use MacPherson struts with integral front springs and shock absorber units. Their security in terms of attachment to the vehicle is vital for safety, for detachment from the mountings (not unheard of!) means no steering, no suspension and no brakes . . .!

So, when surveying any Escort or Cortina, put the front suspension mountings high on your list of areas to examine closely. Start by opening the bonnet, and look carefully at the tops of the inner wings. The upper mountings for the suspension legs are marked by the three securing bolts, placed around the top of the strut. The surrounding metalwork should be absolutely sound, with no flaking, and without any rusty holes. Any weakness in this area can be very dangerous, especially if the reinforced suspension turret webs, below the wing tops, are also suspect, but more about these later.

On most cars more than a few years old, you will find that the original inner wing tops have rusted through from below, and have been reinforced by the addition of a plate attached to the top of the inner wing. This may look fine, but it is important that this plate should have been attached to the original metal by continuous welding, around the plate, and by no other method.

If the plate has simply been tack welded at intervals, or brazed, or riveted, then further attention is necessary to do the job properly. It is also possible, although extremely difficult to check from a visual examination, that although the area has been repaired by welding a plate on top, the metal below could still be extremely rusty. The natural cavity between the new plate and the original metal is, of course, a

breeding ground for rust, as are all such 'sandwiched' metal joints, and the surrounding metal can rust through again later. Therefore, look hard for evidence of rust eating through around the edges of the plate.

Many people mistakenly believe that simply welding a plate to the top of the inner wing cures all ills with regard to rusted MacPherson strut mountings. Unfortunately this is not the case. For when these cars were new, the weight of the vehicle, and the loads imposed by the suspension system, were spread along the inner wing structure by means of a stiff turret web, around and behind the suspension unit at each side of the vehicle.

As the cars age, moisture and salt accumulate around the tops and sides of these webs, eventually eating through the metal and dangerously weakening the structure, as, increasingly, the loads are taken by the upper mounting and inner wing area. This eventually bends or breaks under the strain, giving rise to the unusual spectacle of the suspension struts trying to escape upwards through the bonnet!

So, apart from checking that the upper mounting appears to be solid, from under the bonnet, look hard to establish that the inner wing plate is not distorting upwards, and then closely examine the under-wing area, around the suspension turret webs. Look particularly hard at the top, where, in bad cases, the inverted dish, into which the suspension leg fits, may be parting company from the web sides and the upper part of the inner wing. Brush away accumulated mud for a better look, and suspect any car on which these areas appear to have been treated with a heavy, recent dose of underbody sealant – it could just be filling up rusty holes here!

Apart from obvious safety considerations, these areas are among the most vital to examine

if you are buying the car with a view to immediate use. Rectification is quite tricky, and expensive if you are not doing the job yourself. It is also time-comsuming, since to do the job properly, the front wings need to come off – this in turn can be expensive, since they are welded on and can often be destroyed in the process of removing them!

The good news is that if you are contemplating a major, 'off the road' rebuild anyway, the job will probably not put you off buying the car, which should be priced accordingly. In addition, kits to rebuild the turrets are available from panel manufacturers such as LMC Panels, for all Mark I and II Cortinas and Escorts.

It should go without saying that a car with serious rust in this vital area will be a sure candidate for MoT failure, so think carefully before buying such a vehicle!

Apart from the MacPherson struts, the anti-roll bar attachments to the bodywork, and the track control arm or compression strut mountings must all be secure. If any serious corrosion exists within twelve inches of such mountings, the car will fail the MoT test. Make sure too that the prefabricated type track control arms used on some cars (compared with the heavy duty forged type used on others) have not corroded around each end.

Rear suspension mountings

The strength of the attachment points for the rear springs and the shock absorbers are also vital, of course, and any serious corrosion within 12 inches of these will, again, prevent the car from obtaining a legitimate certificate of roadworthiness.

Look first at the areas around

each end of the road springs, from below the car. The springs are attached to the 'chassis' by means of short hangers, and it is important that all metal in the vicinity of these hangers is sound. The rear ends are best observed from under the back of the car; the front mountings are best studied from in front of each rear wheel. When carrying out this check, pay careful attention to the channel sections of 'chassis' that sweep down each side, just inboard of each rear wheel; mud and salt from the road can accumulate here and eat into the main structure. This applies equally to Escorts and Cortinas.

The rear shock absorber mountings also need to be strong, and of course the bodywork surrounding them, so pay careful attention to these areas too. All saloon models, and Escort estates, employ telescopic type shock absorbers. With these, the upper end of the tube is attached to the car floor by bolting it through a reinforced mounting plate. On saloons, the upper part of the mounting is best observed from inside the luggage boot, followed by a close survey of the underbody condition in this area, from below the vehicle. Of course it is easiest, for this and other underbody checks, to have the vehicle raised, on car ramps or axle stands.

Cortina estate cars, both Mark I and Mark II models, employ lever arm type rear shock absorbers, bolted directly to webs within the rear bodywork. Make sure that the metal surrounding the shock absorber is sound, particularly behind the unit. This will normally be obvious from a visual examination.

The 'chassis'

Like most modern cars, the Cortina and Escort were built on unitary construction principles, with no separate chassis as such. Nevertheless, the bodywork is reinforced by having hollow box section members running along and across the vehicle, giving strength and rigidity.

Assuming that the suspension mounting areas, already described, are sound, you should continue by looking along the length of each of these members, watching for corrosion damage, and also for evidence of twisting or other deformation, perhaps the result of accident damage.

The underbody layouts of the Cortinas Mark I and II are similar, and the following checks apply equally to both versions; the Escort 'chassis' is slightly different.

Starting with the Cortinas, the danger areas to examine first are those in direct 'line of fire' from spray thrown up by the front wheels.

So, look first around each front bumper mounting, where the vertical panel meets the 'chassis' section at this point, just adjacent to the anti-roll bar attachments.

At the opposite end of the wheel arch, just inboard of and behind each front wheel, the vertical sections of the hollow, integral 'chassis' section here are particularly prone to rust damage. Also at serious risk are the rear sections of the inner wings, the jacking points (the jacking points and adjacent floor sections normally rust in unison on Cortinas!), and the whole of the front chassis extension channel sections, all immediately behind the wheels. Other danger areas in this vicinity are the 'outrigger' channels, running across the vehicle on each side, from the inner sill towards the centre of the car.

Make a very close scrutiny of the inner sill area, particularly where it joins this outrigger; normally if the outrigger is rusted, so will be the inner sill, for moisture and mud soon enters holed channels, and rusting accelerates between adjacent sections.

Look at the continuation of the main longitudinal members, where they pass over and behind the rear axle, and be sure to examine BOTH sides of each member, as well as the bottom plate, for small holes on either side can spell a seriously weakened section. While you're under the car, look too at the main floor pan, especially in the vicinity of reinforcing beams. Again, rust in one section normally spreads quickly to adjacent panels.

Make sure that any repairs to the floor or to 'chassis' members have been carried out only by continuous welding, around the entire perimeter of the repair section; anything less will be frowned on by an MoT examiner, and anyway may allow moisture in.

Even if all seems well from below the car, don't assume necessarily that the vehicle structure is sound. Always double check by closely examining the floor of the vehicle from above.

This often means disturbing carpets which may be very firmly attached; nevertheless the effort is well worthwhile, for many apparently sound cars have horrors lurking beneath their floor coverings! In particular, check around the seat and safety belt mountings, and at the joints between the floor pan and the inner sill panels, all favourite places for corrosion to take hold. In addition, check that all sections of floor directly above the integral channel sections of 'chassis' are sound.

Look hard at the condition of both inner and outer sills, since large holes or areas of rust in either will obviously weaken the box section formed by the two panels. Small holes may not be so serious, but if several are evident, along the length of the sill, the chances are that it won't be long before gaping holes

appear. New outer sill panels are available, however, and very cheaply, fortunately.

Finally, as far as the main structure on the Cortina is concerned, look closely around the front door support pillars, and up into the corners between the bulkhead and the side panels, from below the dashboard, with the aid of your torch. Also examine the front edges of the door pillar areas, from under the front wings. Serious rusting here means major repair work is needed, involving, again, removal of the front wings for access to the affected areas.

Much of the foregoing applies equally to the Escorts, although the construction varies slightly from that of the Cortinas.

On the Escort, the main 'chassis' members comprise two longitudinal channel sections, running the length of the car, with a cross-member at the front, but without the outriggers as used on the Cortina.

Check the entire length of each of these channels, including the sides, and look particularly closely at the sections which lie inboard of the rear wheels, where salt-induced corrosion is prevalent. As with the Cortina, the areas of these chassis sections supporting the rear spring hangers are vitally important and, again, need careful inspection.

The body sills on the Escort also need very careful checking, starting with the outer elements, below the doors, and following the entire length of the body between the front and rear wheels. Small holes or evidence of minor filling MAY be acceptable, but beware – if holes have started to appear it means that rust has taken a hold, and the probability is that the rest of the panel won't be far behind the first area, in displaying perforation. Check that the areas of body sill which extend below the floor, are sound too. If repairs have been carried out – and they almost certainly will have been

on a well-used early Escort – make sure that the new sections or panels have been welded on properly, and have not just been 'tacked' on.

As with the Cortina, the areas of the Escort most at risk are those which receive spray from the road wheels. Therefore examine all the wheel arches carefully, especially the areas immediately behind the front wheels, where the floor meets the wheel arch, and holes are often evident! Look closely, too, at the front inner wings, near the anti-roll bar mountings.

It is particularly important to examine the state of the floor from above as well as below. The front seat mounting channel sections can part company with the floor panel, and the inner sills often separate from the floor too, especially around the seat belt mountings, and in the front footwell areas. Rust is encouraged by mud thrown up from the front wheels.

It is a good idea to lift out the rear seat base and check the state of the floor from here, forwards, following the line of the 'chassis' channel section, below the floor, each side. Even on fairly late Mark II Escorts, you are likely to find that the top of this channel, formed by the floor, has collapsed, leaving a rusty, open and weakened structural member! The degree of rectification necessary depends on the extent of the damage, but it is better to discover it before you buy the car, than afterwards!

The front door pillars need close examination, as described for the Cortina, for, especially on early cars, corrosion here can be quite spectacular, even though, from a casual glance, all may seem well.

Bodywork

If all is well underneath the car, make a very thorough

examination of the main bodywork. It is important to do this before moving on to examine the running gear of the vehicle, since the restoration of bodywork is, almost without exception, far more costly and time consuming than rebuilding mechanical components. If you intend to carry out a full rebuild, this may not be so important, but if you intend using your 'new' Ford for a running restoration, it pays to get one that is bodily intact!

Start by looking around the front wings. In particular, the areas surrounding the headlights are prone to rusting. The Cortinas and Mark I Escorts are especially susceptible to holes appearing on top of the headlight, and around each side, due to the collection of mud and salt from the road in these areas. The upper sections at the rear of the front wings, adjacent to the bulkhead, are also danger points. Mud from the road collects on the ledge just below the wing top, and holes eventually appear. In severe cases, the bulkhead will also rot through, leaving an open passageway for water to enter the vehicle by, eventually causing rust in the door pillar and front floor pan!

Therefore, even if the wing looks sound, examine it from below with the aid of your torch, for evidence of bodged repairs. Many Escorts and Cortinas have had these areas simply filled with filler, placed on top of the rust – such repairs seldom last very long.

Normally, filled wings will be obvious, but checking with a magnet will help, as will looking carefully along the surface of the wing with the light behind it; slightly less than perfect repairs will show up as ripples.

With the bonnet open, examine the edges of the wing tops; where rusting is serious, the wing flanges will be separating from the engine bay side panel lip; this is difficult to disguise.

Finally, look down the rear edges of each front wing, where

they meet the front edges of the doors. Water trapped behind the panel can rust the wing through here, especially towards the bottom of the panel, and corrosion here will usually be obvious.

The front panel, below and behind the front bumper, is another area to look at closely. Strangely, some cars have suffered badly in respect of rust here, while others seem to have survived intact – even early models. So, look carefully, in case your 'guinea pig' vehicle has rusted here. It is not unusual to find dents and scrapes in this lower panel, from careless parking, for example, and it can often give a clue as to how well the car has been cared for.

The bonnets are all prone to rusting along the front edge, and the extent of this is best gauged with the lid open. On some cars, there are gaping holes all along the inner lip, and it won't be long, in such cases, before the rust eats its way through to the outer panel. If the bonnet is stiff to open, or flexes from the rear edge, look around the hinge brackets, where they bolt onto the bonnet panel. Sometimes rust weakens the metal here, or, in some cases, lack of lubrication of the bonnet hinges means that the bonnet lid actually pivots by flexing, instead of opening by its hinges!

The windscreen pillars should be looked at closely; these are vital for holding the roof up, of course, and cars which have suffered from severe rusting in the area of the bulkhead and door pillars can also suffer from spreading rot; this travels up the windscreen pillars and can almost sever them. Shoddy repairs in this area should be apparent; look for evidence of filler flaking away. Proper rectification involves welding, after removal of the windscreen.

Doors on the Escort and Cortina can be found to be rusty in several areas. First, open them wide and look around the hinge area; also check to see if the hinge pins are worn (a straightforward replacement job) by lifting the door up and down by its rear edge; if the door moves more than just perceptibly, the pins are worn, with detrimental long-term effects on the door catch, as well as increasing difficulty in shutting the door.

The lower door edges should be checked carefully, for water collects here and eventually rusts right through the door skin, from the inside.

Other suspect areas include the bases of the window frames. especially in the corners. In severe cases, the top section of the door can actually break off. These comments also apply to the tailgates on estate car models, with particular problems occurring along the lower edges.

The rear wheel arches can suffer badly from rust, and in many cases not only does the outer flange completely disappear, but the outer section of the rear wing can part company from the mudguard panel. Once this happens, water and mud are free to travel along the inside edges of the wing and adjacent panels, with catastrophic results. Therefore this is a very important check, best made with the aid of your torch. Even then, it is difficult to see the full extent of any damage without removing the rear wheels. However, be particularly cautious if the outer wheel arch edge looks moth-eaten, or has obviously been heavily filled.

The lower sections of the rear wings, behind the wheels, also suffer from serious rusting, especially on early cars, be they Cortinas or Escorts. In bad examples, the lower edges are completely missing.

I have already covered examination of the body sills in the 'Chassis' section, so I will simply say here that any holes spell problems, and that if there are more than just one or two small ones, the best course is to replace the sills with new items.

The state of the inside of the boot can be quite revealing about how a car has been looked after through the years. If the one you are looking at is clean and tidy, it bodes well. If, on the other hand, it is full of sand, dents and rust, the previous owners may not have looked after the car too well. Not conclusive evidence, it's true, but another pointer, at least.

Anyway, lift the boot mat or carpet, and make sure that the floor is not rusty or wet, especially in the corners. If it is, the boot lid seal may be leaking, which means more rust problems in the long term.

Paintwork

If the paintwork on your potential purchase is merely a little dull, especially on the roof, bonnet and boot lid, which tend to catch the sun, it may be salvageable by the use of cutting compound, followed by a liquid haze remover, and finally a good quality car polish. However, if large areas of the bodywork are affected by rust, dents, or flaking paint, a respray is the only answer to get such a vehicle looking smart again. Again, this may not be a reason for not buying the car, depending on how much restoration work you intend to carry out, and of course the asking price.

Interior

The condition of the interior trim is probably more important than many people realise, when starting out on a restoration. For the seat facings and panel coverings for early cars may be almost impossible to obtain now,

at least if you are attempting to bring the car back to original specification. Of course, motor vehicle dismantlers can provide some items of trim, but with the first Cortinas dating back to 1962, and even the early Escorts to 1968, such cars are becoming increasingly difficult to come by as a source of trim parts in a decent state.

So, if the door panels and seat coverings are in good condition, so much the better. Again, the state of a car's interior can tell you much about the way in which it has been looked after. If, as many are, it is ankle deep in rubbish, with tears in the upholstery and worn out panels hanging off the doors, the chances are that it has been neglected in other areas, too.

Of course, if you are not too concerned about originality, even very tatty seats can be rebuilt, and trim panels re-faced with material which may be close to, if not exactly like, the original. The same applies to headlinings and floor coverings. The original rubber matting on early cars may be difficult to reproduce exactly, unless you are lucky enough to find another scrapped vehicle with a good interior.

The seats on early Cortinas and Escorts were prone to collapsing, especially the driver's seat in well-used examples. These tended to drop at the rear first, and you will soon know if your potential buy is suffering from this problem – if you sit in the driving seat and feel you are sinking, the seat needs renovation.

Power units

The engines used in Cortinas and Escorts changed over the years, and it is easiest to start at the beginning, with the non cross-flow units fitted to the Mark I Cortina.

The first engines used were the three bearing, 1200cc units, also used in the Anglia Super. These engines gained an unfortunate reputation for main bearing problems, due to excessive flexibility of the crankshaft. Of course a lot depends on how the car is driven, and on the maintenance it has received, but on any high mileage Mark I Cortina 1200, listen for a rumbling from the 'bottom end' of the engine when warm. In addition, look for evidence of fuming from the engine, particularly at speed or when under load, and, after a test run, take off the oil filler cap and watch for oil fumes emerging as the engine is revved gently. If serious fuming is evident, the chances are that the pistons, rings and cylinder bores are worn, or that one or more of the piston rings has broken. In this case, an engine stripdown or replacement will be required.

The five bearing, 1500cc engine, first offered on the Cortina in 1963, was a far stronger unit. With the crankshaft more firmly anchored, main bearing problems were overcome.

However, even on 1500cc engines which have seen much more than 60,000 miles, piston slap may be evident, and a stripdown and overhaul is advised as soon as this occurs; another 10,000 miles or so without attention, and the engine, if used in this condition, may start to break its piston rings.

The timing chains on engines of either capacity have a tendency to rattle after high mileages. This is due to wear on the chain, and on both camshaft and crankshaft sprockets. If the car you are considering buying exhibits this rattle, it is best to think in terms of replacing the chain, both sprockets and the chain tensioner, for a complete cure.

The cross-flow engines fitted to later Cortina Mark IIs, and to mainstream production Escorts, all have five bearing crankshafts,

and there are no particular problems with crankshaft or bearing wear. High mileage engines, or those which may have been thrashed and therefore are prematurely worn, will start to show their condition by fuming from the engine breather when hot. This occurs particularly under load, when blue (burnt oil) smoke may also be emitted from the exhaust. This smoke will be especially obvious after a long downhill section with the car on 'over-run' – when the car accelerates at the bottom of the hill, appreciable smoke means that the pistons, rings and cylinder bores are seriously worn.

Another serious problem to watch for on the cross-flow engines is premature break-up of the cam followers (tappets). The faces of the cam followers wear thin, and can eventually split in two, causing a 'clack clack' noise from the engine. This may start quietly, and be intermittent to begin with. However, the intensity and frequency of the noise will increase as the trouble worsens. An engine with this condition should be attended to immediately, for if the car is driven any appreciable distance with one or more cam followers broken, the camshaft will be quickly ruined. Unfortunately rectification is not straightforward. The engine must come out of the vehicle and be inverted, and the camshaft removed, to enable the stepped cam followers to be extracted from their bores in the cylinder block. They should all be replaced as a matter of course, preferably along with the camshaft. Unless the engine has been taken out of service as soon as the noise started, the chances are that the surface of the shaft will have been damaged anyway.

Therefore, beware the seller who advises you that the car is suffering from a 'wide valve clearance' that only makes itself heard occasionally – the chances are that the culprit is a broken cam follower, with all that entails.

A wide valve clearance in any case will be audible all the time, not just intermittently.

The twin camshaft engines used in the Cortina Lotus and Escort Twin Cam models normally present few problems, PROVIDED that they have been properly serviced, including an engine oil change, at the specified 2,500 mile intervals. Apart from the engine being 'off tune', serious troubles in these units result mainly from them being continually thrashed, or lack of regular attention – in particular with regard to lubrication. Either area of lack of care on the part of one or more previous owners will result in a 'smoky', oil burning engine, although it has to be said that these engines were never particularly frugal in their appetite for oil, even when new.

The same general comments about lack of owner care, in maintenance and driving manner, apply equally to the other fast Escorts, including the BDA engined RS 1600.

Cars with the 'Pinto' overhead camshaft engines do suffer from heavy camshaft and follower wear, after high mileage. The problem is identifiable by a loud and continuous clatter from the top of the engine. The mileage at which the trouble starts varies according to the type of use to which the car has been put, and the frequency of oil changes. Rectification is not particularly easy, nor is it cheap, as inevitably it will involve the purchase of a new camshaft and followers.

There are several general checks to make on the engine of your prospective purchase, regardless of the size and capacity.

Start by looking around the engine bay for evidence of oil and coolant leaks. There is no particular evidence of either being a general problem, but, on older cars in particular, the cooling system can accumulate debris, and the resulting continuous

overheating can push anti-freeze mixture out of the overflow pipe. Therefore, with the engine cold, take off the cooling system filler cap, and look at the condition of the coolant. If it is murky, with muddy looking particles, it cannot do its job properly – it should be clean looking, and at least translucent, if not transparent!

If the walls of the engine compartment are covered in fresh-looking engine oil, as well as the power unit itself, the chances are that the engine is blowing out oil fumes. The problem could be a failed crankshaft front oil seal, or excessive crankcase pressure, caused by piston 'blow-by', due to worn pistons, rings and cylinder walls. Oil and vapour can be forced out of the dipstick tube and breather, creating a dreadful mess. Any engine showing these signs is well overdue for overhaul, no matter what excuse the seller may give!

If you can, try to hear the engine start from cold. It should fire immediately, if the engine is correctly tuned. Having said that, Escorts and Cortinas of this era often do exhibit reluctance to start when cold or wet. If, however, treating the high tension ignition leads to a spray of moisture-displacing fluid does not get the engine running straight away, it indicates the presence of a fault which will need sorting out before you can rely on the car.

The oil pressure should build up virtually instantaneously from a cold start, as indicated by the oil pressure light extinguishing as soon as the engine has started. It should also remain extinguished with the engine ticking over when hot. If an oil pressure gauge is fitted, this too should spring into life as soon as the engine fires, and the needle should not hover around the 'zero' mark with the engine hot and idling. If the engine on the car you are looking at shows reluctance to register pressure,

wear will accelerate rapidly, and an early overhaul is advisable.

Transmission

The manual gearboxes fitted to all rear wheel drive Cortinas and Escorts were four-speed, all synchromesh units, although of varying design between the models. However, all the gearboxes used gained a reputation for being smooth and slick in operation, particularly the single rail type employed in the Escorts.

On high mileage cars, whine, rumble or growling from the gearbox bearings can become evident, and, provided the synchromesh is not worn, repairs can be effected at fairly low cost, simply by changing the worn bearings, although of course this does necessitate a gearbox stripdown.

Cortina gearboxes do have a habit of gradually 'losing' top gear as they wear – the gear lever will increasingly jump out of the selected position when under load, until eventually the lever has to be held in position – not ideal on long journeys! While this could just be due to a broken spring in the gearchange fork rod, or to the selector fork rod screw and locknut coming loose, it could equally be due to serious wear in the selector fork rod or gearbox coupling dogs. If this is the case, the chances are that the rest of the gearbox is also badly worn, and an exchange unit will probably be the most effective (and most economical) cure.

The automatic gearboxes, whether the early Borg Warner units, or the Ford 'Bordeaux' boxes fitted to the Mark II Escorts, are very reliable, and give little trouble. If an automatic does misbehave, with, for example excessive slipping when accelerating, adjustment may cure the problem, but, if the car has

been driven for some time in this condition, the chances are that irreparable damage has been done to the internal clutches, and a rebuild or replacement unit will be the only sensible answer. However, troubles are rare; one of the Mark I Cortina estate cars I 'met' in the course of preparing this book had covered more than 182,000 miles on its Borg Warner 35 gearbox, and was still going strong!

The clutches fitted to manual gearbox models are of conventional design, and are generally up to the job, with no specific problems. However, the 1100cc Escorts fitted with the smaller, 6$\frac{1}{2}$ inch diameter driven plates can show rapid clutch wear, especially if the car has worked hard for much of its life, in traffic. On any model, to check for clutch slip, stop the car on a moderate slope and then drive away, accelerating quickly upwards through the gears. If the engine revs rise readily at each gearchange, and take several seconds to fall again, the chances are that the clutch is due for replacement.

The Escort clutch cables can give trouble from time to time, and difficult engagement of the gears, especially first and reverse, can often be attributed to a cable needing replacement. The same trouble on a Cortina is normally due to air having entered the clutch hydraulic system, often through the seals in the clutch master or slave cylinder having softened through age. Neither problem is difficult to rectify, however.

The propeller shafts fitted to Cortinas and Escorts do not, unfortunately, have provision for the fitting of grease nipples. The 'sealed for life' universal joint bearings therefore have a limited lifespan, which is usually in the region of 35,000 to 40,000 miles. Fortunately the bearings fitted to the Cortinas and early Escorts are relatively easily replaced, since the joints are secured by circlips. Later types, however, have staked

joints which are more difficult (and expensive) to replace.

On Mark II Escorts, the propeller shafts are in two sections on 1300cc and larger engined models, with a centre rubber bearing and, on 1600cc cars, an additional constant velocity joint.

Any of these bearings, when worn, give unpleasant vibrations through the vehicle, and replacement is expensive and time-consuming. If your test drive reveals vibrations which appear to come from directly below the floor, if will almost certainly be due to a propshaft problem.

The differential units fitted to Cortinas and Escorts do not suffer from problems of noise, whine, or excessive wear until they have covered considerable distances – normally in excess of 60,000 miles or more. Fortunately the differential units are easy to change (except on some Mk II Escorts, with 'Salisbury' type axles), having withdrawn the half-shafts from the axle casing. The differential simply bolts into the casing, from the front.

However, the axle hub bearings can wear, especially the outer race, giving rise to a ticking or droning noise which varies with road speed. This needs attention at once, for if the bearing should break up, the half-shaft, complete with inner race still attached, can come out of the axle case; since the road wheel will come with it, this can be dangerous.

Replacing this bearing can be tricky, since the new one has to be pressed onto the shaft with a pressure in excess of 1,200 lbs; not really a d-i-y operation. So listen for ominous noises from the rear of the car, during your test drive.

Another visual check to make is to look at the front of the axle and under the floor of the car, for signs of oil leakage from the differential pinion seal. A severe leak here can quickly empty the axle of oil, with obvious, disastrous effects on the gears

and bearings within. Fortunately, changing the pinion seal is a job which can be tackled on a d-i-y basis.

Suspension

The suspension on all models covered by this book comprises MacPherson struts at the front, with leaf springs at the rear, apart from early Cortina Lotus models, with coil springs at the back.

The shock absorbers are usually the first items to wear, and the normal 'bounce' test should be applied, to gain an idea of how effective the units are. Push down hard on each corner of the car in turn, and let go. The body should rise slowly back to its original ride height. If one or more corners of the vehicle continue to bounce up and down, it indicates a worn damper.

It is also worth examining the exterior of each shock absorber. If the front struts appear to be wet with oil, especially around the point where the piston rod enters its operating cylinder, the integral shock absorber unit is leaking. Even if it is providing effective damping at the moment, which is unlikely, it will cause failure at the next MoT test. The same applies to the rear shock absorbers – if leaks are evident, whether from telescopic types fitted to all the saloons, and Escort estates, or from the lever arm units fitted to Cortina estates, ride quality and handling will deteriorate, and MoT failure is assured.

Your test drive will also tell you a great deal about the state of the shock absorbers – if the car is excessively bouncy, and leans hard on cornering, combined with a general 'uncertain' feel about the suspension, it needs new units. Fortunately, the rear ones are fairly straightforward to change. The integral shock absorbers incorporated into the front struts are a little more tricky to deal

with, since the struts have to come off, and the coil springs must be compressed. Nevertheless, it is a job which can be tackled at home.

The front coil springs seldom give trouble, while the main problems experienced with the rear leaf springs are that they eventually tend to go 'flat', or they can crack. The single leaf variety are generally not as long-lasting as the multi-leaf types, and the strongest of all are the heavy duty items fitted to the estate cars.

If the car you are looking at appears to be very low at the rear – particularly if it has a tow bar fitted, the rear springs may be weakened, or even cracked, so look carefully. Older Escorts in particular, suffer from this trouble, and the suspension can 'bottom' when the car is heavily laden.

On any model, rattles and clonks heard when the car travels over rough surfaces can be due to a number of causes. Favourite culprits are loose MacPherson struts, worn or loose front anti-roll bar or rear spring/shock absorber bushes, or slack steering joints. Only a careful examination, by a process of elimination, will discover the source of the noise.

Steering

The steering on the Escort models is always more positive than on the Mark I and II Cortinas. This is due to the use of rack and pinion set-ups on the Escorts, compared with the worm and recirculating nut steering box systems employed on the Cortinas. Therefore, even on a Cortina with little wear in the steering system, you can expect to find some free play at the steering wheel rim – an inch or so is typical. On the Escorts, however, free play at the wheel rim should be minimal; any more than a little slack movement here will be due to wear – probably in

the steering rack or ball joints.

On either model, pin-pointing the exact source of wear is best accomplished by jacking up the front of the car and watching the relative movement of the steering links, while an assistant turns the steering wheel to and fro. However, the extent of wear present is easily assessed by a test drive. If the car tends to wander, and is easily deflected by road surface imperfections, the steering needs attention.

On early Cortinas (up to August, 1967), the MacPherson strut upper mounting incorporated a thrust ball race bearing, which can suffer, due to the ingress of water (and lack of lubrication), after some time in service. When this happens, the steering can become extremely stiff, the cure being to replace the bearings. Later models employed tapered rubber bushes, bonded to the upper mountings, instead of the bearings – check that the bushes are sound.

Brakes

Only a thorough examination of the braking system, including detailed checks of the hydraulic cylinders and the brake pads/ shoes, will reveal exactly how well maintained it has been. However, if serious defects are present, they may become evident during your test drive.

If excessively high brake pedal pressures are needed, even to make the car slow down, let alone stop, it is likely that some of the brake cylinders are seized, or partially seized. This problem often occurs on cars that have been standing, unused, for some time, so take care on any test drive. A tendency for the car to pull to one side under braking indicates that a hydraulic cylinder on the opposite side is not doing its job properly. Again, it is probably seized, or partially

seized, or it could be leaking brake fluid. In any event, it needs IMMEDIATE investigation, for the brakes could cease to operate at any time. Any necessity for the brake pedal to be pumped before a 'firm' feel results show the presence of air in the system, and almost certainly a loss of brake fluid. The fault, causing the air to enter and the fluid to escape, MUST be rectified before the car is driven further, as there is a real risk of sudden and complete brake loss.

It is well worthwhile making a detailed visual check of the state of the brake fluid pipes and hoses underneath the bonnet, and under the bodywork, looking for corrosion damage in particular. Of course, you may be lucky in finding a vehicle which has already had the brake pipes replaced. If they are of long-lasting copper, so much the better. Rusty steel pipes should be replaced forthwith.

Wheels and tyres

Look around the car at the wheels and tyres; bent wheel rims and scuffed tyre side walls indicate a careless owner, and if the front wheels show signs of serious kinks around their rims, there is always the possibility that the steering system may have been bent as well, by a hefty clout or two.

Tyre tread depth is important, of course; ideally all the tyres should have plenty of 'meat' left on them, but just as important, wear should be even, across and around the tyre. Tyres worn on one side only, or in patches around the circumference, show that there are problems, with tracking, worn suspension or steering, or with the brakes.

It may sound obvious, but check that all the wheels and tyres match in size (I've come across cars where they don't!), and with regard to tyre type.

They should be all radials or all cross-plies, ideally, but if a mixture has been fitted, the ONLY legal (and safe) combination is to have cross-plies on the front, and radials on the rear. This is acceptable, but then you really need two spare wheels.

On your test drive, make sure that the car feels smooth at all speeds. Any unevenness could be due to a damaged wheel or tyre. Any regular vibrations felt through the steering wheel could well be due to the front wheels being out of balance. Fords with MacPherson strut front suspension have always been very sensitive to precise wheel balancing, and it is best to have the wheels (and therefore the hubs and brake discs or drums) balanced ON the vehicle, for smoothest results.

General

Provided that you check all the bodywork and mechanical systems in the way described in this chapter, you should be able to avoid buying a rough vehicle, if you are looking for a car to use, and to keep for a long time. If, on the other hand, it is your intention to buy a cheap car for total restoration, the checks outlined here should at least give you a very good idea of exactly how much work you are letting yourself in for.

Whatever condition your prospective purchase is in, it is best to assume the worst about any doubtful aspect, until you can prove otherwise, and that is usually only after you have parted with your money. This applies particularly in the case of long static non-runners, where the owner, for example, might talk enthusiastically about the seized engine, clutch or brakes being 'easy to free off' . . . I've heard it all before!

Finally, if you are buying a running vehicle, take heed of what the instruments tell you, rather than what the seller might tell you. For example, if the temperature gauge shows 'hot', there is probably good reason for this – it may not be 'just the gauge at fault'. Another potential problem can be the oil pressure gauge which 'always runs near the zero mark' – again, it could just be the gauge, but it is more likely that the oil pressure is very low.

Of course, it's nice to think that you can trust everyone, but when buying a car, and laying out YOUR hard earned cash, it always pays to take the greatest care.

B1. The upper front suspension mountings must be strong to avoid MoT test failure, or eventual collapse of the vehicle. Check not only that the top of the inner wing is sound, or has been properly plated, but also that the turret top and under-wing metalwork is solid.

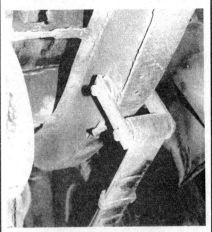

B2. The rear spring supports and surrounding 'chassis' sections MUST be sound. This Mark I Cortina was very strong in this department, with the chassis having been neatly plated in the areas behind the rear spring hangers.

B3. This Mark II Escort looked in good condition, when viewed from below each side. However, from under the centre of the car, the chassis section just ahead of the front support of the offside rear spring displayed evidence of severe rusting. Further investigation revealed serious corrosion of the floor just above the chassis member, as well. Check these areas very carefully.

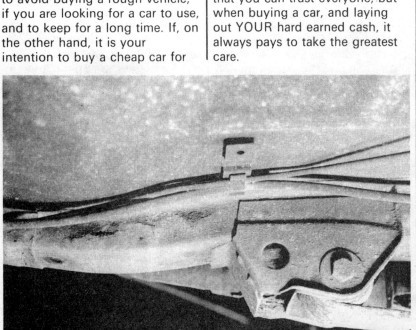

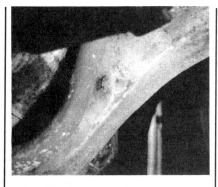

B4. The forward chassis sections also need checking inch by inch; rust was blistering through the main beam on the nearside of this Escort.

B6. This Mark II Cortina has been well maintained generally, and particular attention has been paid to keeping the wheel arches and surrounding metal protected from flying spray.

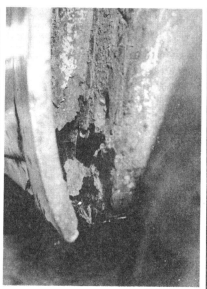

B7. This sad Mark I Escort has been allowed to deteriorate in most areas, and rust has seriously weakened the metal behind each front wheel. The mud and water from the wheels now fills up the sills! Rectification can be tricky, depending on how bad the damage is already.

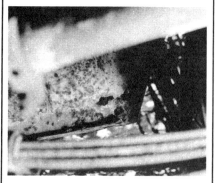

B5. Look closely at the metal immediately behind all four wheels, on all models. This Mark II Cortina had holes on both sides, behind the rear wheels, allowing salt and moisture to enter the hollow sections at the bottoms of the rear wings.

B8. Lift the mats/carpets inside the car and look for rust . . . this same Escort has lost much of the front floor, along with the inner sill! A rag had been stuffed into the holes in the wheel arch to stop the driver from getting wet feet. Amazingly, the car had been in daily use, with a current MoT certificate, until just before this photograph was taken!

B9. The seat mounting points are of course critical on all models. The seat mounting cross-members on Escorts are especially prone to parting from the floor. Careful delving among the debris in the bottom of this Mark I revealed that the cross-member was not, in fact, attached to the car at all!

51

B10. Holes like this in the sills can sometimes be patched by welding in small sections of new metal. The problem is that by the time the rot has reached this stage, most of the sill is likely to be affected, and fitting a new one is the best answer. Check carefully for evidence of bodged repairs.

B11. All Cortina and Escort models are prone to rust breaking through around the headlights, particularly at the top edges of the front wings, where mud collects and moisture held here attacks the metal. This is usually very obvious, unless the damage has been simply disguised with body filler. ▶

B12. The rear edges and tops of the front wings also suffer from attack from behind, due to trapped mud, with rust eating its way through the panel, as on this Mark II Cortina. Although such damage can be repaired, it is not a straightforward job, and a new wing, if obtainable, is often an easier, if more expensive, answer.

B13. Look at the front valance, below the bumper. This area is often dented, through careless parking, and may well be blistering at the edges, because of rust damage, like the one on this Mark II Escort. ▶

B14. Corrosion affects the bonnet lids on all these Fords, particularly the leading edges, and sections where metal is folded – along the edges and around the strengthening ribs. In severe cases, another bonnet may be needed.

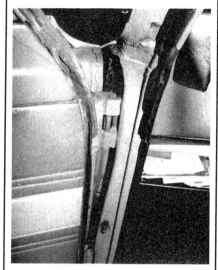

B15. Open each of the doors and look at the pillars and the door edges, for signs of rust. In serious cases the pillars can be almost non-existent! Attempt to rock each door – particularly the driver's door – up and down on its hinges. If the door moves more than a fraction of an inch, new hinge pins will be needed. Wear here is very common.

B16. While the doors are open, look carefully at the door trim panels and sealing rubbers, the kick plates, and the trims around the door apertures. This Mark I Cortina was obviously cared for.

B17. The wheel arches suffer from rust damage if neglected. It is particularly important to check the inside edges of the arches, since signs of damage on the outside of the car are often symptoms of a far more serious problem affecting the bits you can't see! Where corrosion has taken hold, it is not uncommon to find that the rear mudguards have parted company from the wheel arches. When this happens, road salt, mud and water spread inside the wing panels and along the sills, creating havoc here too.

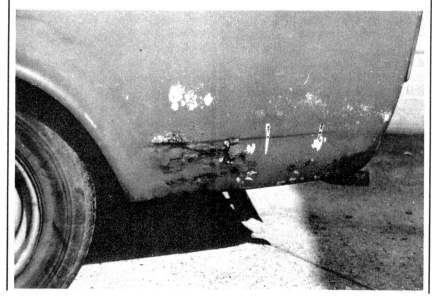

B18. This Mark II Cortina had serious rust in the lower rear wings, due to the problems described in captions B5 and B17. The wings can be plated, but the causes of the problem must be tackled first. As I later found out, this wing had been previously 'repaired' with newspaper, rag and body filler!

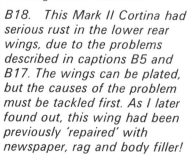

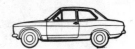

B19. Always inspect the deepest corners of the boot, and lift the floor mat to see what lies below. This Mark II Cortina was in good shape generally, but the owner had used the car for carrying hay for her horses, so the boot corners were full of damp fodder! Fine for the horses, but not so good for the long-term benefit of the car.

B20. Check the upholstery! The driver's seat in this Escort was beyond a joke, with very little left to sit on. In fact, when viewing this car, I sat inside and disappeared! Most examples haven't got to quite such a state, but nevertheless check for sagging, cuts and tears, and broken springs below. ➤

B21. The rear seats also need looking at carefully, especially those in estate models, which tend to suffer more from scuffing and accidental damage than those in saloons. Having said that, the ones in this Mark I Cortina estate were in excellent condition.

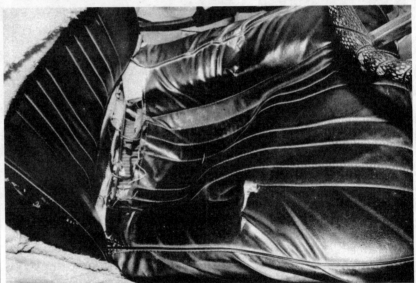

B22. The appearance of the engine and underbonnet area can tell a great deal about how a car has been looked after. Generally speaking, a clean and tidy engine bay bodes well. Look in particular for signs of oil leaks, and fuming from the valve cover. If the engine and its compartment are smothered in what looks like a recent covering of thick, black oil spray, it is likely that the engine is due for overhaul or replacement. ➤

B23. The suspension must be in A1 condition, front and rear, for a smooth ride and safe handling. The springs and shock absorbers need close scrutiny; look in particular for signs of fluid leaking from the MacPherson strut units and the rear dampers. Although the upper section of this Escort's rear shock absorber was rusty, it wasn't leaking, and was still doing its job.

B24. If possible, always jack up the front end of your prospective purchase and, with the car supported on axle stands, check the steering gear for wear, with the aid of an assistant inside the car, to operate the steering wheel. Attempt to rock the road wheel in a vertical plane, and from side to side. If any more than just perceptible play is present, it needs rectification.

B25. Check the state of all the brake pipes, front to rear, and side to side. If the metal pipes show signs of anything more than superficial rust, they need replacing. There is a good case for fitting non-corroding copper brake pipes like those supplied by Automec, if you plan to keep the car for a long time.

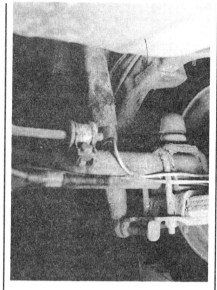

B26. Under the front end of the car, check for signs of oil leaks from the engine, and, on Escorts, from the steering rack gaiters. If these are split or perished, the rack will run dry and wear rapidly, especially if dirt has entered. If the rack gaiter(s) look as if they have been damaged for some time, it is wise to plan for replacing the rack if you buy the car. Cortinas have steering boxes, which can leak from the lower seal, but this can be replaced without removing the box from the vehicle.

B27. If you are looking for a Mark I Cortina and can find one in this sort of (superb) condition, for a fair price, it may be cheaper in the long run than buying a rough one and restoring it from scratch. There is plenty of enjoyable work involved in maintaining a good car in tidy order, or on improving a basically sound vehicle as a 'running' restoration.

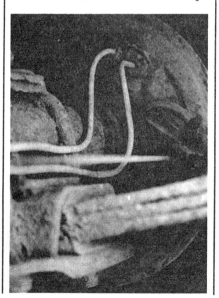

B28. You may be more interested in buying a newer car like this late Mark II Escort. They can still provide plenty of scope for restoration, especially if you can find a neglected example at the right price. The later cars like this do have the advantage that spares are more readily available than for earlier models.

B29. This is how you find 'em . . .! If you are a bit more ambitious, how about a Mark II Cortina which is 'ripe for restoration'? I intercepted this one literally on its way to the scrapyard, and the poor thing displayed most of the faults which should normally put one off buying a Cortina (or any car!). These included a seized engine, rotten floor, non-existent inner wheel arches, rear accident damage, corroded wings and sills, collapsed suspension mountings, rusted brakes, and see-through bulkheads/door pillars. In fact, it was just what I was looking for . . .!

B30. Or how about this MoT-expired Escort Mark I? Again, I salvaged it within an hour of it departing for the local breaker's yard. It looked FAIRLY sound at first glance, but this car provided several of the photographs taken for the 'Buying' section of this book . . . It will therefore come as no surprise that it had ventilated front wings, an open 'sunshine' floor and inner sills, detached bulkheads and so on. The driver's seat had collapsed and was not even attached to the floor! The engine wouldn't run, which was probably just as well, since the brakes had lost nearly all their fluid, and the steering was lacking in direction, through wear . . . Another machine I couldn't resist, and 'perfect' for restoration!

4 Bodywork

The restoration of most 'modern' cars (in this context I am referring to post-War vehicles) hinges around the state of the bodywork. With very few exceptions, 'everyday' cars (as opposed to some luxury vehicles and limousines, etc.) of this era have been built on the 'chassis-less' construction principle, where the car's bodywork is 'fully stressed', and has integral strengthening members, rather than having a separate backbone, or chassis. Therefore the vehicle's inherent strength, and ability to stay in one piece, is dependent on the major part of the body shell, and in particular its 'load-bearing' sections, being in good condition.

This applies to all Ford Escorts and Cortinas, and should be borne in mind when looking for a vehicle to restore, taking into account your own facilities, abilities, and the size of your bank balance, as outlined in the 'Buying' chapter. If you are restoring a car with a view to keeping it long-term (as opposed to driving it just until the MoT runs out), it is essential to tackle the body repairs very carefully – particularly those which affect structural rigidity. For such repairs, welding is the ONLY acceptable method of rectification, so you will need the

necessary equipment (more about which later). Alternatively, you may prefer to prepare the car as far as possible yourself, leaving the welding operation to an expert. For example, very often, by removing trim, carpets, etc, you can save a great deal in labour costs, even if you cannot undertake the actual welding yourself.

Ways and means

The Fords covered by this book will be found to vary greatly in condition. Methods of restoration vary too, of course. What may seem 'sacrilege' to a perfectionist may be quite acceptable to someone trying to keep his car on the road at minimum cost. There are no definitive rules to cover this, unless you are seeking to win prizes in certain concours competitions where originality is the prime yardstick; in such cases, of course, nothing short of perfection, and with the car completely 'as original', will do. In other cases, departures from original specification may be considered in order – for example the use of an anti-rust paint or wax on the underbody, or the hand-painting of this part of the car. In the final analysis, the

decision is yours. It is, after all, your car, and if you are happy with the end result, then this is the main concern. The only note of warning that I would sound in this connection is to say that, in general terms, the more departures from 'standard' which are made, particularly where the bodywork is concerned, the lower will be the vehicle's intrinsic value to enthusiasts. This problem takes on greater proportions as the car ages. Of course, if the value of the car in sheer monetary terms does not concern you, then this will obviously be of less importance.

To what extent you intend to restore a car will depend, largely on what use you intend to put it to. For example, you may buy a car which is structurally sound, but which needs cosmetic surgery to 'tidy it up', for everyday use. On the other hand, you may have bought a completely rusted out wreck, and hope to restore it to 'concours' condition. In this chapter we cover jobs ranging from fairly simple 'patch-up' operations to full-scale bodywork rebuilding. So, whatever the state of your particular vehicle, and whether you are carrying out a 'running' restoration when time and cash permits, or an all-out rebuild, there is plenty of information to help you.

Before you start, though, you should form a plan of action. This is especially important where you may rely on the car as transport during the week, for example; whatever you do to it on Saturday and Sunday, you must make sure it's back together for Monday morning! So, don't try to be too ambitious; tackle only what you think you can handle in one go.

Another, vital point, is NEVER to cut ALL the rusty metal out of a wreck in one session – the car will almost certainly collapse. The metal may be rusty, but it might be all that's holding the thing together. Therefore, tackle one section at a time, preferably leaving one side of the vehicle intact so that you have patterns to work to.

Another, important point, for cars requiring total bodywork renovation, is that it is always best to tackle the major work first, before carrying out the 'cosmetic' jobs.

Whether you are carrying out minor 'touch-up' work only, or more serious, structural operations, time spent on the bodywork is time well spent – a car with a solid, attractive body shell looks better, feels better to drive around in, and is worth more!

Equipment

Basic bodywork restoration can be attempted with a very few basic tools, with the range of jobs extending as the number and variety of implements are added to.

A hammer, bolster and cold chisels, universal tin snips and a range of spanners and screwdrivers are handy items to start with. An electric drill is also useful for any number of jobs, and, for patching non load-bearing panels, a blind riveting gun is helpful.

For bending and shaping metal panels, various tools can be used. For straightening bent panels on the vehicle, it is worth investing in a small set of panel beating tools, such as those made by Sykes-Pickavant, who also make an excellent slide hammer for removing dents from inaccessible panels. If your vehicle is even half as dented as the ones restored for this book, such tools are invaluable. Sykes-Pickavant also make a wide ('Speedline') range of other tools to help the d-i-y body rebuilder, ranging from metal benders and cutters, to welding clamps.

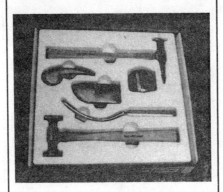

E1. This panel beating kit by Sykes-Pickavant contains all the tools required for dealing with any dents likely to be encountered on your Cortina or Escort. Their 'Speedline' range includes many useful bodywork restoration tools for the d-i-y person.

If you are going into restoration on a fairly large scale, it is well worth spending money on an electric grinder; invaluable for cleaning up rusted metal flanges, it is also ideal for smoothing off welds, where a level surface is required, and for a number of other jobs, including preparing doors for re-skinning, grinding through spot welds in inaccessible areas, etc, etc.

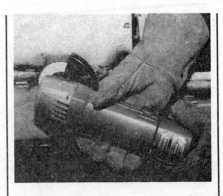

E2. This electric grinder should last for many years, given a little care. For prolonged use, it is worth spending a little more to get a 'professional' or 'heavy duty' unit, like this one.

For working underneath a car, where much of the corrosion damage occurs, a trolley jack and axle stands are the easiest means of getting and keeping (respectively) the vehicle airborne. The jack (of whatever type) should only be used to get the car off the ground, never for holding the vehicle up while you work on it; the stands are for that job!

E3. This well-used Draper trolley jack has lifted many cars, and the inexpensive, secure axle stands alongside have worked equally hard in holding many a wreck airborne as it has gradually been 'sewn' back together!

Welding

It is well worthwhile learning how to weld, even if the thought appears daunting to start with.

The many benefits of being able to weld a rusty vehicle yourself include 1) you don't have to pay anyone else to do the job, 2) you don't have to wait for someone else to do the work and 3) you will have the satisfaction that the job has been well done – by yourself!

So, how does one learn? Well, if you buy any kind of welding gear, comprehensive instructions are normally included with the set. Failing that, the supplier should be able to supply you with basic information at least.

You may also know a welder, who is willing to instruct you, or a friend who is proficient in welding, who may be able to help. Make sure, though, that they really do know what they are talking about, particularly when it comes to safety. Far better, in my opinion, to learn by attending evening classes at a local college or school, where thorough instruction is given on safety and correct methods of working. Contact your local adult education centre for details of courses held near you.

Knowledge thus obtained can, of course, be backed up by reading, and there are many interesting books about welding to be found in your local library or bookshop. The theory complements the practical work, and vice versa.

Welding kits

Electric, or arc welding kits can be purchased very cheaply, and are ideal for work on heavy gauge metal, for instance as employed on 'chassis' sections below the car. The problem as far as work on outer panels is concerned is that most d-i-y arc welders are too fierce. It is therefore very easy to burn holes through the metal, and to cause distortion. You really need a machine which operates at 20 amps (or less) to weld body panelwork. There are adaptors available for larger capacity machines, to enable them to successfully weld such metal. The alternative is to use a carbon arc brazing attachment, which is fine for non-structural areas, but which cannot be used on 'structural' sections of the car body.

E4. A small arc welding set like this is inexpensive and can tackle all the 'structural' repairs necessary below the car. It's a bit fierce for outer panelwork, though.

Gas welding is more useful as far as general bodywork repairs are concerned, and there are a number of small gas kits available. Choose carefully, though, for some of the cheaper sets do not produce a flame which is hot enough for successful welding. Another problem, if you intend to do a lot of welding, is that the cylinders, being small, are exhausted fairly quickly, and can be expensive (or difficult) to exchange. For just occasional use, such disadvantages may not be so important.

For someone carrying out a full-scale restoration, a small oxy-acetylene welding kit, such as the well-known 'Portapak' is ideal. The gas bottles, although small in comparison with industrial bottles, hold enough gas for a weekend's welding, for example, and can be exchanged at BOC gas centres. The welding kit is purchased, by the user, while the cylinders have to be rented (on a seven year basis) from BOC. The beauty of such a welding kit is that the gun is the same as used in the trade, and will accept the full range of nozzles, etc., to give maximum flexibility in use, to cope with materials of varying thicknesses. for example. In addition, the gun can be used for cutting out rusty metal, as well as for welding in new sections.

Slightly cheaper alternative systems are available these days, and it is worth shopping around, and talking to welding equipment suppliers and users, before you purchase.

E5. This Portapak set, purchased second-hand, has already saved eight cars from the scrapyard! Spares are readily available and gas supplies are fairly easily obtained around the country.

The revolution in welding today centres on MIG (standing

for 'metal inert gas') welding. This employs a continuously fed wire, which is melted onto the workpiece within a shroud of inert gas (normally argon or carbon dioxide). The gun can be operated with one hand, and distortion to surrounding metalwork is minimal – far less than with gas or arc welding. A clean weld results, which needs no 'de-slagging', as with arc welding. In addition, the process is at least three times quicker than oxy-acetylene welding.

It is therefore an excellent means of welding for restoration purposes (and, for many newer cars, built with special steels, it is in fact the only acceptable method).

There are a number of small, comparatively cheap MIG welders on the market today, all doing the same basic job. The level of sophistication obviously rises in line with the price ticket, but you don't need to spend a fortune to achieve good results. Machines in the 'Migmate' range from SIP are ideal for do-it-yourself restorers.

E6. This SIP 'Migmate 150 Turbo DP' MIG welder from the company's 'Migmate' range is an affordable, compact and portable, yet highly effective machine capable of dealing with all aspects of car bodywork restoration. It is a versatile dual-purpose machine, capable of welding in both conventional MIG and 'gasless' modes. If looked after it should give many years of useful service.

It is of course possible that you cannot afford to buy new equipment of the type described. Much good equipment can be purchased second-hand, but always take someone with you to make sure that it is safe, before you buy. Many welding centres can supply used welding gear at reasonable prices, so it is worth asking.

Always remember to disconnect the battery on alternator-equipped cars, before using an arc or MIG welder, or the alternator could be damaged.

Spraying

Another aspect of bodywork restoration is applying the paint to the prepared bodyshell. If you are reluctant to have the car resprayed professionally, there is no reason why you cannot do an excellent job yourself. The choice of equipment is enormous. Cheap, electric sprayguns can produce excellent results, and, as an example, the author still uses a ten year old Wagner 'airless' gun for spraying, and is pleased with the results. Alternatively, there are many compressor type sprayguns on the market, with price labels varying enormously. Shop around, and ask the opinion of spraygun sellers AND users before you buy.

As with many aspects of car restoration, the quality of paint spraying varies not only with the sophistication of the equipment, but more often than not with the degree of determination and patience of the operator!

Whatever equipment you use, it needs to be kept scrupulously clean for good results.

Read all about it

If you are unfamiliar with basic

bodywork rebuilding techniques, it pays to read up about the various methods which can be used. Workshop manuals don't normally cover this area in detail, but there are many books about bodywork repair. Try your local library or book shop. One of the most comprehensive books available on this subject is the *Haynes Car Bodywork Manual,* written by Lindsay Porter – it is a complete, easy to follow guide to all aspects of car body repair, including sections on welding and spraying.

Plan ahead

Once you have made a thorough examination of the car, you should have a good idea of which major panels need replacing, and it is always a good idea to arrange for the purchase of these, before you start work. That way, you will avoid the delays which sometimes occur, especially when dealing with the early Cortinas and even, now, the first Escorts. With panels for the older cars ever more difficult to get through Ford dealerships, 'pattern' panels, or those reproduced by the clubs, or old 'unused' stock available through specialist suppliers are increasingly becoming more relevant to restorer's needs. The panels ARE about, but you may need to look for them harder than you might at first imagine, and it is essential that you start well in advance of when you need the particular sections.

Safety

NEVER take chances when working on your car. Extensive notes are included

in Appendix 1 – PLEASE READ THEM NOW. Of course, these cannot cover every eventuality, and it is up to each individual restorer to take common-sense precautions at every stage of the job. No reponsibility for the effectiveness or otherwise of advice given here, nor for any omissions, can be accepted by the author. 'Safety' notes are intended to include some useful tips and no more.

ALWAYS wear goggles when working underneath the car, particularly when poking dirty and rusty sections, and when using any form of grinding or cutting tools – hand operated or power tools.

Wear protective overalls, fully buttoned, at all times, and 'gauntlet' type gloves when welding. Never weld without the correct shielding goggles for the type of welding you are carrying out – 'arc eye' is a painful result of watching welding with the naked eye. In addition, there are serious risks from flying molten metal and sparks – the results are horrific to contemplate.

Take particular care when dealing with jagged – and, particularly, rusty – edges, or freshly cut metal; the razor sharp edges can inflict devastating wounds.

Always try to make sure that someone else is around when you are working on the car. Then if anything unfortunate should occur, there is someone else to help you, or raise the alarm.

PLEASE TAKE CARE – YOU KNOW IT MAKE SENSE. The whole point of restoring a car is to be able to enjoy it when it's finished – the whole thing would turn very sour if lack of a few simple precautions, or the thought that 'It'll never happen to me' led to a serious accident.

Initial work

It is always necessary to remove items of trim from the vehicle, prior to work on the body. The extent to which you have to go depends on the extent of the damage, and which area of the car you are tackling. Inevitably, however, areas of bodywork round the grille and lights tend to suffer from corrosion damage, and so to start with, it is worth looking at how these items come off!

Cortina

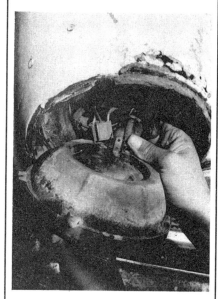

IWC1. The headlight rims on Cortina Mark Is are secured by a single securing screw, whereas those on the Mark II have four screws. Take these out, then pull the rim out at the bottom, and upwards, to clear the front of the lamp.

IWC2. The sealed beam unit is normally released on its own, by taking out the three screws around the rim. However, if the screws are rusted and will not budge, the lamp can be withdrawn complete with its backing unit (push assembly and twist), so that penetrating oil can be applied to the screw threads more easily. Unhook the spring (take care not to over-stretch it), and disconnect the wiring at the back of the lamp.

IWC3. The wiring is unplugged at the snap connectors inside the engine bay (at the centre, front on Mark Is, at each side on Mark IIs); don't forget the earth connection, bolted directly to the car's bodywork. Now the lamp body can be released after taking out the three securing screws; penetrating oil is usually necessary. If all else fails, drill them out, using a $^1/_8$ inch drillbit.

IWC4. The side/indicator light lenses on Mark I cars simply unscrew from the front. The lamp bodies are held from behind the front panel by nuts. These are usually badly corroded, and removal can be difficult. It is very easy to damage the lamp body, so unless you really need to take it out, it is best to leave well alone, at least until you have obtained a replacement.

IWC5. The side/indicator lamps on Mark IIs are attached to the headlight surround by three screws; two (top and bottom) come out when the headlamp surround is removed; the third, on the outside edge, just holds the side/indicator lamp to the surround. A rubber shield protects the unit from the rear, and can be prised out of its aperture, once the wiring has been withdrawn.

IWC6. The grilles on Mark I and II Cortinas are held on with rivets at the top, and rivets (Mark I) or screws (Mark II) at the lower edge. Drill out the rivets, using a 1/8 inch drill, and remove the screws, so that the grille can be lifted clear. On replacing the grille, self-tapping screws can be used in place of blind rivets, for easier dismantling in future.

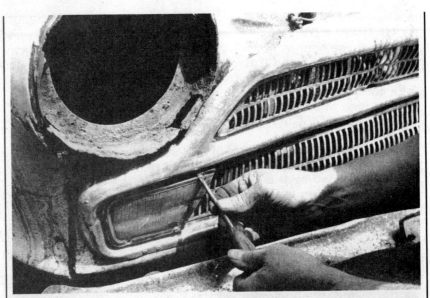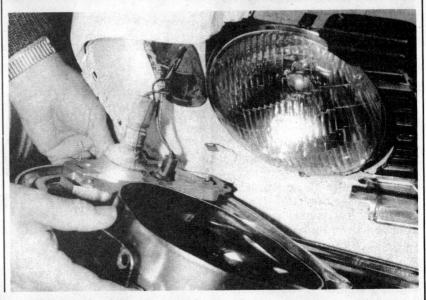

IWC7. The circular trim around the rear light clusters on Mark I saloons is held with a single screw at the bottom edge. Remove this, then lift the trim up, to release it at the top, then outwards.

IWC8. The individual lenses can be released after taking out the single central retaining screw and washer, then removing the two screws holding each lens to the lamp unit.

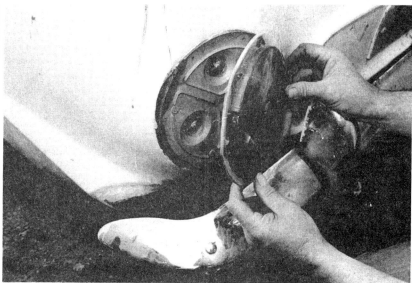

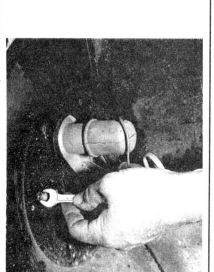

IWC9. To remove the lamp body from the vehicle, unplug the wiring connectors from the unit, inside the boot, and release the three securing nuts. The rear lamp assemblies on Mark II Cortinas also unscrew from inside the boot.

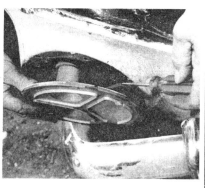

IWC10. The lamp unit can now be pulled away from the car – gentle persuasion with a screwdriver may be necessary, to start things moving.

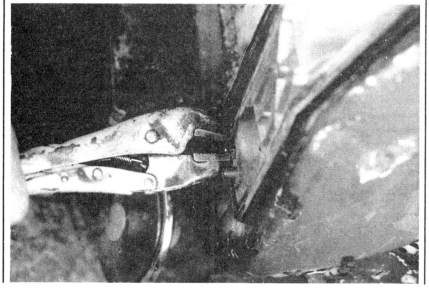

IWC11. The rear lamp units on Cortina estates are held to the vehicle by screws and nuts; once the lens unit has been removed – this simply unscrews from the outside – the fun begins. Apply lots of penetrating oil to each screw, then, holding the head with a large screwdriver, release the nut from behind the panel. At least, that's the theory, but in practice . . .

IWC12. . . . it is often necessary to use a self-grip wrench on the screw heads, since the screwdriver slots soon crumble, and the nuts are usually corroded in place!

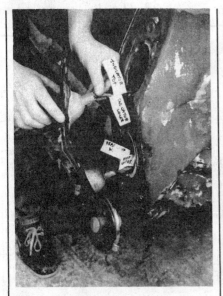

IWC13. As the lamp units are withdrawn, it is helpful to mark each wire very clearly, to aid re-assembly. This will save a lot of time later on! I use short lengths of masking tape for this purpose, wrapped around each wire and labelled with a felt-tip pen.

IWC14. When dismantling any car – especially for a total rebuild – keep all the parts removed from the vehicle in suitable containers, and mark each clearly. It may take a few minutes longer at each stage, but it is better to have a neat stack of cartons than a heap of bits all over the place! Careful packing can help avoid breakages of delicate components. A logical system of dismantling will save hours in the long run.

IWC15. Cortina bumpers are removed by releasing the retaining nuts, located behind the bumper, in line with the dome heads of the securing bolts. At each end of the bumper is a longer bolt, which passes from the car body, through a spacer and into a captive nut in the bumper. Use penetrating oil and a slim spanner to tackle these! Keep all parts together. The bumper support brackets can be removed, if required, by releasing them from the 'chassis', from inside the wheel arches. The same procedures apply to Escorts.

Escort

IWE1. Escort Mark 1 models must have the grille removed before the lamps can be reached. Nine screws hold the grille on; these normally come out fairly easily.

IWE2. On cars with round headlights, three Phillips screws hold the inner ring and lamp unit; with these out, the light can be pulled forward . . .

IWE3. . . . and the three pin connector block is removed from the back of the unit, together with the sidelamp bulb, mounted just below the block. Cars with rectangular headlights require similar dismantling procedures, except that headlamp bulbs, rather than sealed beam units, are fitted. These are simply unclipped from the unit, and withdrawn from the three pin plug.

IWE4. The front indicator lenses on Escort Mark 1 models simply unscrew for removal, using a Phillips screwdriver.

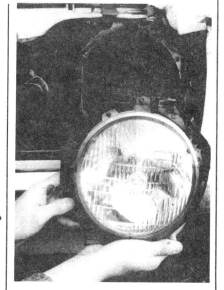

IWE5. The body of the indicator is withdrawn from the front, after taking out the two retaining screws, and releasing the wiring, from under the bonnet.

IWE6. The radiator grille on Mark II Escorts is retained by 12 screws. With these removed, the grille panel can be eased away from the car, for access to the headlight units. These are removed as for Escort I models. The indicator lamps are bolted to the front bumper, and the lenses retained by screws; removal is easy.

IWE7. If desired, the headlight bowls can be withdrawn complete with lamp units and wiring, after removal of the headlamp bowl retaining screws.

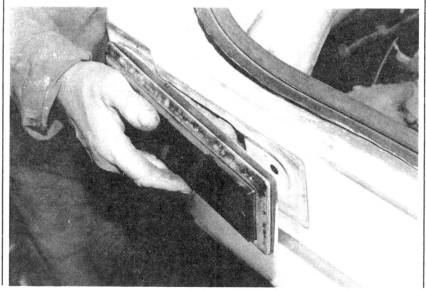

IWE8. To detach Escort Mark I rear lamps, unscrew the retaining nuts from inside the boot, then prise the lens assembly away from the outside of the car.

On Mark II models, the lenses unscrew from the outside, and there is an extra retaining screw holding the offside lamp unit, inside the boot. The lamp units on Escort estates are of similar construction to those used on the Cortinas, and they are removed in the same way, as previously described.

General

IWG1. Bonnet and boot removal is straightforward on Cortinas and Escorts, and re-assembly is not difficult either, provided that the position of the hinges is marked on the bonnet panel before you start. Use a soft ('B' grade) pencil to mark the hinge outline, if you are not going to respray the panel, or use a screwdriver to scribe the metal if you are intending to apply paint before the panel is re-fitted. Then your marks will still be visible when you need them!

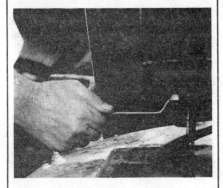

IWG2. Use a ring spanner to loosen the securing bolts; have an assistant on hand to take the weight of the bonnet or boot lid as the bolts come out. Cover the wings and bulkhead areas with cloth, unless they are going to be changed/resprayed anyway.

IWG3. Badges need very great care to avoid damaging them during removal. Gentle prising with a screwdriver, at intervals around the edges, is far less likely to cause damage than levering from just one end. On Cortina badges like this, and the individual lettered types used on later Cortinas and Escorts, the securing clips remain in the bodywork as the badge is lifted away.

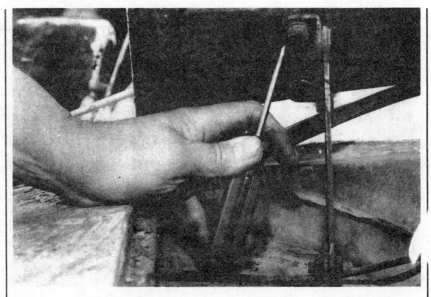

Minor bodywork repairs

Later in this chapter I shall be dealing with major bodywork restoration operations, involving replacing complete panels, fabricating metal sections, and so on. However, you may be lucky, and your Ford may only need comparatively minor cosmetic surgery to put it to rights. As already mentioned, complete information on all aspects of bodywork restoration is contained in *Haynes Car Bodywork Manual*, and it is well worthwhile purchasing a copy if you have not tackled bodywork repairs before, or indeed if you want to improve your technique.

However, in this section, I shall be outlining how to tackle typical bodywork 'tidy up' jobs, on a budget basis. This can be useful where perhaps time and/or funds are limited, for example, and where repairs are a practical alternative to changing a complete body panel. The idea is to enable you to keep your car on the road and presentable, without having to spend a great deal of time and money, or invest in expensive equipment. The techniques are illustrated on a front wing, but can be applied equally to any of the outer bodywork panels. It must be

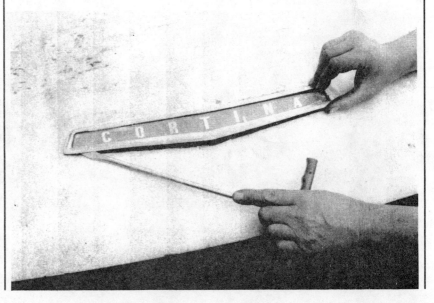

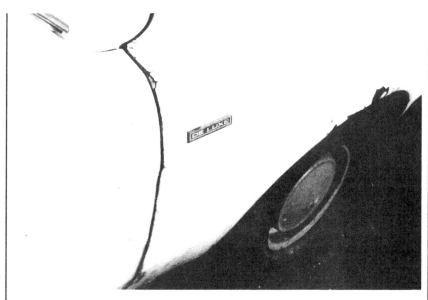

stressed, however, that these methods are ONLY appropriate for cosmetic body repairs, and MUST NOT be used to patch areas of structural importance. For these, rectification by welding in new metal is the only acceptable method.

'Special' tools needed

A rivet gun.

MBR1. Many people would simply write off this Escort wing, which had rust blistering through the wheel arch, and separation of the metal, at the rear edge. However, these are typical problems on all Mark I and II Escorts and Cortinas, and not everyone has the necessary time/money/inclination/ability (delete as appropriate!) to cut a complete wing off and replace it with another panel. If you fall into one of these categories, read on . . .

MBR2. With a bolster chisel, or an old screwdriver, carefully remove layers of loose rust and old body filler, to see what lies beneath. Starting at the rear edge of this wing, we soon found that the area had been filled at some time in the past, with little attempt at rust prevention. A steel plate had been added by a previous owner, as well! Things usually get worse before they get better with this type of job, and so it was in this case; we had soon destroyed what was left of the rear wing flange! Stop scraping when you reach solid metal.

MBR3. Don't panic! Lay a piece of thin card or thick paper on the wing, so that it overlaps the door and the damaged area by a good margin (at least two or three inches each way), then mark the positions of the front and lower edges of the card, on the wing. These datum lines will be important later.

MBR4. Now mark on the card the profile of the front edge of the door.

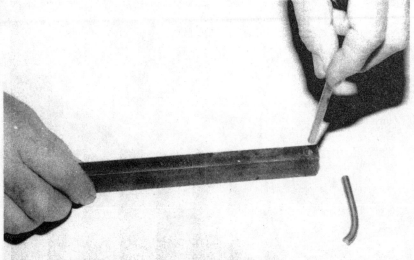

MBR5. Measure the distance between the rear edge of the sound part of the wing and the front edge of the door (the gap varies from car to car!). Now mark a line on your card parallel to, and forward of, the door profile line previously drawn, at a distance exactly the same as the gap measured between the door and wing. Cut the card along the second line, and offer up your completed template to the car . . .

MBR7. The doors on Cortinas and four door Escorts can be unbolted from the car, whereas those on two door Escorts have their hinges welded in place. The hinge pins can be driven out on the two door Escort using a special tool for the job (these can be purchased at most accessory shops). We chose to make a tool by drilling a hole in a flat steel bar, and using two short lengths of $1/4$ inch round steel rod; more of this later.

MBR8. First, extract the locking clip and lift the door check strap retaining pin from the pillar-mounted bracket.

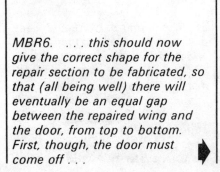

MBR6. . . . this should now give the correct shape for the repair section to be fabricated, so that (all being well) there will eventually be an equal gap between the repaired wing and the door, from top to bottom. First, though, the door must come off . . .

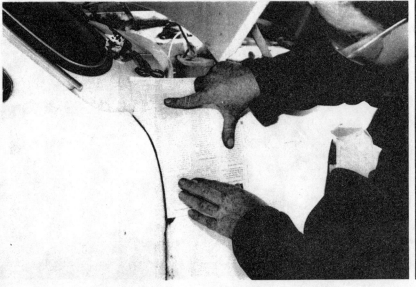

MBR9. The lower hinge pin is easily knocked out, using one of the lengths of rod, inserted in the hole in the steel bar. The hole should be just large enough to accommodate the diameter of the rod, and about $^1/_2$ to $^3/_4$ inch deep. The bar is then hit downwards with a hammer, and the hinge pin should drop out.

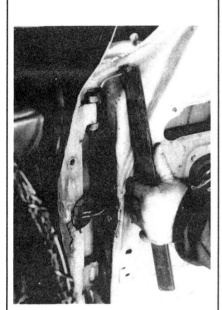

MBR10. Bend the second rod at one end, so that when the other end is inserted into the hole in your steel bar, it will sit comfortably on the upper hinge pin, within the shape of the upper door edge at this point. Knock the hinge pin DOWNWARDS, taking care not to scratch the paint on the door, in the process. Get an assistant to take the weight of the door as the pins are driven out . . .

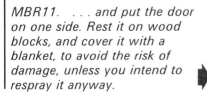

MBR11. . . . and put the door on one side. Rest it on wood blocks, and cover it with a blanket, to avoid the risk of damage, unless you intend to respray it anyway.

MBR12. The main part of the rebuilding exercise involves fabricating a new wing edge to work to. First, measure the depth of the damaged section of wing, using your card/paper template as a guide.

MBR13. Now scribe this depth dimension, just obtained, onto a sheet of metal, to outline a strip of uniform width – approximately one inch is ideal.

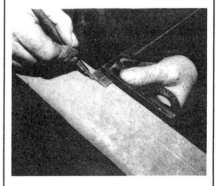

MBR14. Measure the exact width of the strip, and mark a point at precisely half way across each end. Then scribe another line between these two points.

MBR15. The whole area of metal previously outlined can now be cut out, using tin snips, and will, when doubled over along the second scribed line, form a 'rolled' over wing edge, to match the original, as far as possible.

MBR17. Turn your steel plate, now angled, so that the two edges are squeezed between the angle iron in the vice jaws. Tighten the vice . . .

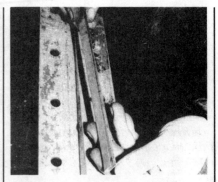

MBR18. . . . so that the 90 degree bend becomes a uniform 180 degree turn, with about $1/16$ to $1/8$th inch gap between the turned over edges.

MBR16. Using the 'midway' line on your steel plate as a guide, lock it in a vice, between two lengths of angle iron (or aluminium), with one half of the plate protruding. Knock this over with a hammer, a little at a time, until it forms a neat 90 degree angle.

MBR19. The doubled over plate now needs to be contoured to follow the original line of the wing. The wing edge is shaped in two directions – rearwards and inwards, so to start with, we dealt with the rearward contour. This is achieved by stretching the metal to shape, and is not as difficult as it sounds. Slide a spacer into the folded metal, to prevent it closing up on being hit. We used the spanner from my angle grinder for this job! Using a metal block, held in the vice, hammer the top surface of the metal plate until it thins and stretches. Continue . . .

MBR20. . . . and make regular checks that the contour is developing as planned, by comparing it with the profile on your template. By gradually moving the hammer along the metal, and hitting particular areas for varying lengths of time, the curve can be made uniform, or emphasised, depending on the section you are dealing with.

MBR21. To achieve the correct line for the inward curve at the back of the wing (towards the centre of the car at the top) is more tricky, but not difficult. Find some thin strips of scrap metal, and feed them into your newly formed wing edge section. This will prevent the edges from closing up when being bent.

MBR22. The panel can now be tapped to shape, a little at a time, frequently comparing the profile with that of the wing.

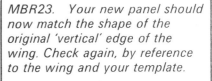

MBR23. Your new panel should now match the shape of the original 'vertical' edge of the wing. Check again, by reference to the wing and your template.

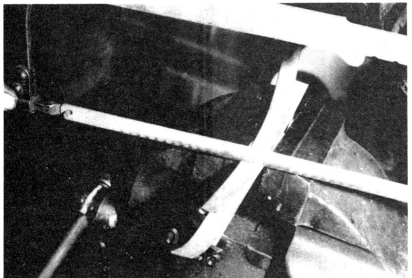

MBR24. This Escort wing had rusted so that the angled top edge was affected, as well as the 'vertical' panel. Our fabricated wing edge therefore had to follow this line. To achieve this, we hacksawed through one side of the doubled over metal plate, so that . . .

MBR25. . . . our repair section could then be bent to the exact shape of the wing; as the metal is bent over, the hacksaw blade slot closes up, avoiding unwanted rippling of the metal.

MBR26. Now check that the new panel fits perfectly over the wing; the existing edge may have to be 'relieved' slightly with a file, so that the new section sits flush with the rest of the wing. De-rust and prime the old wing edge.

MBR27. Position the plate finally, by reference to your template and the datum lines made on the wing, so that the new section is in precisely the right place.

MBR28. The new wing edge must now be attached to the wing. Welding, brazing, or 'blind' rivets (which clamp two pieces of metal together from one side of the panel) can be used. If welding, be careful not to distort

the surrounding metal by overheating. If your car has an alternator, and you intend to use electric (arc or MIG) welding, always disconnect the battery before you start, to avoid damaging the alternator. If using rivets, first prime the inside of the plate. When dry, drill a $1/8$ inch hole, to accommodate each rivet, through the new plate and into the good metal below, at each end. File off rough metal behind the hole, after drilling.

Self-grip wrenches are useful to hold the plate in place while it is drilled and the rivets attached. Use a small paintbrush to apply a little primer to the inside of each hole.

MBR29. Use a good quality rivet gun to fasten the rivets. The stalk of the rivet is simply placed in the gun, and the other (wider) end is fed into the hole through the metal plates. The rivet gun handles are then squeezed together. This action pulls the stalk of the rivet back through its body, firmly clamping the metal plates together, and breaking the stalk off as it does so. If possible, buy countersunk rivets. By counter-sinking the holes in your steel plate first, and using such rivets, final surface filling is much easier, since there is less of the rivet head to disguise!

MBR30.   The next step is to fill any remaining holes. The methods available are numerous, and depend on the size of the holes! For large ones, over a few square inches in area, rivet, braze or weld suitable plates in position. For smaller holes, reinforced glass fibre paste, mixed with a hardener, can be used. First use a wire brush (WEAR GOGGLES!) to clean remaining surface rust, filler and paint from the area. Smooth the reinforced paste into the holes, so that the surface comes to just BELOW that of the surrounding metal, for this paste is incredibly difficult to rub down – it is a waterproof reinforcement, not a surface filler.

MBR31.   Final filling is carried out using standard body filler, applied with a flexible plastic spatula, supplied with the filler.

MBR32.   When it has hardened the filler should be rubbed down with 150 grade 'wet or dry' paper, used dry, followed by 400 grade, then 600 grade, until all imperfections are removed. Re-fill any small holes which appear, and rub down again.

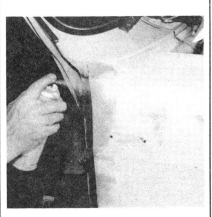

MBR33.   When the surface is perfect (no ridges or lumps should be evident; check with your fingers as well as visually), spray with primer and top coats of paint. Aerosol cans are most convenient for small areas; larger 'panel size' cans can be bought if necessary, although with either size you may have trouble obtaining the correct colour for the older Fords.

MBR34.   A similar repair technique can be used to repair rusted wing flanges. Start by grinding or chipping away all loose, rusty debris, until good, bright metal appears at the edges of the affected area. Then cut out a new metal plate (again, first making a template) to extend well beyond the damaged section at either end. This repair plate can be flat, or right-angled, depending on the damage.

   An electric drill and a few rivets can be used to attach the plate to the wing, if you don't have the necessary welding/ brazing gear.

MBR35.   Use further metal plates, as necessary, together with fibre glass paste/mat to bridge remaining holes. Smooth the surface of the fibre glass before it hardens.

73

MBR36. The final surface is achieved using a thin coating of body filler. Once hard, this can be rubbed down, then primed, and sprayed with top coats, as already shown.

The same basic procedures can be applied to any holes in the car bodywork. Fibre glass paste is waterproof and strong, and is therefore ideal as a reinforcement. Standard body filler is designed for surface finishing only, and is only resistant to water once painted. Always treat the rear of such repairs with a good coating of anti-rust paint, on completion – especially on wings.

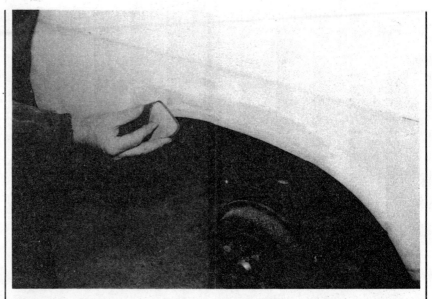

Front wing top repairs

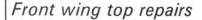

Sometimes there really is no practical alternative to changing a damaged body panel. That is, of course, assuming that you can obtain a replacement panel. As a general rule, the later the model, and the more numerous it was when originally produced, the easier it will be to buy body panels for.

New wings are a case in point. Generally speaking, you should have few problems in buying wings for Escorts, either Mark I or II models, while those for the Cortinas are becoming

increasingly difficult (and expensive) to obtain – especially the Mark I cars, the latest of which date back to 1966.

The alternative, where availability or price are problems, is to repair the existing wing. This can be easier than it sounds. To start with, and looking on the positive side, in most cases, 90 per cent of the wing will be in good condition!

An advantage of repairing, rather than replacing, is that you are less likely to have problems with re-aligning door shuts, bodywork lines and trim mouldings, on completing the job.

Minor repairs, as described

earlier in this chapter, can deal with a variety of small, rusty sections of the body panels. However, it is almost certain that, on a wing affected at all by rust, the area above and immediately behind the headlight will have suffered, whether Escort or Cortina, and more extensive renovation may be needed. Often the damage is worse than it appears initially, and, in extreme cases, the security of the light units will be affected. This means MoT test failure. Repair procedures are similar for either model, and can be varied according to the damage found.

If welding on a car fitted with an alternator, the battery should be disconnected first. Always cover the windscreen and door windows when welding or grinding near them, or the sparks will burn into the glass.

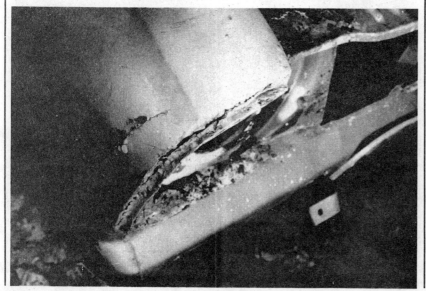

FWT1. The driver's side wing on this Cortina looked reasonably sound, but rust was showing its ugly head around the headlight – common on Fords of this era.

FWT2. First take out the head and side light units, and remove all paint from the rusted area (use a sanding attachment on your drill, or angle grinder – WEAR GOGGLES), to see what lies beneath. This car had already been plated and filled, but rust was breaking through all around the filler, and the wing flange.

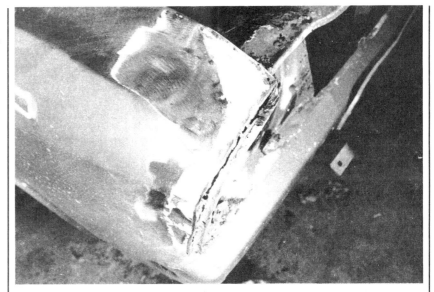

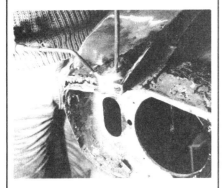

FWT3. The next step is to remove the filler and damaged metal. We used a small gas torch (WEAR WELDING GOGGLES) to melt away the braze from a plate which had previously been inserted.

FWT4. With this out of the way, it was obvious that the metal surrounding the lamp apertures was badly eaten away.

FWT5. Both inner and outer sections of the bodywork were seriously affected, and the main problem at this stage is to decide what to do about it!

FWT6. The inner shell is the place to start, and, while it could have been rebuilt using patching techniques already described, we decided it would be easier to obtain a unit from a scrapped car, which we duly did. Offer up the 'new' unit to your vehicle before doing any cutting. The replacement panel was good on the outside edge, but rusty towards the centre of the car, where our old panel was strong. We therefore decided to use the best parts of both, to make one good unit; such techniques are often necessary when new parts are unobtainable. In fact, LMC Panels can still supply these headlamp backing shells.

FWT7. We first made a hacksaw cut down through the old shell, below the headlight aperture. Make sure that the metal immediately below the shell is not damaged by the saw blade.

FWT8. Use a slim chisel or bolster to 'prise' the shell from the surrounding panels, then . . .

FWT9. . . . carefully ease the shell away from the vehicle. Measure the distance from the outer edge to the hacksaw cut at top and bottom, and mark these points on the 'new' panel. Scribe a line between the two marks. Put the old panel out of harm's way, in a bin where children and animals cannot find it – the edges will be very sharp.

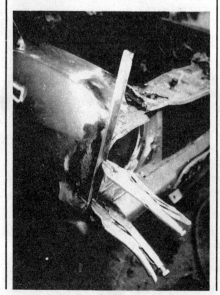

FWT10. Cut the replacement panel along the line marked, so that it matches the original, and tack weld, braze or rivet it in place. Then measure the length of the outer flange, and cut a strip of new steel to this dimension, and approximately 3/4 inch across. Bend it at right angles and clamp firmly to the new inner shell, using self-grip wrenches.

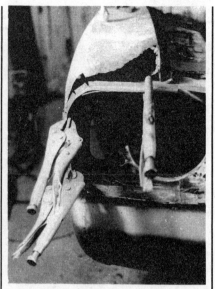

FWT11. Make a series of 'V' cuts on the vertical flange, to allow the metal strip to be bent to follow the wing contour. Clamp the top, inner end, to the 'new' shell; it must fit snugly. Minor adjustments can be made at this stage, using a hammer.

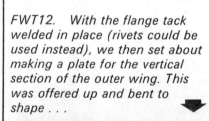

FWT12. With the flange tack welded in place (rivets could be used instead), we then set about making a plate for the vertical section of the outer wing. This was offered up and bent to shape . . .

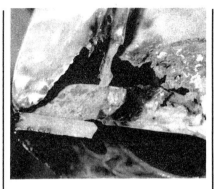

FWT17. . . . holes which looked like this! This sort of rust damage really needs new metal to strengthen the area.

FWT13. . . . then positioned so that it fitted just below the original wing contour.

FWT15. The finished weld should be carefully ground off, using an angle grinder (WEAR GOGGLES), leaving a relatively smooth surface, to await final filling.

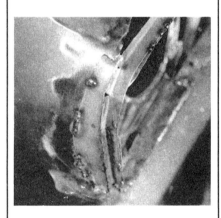

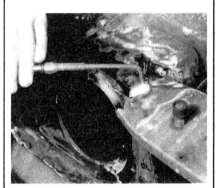

FWT18. Once again, the first step is to cut or burn out the rusty metal. A hacksaw, sharp chisel or jigsaw (WEAR GOGGLES) could be used as an alternative to the gas torch we used.

FWT14. The plate was then tack welded at intervals around the edge, using a MIG welder (USE A PROPER WELDING EYE SHIELD). Once firmly in position, the plate was welded all around its edges. If you use gas welding, employ damp rags, placed on the wing around the working area, to absorb heat and save the wing from buckling. Get an assistant to re-dampen the rags at frequent intervals, and watch for fire! Weld a little at a time, in sequential fashion around the plate, to avoid excessive build-up of heat.

    Rivets can be used equally well if you have no welding gear.

FWT16. So far, so good, but what about this area, between the wing top and the upper cross-member? Gentle finger pressure brought this piece away from the car, leaving . . .

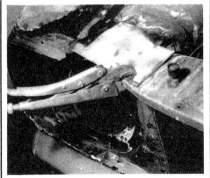

FWT19. Make a template, and apply this to a suitable piece of metal sheet, of the same gauge as the original bodywork. Cut out the repair section, clamp it in position, and weld in place.

FWT20. A plate was now needed to fill in the gaping hole at the extreme front edge of the wing. This was again made from a paper template, cut to size, and offered up to make sure it fitted exactly.

FWT21. Tack welds were then applied, to hold the plate, although, again, rivets could be used with equal success.

FWT22. With the new plate welded around its edge, then the excess metal around the edges ground back smooth, the restored wing corner now only needs a little body filler to complete the job. The wing is now strong, and, with the repair coated liberally with anti-rust paint from below, should last for many years. Total time taken, about four hours; total outlay, virtually nil! Although our 'guinea pig' car for this repair was a Cortina, the techniques used apply equally to the Escorts, which suffer from corrosion in the same area.

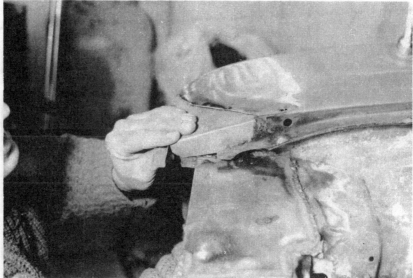

Body panels

Before undertaking any major vehicle restoration, it is useful to know the availability of body panels for your car, since these are usually more difficult to find than mechanical spares.

Luckily, the Fords covered by this book were built in considerable numbers, which at least helps the supply situation, and, to a certain extent, keeps the prices competitive.

Generally speaking, the later the car, the easier it will be to obtain bodywork sections for. Therefore Mark II Escorts present few problems, and even the Mark I models, dating back to 1968, are still provided for. The situation is a little less rosy for Mark II Cortinas, and panels are rather scarce for Mark I Cortinas, although, for example, front wings are still obtainable – at a price!

Fortunately, there are several avenues to explore in your search for new panels. It is worth trying your local Ford dealer, although it has to be said that, by now, most of the bodywork spares for early models will have long since gone. If you do strike lucky, however, the panel will, of course, be a genuine Ford item. Autojumbles are another useful source of 'original' type panels.

There are also, now, several specialist suppliers of Ford parts, listed in Appendix 6, and they often have body sections for sale; it's worth a 'phone call.

Another source could be your 'High Street' motor accessory shop, or local parts factor – they often supply body panels, as well as mechanical spares.

Several firms specialise in producing vehicle body

sections and complete panels for the vehicles covered by this book, including Ex-Pressed Steel Panels Ltd. and LMC Hadrian Ltd.

BP1.   The diagrams illustrate just how many panels can be obtained for the models covered by this book, from one supplier alone – LMC Hadrian Ltd., of Westbury, Wiltshire. The Escorts are particularly well catered for, since, of course they are more recent models.

Reproduced by kind permission of LMC Hadrian Ltd.

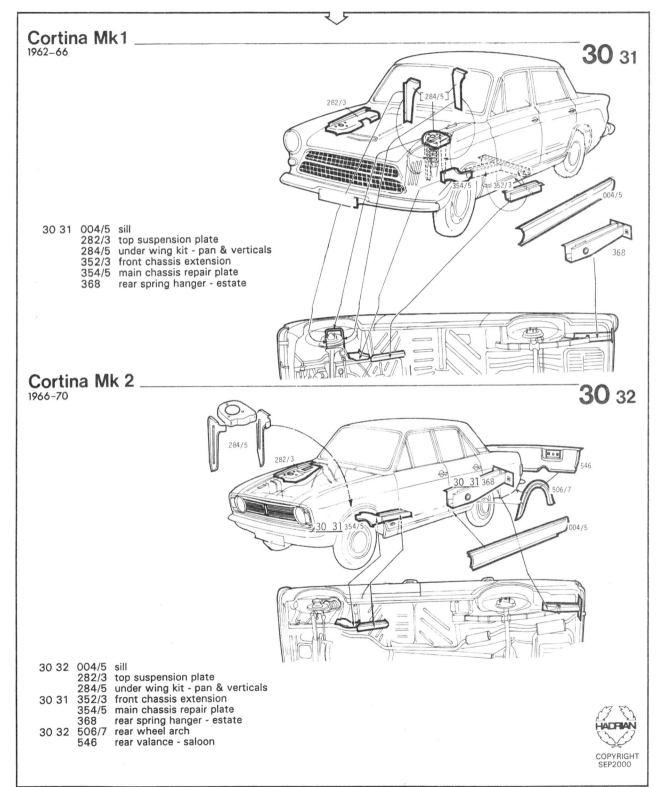

Cortina Mk 1
1962–66

30 31

30 31 004/5 sill
282/3 top suspension plate
284/5 under wing kit - pan & verticals
352/3 front chassis extension
354/5 main chassis repair plate
368   rear spring hanger - estate

Cortina Mk 2
1966–70

30 32

30 32 004/5 sill
282/3 top suspension plate
284/5 under wing kit - pan & verticals
30 31 352/3 front chassis extension
354/5 main chassis repair plate
368   rear spring hanger - estate
30 32 506/7 rear wheel arch
546   rear valance - saloon

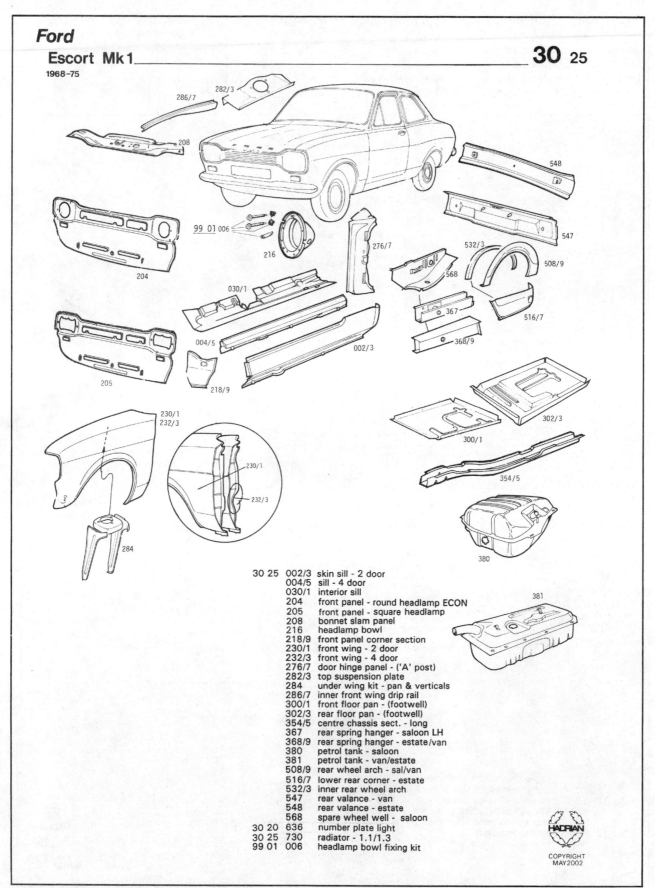

30 25	002/3	skin sill - 2 door
	004/5	sill - 4 door
	030/1	interior sill
	204	front panel - round headlamp ECON
	205	front panel - square headlamp
	208	bonnet slam panel
	216	headlamp bowl
	218/9	front panel corner section
	230/1	front wing - 2 door
	232/3	front wing - 4 door
	276/7	door hinge panel - ('A' post)
	282/3	top suspension plate
	284	under wing kit - pan & verticals
	286/7	inner front wing drip rail
	300/1	front floor pan - (footwell)
	302/3	rear floor pan - (footwell)
	354/5	centre chassis sect. - long
	367	rear spring hanger - saloon LH
	368/9	rear spring hanger - estate/van
	380	petrol tank - saloon
	381	petrol tank - van/estate
	508/9	rear wheel arch - sal/van
	516/7	lower rear corner - estate
	532/3	inner rear wheel arch
	547	rear valance - van
	548	rear valance - estate
	568	spare wheel well - saloon
30 20	636	number plate light
30 25	730	radiator - 1.1/1.3
99 01	006	headlamp bowl fixing kit

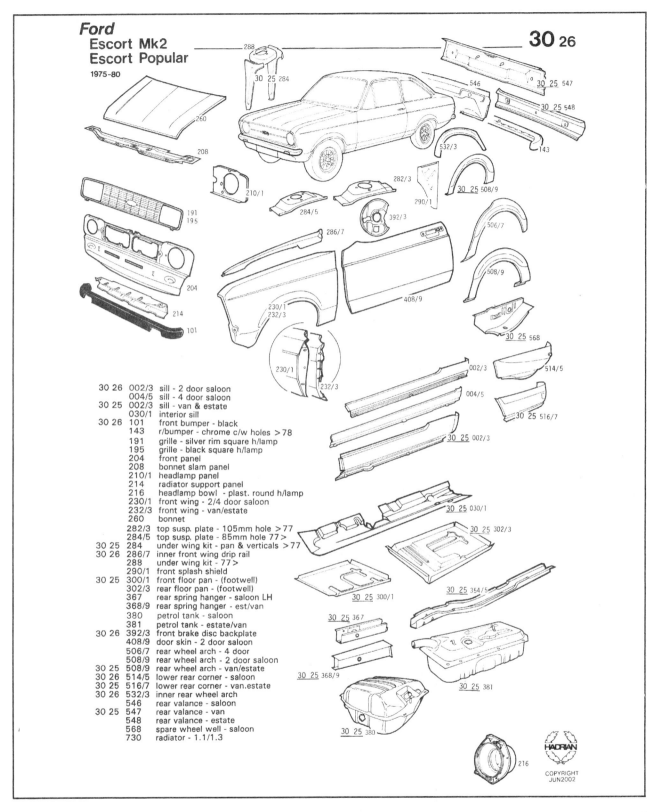

Ford
Escort Mk2
Escort Popular

1975-80

30 26

30 26 002/3   sill - 2 door saloon
       004/5   sill - 4 door saloon
30 25 002/3   sill - van & estate
       030/1   interior sill
30 26 101   front bumper - black
       143   r/bumper - chrome c/w holes >78
       191   grille - silver rim square h/lamp
       195   grille - black square h/lamp
       204   front panel
       208   bonnet slam panel
       210/1   headlamp panel
       214   radiator support panel
       216   headlamp bowl - plast. round h/lamp
       230/1   front wing - 2/4 door saloon
       232/3   front wing - van/estate
       260   bonnet
       282/3   top susp. plate - 105mm hole >77
       284/5   top susp. plate - 85mm hole 77>
30 25 284   under wing kit - pan & verticals >77
30 26 286/7   inner front wing drip rail
       288   under wing kit - 77>
       290/1   front splash shield
30 25 300/1   front floor pan - (footwell)
       302/3   rear floor pan - (footwell)
       367   rear spring hanger - saloon LH
       368/9   rear spring hanger - est/van
       380   petrol tank - saloon
       381   petrol tank - estate/van
30 26 392/3   front brake disc backplate
       408/9   door skin - 2 door saloon
       506/7   rear wheel arch - 4 door
       508/9   rear wheel arch - 2 door saloon
30 25 508/9   rear wheel arch - van/estate
30 26 514/5   lower rear corner - saloon
30 25 516/7   lower rear corner - van.estate
30 26 532/3   inner rear wheel arch
       546   rear valance - saloon
30 25 547   rear valance - van
       548   rear valance - estate
       568   spare wheel well - saloon
       730   radiator - 1.1/1.3

HADRIAN
COPYRIGHT
JUN2002

Front wing change

If a front wing (or wings) on your Ford is badly rusted in all the normal places (as outlined in the 'Buying' chapter of this book), it may be that there is less work involved in replacing it with a new panel, than attempting to repair it with a multitude of patches. If you are carrying out a major restoration on your car, you may not be prepared to settle for anything

less than new panels, anyway.

The front wings on Cortinas and Escorts were welded onto the vehicle when new, and therefore changing a wing involves breaking the original metal to metal joint, to remove the old wing.

In theory, it should then just be a matter of lining up the new panel, and attaching it to the car. However, as with most jobs on old cars, you can come across problems. The usual troubles arise from rust, which often turns out to be worse than expected, in the inner wing, suspension mountings, bulkhead and door pillar areas. This should obviously be rectified before the new wing is fitted, and, of course, access is much easier with the wing off the vehicle. Therefore it is wise to allow much more time than you expect the job to take, especially if you rely on the car to get to work, for example. What starts out as a 'one evening' job might turn out to have been better tackled over a long weekend!

Despite the fact that the wings are welded on, no special tools are needed for their removal. A sharp bolster, or slim chisel is the best implement for separating the old wing from the car. A hacksaw and a pair of tin snips also come in handy for dealing with recalcitrant bits of rusty metal! Welding apparatus will also be needed, of course, to attach the new panel to the car. If your Ford is fitted with an alternator, it is wise to disconnect the battery, to avoid damage to the alternator.

Before you start chopping the old wing away from the vehicle, it is most important first to look at the new panel, and assess the exact positions and shapes of the edge flanges. If this information is borne in mind as you remove the existing wing, you can be sure of leaving sufficient metal in place on your vehicle, so that the new panel can be attached to it! The last thing you want is great gaps between the car and the new

panel, where you were a bit too enthusiastic with the chisel. If in doubt, err on the side of safety, leaving a little more metal on the car than you think you need. Then, with the old panel off, offer up the new one so that you can see exactly where flanges on the vehicle need final trimming.

Of course, you may find it impossible to find (or afford)!) brand new panels, in which case one alternative is to make a detailed search of breakers' yards in your area, to find a car like yours, but with decent bodywork. It may take some time, and you will probably have to remove the panel yourself when you find it, but with the average cost of second-hand front wings running at between one tenth and one fifth of the price of new ones, it is well worth the effort.

You will, of course, find that around half of the Fords in breakers' yards are rusty anyway, but, of the other half, many of the wings will be undamaged, especially where, for example, an otherwise well cared for car has met its fate through serious mechanical failure, or a rear end shunt, for example. Such cars are ideal as 'donor' vehicles for your front wings!

An important point to bear in mind, if considering the use of secondhand body panels, is that any cuts made to remove them should be made with a generous margin around the panel edges. This will ensure that you don't damage your 'new' body section when removing it. Cleaning up the flanges, removing spot welds, etc., can be left until you get the panel home.

ALWAYS wear heavy duty protective gloves when cutting panels from a vehicle, and remove all jagged bits of metal immediately, to avoid accidents.

It is worth noting that although the operations shown in this section are split between the models, to highlight differences, the wing and underwing construction of Cortinas and

Escorts is almost identical. Therefore the techniques used for rectification can be applied, generally, to all models. For example, the restoration of suspension mounting and bulkhead/door pillar areas, depicted in the 'Cortina' section, applies equally to Escorts.

Cortina

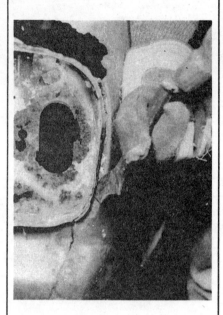

FWC1. This Cortina Mark II had serious rust in all the usual places around the front wings, and it was decided that, due to the extent of the damage, replacement would be a better solution than patching.

The first job was to remove the grille and the front lights, as described earlier in this chapter. A start was then made on the cutting, by separating the wing from the vehicle, around the headlight area. A slim bolster, which had been abused and broken in an earlier life dealing with masonry, was the ideal tool for the job. In places, there was not a lot of metal to separate!

Take care not to damage surrounding metal by proceeding with caution, especially where the adjacent panels are weakened by rust; it is important to retain their shape, as far as possible.

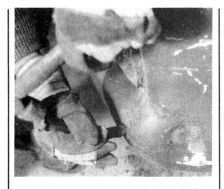

FWC2.   Special care is needed when splitting the wing from the front valance. The slimmer the bolster (or chisel), the better, since otherwise the metal at either side of the joint line can get damaged very easily.

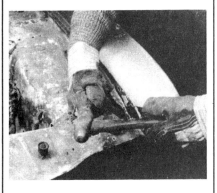

FWC3.   We then worked backwards from the headlight area, along the top, inner edges of the wing. The flange could be separated along the welded joint between the wing and the inner wing, alternatively (as here) the wing can be cut just above this flange, on the OUTER wing side of the joint. Surplus metal can be ground or filed from the inner wing flange later.

FWC4.   This wing had previously been repaired by having patches brazed between it and the bulkhead, so removal was more tricky than usual. However, even if your car has not been repaired in this way, the wing should be cut from the bulkhead panel with great care. Again, we erred on the side of safety, leaving small areas of metal to grind back later, rather than risk damaging the adjacent metal with hammer blows.

FWC5.   Having separated the wing along the front and upper seams, the next step is to split it from the car, down the rear edge. Take out the door check strap pin and open the door as wide as possible, for better access. On Mark II models, DON'T remove the door from the car, since its front edge will be an important datum line when fitting the new panel.

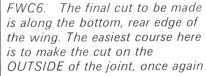

FWC6.   The final cut to be made is along the bottom, rear edge of the wing. The easiest course here is to make the cut on the OUTSIDE of the joint, once again

leaving the flange to be trimmed once the old wing is out of the way. There remains a single nut to release, from inside the car – this holds the wing to the top of the door pillar, and is accessible from under the facia.

FWC7.   Now lift the wing from the car, still using those thick, heavy duty, protective gloves; the sharp edges of the wing are very dangerous.

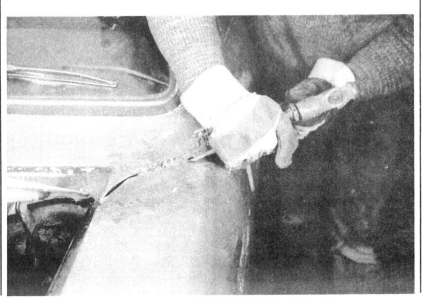

FWC8. The next job is to assess what work, if any, needs doing before the new panel can be fitted. Look closely at the state of the legs and upper web of the suspension strut mountings. Even a cursory examination of this area on the Cortina showed that there was very little left of the top of this front leg . . .

FWC9. . . . and the rear leg was holed, too. Worse still, the suspension strut mounting pan, between the two supporting legs, was rusty as well. In fact, there was very little to stop the suspension unit from departing upwards through the bonnet! Luckily, a suspension top plate had been welded to the inner wing top at some time in the past, which had saved the surrounding metal from deformation.

It was obvious that extensive renovation would be needed to put the suspension mountings to rights, but first we dealt with the rear end of the under-wing area, since this needs to be sound before serious work can begin on the inner wing panel.

FWC10. Take a close look at the bulkhead/door hinge mounting pillar areas. We got quite a shock when we discovered just how bad this secion of the car had become. Water, pouring through the gaps in the bulkhead, had also rusted the floor, but more about floor repairs later. Pull back the sound proofing material and wiring from behind the bulkhead, so that it doesn't catch fire during welding operations.

FWC11. Probe the area extensively with a screwdriver, or gently with a chisel, to rid it of loose material, so that you can get an idea of how much metal needs putting back. Don't,

whatever you do, hit weakened areas too hard, or clear more than a small section at a time, or the front of your car could collapse. Certainly this Cortina was a little rusty here.

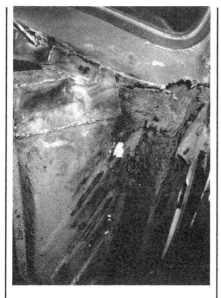

FWC12. Grind or file ALL the rust from the edges of the holes, until solid metal is reached all around. Start reconstruction by making plates to reinforce small areas at a time. This puts back strength so that adjoining sections can be tackled without fear of disintegration. Tack weld the plates at one end, moving along each edge and hammering to follow the shape of the bulkhead as you go. A gas torch can be used to warm the metal to red heat, which makes it pliable and easier to shape, without the use of heavy blows against it. The plates can then be welded in fully, all around their edges.

FWC13. For the door pillar, we shaped one piece of metal, using a paper template, then forming the metal by locking it between two lengths of angle iron, clamped in the vice, and hit with a heavy hammer. The metal used for rebuilding structural parts of the car, like this, must be of AT LEAST the same gauge as the original, for strength. We chose to use slightly thicker material, which of course is also slightly more difficult to work with. Offer up your repair panel to the car at each stage of forming, for a perfect fit.

FWC14. We used gas welding to attach the top of the pillar repair plate to the car, and the gas torch was again handy for heating the metal to a dull red shade, for easy bending. Tack the plate and bend to shape, before continuously welding it around its edges.

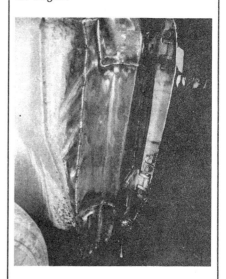

FWC15. On completion, with further 'closing' plates made and fitted to the bottom of the pillar and inner wing, the area looked like this. We used the MIG welder for speed, to complete the welding of the more accessible, lower sections.

FWC16. Before proceeding further with repairs to the suspension turret mountings, it is a good idea to get rid of any metal bits and pieces remaining from the wing removal operations. Use a chisel or bolster, to break remaining welds and skim off surplus wing flange, then grind or file the surface flat.

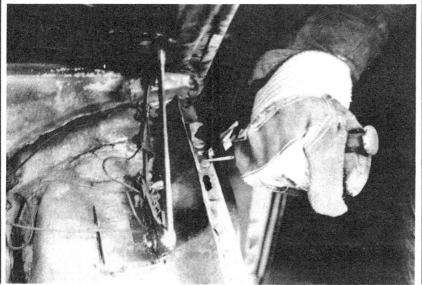

85

Back to the suspension strut mountings, and, to do the job properly, the MacPherson strut suspension unit must be taken off the vehicle, to assess the full extent of rust damage at the top of the mountings. To start with, the suspension leg is detached at the lower end.

On disc braked cars, detach the brake pipe from the hub, or from the inner wing bracket. If you are intending to carry out a brake overhaul, it is also a good idea to take off the brake caliper (full details given in the 'Mechanical Components' chapter); this makes the strut assembly lighter anyway. On drum braked cars, there is no need to detach the fluid hose; simply take off the hub nut and brake drum (described in the 'Brakes' section of the 'Mechanical Components' Chapter), then remove the backplate bolts and tie the backplate out of the way, on the car bodywork, so that the flexible brake hose is not strained. Similar procedures apply also to Escort models; further details of separating the lower end of the suspension unit from the track control arm, on Escorts, are given in the 'Steering and Front Suspension' section of the 'Mechanical Components' Chapter.

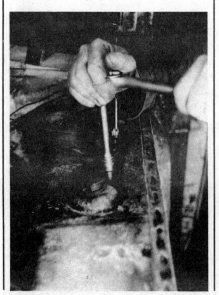

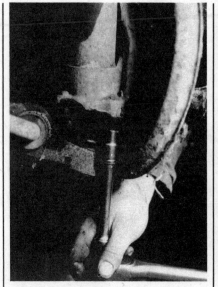

FWC17.   On later Mark II Cortinas, like this one, the lower end of the suspension unit is released by simply knocking back the lock tabs and removing the three bolts securing the track control arm to the suspension assembly. Use plenty of penetrating oil beforehand, on the bolt threads – they are usually corroded.

On Mark I and earlier Mark II Cortinas, the split pin and castellated nut holding the ball joint stud at the base of the suspension unit, must be removed, then a ball joint extractor used to separate the track control arm from the ball joint stud. Use the extractor again to separate the suspension unit steering arm from the track rod end, having first removed the split pin and loosened the nut.

FWC18.   At the top end, release the three bolts securing the unit ◀ *to the inner wing panel. Again, apply plenty of penetrating oil, from above and below the wing top, to make sure that the threads receive plenty of encouragement – the bolts are prone to seizing and breaking.*

FWC19.   Grip the suspension unit firmly, and push the unit downwards, against the track control arm – use your foot to help force this down, if working on your own, then . . .

FWC20.   . . . ease the unit upwards and away from the track control arm – it may need a little encouragement to start with. ⬇

FWC21. With the suspension assembly out of the way, a closer examination could be made of the rusted sections. To start with, it was apparent that the rust extended almost all the way around the inside of the upper suspension mounting pan.

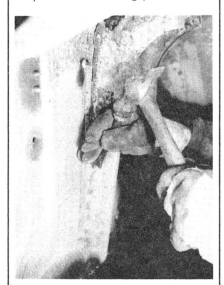

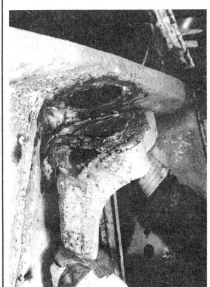

FWC22. In addition, a closer look at, or rather, through, the front mounting leg, following a little poking with a screwdriver, showed that the inner wing panel had disintegrated above and around the mountings. This meant that the suspension mountings had to be taken off, for proper rectification of the damaged areas.

While superficial damage to these mountings could perhaps be plated, it is better to buy new items. New mounting legs and pans, already formed to the exact shape required, are sold as kits by such firms as LMC Panels. These 'under wing kits' are not expensive, and should last for many years.

FWC23. There is no easy way to separate the mounting legs from the vehicle; we used a hammer and bolster, but a cutting disc in an angle grinder might be quicker, if you have neighbours who don't mind the noise! Once again, the easiest approach is to slice the metal just outboard of the inner wing panel, leaving the remains of the flange to be dealt with later.

FWC24. Use protective gloves to hold the suspension mountings as they are carefully withdrawn from the under-wing area. The extent of rust damage becomes evident as the mounting comes away. Layers of metal, 'sandwiched' together, as here, hold water and rust gains ground, destroying the metal from the inside.

FWC25. Use a sharp chisel or bolster to prise the remains of the mounting flange from the bodywork; with luck, it should come off in one strip, away from its spot welds. Afterwards, grind or file the metal smooth.

FWC26. Dig, cut or grind out ALL the rusty metal from the inner wing panel, then find a sheet of metal of suitable size to cover the whole area, overlapping each side by two or three inches. Make sure that it is at least as thick as the original inner wing top; preferably thicker.

FWC27.   Bend the plate to follow the shape of the inner wing, and hold in place with a large 'G' clamp as it is welded into position. Make sure that all wiring and plastic components are removed from the engine bay side of the inner wing, before you start welding! Use a hammer to dress the metal to final shape, before welding the inner edge.

FWC28.   The problem now, of course, is that there is no hole for the suspension unit top to pass through! However, with the plate clamped/welded firmly in place, the exact position for cutting out this hole, and drilling those for the mounting bolts, can be established.

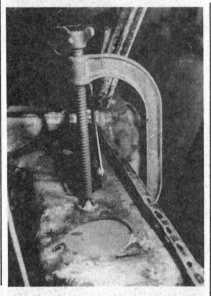

FWC29.   There are several methods of cutting out the hole for the suspension unit top; we chose to use the gas torch to burn through the metal around the edge of the hole. Take care not to damage the surrounding metal, or cause distortion by excessive heat.
   An alternative is to drill a series of small holes around the circumference of the circle, then join them up with a small chisel, finally cleaning up the edges with a file.

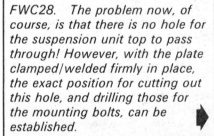

FWC30.   The next part of the job is particularly critical. The three components of the 'under-wing kit' are clamped in position on the vehicle, using the lines of the original panel as a guide. To ensure exact positioning of the upper strut mounting pan, simply bolt this to the inner wing, aligning the three holes in the pan with those in the inner wing. The nuts and bolts used can come off as soon as the welding is completed. It is obviously vital that the welding done here must be to a very high standard, for safety.

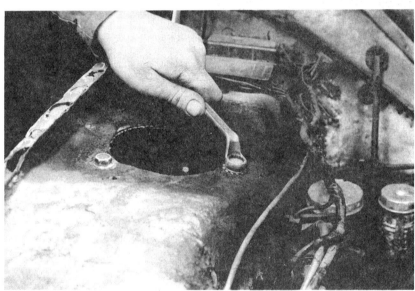

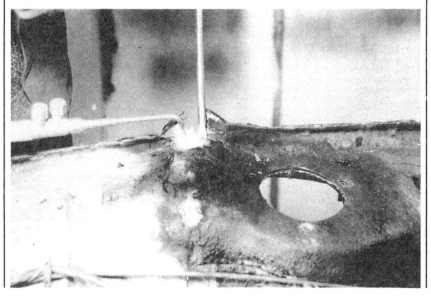

FWC31. On the other side of this car, the upper wing area had already had a 'top plate' welded on, and everything here appeared to be in good condition, with the exception of a few tiny rust holes. However, it never pays to take things like this at face value, as we discovered.

FWC32. We carried out the repair procedure as for the other side, welding a plate into position below the inner wing top, having stripped off the old suspension mountings, and replaced them with an 'under wing kit'. We again used the three existing bolt holes in the inner wing panel to line up the new suspension top pan.

FWC33. Having got this far, you should then normally be in a position to replace the suspension and front wing. However, despite initial appearances, it was obvious that all was not well below the 'replacement' top suspension plate which had previously been fitted by an earlier owner of the car.

When the bonnet was opened or closed, there was considerable movement of the metal where the hinge was mounted, below the replacement plate. It appeared that the hinge was not attached to very much, which was a little worrying! If these symptoms appear on your car, it means trouble – usually rust trouble – which has often been covered up, rather than rectified. So, we used a gas torch, to melt the joint, and a screwdriver, for prising off the repair plate, to see what lay beneath.

FWC34. We tackled the plate in two sections, using the bolster to chisel off particularly stubborn welds. This, of course, is a long and tedious job, but it must be done carefully to avoid damage to surrounding and underlying panels. However, in this case, it was well worth the effort, for . . .

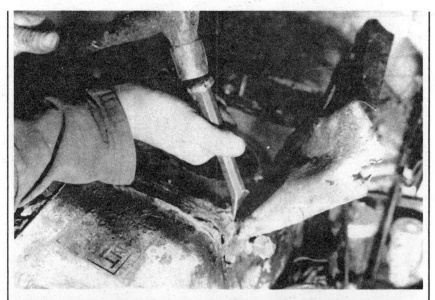

FWC35. . . . underneath the 'repair' plate, and all around the hinge mountings, we found holes! The first step in rectification is to cut out the rust, make up suitable repair plates of your own, using card or paper templates, and weld new metal into the holes that will be covered by your new repair top plate. This puts strength back into the hinge mounting area.

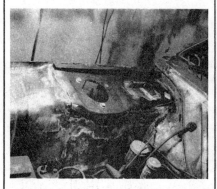

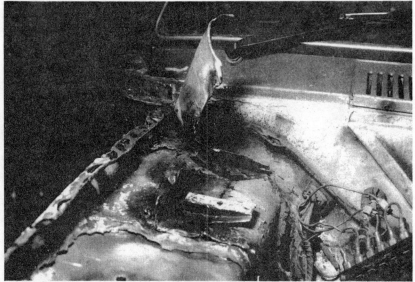

FWC36. Using the same nut and bolt technique that was used on the under-wing plate, locate the new top repair plate on the top of the inner wing. This method can of course be used when fitting a top plate for the first time, and when the suspension unit is in position; simply use the suspension mounting bolts to hold the plate in position. This repair plate, from LMC Panels, fitted perfectly, and was first welded to the metal around the hinge mounting plate.

FWC37. Unfortunately, on this car the inner wing panel was rusty below the lower edge of the top repair plate, so we were obliged to make up our own repair section to deal with this problem. First, offer up the plate.

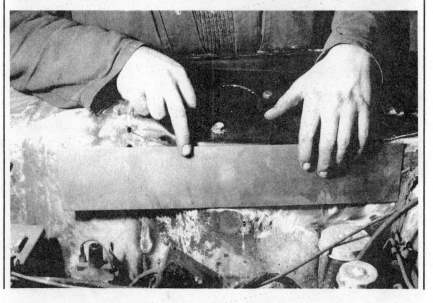

FWC38. Trim the corners of the plate to fit the engine bay, then offer up again, and so on, until a perfect fit is obtained.

FWC39. A large 'G' clamp is ideal for holding the plate to the inner wing as it is welded.

FWC40. The plate is then welded around the edges, starting in the centre of the top and bottom sides, and carefully bending the outer ends to the profile of the inner wing, as work proceeds.

FWC41. A number of smaller plates may also be needed, to strengthen other under-wing areas where rust has taken its toll. The suspension unit can be refitted when the inner wing is sound once again.

FWC42. Before fitting the wing on the passenger side of the vehicle, a repair plate was needed, to strengthen the upper cross-member. The rust was first removed from the existing section, then a plate made and clamped in position, prior to welding.

FWC43. The one remaining job, before the wing goes on, is to make repairs, as appropriate, to the shell surrounding the lamp apertures. It will usually be rusty, as this one was.

91

FWC44.   While patching was possible, we found a good unit on a scrapped car, which of course was already shaped for the job. Using the same basic procedures outlined in the 'Front Wing Top Repairs' section of this chapter, we cut away the rusty (outer) section of the unit, with a small hacksaw.

FWC45.   With the bonnet then replaced, and correctly positioned, we then offered up the 'new' wing panel. We had obtained this from a motor vehicle dismantler; the wing was not very old, and we had taken it from an accident-damaged Cortina.

It is vital that the wing should be a perfect fit for 'line and length' in every direction, so it is worth taking some time to ensure this. Make sure that the bonnet shuts properly, leaving an equal gap at each side between it and each front wing. There should also be a uniform gap between the rear of the wing and the front edge of the door, so that the door will open and close without 'catching' the wing. It helps to have an assistant or two available during these critical alignment procedures.

FWC46.   When all is well, clamp the wing, using self-grip wrenches, at strategic points, so that it doesn't move.

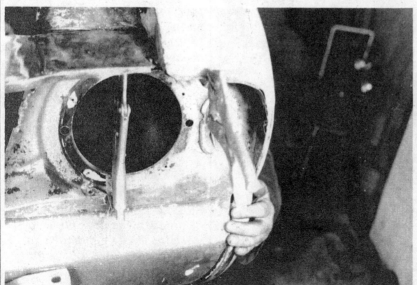

FWC47.   We now introduced the new lamp shell repair section, and clamped it while re-checking wing alignment.

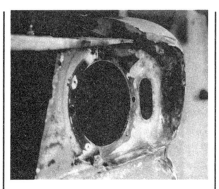

FWC48. The shell was then welded to the outer wing, and to the inner part of the original unit. Use small welds at intervals to start with, then follow up with continuous welding around the perimeter.

FWC49. It can be difficult to squeeze together the inner wing flange and that of the new wing. We used a road wheel nut, clamped with a self-grip wrench, to bring the two together. This makes the job of joining the two panels very much easier.

FWC50. Tack weld at intervals along the remaining flanges. The use of a MIG welder, if available, will reduce the possibility of heat distortion. Since the wing was spot welded originally, there is no need to join up the seams along their entire length, except where water may enter and play havoc. The front and lower edges of the wing are obvious candidates for this.

The techniques described in the foregoing apply, generally speaking, to both Mark I and Mark II Cortinas, including the rectification of rust damage around the suspension mountings, and in the under-wing area. However, there are some differences in design, which mean some variation in the procedures to follow when changing a wing. Therefore the following, additional, points apply specifically to Mark I models:

FWC51. The Mark I Cortinas have a longer seam between the front panel of the car and each front wing, below the headlight. It is therefore especially important to take care as the joint is split, since it is easy to damage the front panel. If you use a chisel for this job, try to make sure that it is very sharp, and as slim as possible. It is not necessary (although to a certain extent it helps access) to remove the front bumper or the mountings on Mark I models, whereas on Mark IIs, at least the outer bumper support at each side must come off.

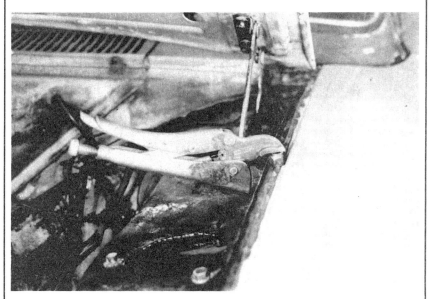

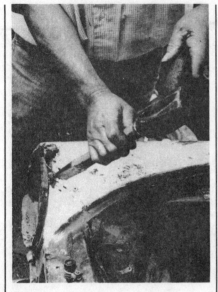

FWC52. There is an additional, short seam just inboard of each headlamp, on Mark I cars. When removing the old panel from your car, make the cut just above the seam, trimming back excess metal afterwards, very carefully. Don't risk using the chisel or bolster directly on this joint, or you may well harm the panel just below, giving yourself further rectification work to do!

FWC53. As with Mark II cars, it is advisable to part the old wing from your car along a line just outboard of the welded joint between the outer and inner wing panels. Be careful, on Mark I models, not to extend this cut further forward than the joint between the upper part of the front panel, and the wing itself.

FWC55. With the door out of the way, access to the rear joint of the wing is much improved. Again, go easy on the hammer blows – use only just enough pressure to break the joint, without harming the surrounding bodywork.

FWC56. The joint between the lower rear edge of the wing and the inner flange at this point may be almost non-existent, due to corrosion. On this Mark I, it was solid, and, again, great care is needed so that metal is not torn unnecessarily.

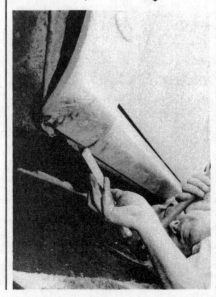

FWC54. The rear edge of the front wing is rather less accessible on Mark I cars, than on Mark IIs. Therefore, it is best to remove the door before you start work on this area, so that damage to the door can be avoided. It does mean that rather more care is needed when offering up your replacement wing, since you will have no datum line to work to, at the rear edge of the wing, unless you temporarily rehang the door. A fiddly aspect, but not difficult to overcome, with a little patience.

The door can be lifted off after removing the two bolts which pass through each hinge and into the door, and the two nuts on each hinge, which are removed from inside the door, after taking off the door panel.

94

Escort

As already stated, the basic design principles of the Cortinas and Escorts are very similar when it comes to front wing construction. Therefore, the techniques needed for most of the work, including dealing with the horrors of rust damage around the suspension mountings, and the inner wing/bulkhead areas, once the wing is removed apply as described in the 'Cortina' section, and reference should be made to this for full details.

However, there are several minor differences in construction, and to outline how these affect changing a wing, the following shows how the job was done on a Mark II Escort which needed a new wing, following a slight altercation with a parked vehicle! The owner of the car had no welding equipment, and, for this reason, and for ease of changing the wing in future (he was worried in case of further 'parked car incidents'!), he specifically wanted the new wing to be bolted, rather than welded onto the vehicle. This is quite acceptable, but, if you decide to adopt this approach, it is important that the wing is bolted securely at frequent points around its perimeter, so that it forms a solid and complete part

of the car. MoT testers will certainly not be too happy about occasional self-tapping screws, for example, scattered at great distances along the seams!

Wing-changing procedures are similar for Mark I and II Escorts. It is interesting to note (although of no consolation to Cortina owners) that new wings for Escorts, both Mark I and II models, are still readily available, and the cost is normally less than half that required for the equivalent Cortina panel. This of course is mainly due to the fact that there are more Escorts in everyday use, and quantities sold are much higher.

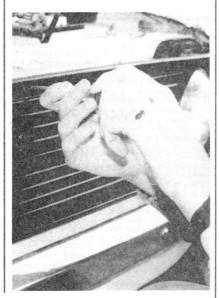

FWE1. It was unfortunate that this wing should need changing because of a minor bump, since it was not visibly rusty, and only the front corners were damaged. However, the creases were more severe than it appeared at first, so a new steel wing was duly bought.

FWE2. To change a wing on any Escort, the headlight has to be removed, and to get at the lights, the grille must come out. Self-tapping screws secure the grille on Mark I and Mark II Escorts. If you withdraw the lamp and its shell as a unit, forward, there is no need to disconnect the wiring; the lamp assembly can be tied to the bumper, out of harm's way.

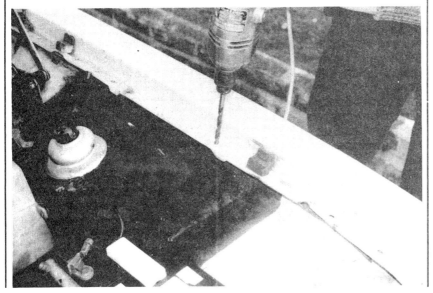

FWE3. The joint between the inner and outer wings was examined very carefully, to find where the spot welds were located. These were then drilled through, very carefully. Use a slow speed on your electric drill, if it is a two speed machine. This method of splitting the wing from the car may take longer, but is useful if you don't possess an angle grinder, for it leave a nice clean flange which requires very little tidying. This technique could also be applied to Cortinas, of course.

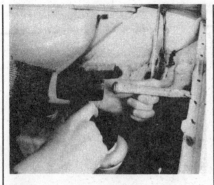

FWE4. Chisel work is still necessary, to make the final break between the wing and the inner wing flange. With care, the outer wing edge can be bent upwards, leaving the inner wing panel intact.

FWE5. The lower edge of this wing turned out to have more rust that it appeared, so parting the wing from the car at this point was easier than expected, having already separated the rear, vertical joint.

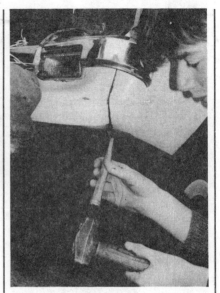

FWE6. The seam between the wing and the front panel is quite deep, and separation needs great care, if damage to the front panel is to be avoided. Use the slimmest, sharpest chisel or bolster available. The bumper doesn't have to be removed, but the outer bolt and spacer do have to come out, since they are normally attached to the wing.

FWE7. The wing can be lifted clear once all the seams are separated; take care not to scratch the paintwork on other parts of the car, as the wing is taken off.

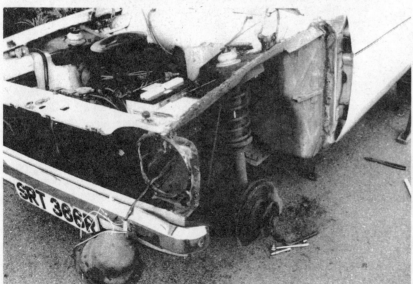

FWE8. Check the inner wing, suspension mountings, bulkhead and door pillar for rust, while the outer wing is off. It is far easier to rectify any damage at this stage, than when the new wing has been fitted. This Escort was in good overall condition in the critical under-wing areas, but if yours is not, follow the guidance given in the 'Cortina' section, earlier in this chapter.

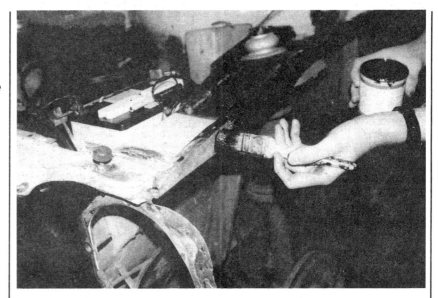

FWE9. It is a good idea to coat flanges and corners which are normally out of sight, with a good coat – preferably two – of anti-rust paint. In fact, if you have time to wire brush the entire under-wing area, and paint all of it, so much the better.

FWE10. Offer up the wing, to make sure that it fits properly, as described in the 'Cortina' section. Mark the positions of the holes already drilled in the inner wing flange (when removing the spot welds), by making a tiny pencil mark by each one, just inboard, on the top of the inner wing, so that when the wing is fitted, you will be able to drill it in precisely the same spots. We then sprayed this wing with a large 'panel spray' aerosal can of primer, prior to fitting, and, when the paint was dry, 'hung' the wing on the car. Holes were then drilled through the wing, in the pre-determined positions, and the nuts and bolts attached, one by one. Don't tighten them fully until all are in place.

Of course, if you have access to welding gear, and you prefer, the wing can be welded on, in the same way as described earlier, for fitting Cortina wings.

Fuel tank removal

Before carrying out any welding work on the rear of your vehicle, or underneath it, it is essential that the fuel tank is removed and that the fuel line is taken off, for safety's sake.

This is not such a major job as it sounds, on any of the Cortinas or Escorts, and it means that you can work safely, without fear of setting fire to the car . . . or worse. **Take care – no smoking or naked flames**

near the fuel system, please!!
Starting with the fuel line, this is clipped to the 'chassis' and is easily removed after disconnecting the pipe from the carburettor, under the bonnet, and from the base of the fuel tank. It is obvious that the fuel level in the tank should be as low as possible before removing the outlet pipe, or else you will lose all the fuel. On Mark I Cortinas, drain plugs were fitted, so it is easy to drain the contents beforehand into a suitable container. Make sure that the cans you have available are sufficiently large, in total, to accommodate all the petrol that's

liable to be in the car's tank, or you will have problems.

On later Cortinas, and the Escorts, there is no drain tap fitted to the tank. One way to drain these tanks is to syphon the petrol out. By dipping a long tube into the tank, and sucking on the outer end of it, petrol will be drawn up the tube. By placing the end into a container placed at the lower level than the tank, the contents of the tank will gradually empty themselves, by gravity, into the container. I don't recommend this method, however, it tastes awful, and there's no need to do it this way. A far better method is, with the

fuel pipe still attached to the tank and carburettor, to raise the rear of the car as high as possible, then disconnect the petrol pipe at the front end. The fuel can then be directed into suitable containers. If you need to stop draining for any reason (to change containers, for instance), the open end of the pipe is simply lifted above tank level, and the fuel will stop.

Once having drained the tank, methods of removing it from the car vary according to which model you have. On all models, the tank filler pipe has to be separated from the tank, after releasing the hose clips. If the filler cap is taken off, the outer section of the filler pipe can be pulled out, having released the securing (Phillips) screws.

On Mark I Cortina saloons (except 1500 GT cars), and Mark II Cortina saloons, the tank is screwed to the floor pan, and is extracted from inside the boot, upwards, away from the floor. The fuel gauge sender connections must be disconnected before lifting the tank out. Use a waterproof sealant between tank and floor, on replacement. 1500 GT Cortinas, and the estate models, have their fuel tanks slung below the vehicle. Removal involves unbolting the tank cradle (where fitted), or releasing the tank bolts from the underfloor crossmembers. The fuel gauge sender wires and vent pipe clips need to be disconnected as the tank is lowered. Make sure that any insulation strips fitted between the tank and the floor, or support cradle, are re-fitted on replacing the tank.

Escort saloons have the fuel tank mounted in the right-hand side of the boot, and removal is only possible after disconnecting the gauge sender wires (at the front of the tank), and the vent pipes (at the rear of the tank), which are held on with spring pipe clips. It is a good idea to remove the fuel filler pipe from outside the car, before taking out the tank, having slackened the hose clips and released the three Phillips screws.

The tank is retained by two bolts at the top of the tank, and two more at the base – these are accessible from underneath the car, and usually corroded in place, so apply plenty of penetrating oil, before you start. The tanks are extracted from inside the boot. The job isn't difficult, but rather fiddly.

The tanks on Escort estates and vans are bolted to the underframe, as with Cortina estates, and are removed in the same way.

At the risk of repeating the obvious, don't smoke when working on fuel systems, and keep naked lights well away from the car while any part of the system is disconnected.

FTR1. This diagram shows the general layout of the Mark I Cortina fuel system. The tank is released from inside the boot, after lifting the mat. Grease the screws on re-assembly; they become rather tight after a few years in service! The layout on Mark II cars is almost identical.

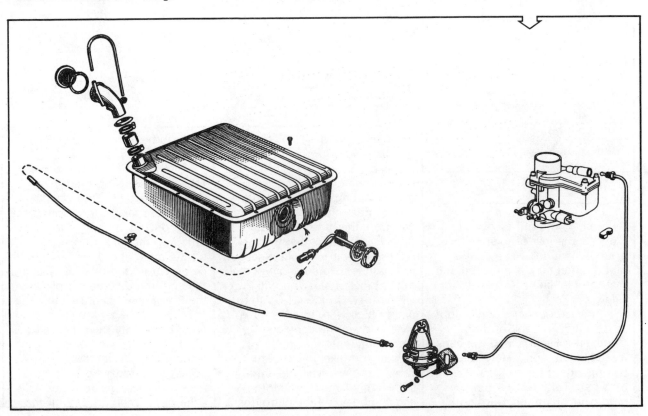

FTR2.   The estate car fuel tanks on both Mark I and II Cortinas are held and released from below the vehicle. After releasing the cradle and supporting bolts, the tank comes out from beneath the car.

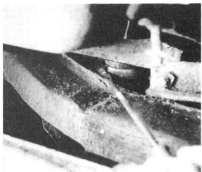

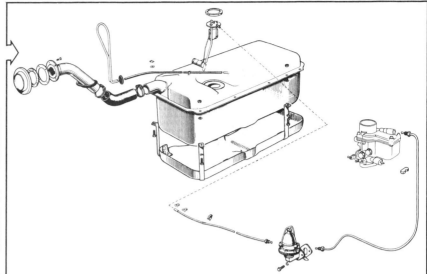

FTR3.   The biggest problem, on Cortina estate cars, is releasing the fuel filler pipe hose connections. You need a very long screwdriver to reach past the chassis members, and plenty of leverage to shift the screws, which are often seized!

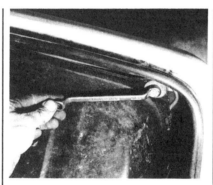

FTR6.   On Escort saloons, first release the gauge connection and the vent pipe, then slacken the mounting bolts. There are two at the top, inside the boot, and two below the boot floor.

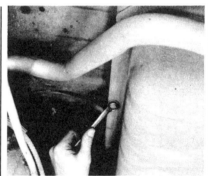

FTR7.   The tank on Escort estate cars is released from below the vehicle, as for the Cortina estate models. The tank is easy to take out, once the electrics, vent pipe and securing bolts have been released.

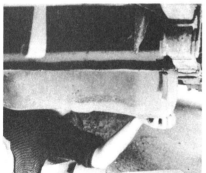

FTR4.   On Cortina saloons, the tank comes out from inside the boot, whereas on estate cars, it must be released from below the car. The tank is not heavy, once empty, and there are no problems, once the wires and pipes have been disconnected.

FTR5.   Escort fuel tanks sit upright in the boot. This diagram depicts the arrangement of the fuel system for Mark I models, but Mark IIs are very similar.

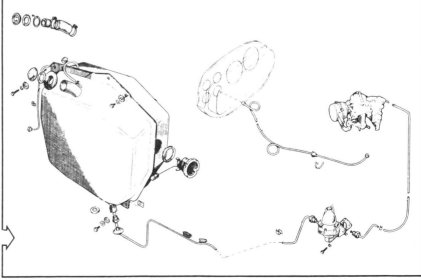

FTR8. There are likely to be dregs of fuel left in the tank, even if you have drained it prior to removal. Pour the remaining fuel into a secure can, and keep the tank well out of the way of naked lights – the vapour inside the tank remains for a very long time. Store the tank, its contents and the car's fuel pipe well away from the working area.

Rear wing and wheel arch repairs

The rear wings form an integral part of the body structure, on Cortinas and Escorts. Common problems include rust around the lower edges and wheel arches, and trouble in these areas needs dealing with as soon as possible, to avoid water and mud travelling along the inner wing area, into the sills and luggage compartment.

The rear quarters on these cars are large panels, and they seem to attract more than their fair share of dents. We have therefore shown basic steps which can be taken to rectify such damage. It is important that any bent panels should be straightened before attempting to fit, for example, new wheel arches, since otherwise the new panels could be welded in place 'out of line' from the start!

The repairs shown were carried out on a Cortina estate car, for which model lower wing repair panels have to be fabricated from scratch, whereas they are commercially available for Cortina saloons, and all Escorts, including vans and estates.

The principles of fitting wing sections and wheel arches apply equally to Cortina saloons, and to Escorts. The notes on removing dents can be applied to any external panel on the car.

It is important to disconnect the alternator, where fitted, before using an electric welder.

'Special' tools needed

Crow bar, wood blocks, rivet gun, panel beating tools.

RW1. This rear wing was badly crumpled, following an assault by another vehicle, but it was also rusted out along the bottom edge. This can be an advantage, since very often the impact dislodges debris, creating a gap at the bottom of the wing, and allowing a crow bar to be inserted, to lever out the worst of the damage.

RW2. With an assistant supporting a stout wooden block on the outside of the wing, use a length of wood and a heavy hammer to rid the bodywork of the worst indentations, having first removed the interior trim panel. Fortunately, access to the inside of the rear wings is fairly good on all Escorts and Cortinas. Take out the rear lamp bulbs before you start hammering.

RW3. The remaining lower flange of the inner rear wing was straightened using a self-grip wrench, giving an indication of the original line, to work to. Reference can also be made to the other side of the vehicle, where this is undamaged, as a guide to how the bent section should look.

RW4. Using the dollies provided in the Sykes-Pickavant panel beating kit, we then started work on the smaller dents at the top of the panel, gradually tapping to even out high and low spots. The spoon in the kit was ideal for reaching into the less accessible areas on the other side of the panel. Precise instructions on the correct use of each of the tools in the kit is provided with it. The exact technique depends on the nature of the damage. In this case, we first eliminated the minor 'tributary' ripples checking . . .

RW5. . . . by hand at frequent intervals, to avoid over-stretching the metal. The aim at this stage is to eliminate most of the dents, down to the original body crease (moulding) line. This line can be re-instated later, by careful use of the two hammers supplied in the kit.

RW6. This special slide hammer (or 'panel puller'), another Sykes-Pickavant tool, was then used to pull out the deeper dents in the lower part of the wing. A special 'self tapping' screw is screwed into a hole made in the panel, then the hammer action of the tool is used to 'bump' the metal back to shape – DON'T stand behind the tool when it is in use, in case the screw should fly out of the hole! Bolts and washers could be used as an alternative, on tricky sections.

RW7.　Repeat the procedure over the entire area, until most of the valleys are nearly back to the level of the surrounding bodywork.

RW8.　The next step, having previously removed the fuel tank, but leaving the filler cap in the wing, was to cut off the rusty, lower edge of the wing, to give . . .

RW9.　. . . a neat line to work to. This would eventually form the upper line for a new bottom section of the wing, after final straightening.

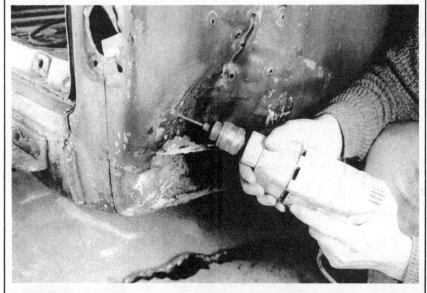

RW10.　We had particular difficulty in extracting the deepest dent, so we continued to drill a series of holes along and around the dent, so that . . .

RW11.　. . . the panel puller could be used again. To help things along, we applied heat to the wing at the same time. This method succeeded in making the wing surface less of a 'mountain range'. A small gas-welding set is a great asset for helping to 'heat shrink' the metal back to shape.

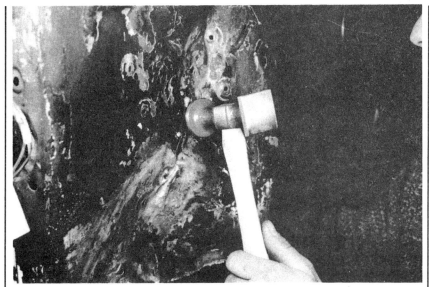

RW12. Final flattening can be carried out when the major creases have been pulled out. We started with the large dolly, tapping this against the metal (watch your fingers), followed by a similar technique with the small dolly, with the large spoon behind the panel in both cases, to react against. The finishing hammer helps bring the minor ripples into line. Hit the metal lightly, swinging the hammer from the wrist, not your elbow. Patience and practice bring good results; you cannot expect to become an expert panel beater overnight.

RW13. The next step was to measure the length of the bottom edge of the wing, and the depth required (allowing for the inward sweeping curve) to meet the previously straightened lower flange, for cutting out new metal to make a repair plate. We allowed an extra half inch on top of the depth measurement, so that our repair panel could be bent around the existing, weak, bottom flange line, to form a new, solid edge. This could be used later, to join to the (yet to be rebuilt) inner panel.

RW14. We then removed the remains of the old wheel arch, finding that someone had previously riveted a wide, plastic, external arch in place. Unfortunately we also discovered rust between the inner and outer wings at this point. There was therefore a gap between the two, inviting water to enter. This is a common problem on Cortinas and Escorts.

RW15. The repair plate for the rear wing needs fixing first, so we cut one out from a sheet of new metal (obtainable in various thicknesses from steel stock holders), using a pair of tin snips, to the dimensions taken from the vehicle, and scribed onto the steel.

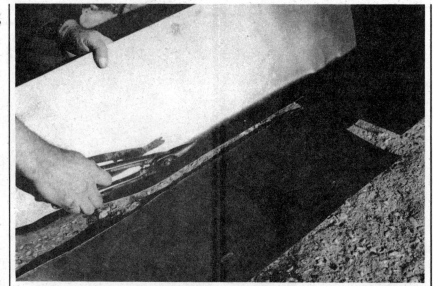

RW16. The plate was then bent approximately to shape, including the under-wing 'wrap around', and offered up to the wing.

RW17. The top edge of the plate was riveted to the lower edge of the wing, to hold it in place.

RW18. The rust was burned away, then the remaining edges of the inner and outer wheel arch sections were clamped together, using a self-grip wrench, and tack-welded in position, using a small gas welding set.

RW19. We obtained a new wheel arch section (LMC Panels make a perfectly shaped repair arch), and offered this up. At this stage, the repair panel at the lower edge of the rear wing was protruding too far forward.

RW20.   A pencil mark was made on the metal, so that the offending piece could then be trimmed off. It is important that the cut is made just BEHIND the line made, so that the wheel arch sits comfortably over the top of the wing repair section.

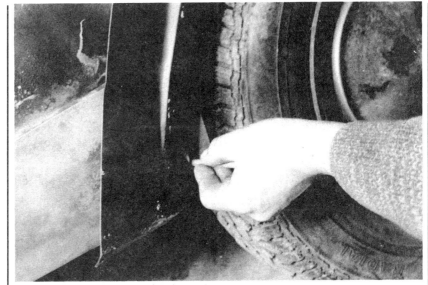

RW21.   Make sure that the panels fit neatly together before proceeding further.

RW23.   Next, using self-grip wrenches along the bottom edge, shape the new section to follow the original body line. Again, reference to the opposite side of the car, as yet untouched, can be very helpful.

RW25.   The metal plate should be marked, in line with the existing body seam at this point.

RW22.   Using the MIG welder, we now attached the repair plate to the wing by tack welding it at intervals along the top edge. This locates it firmly.

RW24.   We used the finishing hammer from the panel beating kit to dress the metal to the final shape of the wing, at the rear corner.

RW26.   Excess metal can now be trimmed off. We again used a sharp pair of tin snips for this job.

RW27. A similar repair plate can be fabricated for the inner wing panel, if (as it is likely to be) it is rusted along the bottom edge, like ours. Trim off corroded metal before riveting the new panel at intervals, then tack weld it. It is best to bend up the bottom lip before fitting to the vehicle, and clamp this to the similar lip on the outer panel, checking alignment of the two before you start riveting.

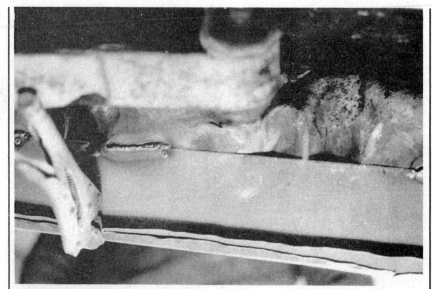

RW28. Finally, clamp the lower edges together with several self-grip wrenches, then tack weld the panels together. Finish off by welding all around the edges of the new repair sections, to form a strong, water tight joint. Excess metal can then be ground or filed off (WEAR SAFETY GOGGLES). The result is a neat repair which will help prevent further rust damage by preventing moisture and dirt from reaching the inner wing.

As already mentioned, we were obliged to manufacture our own wing repair panel for this Cortina, as it was an estate, but lower rear corner panels are available for Cortina Mark I and II saloons, and for all Escorts (including vans and estates) from LMC Panels, for example.

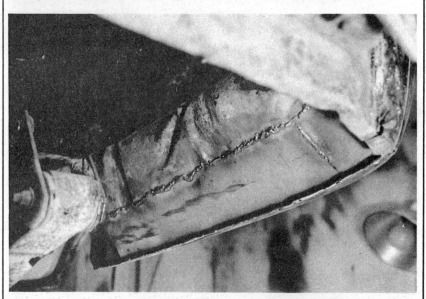

RW29. Back to the wheel arch now, and the first step in fitting this, once aligned with the sill, at the front end, and the new wing repair section, at the rear end, is to drill holes for rivets. Drill one at a time . . .

RW30. . . . fastening the rivets as you go. That way, you won't end up with lots of holes that don't quite line up between inner and outer panels! There is no need to weld the outer edges of the wheel arch to the body; in fact unless you are very careful, the wing panel may well distort because of the heat, if you attempt this with anything other than a MIG welder, or a VERY low flame on a gas welding set.

RW31. Inner wheel arches are available for the Escorts, but not, alas, for the Cortinas, and so we were obliged to make our own panel to bridge the gap between the inner mudguard and the new, outer, wheel arch.

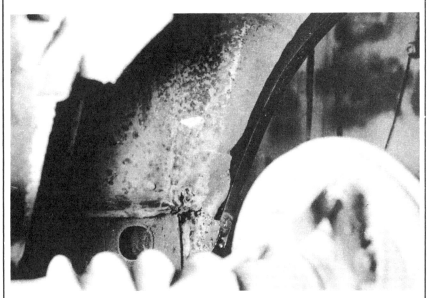

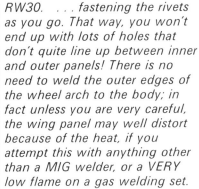

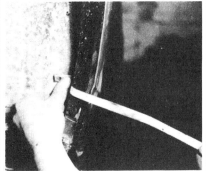

RW32. Allowing a generous overlap of around half an inch (it is better to have a little too much metal, than not quite enough), we measured the distance from the outside edge of the new wheel arch, to the innermost extent of the gap between the two panels. The circumferential measurement from front to back, around the wheel arch, was also taken.

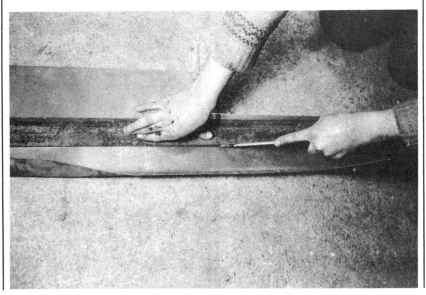

RW33. We then scribed the dimensions onto steel sheet, using an old screwdriver, and cut out the rectangular section so formed.

RW34. Measure the width of the lip on the wheel arch, then scribe a line at a fraction less than this distance (by about, say 1/16th inch) from one edge of your steel strip. Two lengths of angle iron, clamped in the vice, are ideal for helping form a right-angle along this line. Clamp your strip of metal between the two lengths of angle iron, and carefully tap the flange over, along the line. Final shaping can be done with the strip on the ground.

RW35. This strip will be useless as an inner wheel arch repair section, unless it can be persuaded to follow exactly the contours of the outer wheel arch. Therefore it must be able to bend, and, to enable it to do so, notches can be cut every few inches, on both sides of the strip. We cut more notches on the narrow edge of the metal, than . . .

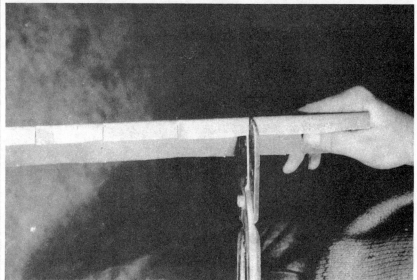

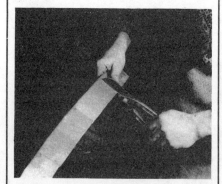

RW36. . . . on the wider side, where the cuts were only necessary at approximately half the frequency.

RW37. The important point is that the repair section should bend uniformly along its length. Check this before fitting!

RW38. When all is well, and the metal strip has been trimmed, where necessary, exactly to length, it can be clamped in position, onto the wheel arch flange, using as many pairs of grips as you can muster.

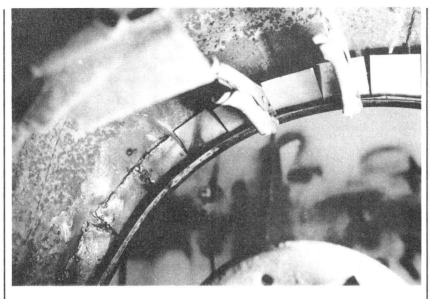

RW39. Then, starting from one end, the repair section can be welded to the inner wing, making just tack welds initially. The grips can be moved around the wheel arch as you proceed, to keep the inner and outer panels lined up.

RW40. When the panel has been tacked into position, fill all the 'V' gaps with weld, to ensure that there are no holes through which water can enter. A good coat or two of anti-rust paint, applied to the new metal, completes this part of the job.

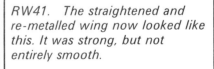

RW41. The straightened and re-metalled wing now looked like this. It was strong, but not entirely smooth.

RW42. Standard 'plastic' body filler can be used to bring back the surface to its original, smooth, level. Build up the surface gradually, in layers – don't apply great dollops of filler in one place. Even the filler out as it is applied to the car, using the plastic spatula supplied.

RW43. It is best to use a coarse grade (around 120 grit) 'production' or 'wet or dry' paper to smooth off the filler between applications, that way, you will achieve a better finish, quicker. Build in body moulding lines by constant reference to the other side of the vehicle, making measurements if in doubt.

RW44. After two applications of filler, the wing looked like this. Continue until completely smooth, rubbing down finally with 280, then 400 grade 'wet or dry' paper, used dry. The filler will completely disguise the wheel arch edge, and any surface imperfections in the wing. It is worth spending some time on this job, to achieve a perfectly smooth surface, suitable for applying primer to. A thin coat of paint, from an aerosol can, will help highlight any rough spots you may have missed, although your fingers are an excellent guide to how smooth the final surface is.

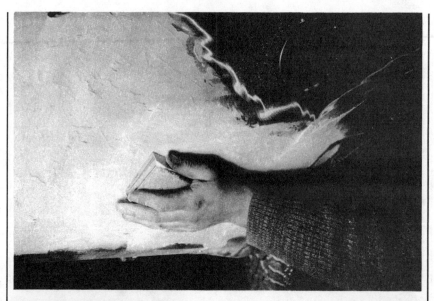

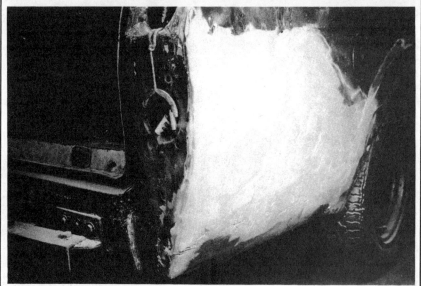

Rear wing change

Changing the rear wing on a Cortina or Escort is not an easy operation, but it is possible at home, on a d-i-y basis, provided that you can first of all find a new panel – not so much of a problem with the Escorts – and secondly that you have plenty of time. It is not a job to be rushed, nor is it for the faint-hearted, since, of course, the rear wings on these Fords form a substantial part of the bodywork.

For illustration purposes, we changed the rear wing on a Mark II Cortina estate car, having first obtained the new panel from Cortina Parts (UK) Ltd. If you cannot buy a new wing for your car, it is of course possible to obtain a second-hand panel,

using the same techniques as outlined in the 'Front Wing Change' section. Although this Cortina was an estate, the procedures are exactly the same for saloon models, except that, instead of aligning with the tailgate, the new panel must line up with the boot aperture. The steps taken can also be applied equally to Escorts.

One important point – rear wings should ALWAYS be attached to the car by welding, as they form an integral part of the body structure, and in any case it is really the only practical means of attaching the panel, anyway.

RWC1. First, the side window must come out. This is easier than might be imagined, and work starts by loosening the rubber seal all around its edges, with a blunt screwdriver.

RWC4. Continue the cuts all around the outside of the wing panel. We worked our way up the seam adjacent to the tailgate. As with the front wings, it is better to make a mess of the old panel than the flange you are to weld the new one to, so cut slightly outboard of the flange line, leaving remaining proud metal to be ground back later.

RWC2. With an assistant applying firm pressure from the inside, the glass, complete with its frame, is eased out along the bottom edge, and withdrawn from outside the car. The headlining material is eased away from the upper section of the rubber seal as the window comes out.

RWC3. Using a hammer and chisel, we then made a horizontal cut immediately below the roof gutter.

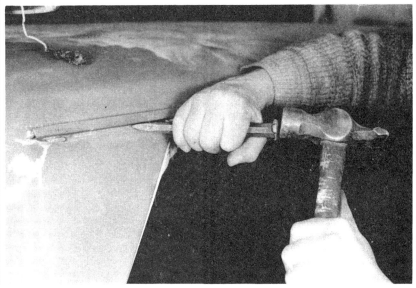

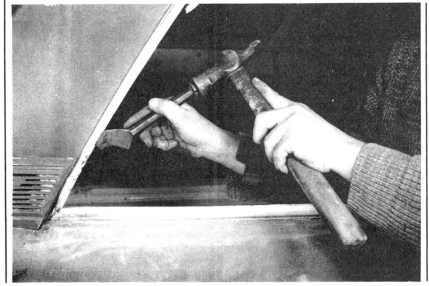

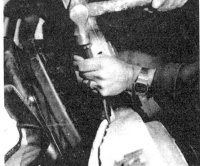

RWC5. The panel must be parted at the rear edge of the rear door frame . . .

RWC6. . . . and around the window aperture.

RWC7.   Careful examination of each flange, before you start chiselling, should indicate exactly where each cut must be made. It is also vital to check first against the new panel, to make sure that you are leaving enough metal on the vehicle in the right places!

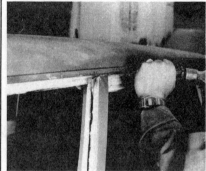

RWC8.   The forward pillar of the estate car rear wing needed to be separated from the roof BELOW the gutter; the panel was now no longer attached to the car.

RWC9.   The wings, even on saloons, are quite heavy, and it is best to have help available to lift the old panel away from the car. Avoid holding the panel by the sharp edges, and put it out of harm's way, away from the working area, children, and pets.

RWC11.   The four Phillips screws on the outside of the body can now be released. This can be tricky as they are normally rusty. Apply plenty of penetrating oil before you start.

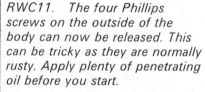

RWC10.   With the wing off the car, the various items attached to it must be removed, for fixing to the new panel. The air grille is released by removing the four nuts on the INSIDE of the car, and NOT by taking out the Phillips screws which can be seen through the louvres in the grille.

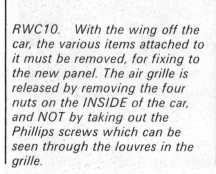

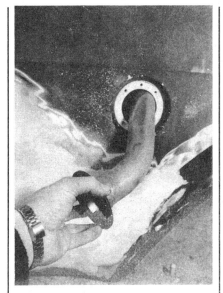

RWC12. The fuel filler pipe needs to be transferred from the old wing to the new one; this is easily released by taking out the four Phillips screws.

RWC14. The surplus metal edges from the old panel can now be prised away from the tailgate/boot surround, using a hammer and a small chisel.

RWC16. Remaining high spots can be smoothed off with a file, an angle grinder, or an electric drill and sanding disc; WEAR GOGGLES. The flange can then be 'dressed' back to a uniform profile, using a hammer and dolly.

RWC13. The rear door lock striker plate must also be removed from the old wing, and attached to the new one, before the old panel is scrapped.

RWC15. Stubborn flange remains can be 'wound' around a pair of grips, to remove them from their spot welds.

RWC17. Now offer up the new panel, to ensure that it fits perfectly, so that it will blend with the existing body lines.

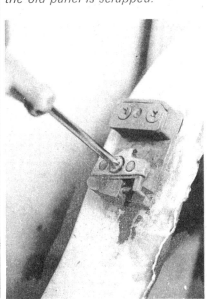

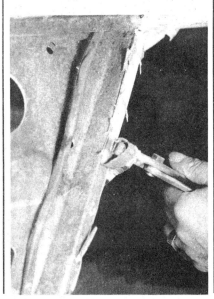

RWC18. Use self grip wrenches, placed at intervals around the panel edges, to clamp the new wing into position. It is important that the lower flange lines up with the inner wing.

RWC19. Minor adjustments are normally necessary to achieve the correct clearance between the wing and the door. This car was no exception, and, to start with, the door touched the wing. Minor movement of the panel restored the required gap here. Use the opposite side of the car as a guide, if in doubt. ➤

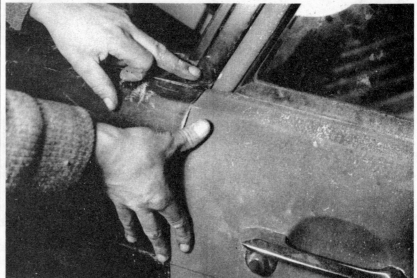

RWC20. The gap between the pillar and the top of the door frame should also be uniform. After making minor adjustments, we were very pleased with the neat gap here.

RWC21. When the panel fits perfectly, tack weld around the edges, to hold it in place. Then double check that the boot or tailgate, and the rear door, still fit. It's too late once the wing has been fully welded, all round!

A MIG welder is by far the most appropriate machine for this job, since distortion is minimal.

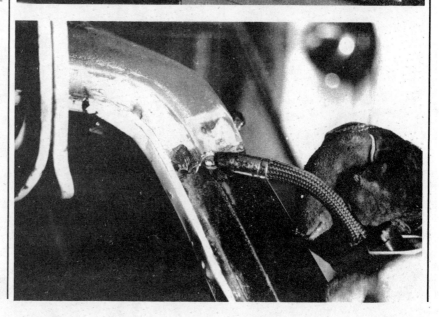

RWC22. It didn't take long to complete the welding required on this wing; again, the MIG welder saved time.

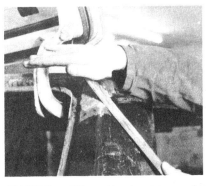

RWC25. When the lead is cool (it doesn't take very long), very carefully trim off high spots with a fine file. Take care not to file off too much, or, again you'll need to repeat the filling operation.

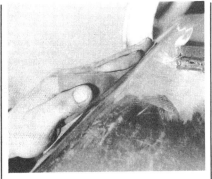

RWC26. Use a sheet of fine 'wet or dry' paper to take out the remaining tiny ripples. A circular motion will give a smooth finish.

RWC23. The joint between the wing and the roof panel was originally filled using lead. To restore this area, the weld is first ground or filed off, to leave the joint slightly below the surface of the surrounding metal. Plastic body filler could be used to restore smooth body lines here, but, being so close to the tailgate, it COULD suffer from cracking before very long. We therefore cleaned the surrounding area to bright metal, warmed the metal with a gentle flame from the gas torch, and 'tinned' the surface, prior to dabbing lead from a stick of 'body solder', into the joint.

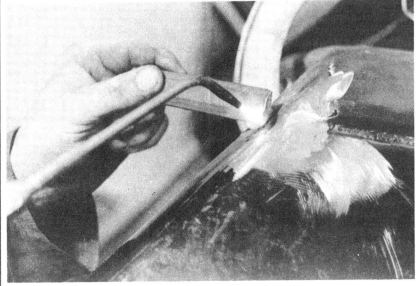

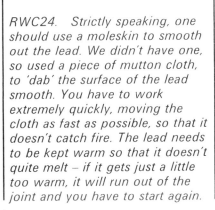

RWC24. Strictly speaking, one should use a moleskin to smooth out the lead. We didn't have one, so used a piece of mutton cloth, to 'dab' the surface of the lead smooth. You have to work extremely quickly, moving the cloth as fast as possible, so that it doesn't catch fire. The lead needs to be kept warm so that it doesn't quite melt – if it gets just a little too warm, it will run out of the joint and you have to start again.

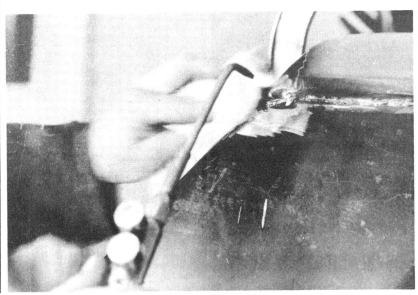

RWC27. *The tips of the fingers can be used to check the surface, finally. The steps are similar when dealing with any leaded joints between the roof panel and supporting pillars.*

If in doubt about your ability to carry out such lead filling successfully (after all, it really is an acquired art), it would pay you to call in professional help for this part of the job, or else risk using plastic body filler. If you employ an elastic type, you should have less fear of it cracking, anyway.

RWC28. *A moment to savour . . . the tailgate fitted perfectly against the new wing panel.*

All that remains is to re-fit the rear side window, using the technique described in the 'Windscreen Pillar Restoration' section.

Changing a rear wing needs time and patience, but it can be tackled successfully at home.

Sills and floor

The floor and sills have been linked in this section, since they are, of course, physically joined on the car, and rust in the floor, for example, almost invariably spreads to the inner and outer sills, and vice versa.

Before you start work you need to know the extent of the damage, and this can only be gauged after removing the carpets and side trims from the footwell areas (screws and clips), and taking out the front seats (four bolts).

There are, of course, many ways in which any repair job can be tackled, and this one is no exception. The main rule to remember is that you should only remove one section of the side of the car at a time, to avoid risk of distorting the body shell – or even its collapse! Therefore, if intending to fit both inner and outer sills, for example, it is best to replace the inner sill and repair the floor first, to restore strength here. The flanged outer sill is best left in position while the inner panels are dealt with. This ensures that there is *some* structural rigidity along the lower side of the car, while work proceeds, even if the outer sill is rusty. With the floor/inner sill restored, it is then safe to cut off the outer sill, and weld a new one on. A useful advantage of doing the work in this way is that there is always an 'original' line to work to, so that the floor and sill edges will start and finish as designed, and line up with the rest of the bodywork.

If the inner sill does not require changing, but merely patching, while the outer sill is badly rusted, it is perhaps more appropriate to leave the repairs to this inner panel until the outer sill has been changed. This way, you will retain the correct 'inner' line to work to, and the outer sill should fit perfectly.

Another tip is *never* to remove the doors when replacing a sill, if you can avoid it. The lower edges of the doors provide an invaluable line to work to, when fitting the new panel(s). If a door is removed, you might possibly end up with a sill that is so high that it prevents the door from fitting into its aperture, or so low that there is a huge gap between the door's lower edge, and the sill's upper lip. Such horrors are almost too awful to contemplate!

If rust is showing its head in more than just an isolated patch on the surface of the outer sill, it is almost certain to have a strong hold in the rest of the panel, and it is better in such cases, to replace the whole sill, than to patch small areas. A close visual examination, combined with probing with a screwdriver, will reveal how much rust is present on your car.

A final word of warning, which may be obvious, but vital – NEVER tackle both sides of the car at once, or it may well fold up in the middle! Always leave one side intact; it is useful for reference during the work on the opposite side, and of course helps to keep the body rigid.

Cortina

There is quite a difference between the construction of the Cortinas and Escorts with regard to the body sills and floor, so to start with, we shall deal with rectification of these areas on the Cortina models. The design of the Mark I and Mark II models is virtually identical, so working procedures apply equally to both cars. No special tools are required, apart from the 'standard' bolster or chisel, and of course welding equipment. Sills should ONLY be attached by welding.

SFC1. With the floor and sill coverings out of the way, and the 'kick' plates removed, it is possible to make a detailed examination of the floor and inner sills on the car. This is what we found on this 'guinea pig' Cortina. The floor was badly holed, and the inner sill panel had separated from the floor at the front, as far back as the driver's seat. Further back, the inner sill and floor were in perfect condition. Since the inner sill panel was only rusted at the lower edge, and only at the front, it was decided that patching was more appropriate than replacement. The decision was therefore taken to deal with the outer sill first, and work inwards, towards the centre of the car. The inner sill patches could be then tailored to fit in with the correctly positioned outer panel.

There was still some strength remaining in the inner sill, to keep the car rigid while the outer sill was tackled.

SFC2. The outer sill on this Cortina was rusty at the front, in the centre, and at the back, so we abandoned all thoughts of patching, in favour of a new panel, from LMC. Before you make any cuts on the vehicle, offer up your replacement panel, to ascertain the highest point; some panels extend to the inner sill joint, at the top, while others finish level with the door bottoms. Unless the horizontal, top section of your sills are badly rusted (and this is fairly unusual), the shallower sills will be entirely adequate. Starting at the rear end, and with the doors still on the car, we opened up the top of the sill, using a hammer and bolster. Leave sufficient metal at the top for attaching the new sill to.

SFC3. Continue the cut to the front of the sill, keeping the line as straight as possible.

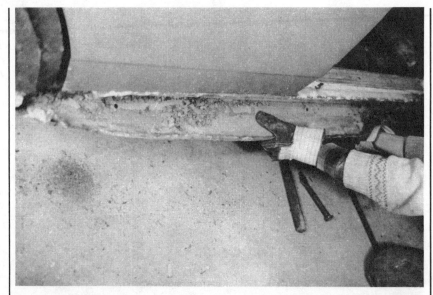

SFC4. WEARING THICK PROTECTIVE GLOVES, because of the sharp edges, prise the sill away from the car at the top edge. As the sill comes away, there will probably be a lot of loose rust inside it, so take care.

SFC5. STILL WEARING THE GLOVES, because of the sharp metal edges above and below your hand, cut the outer sill away from the inner sill, just outside the lower joint line. Remaining bits of the outer sill can be cleaned from this joint afterwards.

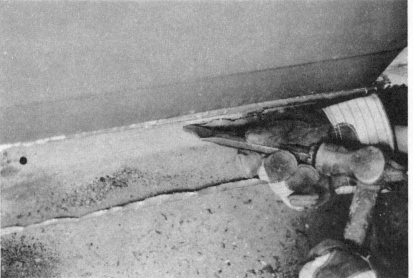

SFC6. The outer panel can now be pulled away from the car, and discarded.

SFC7. With care and patience, the remains of the outer sill flange can now be sliced away from the inner sill.

SFC8. Loose, rusty remnants will probably be fairly easy to remove by hand.

SFC9. Grind or file off remaining rust and protruding metal (WEAR GOGGLES), then dress the lower, inner flange to a uniform, flat profile, using a hammer and dolly.

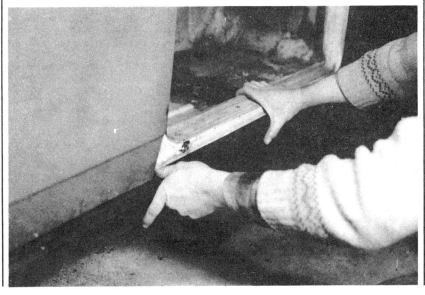

SFC10. The new sill can now be offered up to the car, making sure that it will sit flat against the existing bodywork, and will fit around the door pillars – especially important on four-door cars. If all fits properly, rub down the inner sill panel with a wire brush and coarse emery paper, before painting the panel, and the inside of the new outer sill, with an anti-rust paint. Keep the paint away from edges which are to be welded.

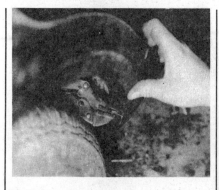

SFC11. Self-grip wrenches can then be used to attach the new panel to the existing flanges.

SFC12. Before the sill could be attached at the lower edge, the flange had to be relieved to accommodate the existing jacking point. We used tin snips to make cuts in the flange, around the jacking point, then clamped the sill to the car with another self-grip wrench, as close as possible. A screw jack was placed on the other side of the jacking point, to help push the sill upwards (under very slight pressure only) into position.

SFC13. Tack weld the sill in place, checking again that alignment is correct (shut the doors and check for clearance between them and the sill top), then weld the edges of the sill to the car, a little at a time, to avoid heat distortion. MIG welding is best for this job, if available, especially if you have painted the inside of the sill. The heat from a gas welding torch could well ignite the paint inside.
The welds now need smoothing off, using an angle grinder, if available (WEAR GOGGLES). Don't overdo it, though, or you can very quickly grind away the weld and the sill. If you go too far, the weld will be weakened.

SFC14. Back to the inside of the car now, and the floor was re-examined in some detail. Apart from the obvious hole through the floor, the 'chassis' members below were completely eaten away by rust, and needed to be changed. The problems here stemmed from an aerial hole in the bulkhead, drilled many years previously. There had been no grommet around the aerial cable, and mud, thrown up from the front wheel, had built up on the floor of the car, rusting it and the chassis below, from inside the vehicle! Two bucketfuls of mud and road salt had to be shifted from this area before we could see the full extent of the damage!

SFC15. The chassis sections normally affected in this area are the forward running front chassis extension piece, and the centre outrigger, which runs across the car, at each side. The front section of the chassis, which extends into the under wing area, may also be rusty, and repair sections can be obtained for all these areas. The construction of Mark I and Mark II models is virtually identical here.

Having bought the chassis sections, we then found a suitable piece of steel plate, which overlapped the rusty area all round. We first turned up a right angled flange along the edge adjacent to the sill (by clamping the plate in the vice between two lengths of angle iron, and knocking it over at 90 degrees with a hammer). We then marked around the outside edges of the plate on the floor, with a piece of chalk.

SFC16. We now cut out the rusty remains of the floor within this area, up to the INSIDE edge of the chalk line, using the gas torch.

SFC17. We also cut through the remains of the chassis members — there wasn't much good metal left!

SFC18. The next step was to make a new section of the inner sill. Another length of steel was found, and cut to length.

SFC19. This was then slotted into position (having cleaned remaining rust from the existing inner sill), and held, using two pairs of Sykes Pickavant special 'extra large' welding clamps, which have very deep jaws; these are ideal for working around sills, etc.

SFC20. When the repair section lines up exactly with the lower edge of the new outer sill, and the rear half of the old inner sill, it can be welded in place – again, MIG welding is ideal, because of its minimum heat distortion. ➤

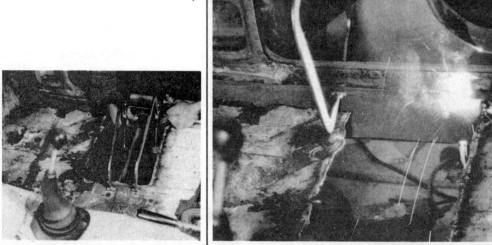

SFC21. The new chassis sections were then offered up from below the floor, starting with the outrigger. This was held in place, again using the large clamps, and tack welded to the inner sill.

SFC22. The forward running chassis extension section was then clamped to the front part of the existing chassis, and, at the rear end, to the outrigger just attached.

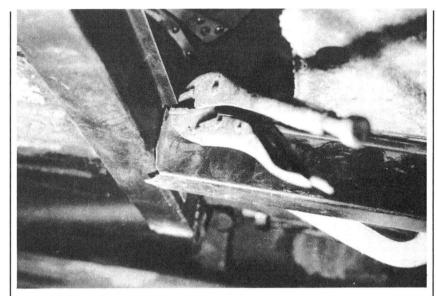

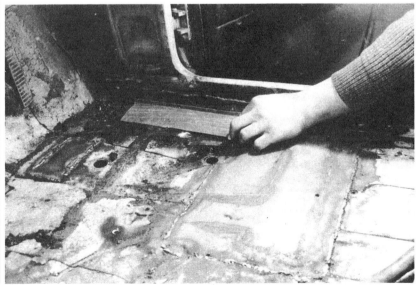

SFC23. From below the vehicle, the two sections joined like this. The chassis extension piece was tack welded in position at the front edge, first, and then, after final shaping of the flanges with a hammer, at the back. The new chassis members were then permanently fixed together by a 'continuous' welded seam.

SFC24. The floor plate was then placed in position in its pre-cut aperture in the floor, and held there with the large clamps. You may find it necessary to trim the edges of the hole, or the plate, slightly, so that it fits perfectly.

SFC25. The MIG welder was then used again to join the plate to the floor. We used tack welds at first, at intervals around the edge, gradually filling in the gaps, a little at a time (to avoid distortion). With most of the work now done, the remaining unattached flanges of the chassis sections can be welded to the floor of the car from below. Take EXTREME care when welding underneath the car; gravity brings sparks and molten metal DOWN!

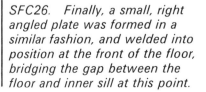

SFC26. Finally, a small, right angled plate was formed in a similar fashion, and welded into position at the front of the floor, bridging the gap between the floor and inner sill at this point.

Escort

The floor and under-floor construction on Escorts is rather different from that on the Cortinas. The Escorts have two chassis members running from the front to the back of the car, each side, and welded to the floor pan. The floor joins the inner sill, and the outer sill wraps around the lower edge of the car, below floor level.

While the sill profiles of Mark I and II models vary slightly, and techniques involved in assessment and rebuilding are similar.

As with the Cortinas, the first step is to assess the degree of rust damage, in order to decide the best method of rectification.

SFE2. For a proper examination, the seat belt mounting must come out; this is simply unbolted from the rear of the inner sill.

SFE3. The seat mountings are held by two bolts, which are normally easy to release with a socket spanner.

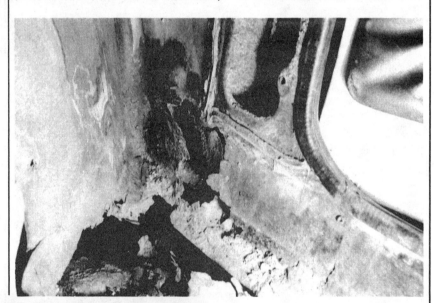

SFE1. We didn't have to look very far on this Escort to find out that the floor and inner sill on the driver's side were extremely rotten. In fact, only the rubber mat and a lump of rag had been separating the inside of the car from the outside!

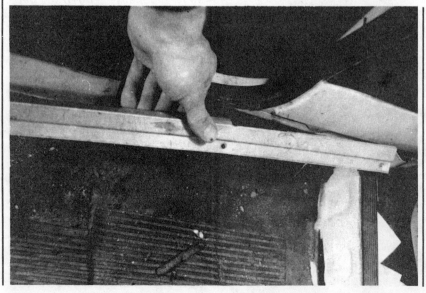

SFE4. The aluminium protector, from the top of the sill, can be taken out after removing the Phillips screws. This releases the floor covering.

SFE5. To establish exactly how bad the floor is, probe at the remains of the soundproofing with a screwdriver. If the screwdriver continues downwards, the floor is not as solid as it ought to be!

SFE7. Small rusty areas are fairly easy to deal with; simply cut the surrounding rust away, until you have a uniform hole, with firm metal all round it. A gas welding torch is an ideal tool for this.

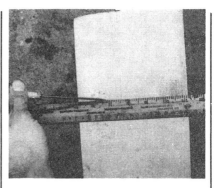

SFE8. Take the measurements of the hole, and transfer them to a sheet of steel, using a scriber, or an old screwdriver.

SFE6. It is usually obvious by now whether the job is going to be a major one; this one was! Therefore the car should be raised as high as possible, and supported on strong axle stands. If you haven't already done so, drain the fuel tank and remove the fuel feed pipe from the chassis, as described in the earlier section on Fuel Tank Removal.

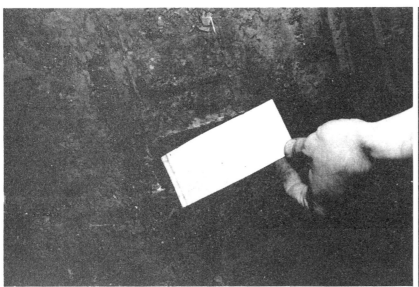

SFE9. The plate can then be slotted into its hole, and welded around its edges. It can, of course, be difficult to hold plates in position while attaching tack welds to them. Either use a 'bottle' jack from below, with the plate sitting on top of it, in the correct position, or strong magnets can be used to hold the plate to the floor. Apply heat away from the magnet, or it may melt, or at least lose its magnetic effect!

SFE10. However, it may be that your exploratory probings with the screwdriver keep on uncovering disaster areas like this. If so, patching may be a waste of time, or even impossible!

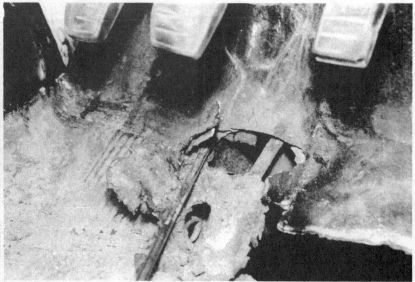

SFE11. We soon had holes in our Escort floor which looked like this. There is nothing for it, in cases like this, except . . .

SFE12. . . . to cut the whole floor away, back to good metal, wherever that appears. A word of caution here – only clear one side of the car at a time, and don't touch the rotten outer sills at this stage. If you do, the car may literally fall apart.

A large chisel is handy to chop out the 'soft', rusty metal, while a gas torch is quickest for cutting through the rest. It is worthwhile releasing the brake fluid pipe fom the chassis, below the floor, before you start, to avoid damage from the cutting operations.

SFE13. After a while you may end up with a floor which looks like this; the metal on top of the chassis beam is not so easy to remove, since the chassis and floor were originally spot-welded together, along the chassis edges. Therefore, it is best to cut the floor away from each side of the chassis, to start with.

SFE14. The metal remaining on top of the chassis must be completely removed, for the new floor sections to sit correctly. A mixture of methods can be used, including chiselling, grinding (WEAR GOGGLES) and burning with a gas torch. Deal with the centre section first, then the edges. Take care not to damage the chassis flanges during this operation.

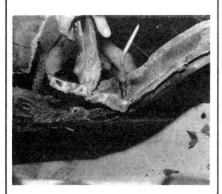

SFE15. Stubborn bits of metal are removed by warming them to red heat with the gas torch, then twisting the metal clear, using a self-grip wrench.

SFE16. An alternative is to 'roll' the edges of the metal adjoining the spot welds, and pull it clear by using a wrench.

SFE17. Any remaining metal fragments can be filed or ground off the chassis member (WEAR GOGGLES), to leave the surface smooth and clean.

SFE18. Once the chassis beam has been 'opened up', inspect the bottom and sides of it, for evidence of rusting. Surprisingly, in view of the state of the rest of the car, the chassis on this Escort was entirely sound on the driver's side, and had only a few small holes on the passenger side. Any holes found should be plated before proceeding with the floor repairs, using metal of at least the same gauge as the original.

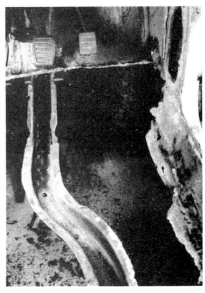

SFE19. You won't often get the chance to protect the inside of the chassis members, so take the opportunity to rub down the inner surfaces with emery cloth, and give them two good coats of anti-rust paint. Leave the edges, to be welded, clear of paint.

SFE20. Before rebuilding the floor, we needed an 'outside edge' to work to, in the form of a solid inner sill panel. We already knew that the existing inner sill needed to be completely replaced, since it was holed virtually all along its length, but we hadn't yet examined the outer sill in detail. At first glance, it has appeared to be in reasonable condition, but probing with a screwdriver soon revealed a thin coating of filler, covering an even thinner skin of metal, complete with holes and various plates which had been added over the years. The decision was therefore taken to 'start again' and replace the whole lot, rather than to attempt patching.

However, before taking the outer sill off, we had the inner panel to deal with.

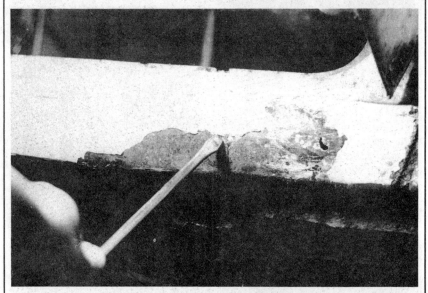

SFE21. Bearing in mind the earlier comments about preserving the car's rigidity while working on this area, we left the outer sill intact, while we used the gas torch to cut off the remains of the inner sill, just below the top edge, which was still in excellent condition – the rust had crept up the panel from the bottom, rather than down from the top.

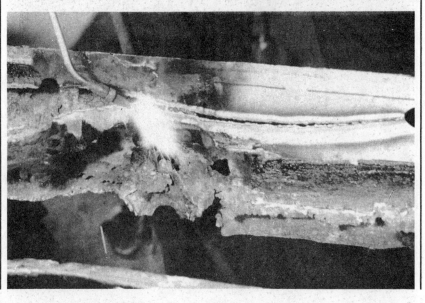

SFE22.   At the rear end, it is helpful to preserve the seat belt mounting plate/threads in the correct position, so we made a 'detour' with the torch, around this area, which was in good condition.

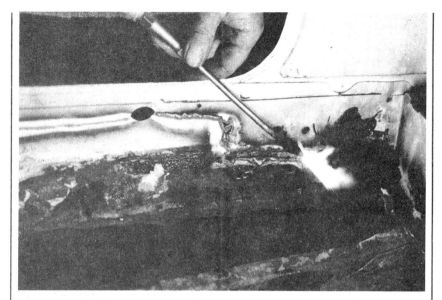

SFE23.   Another vital point is that the jacking point will disappear, unless you make positive steps to save it. By fitting the jack into its socket, and the hole designed for it, in the chassis member, you can establish exactly where the jacking point must sit; make measurements from the top and end of the inner sill, to ensure precise positioning. In fact, on this car, the bottom edge of the original jack mounting was still intact, and we made use of this later.

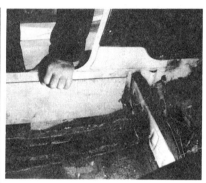

SFE25.   . . . as far back as the rear seat.

SFE24.   Inner sills (and also 'under' sill sections for the Mark I models) can be purchased commercially, if desired. However, there is no reason why you shouldn't fabricate your own inner sill from a flat sheet of steel, providing that it is at least as thick, and preferably thicker, than the original. We made this panel from a large offcut of steel sheet, having measured and trimmed as necessary. Make sure that it extends right to the toe board, and . . .

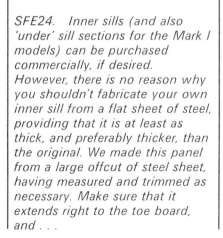

SFE26. Final trimming can be carried out, then the panel is clamped to the vehicle, and 'adjusted' so that it is perfectly level, and so that the bottom edge will align with the outer sill, when fitted. In fact, at this stage, it doesn't matter if the inner sill is a little low at the bottom; it can always be trimmed later. It is, however, vital that the panel is not too short!

SFE29. Drill these, and offer up the new inner sill to the vehicle, to check that they line up with the original threaded holes.

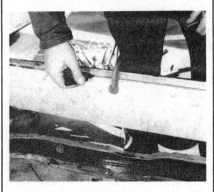

SFE27. Mark the position of the top of the new panel, with a felt tip pen. This is your 'base line' for future reference.

SFE28. By very careful measuring, and transferring these readings onto the panel, mark the position of the seat belt mounting holes.

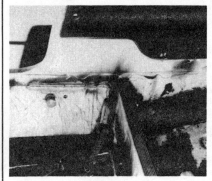

SFE30. If all is well, screw in the seat belt securing bolt and its spacer, and clamp the panel at the front, so that it can be welded in position.

SFE31. With the inner sill firmly welded in place, the floor can be reconstructed, with firm boundaries! We bought a new floor panel for the front of the car; they are also available for the rear, although, on our Escort, the floor aft of the driver's seat wasn't quite as bad as the front part of it, and only needed a panel across half its width! However, we did have one problem; the new front floor panel didn't extend up the toe board as far as the rust damage did! We therefore fashioned a sheet of steel, to fit between the original toe board, and the new floor panel, and sat it in position.

SFE32.   If you find, as we did, that the new floor section doesn't reach back as far as the extent of the rust, the rear edge of the panel can be hammered flat, against a block of wood, so that it will readily join up with a new rear floor section, yet to be fabricated, to bridge the remaining gap.

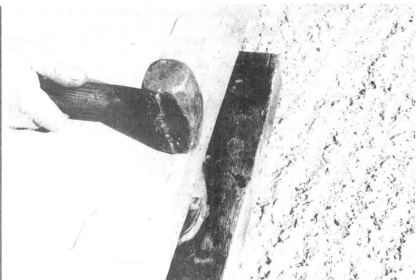

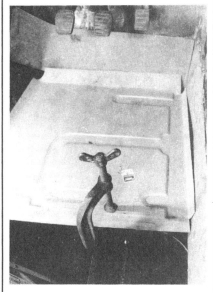

SFE33.   With the new panels at the front end of the floor in the correct position, we clamped the main floor section, at its rear edge, to the chassis member.

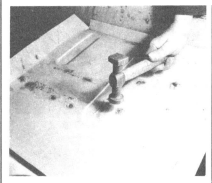

SFE35.   Tap the welds down, so that the floor section remains flat, and is kept in contact with the chassis member, all along its length.

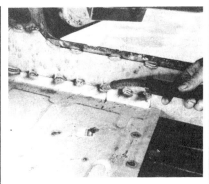

SFE36.   Next, tack the outer flange of the floor panel to the inner sill.

SFE34.   At the front end of the floor, we used a crow bar, levered down between the edge of the toe board and a small block of wood, to hold the floor panel against the chassis, while it was tack welded in place from below the car.

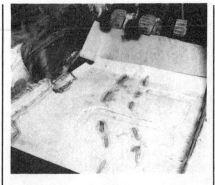

SFE37. Use further welds below the floor, to attach it firmly to the chassis. The path of the chassis is then clearly visible from above, if the weld penetration is sufficient.

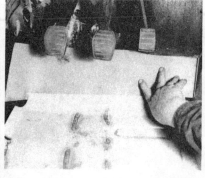

SFE38. Position the toe board panel exactly, by hand, clamping in place if necessary.

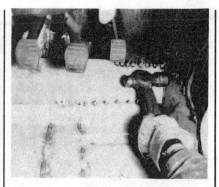

SFE39. We then tack welded the plate to the existing toe board, at the top, and the new floor plate, below, before tapping the outer edge to meet the inner sill, so that it could be tacked in place here too.

SFE40. If working on your own, you need a means of keeping the repair panel in place while you attach it. A block of wood and a hammer, wedged under the clutch pedal, overcame the problem on this Escort. To quote a much later Ford phrase "Simple is Efficient". . .

SFE41. A new floor section was fashioned from a piece of steel, to fit between the inner sill and the remaining original floor, at the rear. We used wood blocks and a hammer to achieve the required contours. We cut slits in the turned up flange, along the inner sill edge, to allow it to bend around the floor contours. Had the whole of the rear floor been rusty, it would have been easier to buy a complete new rear floor panel.

SFE42. The new panel was then welded to the existing floor, and to the inner sill, to form a watertight and strong part of the car. Further small plates were made as necessary to bridge remaining open areas. Any proud metal resulting from the welding operations can be filed or ground down afterwards (WEAR GOGGLES). Don't grind too much metal away, or the welds may be weakened.

SFE43. The next job is to reinstate the seat mounting channel. The old one was extremely weak on this Escort, so we made up a new supporting section, using the original one as a guide, and frequently comparing the new, home-made item with the old, and with the profile of the floor, inside the car. The nut plates were chiselled from the original seat mounting, and welded to the new one.

SFE46. The side flanges can now be welded to the floor; we applied tacks at intervals, first. We used a hammer for final shaping of the flanges.

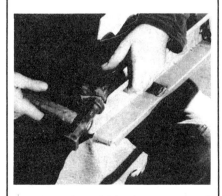

SFE44. Wood blocks were used, both in the original shaping of the new section, and in final 'dressing' of the end flanges.

SFE45. When all is well, weld both ends of the new section to the car.

SFE47. With the floor and inner sill complete, it was now safe to cut off the outer sill, to replace this. An angle grinder, with a cutting disc, can be used to open up the lower edges of the old sill (WEAR GOGGLES).

133

SFE48.   We then used the gas torch to slice through the upper part of the sill. Make sure that you are cutting slightly below the line of the top of your brand new sill panel, or you may end up with a gap between the existing bodywork and the sill! On two door Escort saloons, make the cut slightly below the natural body crease line, just ahead of the rear wheel; the surface will be far easier to fill than if the cut is made on the crease line. It is always best to offer up the new panel to the car, before you start cutting, to see where the top edge comes at this point. This old sill was extremely rusty, and needed little encouragement to fall off!

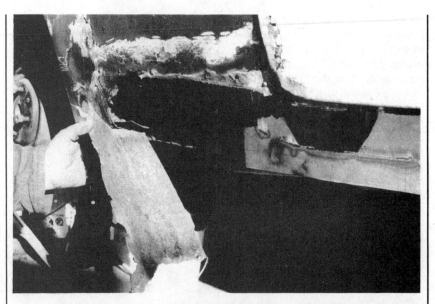

SFE49.   With the old sill out of the way, the first job is to complete the welding of the seat belt mounting plate to the new inner sill; you cannot do this until the outer sill is off the car, or a hole has been cut through it! ➤

SFE50.   The next step is to build in the jacking point; we used the shaped, lower piece of the old jack mount, which was still sound, and welded it to a new, strong piece of steel, approximately double the thickness of the inner sill panel.

SFE51.   The steel plate was a little deeper than we needed it to be, so we marked and cut the panel to exact size by reference to the car, and 'trying' the new section in place.

SFE52. Before welding the new jacking point to the inner sill, clamp it in place (we used the large Sykes Pickavant clamps again for this), and try the jack in its new location.

SFE53. When perfectly positioned, remove the jack and use a 'G' clamp to pull the inner sill and jacking point together.

SFE54. The new section can then be welded in place, all around its edges, for a strong, permanent job. The entire inner sill, jacking point mounting and seat belt support can then be wire brushed and cleaned with coarse emery paper, and painted with two good coats of anti-rust paint. Avoid painting the flanges which are to be welded to the outer sill.

SFE55. Offer up the new sill panel to the car, making sure that it sits flush around the door aperture(s), and that the rear section, on two door cars, fits tightly against the bodywork above.

SFE56. If all looks good, clamp the sill to the car for more accurate assessment. Always leave the doors on, for then it is far easier to line up the sill panel correctly, and to deal with problems like this – the rear edge of the door was touching the sill.

SFE57. Minor adjustments were made with a panel beating hammer and dolly to relieve the sill at this point.

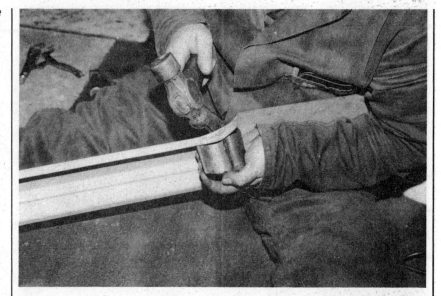

SFE58. With the panel back on the car, and clamped, we were also obliged to use a bolster to tap the sill downwards a little, to give a reasonable gap between the bottom of the door, and the top of the sill. Such adjustments are commonly required when doing this sort of job.

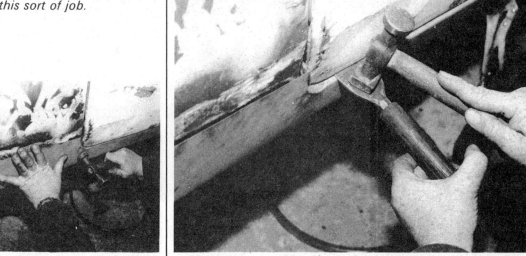

SFE59. With the sill in the correct position on the car, final 'dressing' can take place. The sill now fitted perfectly round the door on our Escort.

SFE60 The sill panel was tack welded in place, using the SIP MIG welder, along top and bottom edges, and then, finally, welded all round.

Windscreen pillar restoration

It is often surprising where rust is found in motor cars, and the windscreen pillars are perhaps not thought of as prime target areas.

However, Cortinas and Escorts do suffer from corrosion problems here, if neglected. Once the outer metal skin is holed, water runs amok, taking with it, eventually, the rest of the pillar, the bulkhead and the floor.

Repairs to the pillars are easier than might be imagined, but there is the complication that the windscreen glass must come out, for rectification by welding, and the repair MUST, of course, be completely watertight on completion.

No special tools are needed for the job, except for a length of stout cord, which is used to re-fit the windscreen.

WPR2. The first step is to remove the windscreen, which means, on some models, extraction of the bright trim, to start with. Simply lever up the joining clip with a screwdriver, then ease each half of the screen surround trim away from the car. Initial encouragement, with a screwdriver, may be needed.

WPR3. Lift the inner lip of the rubber screen seal away from the glass, all the way round, with a screwdriver, before pushing the screen out, starting at the centre, top. Place a cloth on the bonnet, and have an assistant handy, to 'catch' the glass, as it comes out.

WPR4. The rusty edges of the holes should be ground down (WEAR GOGGLES). It is advisable to cover the top of the dashboard, and any glass in the area, during grinding operations, unless these are to be changed.

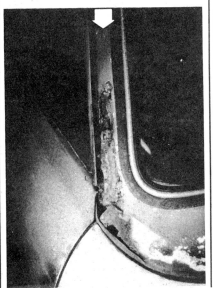

WPR1. The screen pillars usually rust at the bottom end, on Cortinas and Escorts, and when the damage reaches these proportions, there is no barrier at all to the weather. Both sides were equally bad on this car.

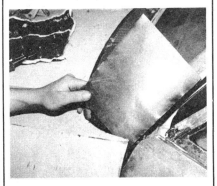

WPR5. Find a sheet of steel large enough to cut the necessary repair plate from. You will need a bigger repair section than it first appears.

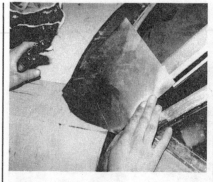

WPR6.   Start by shaping the lower edge, to conform with the curve of the adjoining panel at this point.

WPR7.   Reduce the plate to size and shape by gradually marking the various curves, with a felt tip pen, then cutting the plate edges, one at a time, with tin snips.

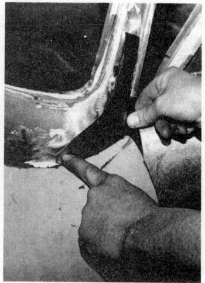

WPR8.   Trim the plate, a little at a time, until it is a perfect fit.

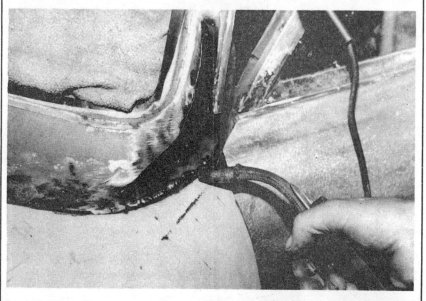

WPR9.   Keep the dashboard top covered during welding operations, or sparks may damage it. We used a MIG welder to join the plate to the car, running a weld along the bottom edge first, then . . .

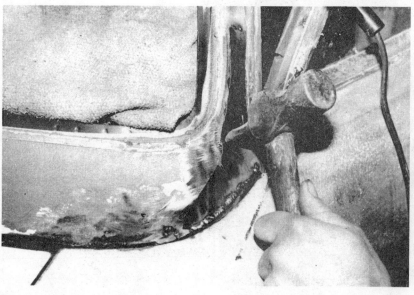

WPR10.   . . . tacking the plate at the top, and tapping the centre section inwards, so that it sits almost flush with the rest of the pillar.

138

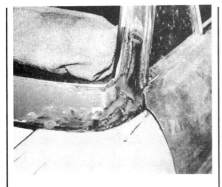

WPR11.   The finished weld looked like this; it was obviously proud of the surface, but . . .

WPR12.   . . . a few minutes' work with the angle grinder made the edges blend with the rest of the pillar.

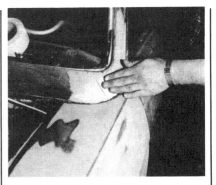

WPR13.   A thin application of body filler was all that was necessary to restore the original contours of the pillar – vital, of course, for the screen rubber to sit flush against the body, on re-fitting. This was smoothed down, using coarse production paper, followed by . . .

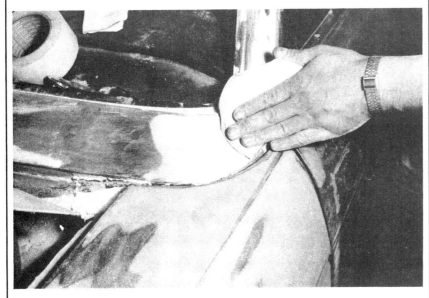

WPR14.   . . . medium grit paper, before final finishing with fine (400 grade) 'wet or dry' paper, used dry.

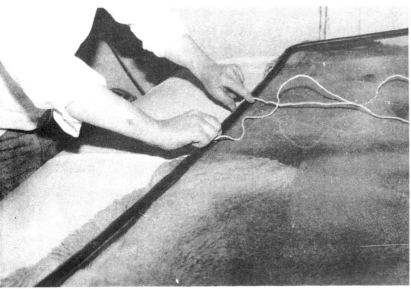

WPR15.   We resprayed the car while the windscreen was out, and then re-fitted the screen, having checked the rubber and cleaned off the remains of the old screen sealant. Place a soft cloth on the bonnet, to protect it and the screen glass from being scratched. Thread a length of stout cord around the screen rubber, in the inner groove, so that both ends of the cord protrude at the centre of the bottom edge of the screen.

WPR16. The screen can then be lifted into place, and pushed, or tapped with the palm of the hand, to seat the sealing rubber against the metal lip.

WPR17. The two ends of the cord are then very carefully pulled in opposite directions, around the screen frame, pulling the rubber seal over the metal lip.

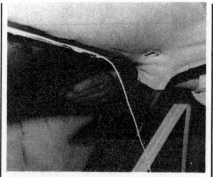

WPR18. It helps to push the screen in from the outside, as the cord is withdrawn.

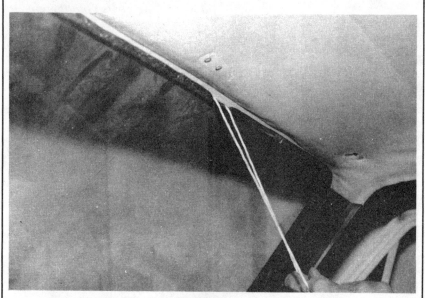

WPR19. All being well, the cord should be fairly easy to pull out, at the centre top of the screen, with the rubber seal neatly in place, all the way round.

WPR20. Finally, seal around the screen rubber, using one of the proprietary sealing compounds available for this purpose. Any of the windows in the car can be removed and re-fitted in the same way as for the windscreen.

Chassis and underbody repairs

The term 'chassis' is perhaps not accurate, strictly speaking, when talking about modern vehicles, of unitary, 'integral' construction, since of course they have no separate chassis, as such. However, the Cortinas and Escorts covered by this book do have channel sections which form a 'backbone' on which to construct the rest of the vehicle. Although the design is rather different between the models, as outlined in the 'Buying' Chapter,

the need for strength in these sections is equally important on Cortinas and Escorts.

The normal problems with these chassis sections is that they rust; sometimes from the outside, sometimes from within. They can deteriorate so far that they are in danger of collapse, or of parting company from the rest of the bodywork. Therefore it is always wise to tackle any rust found, as soon as it is discovered, and to protect the metal from further attack by the elements, using the methods described in the 'Rustproofing' section of this chapter.

You may well also find that

there are other areas of the 'underbody' which have rusted, in addition to the main floor, covered earlier in this chapter.

Advice on tackling such additional floor repairs is also given in this section. Reconstruction of some of these areas can in fact take place from above, from inside the car. It is vital that any repairs to the structural members of the car are ONLY carried out by welding in new metal. NO other method is acceptable if the car is to gain a legitimate MoT certificate.

Welding gear and a pair of tin snips will be needed, but no other special tools are required for this work.

Small holes

CR1. Small holes like this are quite common in the vicinity of the spring hangers. These need dealing with straight away. The important point here is to make quite sure that all the rust is removed from the area, before plating.

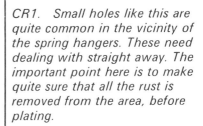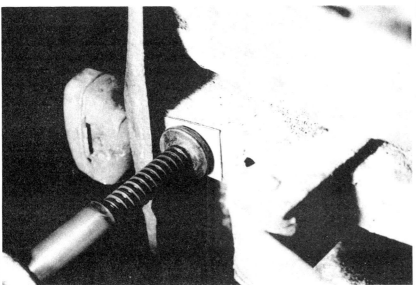

CR2. Cut a plate from a piece of steel AT LEAST as thick as the original chassis beam, and hold it in place against the car with a hydraulic or screw 'bottle' jack. The plate can then be welded continuously around its edges, giving a strong, permanent repair.

141

CR3. Small rusty areas like this can be repaired in a similar way; this flaky area of chassis was immediately in front of the forward spring hanger on a Mark II Escort. Again, remove ALL rust before attempting to weld a plate in place. Always unclip the fuel and brake pipes; remove the petrol pipe completely, after draining the fuel tank, and tie the brake pipe well clear of where you will be welding.

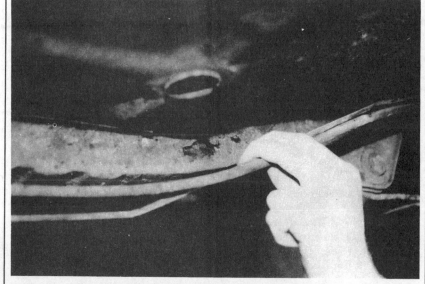

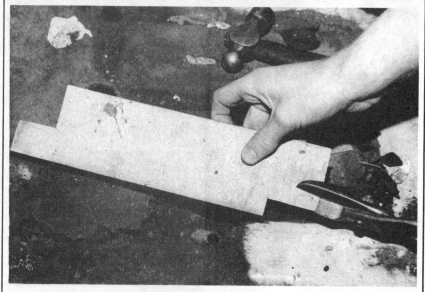

CR4. A repair plate can be fabricated from sheet steel, then welded CONTINUOUSLY around its edges. It is useless to tack weld such plates at intervals, for
a) the water can get in and
b) you will not impress an MoT test examiner.

Top section

CR5. Occasionally, as with this Escort Mark II, the chassis looks good from below the car, but the top section, formed by the floor, has rusted through, from above. This is normally due to water leaks into the car's interior. The danger is that once the floor has been holed, the chassis will literally fill with water each time it rains, with devastating results.

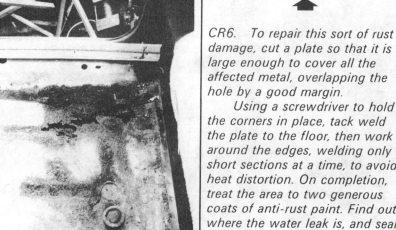

CR6. To repair this sort of rust damage, cut a plate so that it is large enough to cover all the affected metal, overlapping the hole by a good margin.

Using a screwdriver to hold the corners in place, tack weld the plate to the floor, then work around the edges, welding only short sections at a time, to avoid heat distortion. On completion, treat the area to two generous coats of anti-rust paint. Find out where the water leak is, and seal it, to prevent trouble in the future.

Rear chassis

CR7.   The rear chassis members on Cortinas and Escorts pass over the rear axle each side of the vehicle, where they are prone to rusting, owing to the salt spray thrown up from the rear wheels. A common problem is holes which are barely visible, and very awkward to reach, tucked away behind the rear splash shield, as on this Cortina estate car.

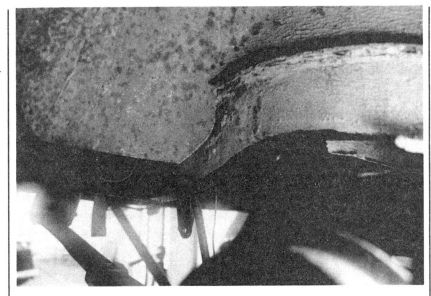

CR8.   To effect a proper repair, the splash shield HAS to be moved out of the way. We therefore used the gas torch to cut a slot in the inside, forward edge of the shield, and 'rolled' it back, out of the way, using a pair of grips.

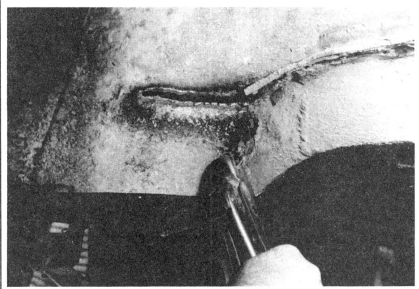

CR9.   With the shield bent back, the hole could be seen more clearly. Unfortunately, much of the metal around the hole was already very thin, where water, mud and salt had been taking their toll.

CR10.   By the time we had cut out all the rust from the area, we had a hole of considerable size to deal with.

CR11.   Because of the awkward, curved shape of the chassis at this point, we first made a template from a piece of thick paper, cutting it exactly to the size of the hole we had made.

CR12. We transferred the template to a sheet of steel, by drawing a line around the edges of the paper. We then cut around the profile thus obtained, using a pair of tin snips. The resulting repair plate fitted the hole perfectly. It is advisable to treat the inside of the chassis to two coats of anti-rust paint, to protect it in future, after rubbing down, and sweeping out all loose rust and debris – an old toothbrush is handy for reaching into corners.

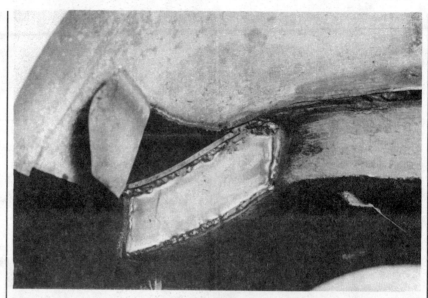

CR13. The top of the chassis beam, at its junction with the inner wing, often rusts, and this car was no exception. We burned away the loose rust with the gas torch, and then welded along the seam, to make it waterproof once again.

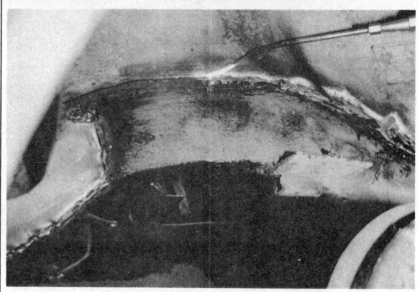

CR14. To complete the job, the splash shield was bent back to its original shape, and the slot cut in it was welded up. It only remains to coat the repaired area with a protective paint.

Rear spring hangers

Rust in the vicinity of spring mountings means certain MoT failure, and of course is potentially very dangerous. If a car is badly affected, the only answer is to cut out the offending section of chassis, and replace it. If you have doubts about your constructional or welding abilities, it is not a job for you. Far better to have this job performed by a professional, than risk lives.

Strangely, although this is a recognised problem area as far as rust is concerned, we found that repair sections for this part of the car were not readily available. It is therefore necessary either to make your own repair section, or buy a complete chassis 'leg', if available, from a Ford dealer. This can work out very expensive, though.

We used an angle grinder, with a cutting disc attached, to cut through the old chassis member, but a chisel COULD be used, although it would take far longer, and not give such a clean cut.

CR15. The forward spring hangers on this Escort estate car were literally crumbling away. Since the owner regularly carried his family, and heavy loads, in the car, he was naturally rather anxious about the state of the chassis at this point.

CR16. The first step was to remove the front end of the road spring from the vicinity. Full details of this operation are given in the 'Mechanical Components' Chapter.

CR17. WEARING GOGGLES, we then used an angle grinder to 'chop' out the rotten chassis sections; we took several 'bites' at the chassis. Although it was rusted, it was surprisingly difficult to cut through.

CR18. It is tempting to leave the spring support on the vehicle, and weld around it. However, the wisdom of removing it can only be appreciated when it is off the car. The multi-thickness edges of the chassis were literally blown apart by rust.

CR19. The easiest way to remove the rotten metal from within the spring support (which was still sound), is to chisel it out, with the support clamped in the vice. Even then, this is a laborious operation.

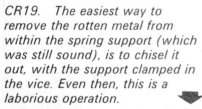

CR20. Under the car, the floor was surprisingly sound in the vicinity of its joints with the chassis. Nevertheless, we had to cut out quite a length of the chassis itself.

CR21. We had to form new sections of chassis from steel plate. These must be AT LEAST as thick as the originals. It is vital that the new sections must fit the spring support exactly, and must also follow the taper of the original chassis. Bending can be achieved using blocks of wood of appropriate thickness and length. The edge flanges can be bent using two lengths of angle iron, clamped in the vice, with the repair section between them, and hammered over to form a neat right angle.

CR22. The making of the repair sections is the most time consuming part of the job, after which it is a case of welding the sections in place on the car. We fitted the new sections in their respective positions, and held them with a jack while they were welded 'end to end'. The spring was re-attached, and supported from below by the jack, in its correct position.

CR23. The flanged edges of the new chassis sections were then tapped against the floor of the car and welded in place, all along their length, to complete the repair.

Front bumper mountings

CR24. The area around the front bumper mountings on Cortinas and Escorts often suffers from rust. Rectification is not difficult, but first the bumper brackets must be removed. Release the mounting bolts, and the brackets can then be pulled forward, through the front panel. We had already removed the bumper, which made the job a lot easier.

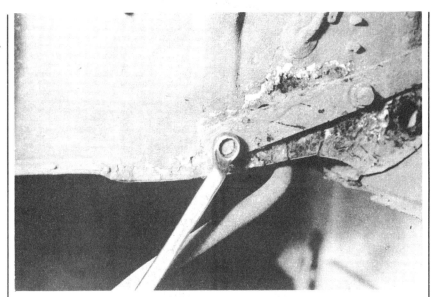

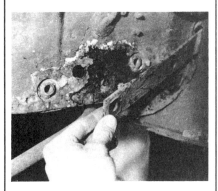

CR25. As is so often the case with this type of job, the rust in this Ford was worse than it had at first appeared. In fact there was very little metal left behind the bracket.

CR27. We used a gas torch to cut away the rusty metal from the area, then made a paper template from a glossy magazine, complete with the correct positions for the bumper bolt holes.

CR28. We then converted the paper cut-out to steel, using an off-cut of steel plate, and a pair of tin snips.

CR26. Disconnect the lamp wiring, and feed it back through the inner wing panel, into the engine bay. In addition, check the other side of the panel, removing anything that will suffer from heat, during cutting and welding operations.

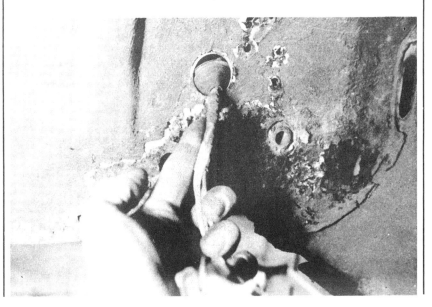

CR29. The positions of the holes were then marked on the steel plate, in their precise positions. Make each hole slightly larger than the diameter of the bolts used – by about $^1/_8$ to $^1/_4$ inch, so that the metal around the hole can be welded to the car without impeding the bolt's progress. If you haven't a drill bit of sufficient diameter, drill a series of small holes in a circle, around the position of the required bolt hole, then join them up with a small chisel, finally shaping the edge of the hole with a round file.

CR30. The plate can then be welded into place on the car. We used the MIG welder, to keep distortion to a minimum. The welds can be ground down afterwards, if desired (WEAR GOGGLES).

Rear floor

On almost every Cortina and Escort examined during the course of preparation of this book, there was rust in the area under or around the rear seat. This needs early rectification, for dirt and water can collect here, eventually rotting the rest of the floor, and the chassis. Since this area is normally hidden, it needs positive steps to make a thorough check. An inspection at least once a year is an excellent idea.

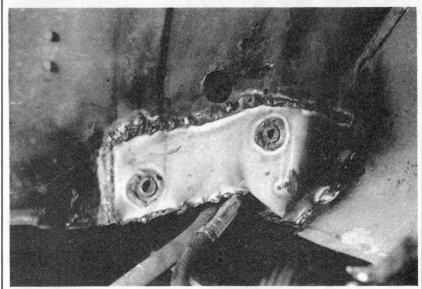

CR31. With the rear seats taken out of this Cortina estate car (details of seat removal are given in the 'Interior' section), it was evident, on lifting the wheel arch coverings, that the floor and wheel arch were no longer joined, at least at the front. The rust needs to be completely cut away from the floor.

CR32. Repair plates are fairly easy to fabricate for this area, since they are largely flat. Right angled flanges are needed where the plates meet the wheel arch, however, and slots need to be cut for the side plate to follow the contours of the floor and wheel arch. The plates are easily welded into place; it is important to rectify any rust damage underneath this area at the same time as tackling it from above.

CR33. This Escort saloon also showed signs of perforation of the side panel, and separation of the floor from the wheel arch.

CR34. Poking with a long scraper opened up the gaps. It is important to find out how far the rust extends.

CR35. Repair plates can be fabricated to suit the contours of the wheel arch; when welded in place, they MUST be weathertight. In the case of this Escort, the repair panel could be viewed from inside and outside of the vehicle.

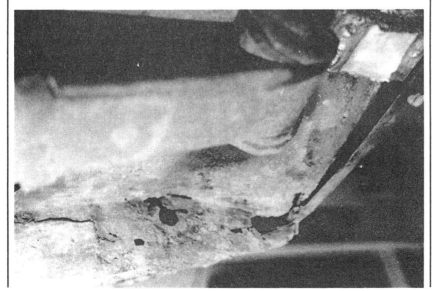

Fuel tank mounting – Escort

CR36. The lower body sections at the rear of Escorts attract mud and water from the rear wheels, and so are targets for rust. The petrol tank attaches to the bodywork at this point, on the driver's side of the car, and the metal around the mountings is often found to be holed, as on this Mark I.

CR37. A repair plate can be fabricated and drilled very easily, using a paper or cardboard template as a guide, and bending the metal around wood blocks, or in the vice.

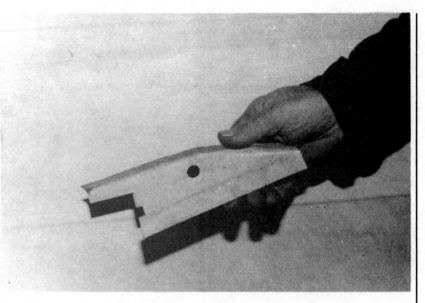

CR38. Since this area is easy to reach from below, it is also a straightforward task to clamp the new section in place, using a self-grip wrench. The repair plate can be welded in place, all around its edges. Needless to say, the petrol tank should be removed beforehand.

Sundry bodywork reconstruction

So far in this chapter, I have covered the 'normal' problem areas that you are likely to encounter on Cortina and Escort bodywork, as far as the main structure is concerned.

However, of course, every individual vehicle presents its own unique difficulties which must be overcome, and there can never by any one set answer which will cover all eventualities. Therefore, included in this section are a few tips which should be helpful when it comes to dealing with some of the challenges you may encounter.

It is also recognised that while, for example, the best way of dealing with major corrosion in the bulkhead and inner wing areas is by removing the outer panel, for better access, there are occasions when less serious damage can be dealt with without resorting to cutting the wings off! This is especially true where the wings are in good condition, and do not need replacing, or where a vehicle is in everyday use, and time 'off the road' must be kept to a minimum. Therefore, included in this section is information on alternative ways of tackling repairs to the underwing areas.

Bodywork jobs

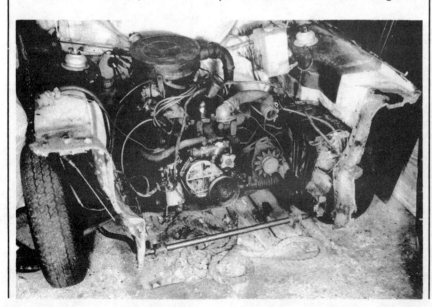

SBR1. Believe it or not, this is a rather tidy Mark II Escort . . . So far in this chapter I have described how many of the bodywork panels can be replaced. Hopefully it isn't often that a complete front end needs to be changed, but, using the same 'step by step' techniques employed on the other panels, this sort of job can be tackled at home, provided the repairs are carried out carefully, and without rushing them.

SBR2. Jobs like this are made far easier if the correct body panels are available, of course, and, with the later Escorts, there are few problems in this direction. Nevertheless, with any of the models covered by this book, always try to obtain the sections you think you will need BEFORE you start the stripdown, otherwise you may have to hold up the job in mid-operation, while a vital section is sought.

SBR3. Some bodywork panels, particularly small brackets, etc., can be fabricated quite easily and quickly at home, using the most rudimentary of tools. It is always worth attempting to make a section yourself, if it isn't readily available. Do make sure that it is of at least the same thickness as the original panel, especially if it forms part of the vehicle's main structure.

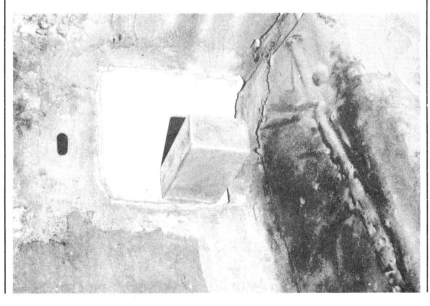

SBR4. It can be most awkward to hold patches in place while welding them to the vehicle, especially if you are working on your own. There are various methods to help overcome this, some of which have already been covered in this chapter. However, ingenuity has few boundaries, and, for example, in this case, a solid block of steel was used to weight this plate down, while it was attached to the floor of this Escort.

Under-wing work

SBR5. Earlier in this chapter, in the 'Front Wing Change' section, I described how to deal with rust problems in the bulkhead and surrounding areas. Now although it is far easier to deal with such rust when the front wings are off the vehicle, repairs CAN be effected without removing the wings. This would be a help where, for example, the wings themselves are in good condition and it is then neither desirable nor necessary to wreck them by taking them off. In such cases, the parcel shelf, interior trim and wiring must be removed from immediately behind the bulkheads; firstly, to accurately assess the amount of damage, and secondly, to avoid setting fire to anything when welding.

The parcel shelf on this Escort was first released from the body by unclipping and unbolting it from its mountings. Cortinas have very similar mountings.

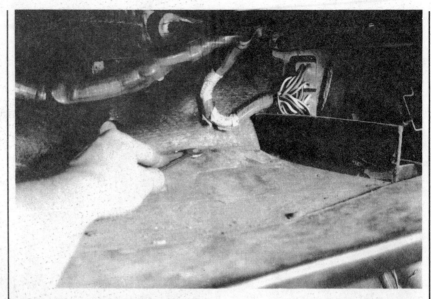

SBR6. The parcel shelf can then be withdrawn from the car, allowing better access to the trim panel, soundproofing felt and wiring on that side of the vehicle.

SBR7. We then unbolted the shelf clips from the side panel, putting all the bits in a box, for safe keeping. This released the side panel, which . . .

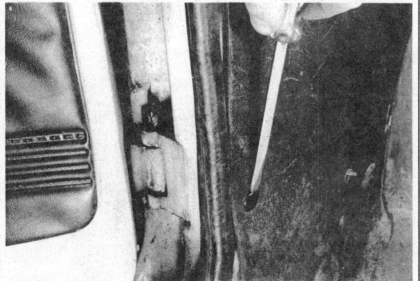

SBR8. . . . then just needed unclipping from the side of the car. A large screwdriver is useful to prise the head of the clip out from the panel, so that it can be withdrawn by hand.

SBR9. The wiring harness has convenient multi-plug connections at the bulkhead; with these disconnected, the wiring can be pulled clear. The soundproofing felt can then be moved away from the bulkhead, and a thorough examination can be made.

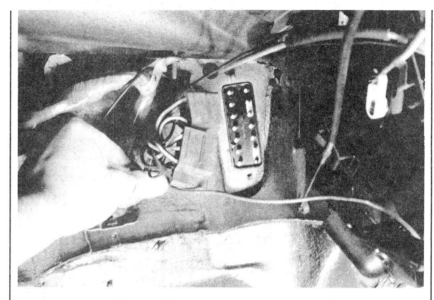

SBR10. As the felt was pulled down, we found a great deal of mud, which had found its way into the car through the inner wing/bulkhead. The area should also be checked carefully from the under-wing side, using a strong light. All rust should be removed before attempting to plate it; if very large areas of the door pillar and bulkheads are missing, the wings should be removed for further checking anyway.

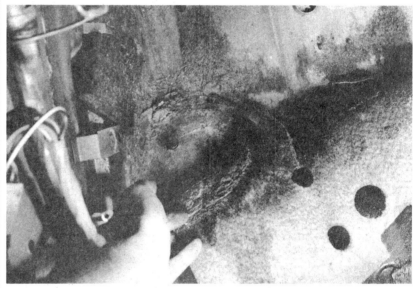

SBR11. This Escort had patches of rust, but nothing too drastic. We therefore fabricated plates to fit individual areas, using paper templates as described earlier in the chapter. We started with the offside front under-wing area, by burning out the rust from a small, triangular area, at the back of the wheel arch.

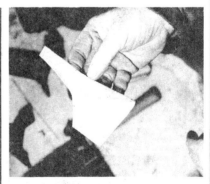

SBR12. We fabricated a repair plate, and angled it to fit the hole. The problem was then, how to attach it, on a near vertical surface?

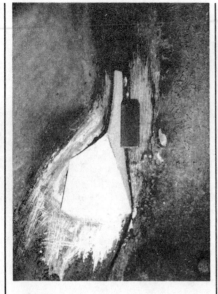

SBR13.   We used a small but powerful bar magnet to hold the repair section in place. The repair plate was then welded in position, during which operation the adjoining metal was found to be weaker than it had at first appeared.

SBR14.   The answer was to burn out another section of the metal, making a square hole, and double checking that the surrounding area was sound, before making up another repair plate.

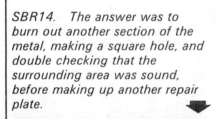

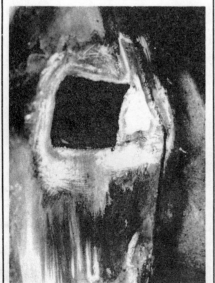

SBR15.   This was then welded all around its edges, after being tack welded in place, initially. The weld must be water tight, or leaks to the car's interior will follow.

SBR16.   The rear extremities of the wing were holed, near the bottom, although the surrounding panel was sound. Because of the angle of the bodywork at this point, we made two small repair sections, and welded them together, prior to fitting, once again following a template. This technique can be used to tackle many awkward shaped repair plates.

SBR17.   The panel was then offered up to the car, holding it in place with a screwdriver, before clamping with the bar magnet, and welding in position.

SBR18.   One of the most serious holes had been at the top of the inner wing panel. To repair this, and to reinforce the area, we made a repair plate so that it was right-angled in two directions. A 'vee' shaped slot, cut in the shallower flange, allowed the metal to bend at this sharp angle.

154

SBR19. The plate was tack welded in place at either end, then tapped to the exact shape of the bodywork, before being welded all along its edges. Beware of falling sparks when welding in confined spaces like this.

SBR20. The bottom of the front wing was very rusty, and had parted company from the car. We therefore made a new section, welded it to the wing, and clamped it in place against the inner sill. Repair plates like this are surprisingly easy to make and fit. The remainder of the wing was patched using the methods described earlier in the chapter; cutting out the rust and replacing it with new metal.

Motor vehicle dismantlers

SBR21. This sad Mark I Cortina had reached the end of the road, but many of the bodywork sections were still good, including the rear wings, bootlid and doors. A trip to the vehicle dismantlers in your area is ALWAYS worthwhile, for it is surprising just how many body panels can be salvaged. Although Mark I Cortinas are now the scarcest of the models covered by this book, we found three in one day, on a tour of local breakers' yards. We also counted four Mark II Cortinas, and approximately 20 Escorts, equally split between Mark I and Mark II models. So, if you are stuck for body spares, there are plenty of used panels to be found.

Doors and door windows

To detail the complete stripdown of every type of door and window mechanism employed on all the Cortinas and Escorts would be enough to fill a book in itself, since the design changed with each model, and even between two and four-door cars, and so on. Therefore, for precise details applicable to your particular vehicle, you should consult a *Haynes Owners Workshop Manual* covering your specific model.

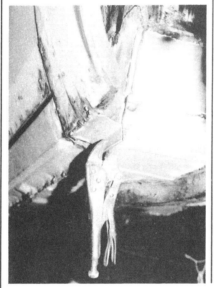

However, although there are differences between models, there are also many areas of 'common ground', and in this section are included tips on how to make the task of dealing with doors a lot easier. In all cases, re-assembly is a direct reversal of the dismantling procedure.

SPECIAL TOOLS: Door hinge pin remover (two-door Escorts); special screwdriver for strike plate screws (later Escorts, with anti-burst door locks).

A tool for driving out the hinge pins can be made very easily at home, as described in the 'Minor Bodywork Repairs' section of this chapter.

Door removal and re-fitting

The doors on two-door Escorts have hinges which are welded onto the doors and onto the body; to remove them, the hinge pin must be drifted out as shown under 'Minor Bodywork Repairs'. It is best to use new hinge pins on re-hanging the door, since, unless they have been lubricated regularly, the old ones will be grooved, giving excess up and down movement.

Four door Escorts, and two or four-door Cortinas Mark I and II employ door hinges which are bolted to the door, and to the pillars, so that the doors may be

155

removed simply by unbolting them, although re-fitting them is more tricky, since they normally need to be aligned within the door frame.

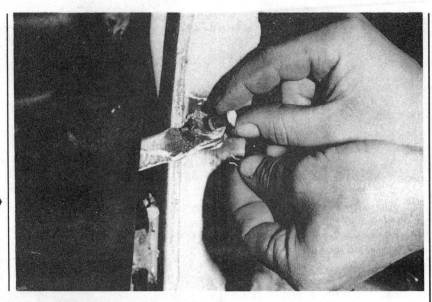

DR1. The first move is to withdraw the door check strap retaining pin, after hooking out the locking spring clip with a pair of pliers, or a small screwdriver. Take care that neither the pin nor the clip are lost.

DR3. Re-alignment on re-fitting is the tricky part of the job, and the first problem is just to get the hinge bolts into their threaded holes in the door! A screwdriver blade, or length of small, round bar, pushed through the door and hinge holes from inside the door, can be used to gently lever the two into line. It is important that any bolts already fitted are left loose, at this stage.

DR2. Use a ring spanner to slacken the hinge bolts, and get an assistant to take the weight of the door as the bolts come out.

DR4. We fitted a second-hand door to this Cortina, but problems can arise even when replacing a door into its original position. The first step is to centre the door, in its aperture, checking by eye, then tighten the bolts. When the door is shut, it will be obvious whether it needs to be adjusted up or down, as the gaps around its edges will be equal, if all's well, or decidedly different, if not.

DR5. Make up and down adjustments by altering the position of the hinges, in the door pillar. Access to the retaining nuts is through a small aperture in the pillar. It is extremely helpful to have an assistant on hand during these operations. Tighten the bolts and re-check after each alteration, until the door fits perfectly within its aperture. This can sometimes become one of those jobs that you wish you had never started . . . However, perseverance eventually pays off!

DR6. Having got the door centralised, you may well find that it doesn't shut cleanly, in which case adjustment can be made to the striker plate, on the door closing pillar. Early cars have three Phillips screws holding these plates; later Escorts, with anti-burst locks, need a special screwdriver. The door should fit flush with the surrounding bodywork when correctly aligned, and the striker plate MUST sit vertically on its mounting panel. Make allowances if the door aperture trims have been removed; final adjustment is only possible after they have been re-fitted.

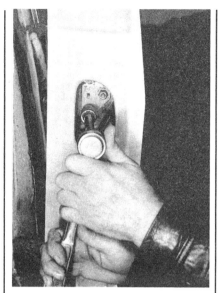

Door dismantling – Cortina

Most of the dismantling procedures are similar for Mark I and Mark II models, although removal of the cylinder lock from the driver's door is different on Mark II cars.

The cylinder door lock fitted to the driver's door on Mark I Cortinas can be removed after taking off the external door handle. This is held by two screws from the inside of the door. The two screws holding the lock cylinder cover plate can then be taken out, followed by the coil tension spring. With the adjuster stud locknut slackened, the plunger stud can be removed. The lock cylinder is then withdrawn, using the ignition key.

On Mark II models, the cylinder lock is extracted by first removing the door handle, then by extracting the circlip, from inside the door. This releases the end plate, spring and lock barrel assembly. The inner end of the barrel is now removed by loosening the locknut and unscrewing the adjusting nut. The cylinder can now be withdrawn, again using the key.

When dismantling a door, take great care that all screws, clips and handle sealing gaskets are kept together in a box or jar, so that they don't get mislaid.

DDC1. The outer weatherstrips, which are clipped in place on the outside of the door frame, at the top, can be gently prised upwards, away from the door. If they are the originals, the rubber will probably be very brittle, and the metal backing strip rusted away. In this case, it is best to renew these strips, and their clips, to make sure that rainwater is kept out of the doors in future.

DDC2. On the inside, take out each single Phillips screw holding the door handle and the window winder.

DDC4. Now, VERY carefully, prise the door panel away from the frame, and, one by one, ease the securing clips from their holes in the door. A slim screwdriver can be used initially, to start the panel moving, but it is safest then to unclip the remainder of the panel by hand.
Heavy-handedness during this operation will split the door panel VERY easily.

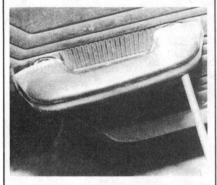

DDC3. The armrests/door closing handles are secured by two Phillips screws, one at each end, UNDERNEATH the handle.

◄*DDC5. If removing the ashtray from the door panel, prise the clips from the rear of the ashtray, before trying to pull the tray out through the front of the panel.*

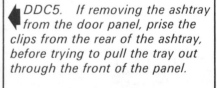

DDC6. The plastic weather shield can now be CAREFULLY eased away from the door frame. These are glued in place, and are usually very sticky, so store them carefully, so that they cannot be stuck together accidentally, or you'll never separate them without tearing the plastic (I know because it happened to me!).

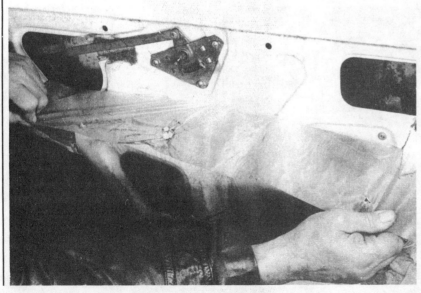

DDC7. On Mark I cars, the bright trim panel along the bottom edge of the door is withdrawn by taking out the four Phillips screws.

DDC8. The window winding mechanism is initially released from the door by taking out the screws surrounding the winder handle, but first, re-fit the handle to the operating shaft, and lower the window glass to the bottom of the door.

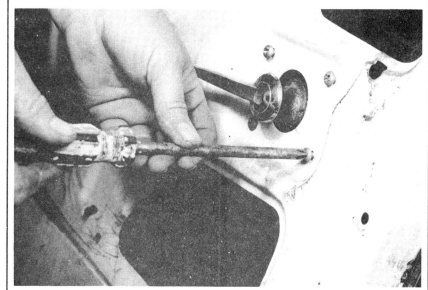

DDC9. Prise out the glass channel at the top of the door, to allow the glass some free movement. Next, release the screw securing the lower end of the rear glass channel, and pull this end of the channel away from the glass. On Mark I cars, take out the two screws securing the lower glass stop.

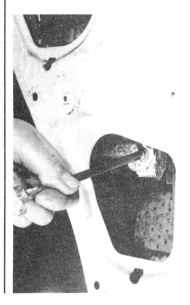

DDC10. The operating end of the window regulator mechanism can now be moved to the widest part of the channel in which it runs, by moving the glass and channel assembly towards it; this is in fact easier than it sounds!

DDC11. The complete window winder/regulator assembly can now be withdrawn through the aperture at the bottom of the door. You will need to turn the assembly to enable it to come out.

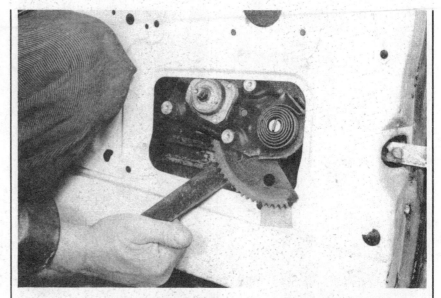

DDC12. Before the window glass can be removed, the quarter light assembly must come out. On Mark I cars, the front quarter light frame is held to the door by three screws. On Mark II cars, the fixed quarter light frame is held to the door by a blind rivet. This must be drilled through, to release the quarter window.

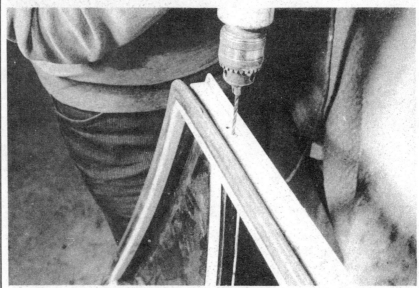

DDC13. The metal window frame is pulled away from the quarter light assembly, taking care not to scratch any of the door paintwork, unless it is to be resprayed anyway.

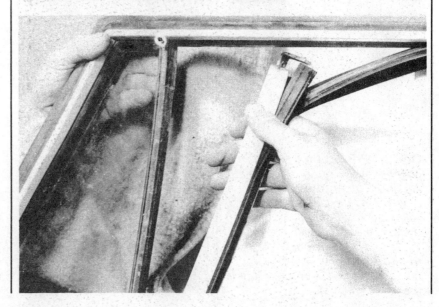

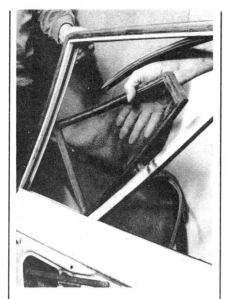

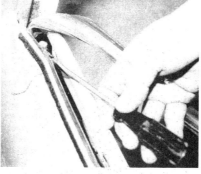

DDC17.   The clips securing the inner felt glass seal are prised apart, to release the seal.

DDC18.   The interior 'remote control' mechanism for the door lock is released from the door by taking out the three securing screws.

DDC14.   The quarter light assembly, complete with its frame, can now be lifted out of the door.

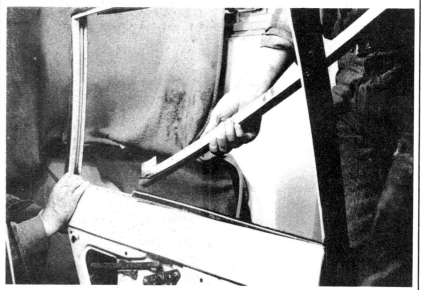

DDC15.   The metal window channel can be eased out through the door frame from above; you will need to prise the inner and outer sections of the door apart slightly, to enable the frame to be withdrawn.

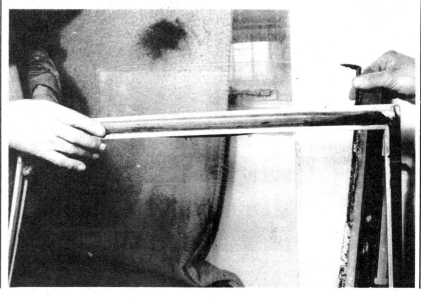

DDC16.   The main door window glass, complete with its metal lower channel, can now be lifted out of the door fairly easily. We found it easiest to turn the glass through 90 degrees, to extract it from the outside of the door. Even then, it was necessary to prise the inner and outer sections of the door slightly apart, to allow the lower channel through.

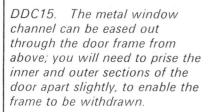
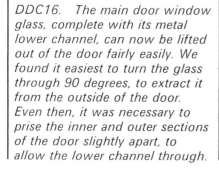

DDC19. The system is similar on Mark I Cortina models, like this.

DDC20. Next, take out the three screws holding the lock to the outer edge of the door.

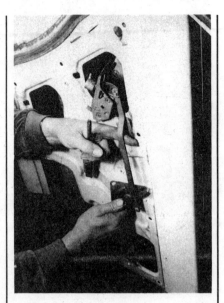

DDC21. The complete lock and remote control assembly can now be fed out of the door. On Mark I cars the remote control linkage must be disengaged from the key lock operating shaft, before it can be withdrawn. If you are taking the remote control mechanism out, leaving the window in, you will need to detach the lower end of the rear glass channel (single screw), and pull this to one side, to allow the linkage to pass through.

DDC22. The door handle is released by taking out the two securing screws from inside of the door. The screws are accessible through the small apertures in the inside of the door panel. If the screws are particularly reluctant, apply plenty of penetrating oil, and try gripping the heads of the screws with a self-grip wrench.

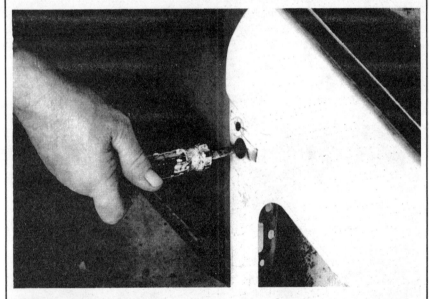

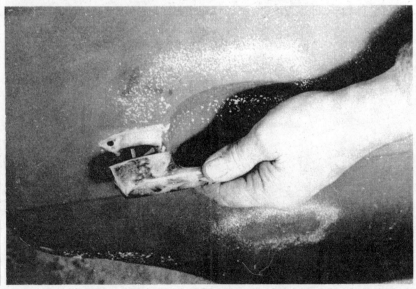

DDC23. The handle can then be extracted from the outside of the door.

DDC24.   The door sealing rubber is clipped to some parts of the door frame, with small plastic clips. These need very careful extraction with a screwdriver, or they can pull out of their holes in the rubber. They are then very awkward little characters to get back in again!

DDC25.   The rubber seal fits into a groove around the top part of the door; it can be removed from the groove using a screwdriver, initially, then by very gently pulling the rubber away from the frame.

Door dismantling – Escort

The basic procedures for stripping an Escort door are similar to those used on Cortinas. However, there are some important differences.

To start with, the window winder mechanisms on the four door Mark I Escorts are of the cable type. These are easily withdrawn from the door, by simply taking out the two screws holding the mechanism to the door panel, and two further screws, attaching the mechanism to the glass carrier. On other Escort models, the set-up is very similar to that used on the Cortinas, and removal is as described for these models.

Removal of the windows from Escort doors involves the same basic steps as described in the 'Cortina' section, but, again, there are some differences. For example, the metal divider between the quarter light window and the main window glass is attached by two rivets, on two door Mark I Escorts (compared with a single rivet on Cortinas), and by screws on the other Escorts. Another point is that the main door window glass is best withdrawn from the OUTSIDE of the upper door frame, on Mark I cars, and from the INSIDE of the frame, on Mark IIs.

The remote door controls are removed in basically the same way as for the Cortinas, except that rods are used on the later Escorts, in place of the 'solid' type connecting bar used on Cortinas and early Escorts. The rods are unclipped from the handle and the lock, when dismantling.

When taking out the remote control door lock from Escort II doors, turn the lock claw to the 'closed' position (with the 'U' facing the ground), while withdrawing the assembly inwards, from the door shell edge, for subsequent removal through the inner door panel aperture.

DDE1.   The door lock and window winder mechanism on early Mark I Escorts is similar to that used on the Cortinas.

1	Screw	16	Clip
2	Window actuating mechanism	17	Clip
3	Escutcheon	18	Door catch mechanism
4	Winder handle	19	Door catch exterior plate
5	Screw	20	Screw
6	Screw	21	Clevis pin
7	Washer	22	Gasket
8	Clevis pin	23	Bolt
9	Escutcheon	24	Washer
10	Handle	25	Gasket
11	Screw	26	Bolt
12	Lock actuating mechanism	27	Washer
13	Clip	28	Exterior handle
14	Screw	29	Lock barrel
15	Washer	30	Keys

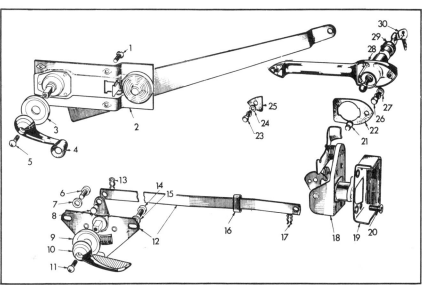

DDE2.   The later Mark Is employed this front door lock mechanism; note the use of a 'U' clip to hold the driver's door lock in place, and rod linkages between the various parts of the locking mechanism.

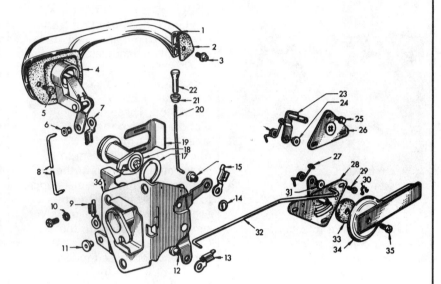

1 Exterior handle	20 Connecting rod
2 Gasket	21 Escutcheon
3 Screw	22 Interior lock
4 Gasket	button
5 Screw	23 Remote control
6 Bush	lever
7 Connecting rod	24 Bush
retaining clip	25 Bolt
8 Connecting rod	26 Plate
9 Connecting rod	27 Spring
clip	28 Door catch
10 Shakeproof	actuating lever
washer	assembly
11 Bush	29 Screw
12 Bush	30 Clip
13 Clip	31 Bush
14 Clip	32 Connecting rod
15 Clip	33 Pad
16 Bush	34 Interior handle
17 Locking ring	35 Screw
18 Lock assembly	36 Door catch
19 Lock barrel	assembly
securing clip	

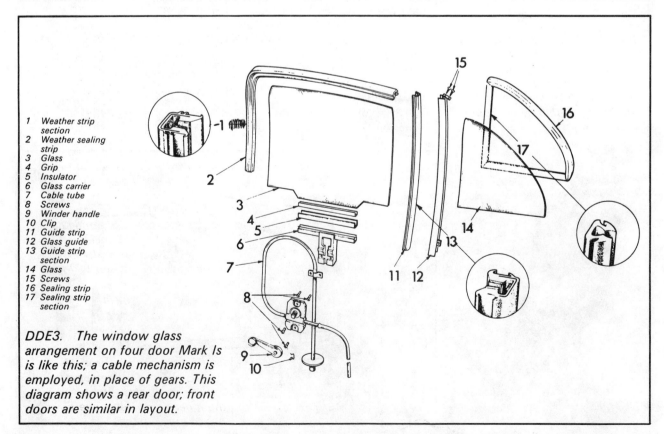

1 Weather strip section
2 Weather sealing strip
3 Glass
4 Grip
5 Insulator
6 Glass carrier
7 Cable tube
8 Screws
9 Winder handle
10 Clip
11 Guide strip
12 Glass guide
13 Guide strip section
14 Glass
15 Screws
16 Sealing strip
17 Sealing strip section

DDE3.   The window glass arrangement on four door Mark Is is like this; a cable mechanism is employed, in place of gears. This diagram shows a rear door; front doors are similar in layout.

DDE4. This diagram shows the door lock layout on Mark II saloons; the system on Mark II estate cars and vans is similar to that used on Mark I cars, apart from a different interior handle being used; plastic, pull type handles are used on Mark II models.

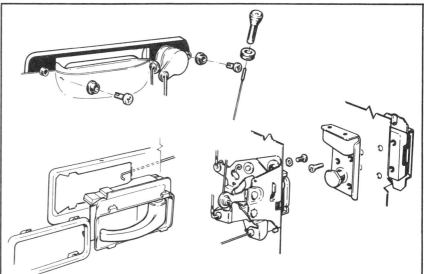

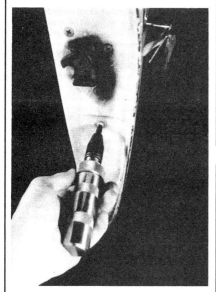

DDE5. To take out the lock mechanism on Mark I or II Escorts, the screw holding the rear glass channel should be taken out (an impact screwdriver may be needed to shift this screw), so that the window channel can be moved to one side, to allow the door lock to pass through.

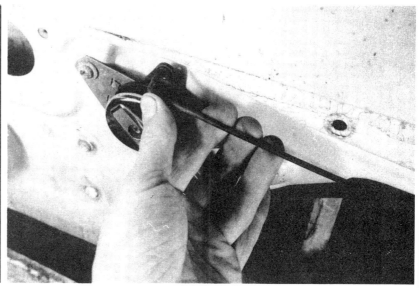

DDE6. Steel rods transmit movement from the remote control handles to the locks, on all but the early Escorts. They fit into bushes in the metal, and are simply unclipped for removal. The rod connecting the locking button with the lock also needs to be unclipped, when taking the lock out.

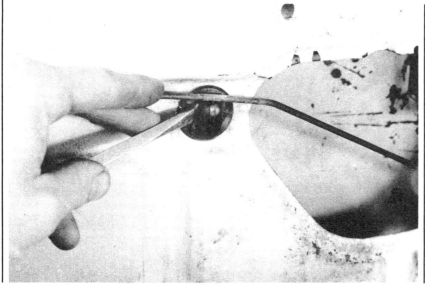

DDE7. A screwdriver is useful for prising the remote control rod out of the support, at the top of the inner door shell. Take care not to break the plastic clip.

DDE8. The lock barrel on the driver's door is released by prising back the 'U' shaped retaining clip, on Mark I Escorts. On Mark IIs, tap the roll pin from the lock barrel's end cap, and take out the end cap 'U' clip, return spring and gaskets, to release the barrel from the door handle.

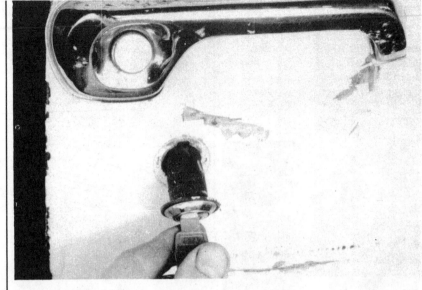

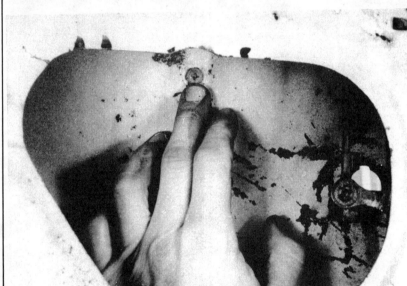

DDE9. The door handles are screwed to the outer door panel, from inside. One of the screws is located here, within the panelwork, and is accessible only when the inner door trim panel is taken off.

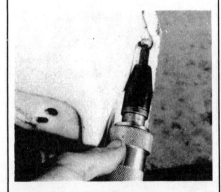

DDE10. The screw at the rear of the handle can be found on the outside edge of the door, and can be rusted in place. An impact screwdriver is usually effective in removing this screw, but . . .

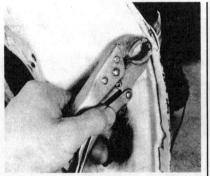

DDE11. . . . if the soft metal head of the screw does become chewed up, a small self-grip wrench is useful for gripping the screw and releasing it from the door.

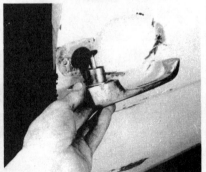

DDE12. The door handle and plunger can now be withdrawn from the outside of the door.

Lubrication

DL1. On Cortinas and Escorts, treat the moving parts of the door locks and window winder mechanisms to a few drops of oil (or grease, where it can be made to reach the working parts) before re-fitting the remote control links and the trim panels. This will help maintain smooth operation, and reduce the chances of the mechanisms freezing in winter, for a long time to come.

The respray

The chances are that you will have to apply paint to at least some of your vehicle, even if it only amounts to using an aerosol can or two, to cover repaired areas on wings and wheel arches, etc.

Once the bodywork is intact, as far as rectification of rust and dents are concerned, the aim must then be to get it in the best possible state to accept paint. This can just mean rubbing down the old paint and body filler which has been applied, so that they present a perfectly smooth surface on which to spray a primer-surface, or it could mean stripping the existing paint right back to bare metal, and starting again. So, how do you decide which is best?

There are several factors. In some cases, you really have little choice. For example, if the vehicle has been painted (usually hand-painted) with an oil-based household paint, there is no way thay you will ever get a cellulose vehicle paint to stick to the old surface, even assuming that you could get it smooth! Other possibilities could be that the

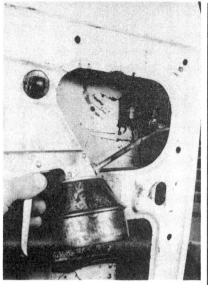

existing paint finish is covered in tiny lumps, about 1mm across ('micro-blisters'), or that the paint surface has lots of tiny cracks running around it ('crazing'). In either of these cases, it is honestly a waste of time and money trying to apply paint on top; the new surface will soon suffer from the same underlying problems that affected the original paint. Therefore, in all these cases, and where the original paint is peeling, don't waste any time thinking – strip the old paint right off the car, back to bare metal. Tedious though this may be (and, believe me, it IS tedious!), it is quicker, cheaper and far better in the long run. You end up with a better surface, for a longer-lasting result that looks right; in short, a proper job.

Another advantage of completely stripping the paint from the vehicle is that this operation will reveal any areas that have been filled previously, since the paint stripper will react with the filler. You can then deal with such areas as appropriate, putting in new metal where this is desirable – for example where rust damage has been simply covered with body filler in the past!

There are two notes of caution to sound in connection with paint stripping.

Firstly, the job will take about a week of evenings, plus a weekend, for a car the size of an Escort/Cortina (allow a day or so more for estate cars – there's more body area to cover!). During this time, the bare metal MUST NOT be allowed to get damp. This means that either the car should be garaged in a dry place, for the whole time the job takes, and then painted, at least in primer, before being used, or, as each panel is stripped, it should be primed straight away, if the car is to be used, or even parked outside overnight. Just one shower of rain, or a night out in damp air, will cause surface rust over the whole of the bare metal areas. This is difficult to remove and you stand to leave at least some of the rust behind, which will then work away at the metal under your new paint.

Secondly, strictly speaking, bare steel should be coated with an 'etching' primer, prior to normal priming and the application of top coats. However, the fumes created by such primers can be dangerous to inhale, and a proper respirator (NOT just a gauze face mask) MUST be worn when working with them. Check with your paint suppliers – normally 'Health and Safety' information sheets about each type of paint sold are available from the suppliers.

If in doubt, use a standard primer, suitable for the top coats you will be using, direct onto the bare metal surface. In practice, the finish should be durable even when an etching primer is not used on the bare metal.

This brings us onto the choice of the type of paint to use on your car. There are arguments for and against the use of, for example, cellulose, acrylic, or synthetic paints. For general use, to respray the models covered by this book, any would do the job satisfactorily. Cellulose finishes are the 'traditional' respray material – for the d-i-y- use they are comparatively easy to apply, are durable (if applied properly!),

and, even if the 'gloss from the gun' is not fantastic – and that depends a great deal on the sprayer, and on temperature, paint mix, and so on – they can be 'cut back' to give a deep shine, and they can be applied without the need for special safety equipment – apart from a face mask and perhaps goggles. Some of the acrylic and synthetic finishes available are very hard wearing, given better initial gloss when applied, and are perhaps more forgiving in some ways to the manner in which they are sprayed. Disadvantages can be, depending on the paint, that cellulose cannot be applied over the top of some finishes (for example when repairing minor scrapes, etc.), that they often respond less well to polishing, after application, and – especially some of the 'two part' paints, with chemical hardeners – they can be poisonous to inhale, and need very careful handling. Special respirators are required for some paints.

Whatever material you choose, talk to your paint supplier before you buy, and in particular find out about the safety implications, and the correct methods of applying and polishing the paint you intend to use. Data sheets are very often available, and these give a wealth of useful information about the

product, which helps you make a better job of your restoration project. As the paintwork is the part that most people see first, this is obviously important.

Paint stripping

Assuming that 'the worst' situation prevails, and that you have to strip the paint from your vehicle, you will need about five litres (perhaps a little more) of paint stripper, so this should be purchased before you start. It is pretty strong stuff, and burns if it touches your skin. Therefore take particular care when stripping paint. Cover your arms and wear rubber gloves; always wear old clothes which don't matter, or an old pair of overalls. It is especially important that you don't get any stripper in your eyes, so don't splash the stuff about. Normally, for the odd spot of paint stripper on your hand or arm, copious quantities of water, applied straight away, will help. If you should splash paint stripper in your face, seek medical aid immediately.

Special tools

Rubber gloves, paint scrapers, old scrubbing brush, empty tin of about 2 pints capacity, for paint stripper.

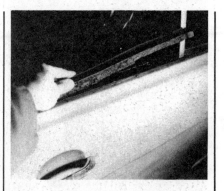

PS1.   Start by taking off any rubber trims and water deflectors, for any spots of paint stripper falling on these will cause damage. The same applies to tyres; it is best to cover them.

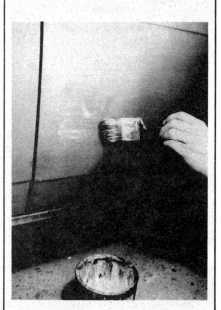

PS2.   Apply the paint stripper with slow, even strokes of an old paintbrush. Give the entire surface a thorough coat, then go over it again, especially where the car has several layers of paint on it.

PS3.   Allow the stripper several minutes to percolate through the old paint, until the surface has bubbled, then use a scraper to peel the paint away from the metal. This is the stage where rubber gloves are handy, since bits of paint, falling from the vehicle, will still be soaked in paint stripper, and will burn your skin.

PS4. On a car like this Cortina, which had several coats of paint, some of them quite thick, you may need two or three applications of paint stripper, to lift all the paint. It is best to tackle the large, flat panels first, moving onto the smaller, complicated bodywork sections later. A small, stiff hand brush can be useful for 'agitating' the paint stripper on the surface, to make it work more quickly, and an old toothbrush is useful for getting into tight corners. Stripping the paint from a large vehicle is one of those jobs where the more friends you have, the better.

When the bodywork is finally back to bare metal, wipe off all the stripped surfaces, using a little cellulose thinners on a clean rag. This will ensure that the surface is free from paint stripper and paint fragments.

Prepare for painting

PP1. It is difficult to paint all the intricate corners of a vehicle when there are lots of bits and pieces still attached. It is therefore helpful to remove as many of these as you (sensibly) can. For example, the air vents, below the windscreen, on Cortinas will unscrew, to allow them to be cleaned (or stripped) and sprayed separately, also the areas beneath them. You are not so lucky here with an Escort, since the grilles are part of the bodywork!

PP2. On the Cortinas, take out the screws and the grille can be lifted forward and away from the car.

PP3. It is also worth taking out estate car tailgate handles (unscrew the inner securing ring to release), and any others which are not difficult to remove. It is a matter of choice whether you feel that the main door handles should come off the car or not.

PP4. Depending on how bad the paintwork is on the inside of the car, you may need to respray the interior paintwork too! You certainly will if you are changing the colour of the car. In any case it is far quicker and easier in the long run to remove the door sealing rubbers, than to attempt to mask them. Gently prise them away from the doors, using a screwdriver. Remove other interior trim items as described in chapter 7, 'Interior'.

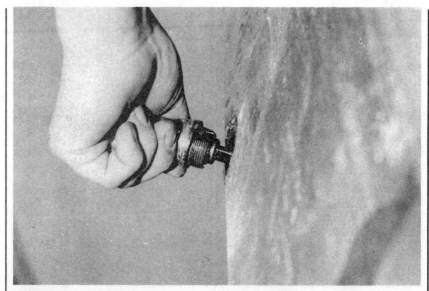

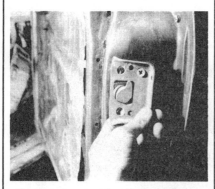

PP5. Items such as the door lock dovetail plates are easily removed, so it is worth taking them off.

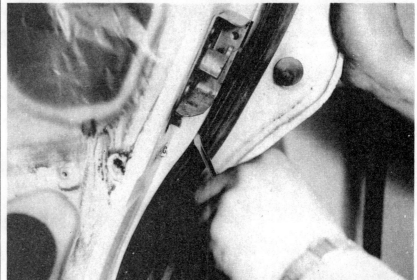

PP6. If you haven't already done so, now is the time to apply thin films of body filler over joints where new panels have been welded on. For example, the body sills need to be sealed along their top edges. This job doesn't take long. Try to get the filler surface as smooth as possible as it is applied. This saves a lot of time in rubbing down later.

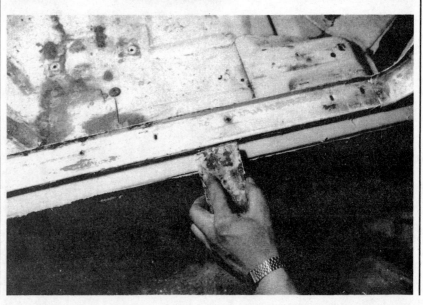

PP7. Flexible sealant is more appropriate to use as a jointing compound between body panels around door, bonnet and boot apertures, etc., where new wings have been fitted, for instance.

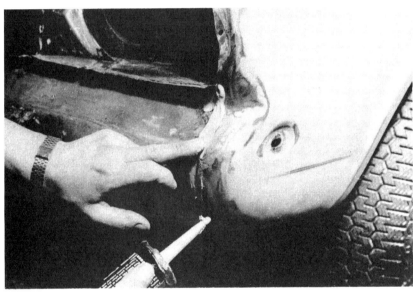

PP8. Make certain that joints which are vulnerable to the elements – like this one, between a replacement wing and the main body – are sealed against the ingress of moisture. We used a flexible sealant here too. Other seams to seal in this way are the rain gutter to roof panel joint, and where the roof pillars attach to the roof.

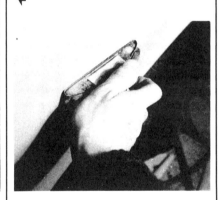

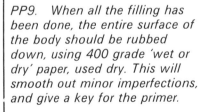

PP9. When all the filling has been done, the entire surface of the body should be rubbed down, using 400 grade 'wet or dry' paper, used dry. This will smooth out minor imperfections, and give a key for the primer.

PP10. At this stage, it is worth having a good tidy up, both inside the vehicle, and in the working area around it. The last thing you need when spraying is to have a lot of dust particles present, so sweep up as much debris as possible.

PP11. The next job is masking up all items remaining on the car, that you don't want painted! Masking tape often doesn't like sticking to rubber window seals, but, if you wipe the seal using a rag with a little cellulose thinners on it (don't overdo it, or you may soften the rubber), the masking tape will adhere a lot better.

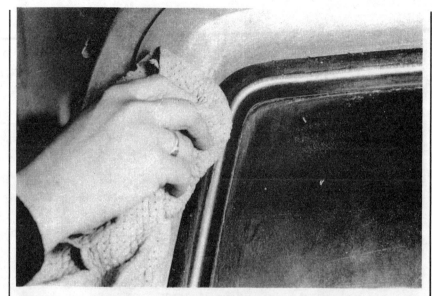

PP12. Start masking the windows by applying a single strip of masking tape, all around the window sealing rubbers. We intended to spray the interior paintwork as well as the exterior of the car, so had to mask the window rubbers on the inside as well. It is vital that the tape fits right to the edge of the rubbers, to give a neat, clean line when spraying.

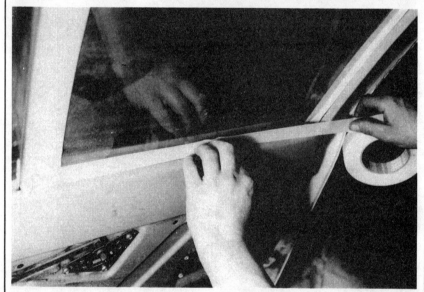

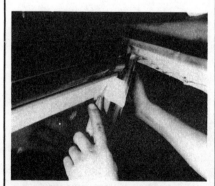

PP13. Excess tape can be trimmed off in the corners, using a very sharp knife.

PP14. Using several thicknesses of newspaper, cover up the exposed glass areas, by taping the newspapers to the previously laid single strip of masking tape.

PP15. When all the excess tape has been trimmed, the windows should look like this. Double check that the tape is where it should be, and that all the window glass area is covered.

PP16. If you are not going to remove the door handles, the easiest way of masking them is to wind masking tape around and along each handle, starting at one end, and working along to the other. Use several short lengths of tape, rather than one long one.

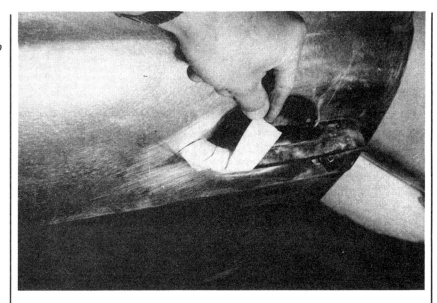

PP17. Cover the wheels and tyres completely. There are several ways of doing this, but we used some old car seat covers. These are easy to fit, and paint spray doesn't pass through them.

Applying the paint

If possible, choose a warm (but not scorching), dry day for spraying the car. Generally speaking, if working outside, or in an unheated garage, the minimum temperature for paint to go on 'properly' is around 15° Centigrade (60° Fahrenheit). It is not impossible to spray a car successfully at temperatures below this, but you are more likely to encounter paint runs and 'blooming' of the surface, and the paint takes far longer to dry.

If you are planning to spray the car outside (and this does have some advantages – mainly that you can move around the vehicle more easily, and the paint fumes are not contained in a confined area) – you need a CALM day. Any more than the slightest breeze will blow the paint spray all over the place, and whisk specks of dust onto your newly sprayed car. This is more than annoying.

Another problem with spraying outside can be insects –

they often land on wet paint, and this obviously causes havoc with the finish, so try to choose a day when the gnats are not about!

At this stage, the car should be almost ready for spraying, but there are a few more final preparations to carry out. Having mixed the primer with the appropriate thinners, and 'timed' the mix through a viscosity measuring cup, according to the working instructions for the paint you are using, the final steps prior to applying the paint involve 'anti-dust' measures. The floor areas around the car should already be swept clean, but

applying a little water will help dampen flying dust. The surface of the car, too, will need wiping. Start by using a 'spirit wipe' solution – obtainable from your paint suppliers. This removes grease, grime and dust from the surface. Don't touch the car again by hand before spraying. Give a final wipe over the vehicle with a 'tacky' cloth (a sticky cloth designed to collect fine dust particles from the surface – again, these can be bought, in packs of 10, from your paint supplier), and the car is ready. Give the primer a final stir before loading the spray gun, then don a suitable mask, and goggles.

ATP1. We used a 'high build' primer-surfacer, applied in several fairly thick coats, starting with the interior, the door shut panels, and the insides of the doors. These areas should always be sprayed before the outside of the vehicle. The main advantage of a 'high build' primer is that it fills minor surface imperfections; the more coats that are applied, the better the tiny holes, etc. will be filled. Allow the paint to harden in between coats. Apply the paint in smooth passes of the spraygun, overlapping each stroke just a little, by the same amount on each stroke, to get a smooth, even finish. The gun needs to be kept at the same angle to the car throughout each stroke. If you swing the gun in an arc, you will finish up with more paint on the car at the centre of each stroke, than at either end!

ATP2. We next sprayed the roof, the upper edges of the doors, and the rain channels, before moving on to the sides of the car, and large, flat panels, like the doors and wings. Keep the spraygun moving all the time, to avoid runs, and apply paint to the panels in strict sequence, the same for each coat. That way, you can't miss any part of the car! It is important that body ridges and sharp edges get more than their fair share of paint, both with primer and top coats.

Opinions vary regarding the correct sequence for spraying, some prefer to start with the roof, bonnet and boot lid, while others leave these until last. Personally, I prefer to get the paint on the roof first. This is normally the most difficult panel to spray, and you stand more chance of getting drips of paint on it from the gun, so take care. If your gun has a tendency to leak when tilted (and many do!), keep a rag held underneath the body of the gun, while you spray the horizontal sections.

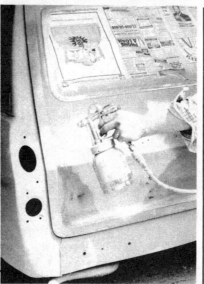

ATP3. When spraying the vertical panels, work your way round the car so that each section has a chance to dry before you reach it again on your next circuit of the vehicle. In any case, it is desirable to leave the paint a few minutes, at least, between coats, or the surface may sag.

174

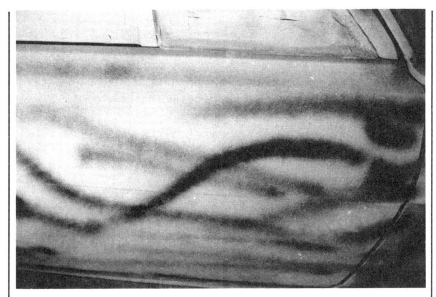

ATP4. When the primer has hardened, go round the car with an aerosal can of contrasting coloured paint, and create your own 'custom' masterpiece! The aim is to produce a very light coating of paint over most of the surface of the primer.

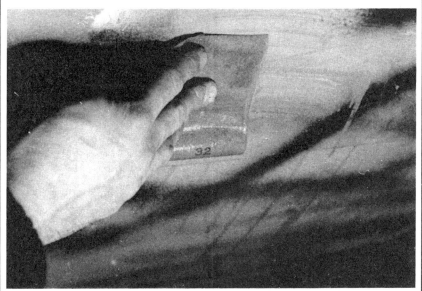

ATP5. Leave the car for several hours (preferably overnight), then, using 600 grade 'wet or dry' paper, rub down the surface of the primer until all the aerosol paint disappears. When all traces of the aerosol paint have gone, even those in the tiny 'orange peel' pits of the surface, you will be sure it is smooth enough to apply the top coats. Use plenty of warm, soapy water to keep the paper lubricated and clean during this operation.

ATP6. This Cortina was almost ready for the top coats, but this job is not one to be rushed. It is helpful to wheel the car out into daylight for a thorough inspection, to make sure that the surface is completely smooth.

ATP7. The car now needs to dry off completely, before you can proceed.

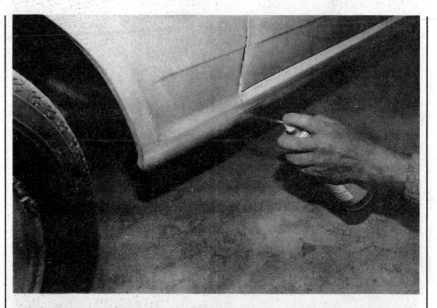

At this point, we masked off the lower sections of the body sills and front valance, and applied an 'anti-stone chip' protective coating, by aerosol can. This 'plastic' coating, once hard, helps bounce back stones, etc., from the road. When 'cured' (it takes several hours), top coats can be applied over it if desired. Or, if you prefer, you can apply it as a contrasting colour, over your final top coat.

ATP8. The car now needs another application of the 'spirit wipe', followed by a tacky cloth or two, to get rid of all dust particles, before applying the top colour coats. Again, paint the interior of the car and the insides of the doors, before moving on to the outside. Three good coats will be sufficient for the interior of the car, but four or five are preferable for the exterior. To achieve a good gloss, the final coats can be thinned rather more than the early ones. You need to get the paint to the point of running, without it actually doing so, for a shiny finish! This is obviously easier on horizontal surfaces than vertical ones.

ATP9. This is how the Cortina looked at the end of the spraying sessions. The best thing to do is to leave the car overnight, if possible, for the paint to harden.

After the respray

One of the most rewarding parts of a major restoration is seeing the car with all the masking paper removed, when it has just been resprayed. It is best to take the paper off fairly soon after the paint has become 'touch dry', since it is still then a little 'elastic', and a bit more forgiving when it comes to 'de-masking'. Nevertheless, great care is required when removing masking tape from the car, or the paint edges can be damaged.

To achieve a good gloss on the paintwork, you will probably need to 'cut back' the top coats, using 1200 grade 'wet or dry' paper, used wet, followed by cutting compound, applied with a foam mop. These can be bought quite cheaply in car accessory shops, for fitting to an electric drill.

AR1. When de-masking windows, tackle the centre first, removing the newspaper but leaving the outer tape in place.

AR2. Pull the outer strip of tape away from the rubber seals at an angle, and don't rush the job. Take your time, and the tape should come away cleanly, leaving the paint where it should be, on the car!

AR3. You may be one of the lucky people who are able to produce a brilliant gloss 'straight from the spraygun'. However, if, like most people, you are not that lucky, you will have to work a bit harder for that deep shine.

Leave the car for about a week after spraying, for the paint to harden fully, then, using 1200 grade 'wet or dry' paper, used very wet, and with lots of soap, gently rub the paint surface down, one panel at a time, until all the 'nibs' of paint are removed, leaving a semi-matt finish. Don't rub too hard, especially on raised body mouldings, panel edges, etc., or you will eventually reach the primer coats!

AR4. Apply a little rubbing compound to a foam rubber 'cutting mop' which, for best results, should be slightly damp. The mop fits in an electric drill, and literally 'grinds' the paint back to a smooth surface, ready for polishing. The slower the drill speed, the better – apply a LITTLE water to the mop head every so often – unplug the drill first, of course. If you use the mop 'dry' you risk burning the paint surface, and the mop head! When you have tackled the whole car in this manner (it takes about a day to do it properly), follow up with a mild liquid ◀ cutting agent ('colour restorer' polishes can be used), and, finally, with a coat or two of wax polish, for a gleaming shine. Wipe off the residues after each stage, with a clean rag, as you proceed through these steps.

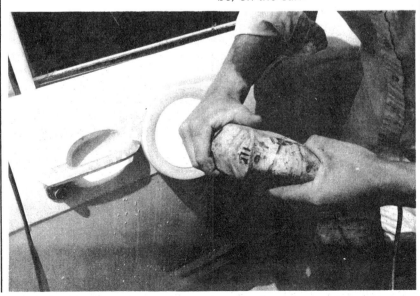

AR5. *The Cortina now looked quite smart, but the wheels had yet to be tackled (always spray those separately), and it was still minus its lights, trims and various other fixtures and fittings.*

Gilding the lily

The overall effect of a car which has been restored depends, to a large extent, on many items which, although small in themselves, are important as part of the whole vehicle. For example, a resprayed car will only look half decent if it has shabby wheels, dirty chrome and bent number plates.

Dealing with the 'odds and ends' can be extremely time-consuming, but it is worth doing properly. The end result will be a vehicle which looks smart, and which is 'tidy' in every respect. Whether you are intending to use the car as a 'concours' example or not, the satisfaction of having done the job properly means that you (and others) will get that much more pleasure from the vehicle.

GL1. *Wheels which exhibit great expanses of rust are ugly, so the first step is to scrape off all loose rust, and wire brush the rim all the way round. Follow this up with progressively finer grades of 'wet or dry' paper, or emery cloth to achieve a smooth finish, prior to application of your favourite rust treatment, and spraying. Wheel masks can be made quite easily from the side of an old cardboard carton. The paint can be discouraged from settling on the tyre by the application of washing-up liquid, spread into the rim well with a finger.*

GL2. *On these (non-original) wheels, we particularly wanted a 'hammered' silver finish, so we applied the paint, which also resists rust, by brush. The tyre was worn out anyway, so masking was unnecessary. If you are not fitting new tyres, clean the walls with soap and water, followed by a wipe with one of the widely available rubber cleaners. It will restore that 'as new' look in seconds.*

GL3. The grilles, whether Escort or Cortina, lose their crisp effect as they age, with stone chips in particular giving a 'spotty' appearance. The best course here is to re-paint all the black areas, using a semi-matt finish, polishing the bright metal sections only after the black paint has been allowed to dry for several days.

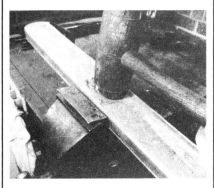

GL4. Minor dents in bumpers can be removed by clamping the bar in a vice, between two aluminium protectors, and tapping with a wooden or rubber hammer. This works wonders, even on quite 'crinkly' bumpers.

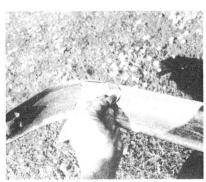

GL5. Rub down all surface rust behind the bumpers, and treat with a rust killer.

GL6. Use warm soapy water and a soft sponge to clean all accumulated grime from a chrome bumper, before attempting to polish it. Black bumpers, as fitted to the later Escort IIs, can be rubbed down and resprayed to restore their looks.

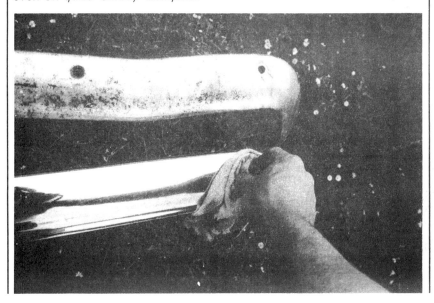

GL7. A proprietary chrome cleaner will clean even pitted rust from the surface; always apply a wax polish afterwards, and paint the back of the bumpers with an anti-rust paint, we chose a hammered silver finish for the rear of our Cortina and Escort bumpers. This looks smart, as well as protecting the metal, and is not too far off the original silvery 'metal' finish.

GL8. A new set of number plates will transform the appearance of the car – far more than might be appreciated. Take care to mount the plates on an even keel. If one end of the plate is higher than the other, it rather spoils the effect!

GL9. It is worth spending some time cleaning up the bodywork badges. A small tooth brush and lots of hot, soapy water are helpful. Use neat washing-up liquid for stubborn marks. Follow up with a dose of chrome cleaner, followed by wax polish.

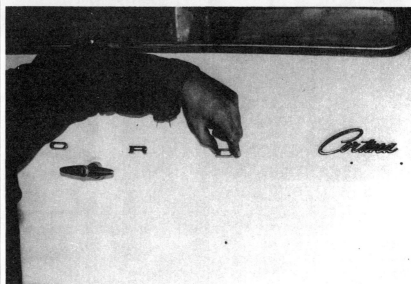

Rustproofing

If you are investing a great deal of time and money in restoring a car, it makes sense to protect the 'investment' by ensuring that it will be preserved well into the future. Therefore steps taken now to minimise the chances of attack by rust are well worth taking. Already, in the text, I have mentioned some of the ways in which you can discourage rust from forming on the car. Treating the inside of exposed chassis beams to a coat of anti-rust paint, during restoration work, the use of stone resistant coatings on the lower edges of the bodywork, and the sealing of bumpers from the rear, by painting them, are just three examples. It is also worthwhile using a seam sealant between newly welded panels, for example on sills and under-wing areas.

The approach to rustproofing can vary a great deal, but the main aim is to prevent moisture and salt from coming into contact with bare metal, or rust will quickly form, and eat the metal away!

You are at a disadvantage at the outset, with an older car, since rust will inevitably already be present over much of the underbody. The first step on any rustproofing operation on an old car is therefore to kill existing rust. This, again, can be tackled in a number of ways, but in all cases, start by grinding, scraping or brushing loose rust from the affected surfaces (WEAR GOGGLES). A chemical rust killer can then be applied. These vary in their contents and methods of application, but, for best results, follow the instructions on the can TO THE LETTER. You then have a good chance of the product giving its best.

Having killed the rust, the metal needs to be protected. Some people like to spray the

underside of the vehicle with old engine oil. This is certainly effective, if repeated, say, annually, but it is rather messy, and makes future maintenance under the car rather unpleasant.

Another approach is to paint the entire underbody with a rust resistant paint, which will prevent water from reaching the steel below it. Underbody seal also keeps out water, but is not normally chemically rust resistant; it relies on total coverage to prevent water from attacking the metal.

Particularly popular these days are the wax based solutions, which can be sprayed over the underbody, into box sections and 'chassis' members, and inside door panels. etc. Such waxes are cleaner than old engine oil, have a 'self-healing' effect if battered by flying stones, and are easy to apply.

Whatever method you decide upon, none are 'forever' treatments – check at least once a year that the *whole* underbody area is protected. Damaged areas of paint, wax or underbody seal should be re-treated immediately, or rust will soon take a hold on the exposed metal.

You can, of course, adopt a 'belt and braces' approach, first applying anti-rust paint, then a wax anti-rust fluid, or one of the new underbody sealing compounds which also contain wax.

Finally, hose down the underside of the car AT LEAST twice a year, to remove all mud and salt.

R1.   Use a wire brush to remove loose surface rust from underbody areas (WEAR GOGGLES).

R2.   Still wearing the goggles, follow up the initial brushing with another rub down, using coarse grade emery cloth, or 'wet and dry' paper, used dry. A chemical rust treatment can then be applied.

R3.   Anti-rust paint can then be applied, and normally, the thicker the coating, the better. I applied two thick coats to the underside of this Cortina estate car.

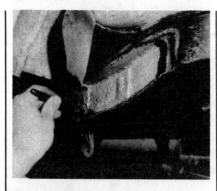

R4. When chassis beams are 'opened up' for repair work, treat accessible parts of the interior of the beam with an anti-rust coating. DON'T use wax prior to welding; it will ignite.

R7. A wax-based anti-rust treatment, like Waxoyl, can be applied on top of existing paint surfaces, if desired. We had already painted the underbody on this Cortina, and applied the wax on top of the paint, for extra protection – especially important where, as in this case, the car is to be used every day, all year round. Newspapers, placed directly underneath the area being sprayed, will stop the garage floor from becoming very slippery!

R5. If any repairs have been made to the floor of the car, coat them before re-fitting the carpets. Finnigan's Hammerite is an ideal finish for this sort of job, and for underbody work. It requires no primer, is quick-drying (10-15 minutes), and resists rust. It also has a 'hammered' finish which conceals all brush marks!

R6. Any metal can be protected by painting, and, while they are off the vehicle, it is worthwhile painting the insides of the hub caps, the fuel tank, and behind the bumpers. The exhaust system needs a special, heat-resistant paint; ordinary paint just burns off.

R8. An extension tube enables the wax treatment to be injected into sills, chassis box members, and so on. By pulling the tube back through the sill, the entire interior surface can be coated. Again, place newspapers around the car to absorb stray wax. If you have any foil containers, or tins, place them under the drain holes to catch the waxy fluid as it drips out; it can then be used to treat other parts of the car.

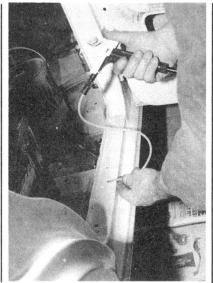

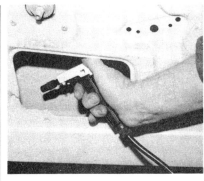

R9. Treat the insides of the doors, making sure that all the surfaces are coated. Always wear old shoes and clothes when doing this job, you are bound to spill some of the wax during application.

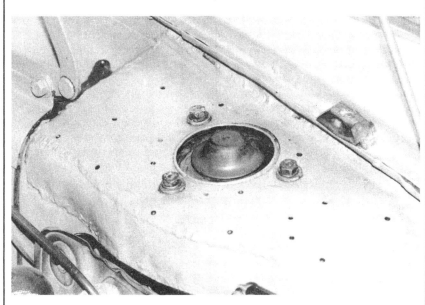

R10. Rust around the upper front suspension mountings is, of course, commonplace on Cortinas and Escorts. One way to be sure of stopping the trouble once and for all is to drill a series of holes around the mountings, JUST through the upper plate, and periodically fill them with Waxoyl. The wax will fill the cavity below the top plate, and prevent rust – if the treatment is repeated, you should never be troubled with rust here again. Fill the bonnet cavities with wax, too. This Mark I Cortina has been so treated for several years, without a sign of rust appearing.

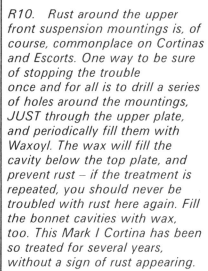

R11. Badges can be potential trouble areas, when it comes to rust, especially if the paint around the badge holes is slightly chipped. A squirt of water dispellant spray, like WD40, applied regularly, will keep rust at bay. The fluid has a creeping effect and will reach parts that thicker fluids cannot get to. Aerosol cans like this, with an extension nozzle, are also useful for reaching into holes in the body pillars, etc., for protecting the metal within. It is important to repeat the application at regular intervals.

5 Mechanical Components

Mechanical components

If your restoration project is a long term one, where time 'off the road' is not too important, it doesn't really make much difference in which order you tackle the various refurbishing jobs. However, you may need the car to be mobile for everyday use, as soon as possible. Therefore, having mastered the bodywork, it makes sense to sort out the mechanical components next, leaving the interior trim until later. You can gain an MoT certificate once the engine, brakes, suspension and steering have been put to rights and then, providing that there are seats in the vehicle, you can use it on the road, tackling the interior on a 'running restoration' basis.

Most mechanical jobs can be tackled using basic tools; with 'AF' spanners for Cortinas and Mark I Escorts, and metric spanners for the Mark II Escorts.

Engine work

Cylinder head overhaul

If you have acquired a car which appears to be lacking power, yet oil consumption is negligible, and all the routine service points have been cleared of blame (valve clearances, spark plugs, high tension leads, contact points, ignition timing and carburettor settings, and so on), the chances are that a cylinder head overhaul is needed. This is a job which can be tackled at home within a weekend, even if you have never previously undertaken such mechanical work. Removing the cylinder head, cleaning out the carbon and grinding in the valves will make a surprising difference, to performance *and* fuel economy.

The principles of a cylinder head or 'top' overhaul are the same for all models, Cortina and Escort, although there are of course detail differences, notably on the 'fast' versions, with respect to the layout of the valve gear and overhead camshaft driving arrangements, where appropriate. For detailed analysis of these areas, reference should be made to the appropriate *Haynes Owners' Workshop Manual,* or to the relevant Ford publications relating to the engine concerned.

The stripdown depicted here was on a cross-flow 'Kent' engine, the earlier non cross-flow engines requiring similar dismantling procedures.

Always disconnect the battery before you start work, to prevent the chance of an accidental short circuit.

The cooling system will need to be drained too before you start work in earnest, either by releasing the radiator drain tap (if fitted), or disconnecting the bottom hose from the radiator stub. Use a clean bowl to catch the coolant in, if you intend to re-use the anti-freeze solution.

No special tools are required, apart from a valve spring compressor, and possibly a valve seat cutter. You may be able to hire these items if you do not possess them.

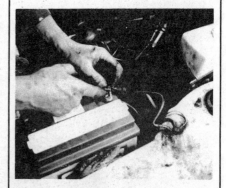

CHO1. ALWAYS disconnect the battery, so that there is no possibility of sparks flying accidentally, when working.

CH02. Take out the securing bolts, and lift off the air cleaner housing.

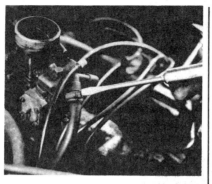

CH04. Unscrew the fuel inlet pipe at the carburettor union, and pull the pipe away, then disconnect the vacuum and vent pipes at the carburettor.

CH06. The whole throttle cable and return spring assembly can then be lifted aside, after taking out the two securing bolts at the manifold.

CH03. Disconnect the choke cable from the carburettor, by slackening the screw in the clamp. Don't take the screw right out – it is easily lost.

CH05. The throttle link rod is separated from the carburettor by prising it out of its retaining clip.

CH07. The coolant hoses need to be separated from the manifold; simply unscrew the clips and gently pull each hose from its stub. If fitting new hoses, a little washing-up liquid, applied to the stubs, will allow the hoses to slide on more easily.

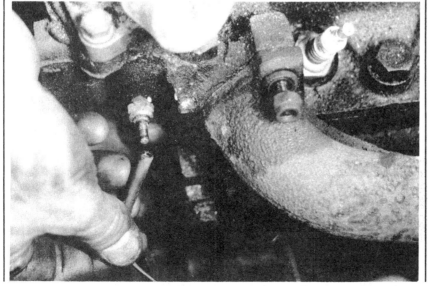

CH08. Disconnect the temperature gauge sender wire (where fitted) from the front of the cylinder head – simply pull the connector away from the head.

CHO9. Slacken the two exhaust pipe retaining nuts, at the manifold to pipe joint. There is no need to take off these two nuts, unless you wish to remove the manifold from the vehicle. Now release the nuts securing the exhaust manifold, and pull this away from the engine. On pre cross-flow engines, the inlet and exhaust manifolds are, of course, on the same side of the motor, and are withdrawn together.

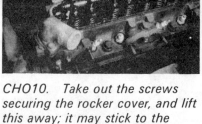

CHO10. Take out the screws securing the rocker cover, and lift this away; it may stick to the gasket, at first, needing gentle 'persuasion' with a screwdriver, or by tapping with a rubber mallet.

CHO11. Starting with the two centre attachment points, release the four bolts/nuts securing the rocker shaft to the cylinder head, and remove the shaft. Check each rocker for side play on the shaft, and the rocker pads for indentations at the points of contact with the valve stems.

CHO12. Carefully withdraw the pushrods, placing them in order on a clean sheet of newspaper, and keeping them well out of the way of grit and dust. An old egg carton, suitably punched and numbered, can be used to store the pushrods until they are cleaned and re-fitted. It is safest to cover them, and any other internal engine components removed, with a clean rag, until required for re-fitting.

186

CHO13. Slacken the cylinder head retaining bolts in the appropriate sequence shown in the diagram, depending on whether your engine is a cross-flow, or pre cross-flow unit (please see CHO14.). When all the bolts are loose, take them out and store in a clean place.

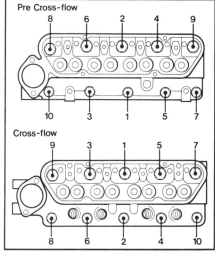

Pre Cross-flow

8 6 2 4 9

10 3 1 5 7

Cross-flow

9 3 1 5 7

8 6 2 4 10

CHO14. The recommended cylinder head bolt loosening and tightening sequences vary slightly between pre cross-flow and cross-flow cars. Follow the sequence applicable to your engine.

CHO15. The cylinder head can now be lifted away from the engine. If it sticks, try 'rocking' it against the cylinder block, or tap it with a rubber mallet. Avoid prising it away from the cylinder block with a screwdriver or lever, of you could damage the block or head surfaces.

CHO16. We left the inlet manifold in place on the cylinder head until this was lifted off, since the securing bolts/nuts are easier to get at with the head off the car.

CHO17.   Carbon must be removed from the piston crowns, and the quickest way to do this is to use a special 'decoke' wire brush in an electric drill (WEAR GOGGLES – the carbon fragments fly around), with the pistons at the top of their cylinders. Use insulating or masking tape to cover the apertures for oil and water channels in the cylinder block, having first wiped the block face with a rag damped with cellulose thinners. The thinners will dissolve gasket remnants, and free the surface from grease, allowing the tape to stick.

Use rag or paper, stuffed into the other two cylinders, to prevent dust from entering. Always wipe the piston tops clean on completion; they can be polished, if desired, using a metal polish.

The ports in the exhaust manifold can also be cleaned by using a rotary wire brush. If you find it easier, remove the manifold, for cleaning on the bench. Blow out all dust afterwards.

CHO19.   The carbon can be cleaned from the cylinder head by using a rotary wire brush, as for the piston tops. Alternatively, you could use an old hacksaw blade or similar, for scraping the flat surfaces clean, and . . .

CHO18.   The cylinder head must be dismantled, in order to assess the state of the valves and their seats, and the combustion chambers. Use a valve spring compressor to compress the springs while the split cotters and valve stem oil seals are removed. The top of the valve spring may need to be tapped gently with a soft faced hammer, to dislodge it.

SAFETY NOTE: ALWAYS keep your face well back from the springs during this operation, and make sure that the valve springs are always pointed AWAY from people. Make sure that the valve spring compressor is correctly aligned before compressing the valve. If it slips, and the spring is released, when under tension, the results could be disastrous.

CHO20. . . . an old, blunt screwdriver, for cleaning the internal passages within the cylinder head. This does take rather longer, though. When the cylinder head is clean, check the valves for side play in their guides. If more than just perceptible movement is evident, the guides (machined directly into the cylinder head) will need to be over-bored, necessitating the purchase of larger diameter valves, to suit, or 'boring and sleeving', if standard valves are to be used again. You will need the help of an engine reconditioning firm, or machine shop, for this.

CH021. Inspect the valve seats; if they look badly pitted, use a valve seat cutter to JUST remove the pits. Don't overdo it; this tool removes metal, and, if you go too far, the valve seat will become 'pocketed', and a valve seat insert will then be needed. A couple of smooth turns under medium hand pressure are usually sufficient, unless the damage is severe. Wipe away all swarf with a clean rag.

The valves and seats will normally need a little light 'grinding in', to ensure an efficient, gas-tight seal. The 'official' Ford recommendation, for their pre-1971 engines, which have a wear-resistant, diffused aluminium coating on the inlet valve faces, is NOT to grind these in. This is because the grinding will remove the aluminium coating. Instead, if pitting is present in the inlet valve faces/seats, they recommend re-cutting the valve seats, or lapping in the valve seats using a 'dummy' valve, and fitting new inlet valves.

However, in practice, the old valves can be lightly ground in, where pitting is not severe, provided care is taken.

CH022. Replace any badly pitted valves (normally the exhausts), and clean up the remainder, using a rotary wire brush or a scraper, then place a little fine grinding paste around the valve seat, with a matchstick. Four small blobs are sufficient. Using a suction valve grinding stick, twist the valve backwards and forwards a few times, then lift the valve from its seat, turn it through 90 degrees, and repeat the operation two or three times. Make sure that NO grinding paste reaches the stem of the valve, or the guide.

It is best to avoid using coarse grinding paste where possible; it is usually only necessary when dealing with deep pits. If you do need to use coarse paste, always follow up with a final lapping-in using fine grade paste.

CHO23. When you are left with a continuous, unbroken ring of paste around the valve seat, wipe the remnants of the paste from the valve and seat, and you should have a smooth, uniform surface on both, like this. Use a rag soaked in paraffin to clean away all traces of the grinding paste. Paraffin can also be used at this stage to rid surplus dirt from the outside of the cylinder head. Make sure that no grit enters the ports and valve guides.

CHO24. Always fit new valve stem oil seals when rebuilding the head; these are included with the 'top overhaul' gasket set anyway.

CHO25. Place the new head gasket on the cylinder block, so that the holes align with those in the block. Apply a little clean engine oil to each of the cylinder walls, to provide initial lubrication on start-up.

CHO26. Always use new manifold gaskets; we assembled the inlet manifold to the head, before re-fitting the head to the vehicle.

CHO27. The cylinder head is now placed very carefully onto its new gasket, so that all the holes align, and the retaining bolts are replaced. Tighten the bolts to 65-70 lb.ft (pre cross-flow and cross-flow engines), in the order indicated previously (please see CHO14). It is best to tighten the cylinder head bolts a little at a time, in stages, to approximately 5 lb.ft., 25 lb.ft., and 50 lb.ft., then 65-70 lb.ft. Re-check after running the engine for about a quarter of an hour, and again after about 500 miles. Check torque figure settings with the appropriate workshop manual.

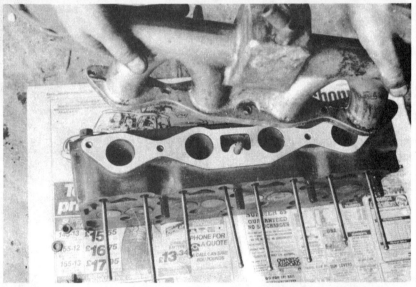

CHO28. The valve clearances need to be re-set once the rocker shaft has been torqued down to 17-22 lb.ft. (pre cross-flow and cross-flow engines). Set the clearances, and then re-check. Conventional screw and locknut adjusters are employed, except on late Mark I, and Mark II Escorts, which have hollow hexagonal adjuster nuts. These self-locking nuts should only be moved with a ring or socket spanner.

Valve clearances

The method of checking the valve clearances varies between the pre cross-flow cars and the cross-flow models.

Pre cross-flow

For pre cross-flow models (i.e. Mark I Cortinas, and Mark IIs to September, 1967), the 'Rule of Nine' may be used. That is to say, turn the engine (clockwise when viewed from front) until the valve no. 1 (counting from the front) is fully open. Check/adjust the clearance on no. 8. Check the clearance on no. 7 with no. 2 fully open, and so on. In each case, the sum of the valve 'numbers' is nine. Alternatively, use the following sequence:

Valves open	Check/adjust Valves
1 and 6	3 (in.) and 8 (ex.)
2 and 4	5 (ex.) and 7 (in.)
3 and 8	1 (ex.) and 6 (in.)
5 and 7	2 (in.) and 4 (ex.)

The clearance should be set, with the engine cold, to 0.008 in. (0.20 mm.), inlets, and 0.018 in. (0.46 mm.), exhausts, except for GT models, on which the clearances are 0.010 in. (0.25 mm.), inlets, and 0.023 in. (0.58 mm.), exhausts. When the engine has been warmed up to normal operating temperature, check again, and if necessary, re-set the clearances to 0.010 in. (0.25 mm.), inlets, and 0.017 in. (0.43 mm.), exhausts, except for GTs, on which the clearances should be 0.012 in. (0.30 mm.), inlets, and 0.022 in. (0.56 mm.), exhausts. There is a little leeway in the (cold) valve clearances quoted. For non-GT engines, it is acceptable for the clearances to be up to 0.002 in. wider than those quoted, but NO TIGHTER. On GT engines, a tolerance of 0.001 in. either side of the (cold) figures quoted is acceptable.

Cross-flow, Cortina

The valves are checked/adjusted in the same sequence as for the pre cross-flow models. The clearances (engine cold) are 0.008 to 0.010 in. (0.20 to 0.25 mm.), inlets, and 0.018 to 0.020 in. (0.46 to 0.51 mm.), exhausts, except for the 1600 GT, on which

the clearances (cold) are 0.011 to 0.013 in. (0.28 to 0.33 mm.), inlets, and 0.021 to 0.023 in. (0.53 to 0.58 mm.), exhausts. The 'hot' settings are identical to the pre cross-flow models.

Cross-flow, Escort

The same valve checking/ adjusting sequence is used as for the Cortinas.

MARK I: The valve clearances (cold) for 1100 and 1300 Non-GT models are 0.008 in. to 0.010 in. (0.20 mm. to 0.025 mm.), inlets, and 0.018 in. to 0.020 in. (0.46 to 0.51 mm.), exhausts. The 'hot' settings are 0.010 in. (0.25 mm.), inlets, and 0.017 in. (0.43 mm.), exhausts.

For 1300 GT, 1300 Sport and 1300E models, the clearances (cold) are 0.011 to 0.013 in. (0.28 to 0.33 mm.), inlets, and 0.021 to 0.023 in. (0.53 to 0.58 mm.), exhausts. The 'hot' settings are 0.012 in. (0.31 mm.), inlets, and 0.022 in. (0.56 mm.), exhausts.

MARK II: The valve clearances (cold) for standard 1.1 and 1.3 litre engines are 0.008 in. (0.20 mm.), inlets, and 0.022 in. (0.55 mm.), exhausts. The clearances for GT models are 0.010 in. (0.25 mm.), inlets, and 0.022 in. (0.55 mm.), exhausts.

CHO29. Finally, lubricate the valve gear with a little clean engine oil, before replacing the rocker cover.

Engine Out?

It is possible to carry out some overhaul operations on the engine while it is in the vehicle. These include, on all models, cylinder head work, and, on the Cortinas, removal of the sump for attention to the big ends and lower part of the engine. However, for a complete engine overhaul, the motor must come out. On Cortinas and Escorts, this involves lifting the engine, rather than, with some cars, 'dropping' the engine and gearbox assembly out from below the vehicle. Therefore heavy duty lifting tackle is a MUST, and it is also a great help to have assistance when you are removing and replacing the unit. Another pair of hands is useful for guiding the engine out of the car, and back in again, and for keeping sharp metal projections clear of the vehicle's paintwork, for example. The procedures are similar for Cortina and Escort models.

Engine clean-up

Engines naturally become dirty in use, unless efforts are made to keep them clean, and, in all probability, the engine on your restoration project will be filthy. It is worth spending some time trying to get the worst of the grime off the engine and the surrounding bodywork, BEFORE you attempt to take the motor out. This way, you will have less

cleaning work to do later, but, more important still, the engine will be more pleasant to deal with, and less dangerous, since it will not be so slippery. A proprietary de-greasing solution can be used; it is sprayed or brushed onto the oily sections, then rinsed off with water. Obviously, the rinse water will contain a great deal of grease, so it is a good idea to lay as many old newspapers and drip trays as possible, beneath the car. This will help keep grease off the drive, and will create a better impression as far as your partner/parents are concerned. Greasy footmarks on the hall carpet tend to encourage uncomplimentary remarks about old motor cars and the people who restore them.

The rinsing operation can be carried out using a garden hose. However, if you don't have one, a good alternative is one of the pressure garden sprayers. These contain a couple of gallons of water, and force it out under pressure. The jet is quite powerful, and, of course, you use much less water than with a hose, so the risk of greasy water running everywhere is far less. Another advantage is that you can fill the container with *hot* soapy water, which helps the grease come away from the engine more easily.

ECU1. Whichever way you looked at this Cortina engine, it was filthy. For a long time it had been blowing black engine oil all over the engine bay, and this grime is always best removed before the engine comes out.

ECU2. Place as many drip trays and old newspapers under the engine bay as you can muster. This helps avoid oily footprints, and the resulting, unnecessary problems that these tend to cause!

192

ECU3. Start by pouring a little de-greasing fluid into a suitable container (foil dishes obtainable with Chinese takeaway food are ideal!).

ECU4. Use an old paintbrush to coat the entire engine and surrounding surfaces with the de-greasing solution, then allow a few minutes for it to 'work' its way into the grease. Repeat the application on particularly thick deposits.

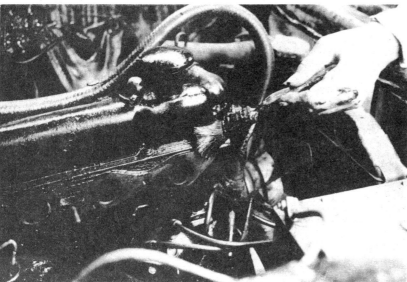

ECU5. Using a garden hose, or a garden pressure sprayer, rinse off the grease. Once dry, the engine will be far more pleasant to work on.

ECU6. The engine compartment on this Cortina was particularly oily. However, an hour's work with the de-greasing solution and garden sprayer left it a lot cleaner. It was then much easier to find items like the engine mountings, and so on.

Engine removal

The engines can be removed from Cortinas and Escorts using normal open-ended, ring and socket spanners. You will also need heavy duty lifting tackle, and a *strong* beam or frame from which to hang it.

The engine can be removed complete with the gearbox, but to do this, the assembly has to be lifted comparatively high over the front of the car, and at a very steep angle. It is for this reason that it is often easier to separate the engine from the gearbox, lifting the engine out first, and releasing the gearbox afterwards. The weight of the 'lump' to lift over the front of the car is also far less, doing it this way.

In addition, on the Cortinas, you may find it necessary to remove the front cross-member and/or steering components, to allow the engine and gearbox to be withdrawn as an assembly.

If you leave the gearbox in place in the vehicle, you must leave a support under the front of the bellhousing, to take the weight of the gearbox, once the engine is clear.

ER1. Start by disconnecting the battery leads and the battery retaining clamp, and lift the battery out of the vehicle. This cuts out the possibility of accidental short-circuits, and leaves more room for working on the engine.

ER2. Next, disconnect the carburettor links and pipework, and release the inlet manifold from the engine. On pre cross-flow engines, the inlet and exhaust manifolds come off together, once the exhaust pipe to manifold connection has been separated.

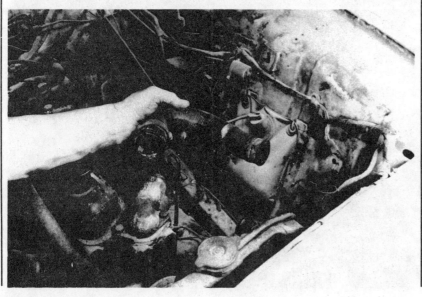

ER3. Slacken the securing clips, and take off the top and bottom hoses, after draining the cooling system. This is achieved by releasing the radiator drain tap, if fitted, or by slackening the lower clip on the bottom hose, and by unscrewing the cylinder block drain tap. This is on the exhaust side of the engine, at the rear of the cylinder block.

ER4. Take out the four securing bolts from the front panel, and lift the radiator clear. Beware of dregs of water draining from the radiator as it is lifted out.

ER5. Disconnect the engine electrics, labelling the wires as you do so. This saves a great deal of time when re-fitting the engine.

ER6. Release the petrol pipe from the fuel tank, at its entry point to the fuel pump. Make sure that the petrol doesn't syphon out from the tank, by securing the fuel feed pipe out of the way, and above tank level, if necessary. DEFINITELY NO SMOKING!

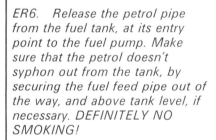

ER7. Slacken the two nuts holding the exhaust pipe to the manifold, and lower the front end of the exhaust pipe down through the engine bay. Make sure that the exhaust system and its mountings are not strained; support the pipe on wood blocks, or tie it to the vehicle, if necessary.

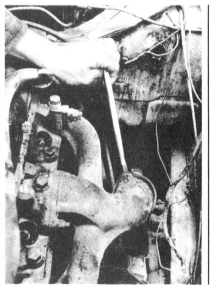

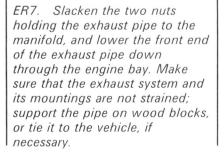

ER8. Release the engine mountings, initially, by taking off the single bolt on the outside of each unit.

ER9. The bell-housing bolts and the starter motor can now be released.

ER10. As a precaution, in addition to a mobile support (trolley jack) below the gearbox, we rigged up an additional support above it. By cutting a timber plank to the width of the engine bay, this was made to sit across the tops of the inner wings. From this we suspended an 'emergency' sling of stout nylon cord, which passed below the gearbox bell housing. This allowed the car to be pushed backwards or forwards, as desired, which helped in positioning the vehicle relative to the engine hoist.

ER11. The bonnet needs to be removed, or else tied right back as far as it will go, to allow clearance for the engine hoist, and for the engine to come out. We made a cradle of stout rope, to support the weight of the engine at four points.

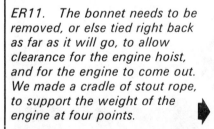

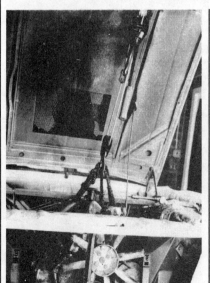

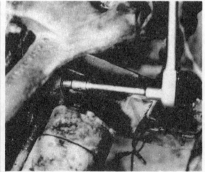

We attached the engine hoist to a reinforced steel girder, built into the garage roof for the purpose of lifting engines. If your garage hasn't got strong beams, or indeed if you have no garage, you need to buy, rent or borrow a proper engine lifting frame. This stands above the front of the car, on legs, and will allow the engine to be lifted out quite easily. You will also need a strong hoist, if not integral with the lifting frame.

ER12. With the engine raised slightly, at least one of the engine mounting brackets can be released from the cylinder block. This makes the engine easier to manoeuvre.

196

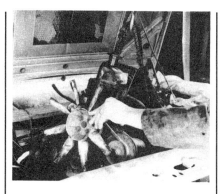

ER13. As the engine is raised, the cooling fan may hit the front panel. Therefore, twist the motor sideways as it is lifted.

ER14. When the engine sump has cleared the upper front cross-panel, push the car back (or wheel your engine frame and hoist forwards, if they will move), so that the engine can be lowered CAREFULLY to the ground. Keep your fingers clear of any pulley mechanisms, and your feet well away from the area immediately below the engine.

Engine stripdown

Once the engine is out of the car, work can begin on stripping it, to evaluate how much work needs doing to it. It is worth pointing out at this stage that if the engine is very badly worn, it may well be cheaper to buy an exchange reconditioned unit, which will also carry a guarantee, than to replace all the worn parts in your own engine. It is impossible to

give hard and fast rules about reconditioning, since engines can vary so much in the degree of wear present. However, if the pistons and cylinder walls are in good condition, and the crankshaft is not scored or badly worn, new oil control piston rings and a set of big-end shells will extend the working life of the engine considerably. If, on the other hand, bore wear is excessive, and the main and big-end bearings are found to be seriously worn, it is best either to fit a reconditioned engine, or to completely overhaul your own unit. The time and money spent now will be repaid in terms of a sweet running, quiet engine, which is reliable and which doesn't burn oil.

The stripdown steps are similar for Cortina and Escort engines, pre cross-flow and cross-flow units. No 'special' tools are necessary, although, as with any engine, a piston ring compressor will be needed when fitting the pistons.

Start dismantling by removing the cylinder head as described in the 'Cylinder Head Overhaul' section, then take off the clutch assembly (please see 'Gearbox Out/Clutch Change' section). Ancillary units such as the fuel pump, dynamo/alternator, oil filter housing/oil pump, and the distributor can

also be unbolted now. When removing the distributor, release the main securing bolt, leaving the clamp bolt in position. This way, the basic ignition timing is retained.

From the rumbling and clattering coming from the bottom of this engine, we were fairly certain that the crankshaft and bearings were badly worn, so we anticipated removing the crankshaft for re-grinding anyway. The first step was therefore to take off the flywheel. Support the engine securely on wood blocks during the dismantling operations; it makes life easier and safer.

ES1. Use a socket and a long lever to release the flywheel retaining bolts; you may need an assistant to hold a long screwdriver or strong bar against the flywheel ring gear teeth, to prevent the flywheel from turning as the bolts are moved, initially. Alternatively, you could fit a ring spanner to the crankshaft pulley bolt, and wedge the spanner against the floor. By holding the engine down with your foot, while pulling on the flywheel bolts, they should come undone! Take care that the spanners don't slip.

ES2. Lift the flywheel from the engine, and examine the ring gear teeth. If they appear to be worn in any section, a new ring gear will be needed.

A new ring gear can be shrunk onto the flywheel at home, after gently chiselling the old one off, WITHOUT damaging the flywheel. Drill between two of the ring gear teeth, then split the ring gear at this point, using a sharp chisel, hit with a soft-faced hammer. The new ring gear now has to be heated up relative to the flywheel, to enable it to be 'shrunk' on. This can be achieved by heating the ring gear EVENLY (on firebricks or similar) with an oxy-acetylene torch or blowlamp. It is VITAL that the ring gear is not over-heated, during this operation, or it will lose its 'temper'. Therefore, for non cross-flow engines, keep the temperature below 204°C. This is indicated when a pre-polished section of the ring turns a light yellow. If you polish four, equally spaced, sections of the outside of the ring gear before you start, it will be easy to identify how the temperature is going. On later cars, the maximum temperature permitted is 316°C, indicated by a polished section turning DARK blue. If it turns light metallic blue, it's too hot! Hold the ring gear at the required temperature for five minutes, then quickly fit it, squarely, to the flywheel, with the chamfered sections of the teeth facing the gearbox side of the flywheel. Tap it gently home, minding your fingers, as it will be VERY hot! On cars with pre-engaged starters, there are no chamfers on the ring gear teeth, so it doesn't matter which way round the ring gear is fitted onto the flywheel. Always allow the flywheel assembly to cool naturally; never quench it.

An alternative is to place the ring gear in a domestic cooker oven for about half an hour (on a 'hot' setting, bearing in mind the maximum permissible temperatures quoted), and the flywheel in the refrigerator for the same period, to get the maximum temperature differential. The ring gear can then be tapped squarely into position on the flywheel (mind your fingers, the ring gear will be VERY hot). The ring gear will then grip the flywheel very tightly, as the two assume the same temperature. Whichever method you use, take care, or the new ring gear could get damaged in the fitting process. If you have any doubts, or if in any case you are 'banned' from using the domestic oven and refrigerator for such technical jobs, it would be best to take ring gear and flywheel to an engineering shop or engine reconditioning firm, and ask them to do the work for you.

ES3. At the other end of the motor, take out the bolts securing the cooling fan, then remove it.

ES4. Take out the water pump, and check the bearings for play, if more than just perceptible movement of the shaft is evident, it would be wise to invest in a new pump. If there are water stains on the underside of the pump, coming from the seal, rather than the gasket face, this again is an 'early warning' sign of the pump's imminent failure.

ES5. The crankshaft pulley is removed by releasing the central bolt; the crankshaft can be prevented from turning initially, by an assistant holding a bar across the flywheel bolts, screwed back into the end of the crankshaft. Use a pair of levers or long screwdrivers to ease the pulley from the shaft. Don't lose the Woodruff key. The timing chain cover is next to come off.

ES6. The engine can now be turned on its side, or even upside down, and the sump pan taken off. Simply release all the securing bolts from the underside of the engine, a little at a time. Unbolt the timing chain cover, too, and remove it.

ES7. Wedge the crankshaft by placing a length of wood or a hammer handle between the shaft and the cylinder block wall. Knock back the lock tabs, and take out the two camshaft sprocket retaining bolts, by using a socket spanner, through the holes in the sprocket.

ES8. Pull the dished oil thrower from the crankshaft, noting that the base of the dish faces the crankshaft.

Check the free play in the timing chain midway between the camshaft and crankshaft sprockets. If this exceeds half an inch, the chain should be replaced. It is best to replace the chain, anyway, as a matter of course, at a major overhaul.

Gently lever the sprockets, still inside the timing chain, from the camshaft and crankshaft. Examine the sprocket teeth, and if badly worn (with a 'hooked' appearance), replace the sprockets, as well as the chain.

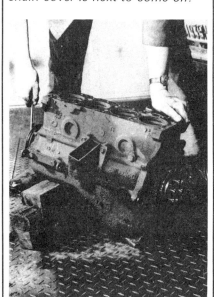

199

ES9.   At the other end of the engine, unbolt the crankshaft rear main bearing cover, which contains the rear oil seal. The oil seal should be replaced.

ES10.   The oil pump pick-up pipe and strainer should be taken off, and cleaned in fresh paraffin.

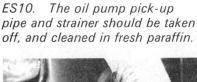

ES11.   Take out the big-end securing bolts, keeping the numbered caps in strict sequence on the bench; they MUST go back with their respective connecting rods, on re-fitting.

The main bearing caps too can be removed, again keeping them in order. Gentle tapping with a soft-faced mallet may be needed, to encourage the bearing caps to part company with the engine.

ES12.   The crankshaft can be lifted away from the cylinder block, and carefully placed on the bench, for subsequent examination and checking for wear.

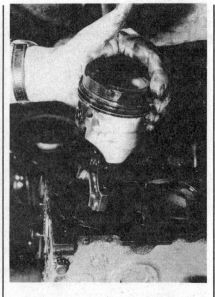

ES13.   The pistons, now free, are withdrawn up the cylinders, complete with their connecting rods. The black marks on the side of the piston are signs of excessive 'blow-by', due to piston ring/cylinder bore wear. However, only careful measurement will determine how badly worn the pistons and cylinders are.

The cylinder bores need to be examined and assessed for taper, ovality, and scoring. Ideally, a micrometer should be used to measure the cylinder bore diameter just under the 'wear' ridge at the top of the cylinder, and then the diameter at the unworn, lower, section of the bore. If the difference between the two diameters is more than 0.006 in. (0.1524 mm.), then special oil control pistons and/or rings are needed, or a rebore and new pistons. If you have no micrometer, the degree of wear can still be assessed. Take the rings from a piston and slide the piston down each cylinder in turn, about 3/4 inch down the cylinder. Then attempt to slide a 0.010 in. (0.25 mm.) feeler gauge blade between the piston and the cylinder wall, on the thrust side of the engine (that is, the exhaust side). If the feeler gauge passes through, either a set of oil control piston rings or a rebore, are required. As a rough guide, provided wear is not too excessive, a set of oil control rings should give another 15,000 to 30,000 miles motoring, dependent on use, before a rebore is unavoidable, at around one third of the cost. Oil control piston rings can normally take care of up to around 0.004 inch of wear for each inch of cylinder

diameter. Therefore, in theory, on these Fords, with a bore diameter of just over three inches, up to around 0.012 in. of bore wear can be dealt with by fitting a set of oil control rings.

If you decide to fit new oil control rings to the existing pistons, the pistons must be in good condition. Take off the old rings, and clean out the grooves very carefully. A short section, cleanly broken from one of the old rings, is ideal for this job. Before fitting the new rings, place each ring in turn about two inches down the cylinder in which it is proposed to fit it, and measure the gap between the ends of the ring. This should be between 0.009 and 0.014 in. (0.23 to 0.36 mm.). Check the gap again at the lowest extent of the ring travel, when fitted on the piston, and make sure that there is still a gap here, in the relatively unworn section of the bore. If the gap is too small when measured here, 'gap' the piston ring by filing the ends away very carefully with a fine file, until the gap, when the ring is fitted, is as quoted. Otherwise there is a danger that the ring might seize when the piston is at the lowest extend of its travel. To ensure that the piston rings are 'square' to the bore when making these measurements, push the piston

ring down the cylinder using an inverted piston.

It is also important that there is sufficient (but not too much) clearance between the new piston ring and the edges of the groove in which it sits. Specific information on this is normally included with the new oil control rings.

If fitting new pistons or rings, without reboring your engine, the shiny surface of each cylinder needs to be roughened, for the rings to grip it, forming an effective seal. A special 'glaze buster' tool can be used, but, alternatively a little fine 'wet or dry' paper, soaked in oil, will do the job. Remove all traces of abrasive on completion of the job, when the cylinder walls have a smooth matt appearance.

Unfortunately, on this engine, the pistons were in poor condition, and wear was well beyond the 're-ringing' tolerance, so the cylinder block was taken to a local engine reconditioner, who re-bored the cylinder block, and supplied oversize pistons to suit the new bore dimensions.

ES14. A detailed examination of the crankshaft and bearings revealed that, as we suspected, the main and big-end bearings were worn out. The surfaces of the bearing shells should not be crazed, like this, but should have an even, matt grey appearance. The crankpins and main bearing journals should be checked for ovality and taper, using a micrometer. If there is more than 0.001 in. wear in either respect, the crankshaft needs re-grinding. For full details of the original crankshaft dimensions, refer to the Haynes Owners' Workshop Manual relating to your model. We took our crankshaft to a local firm for re-grinding, and they also supplied new undersize bearings, and new thrust washers.

ES15. The camshaft must come out, to allow the 'mushroom' shaped cam followers to be withdrawn for examination. Start by taking off the timing chain tensioner and arm. Knock back the locking tabs, and take out the two bolts securing the 'U' shaped camshaft retaining plate. With the engine upside down, turn the camshaft so that all the tappets (cam followers) are fully home, then, very carefully, withdraw the camshaft from the engine. Make sure that the cam lobes do not scrape the camshaft bearings, as the shaft is withdrawn. The cam followers can now be withdrawn, keeping them in strict order. If you decide to re-use them, make sure that they are re-fitted in their original housings.

The camshaft bearings in the cylinder block should be checked for scoring and wear; replacement is achieved by pressing the old bearings out, and the new ones in, making sure that the oil holes in the bearings line up with those in the engine block. This is a job for an engineering company, rather than a d-i-y operation.

Check the camshaft and cam follower faces for signs of wear, pitting and cracks. If any are evident, it is best to fit a new camshaft, together with a new set of followers. Check the condition of the camshaft thrust plate, too. If it is grooved or pitted, replace it. When re-fitting the camshaft and followers, use plenty of clean engine oil, for initial lubrication, and make sure that the followers rotate freely in their housings, before fitting the camshaft.

When the camshaft is in position, ensure that it turns freely, and then fit the 'U' shaped thrust (retaining) plate. The end float on the shaft should be 0.002 to 0.007 in. (0.051 to 0.178 mm.), for pre cross-flow engines; 0.0025 to 0.0075 in. (0.0635 to 0.1905 mm.) for cross-flow units. This can be assessed with feeler gauges. Finally, tighten the thrust plate retaining bolts (5 to 7 lb.ft., for pre cross-flow cars; 2.5 to 3.5 lb.ft., for cross-flow models), and knock over the locking tabs.

Before rebuilding the engine, clean the engine block and all parts that are to be re-fitted (BUT NOT the oil pump), in clean paraffin, making sure that no paraffin remains when re-assembly commences. If necessary, wipe the components with clean rag, prior to rebuilding. Stubborn gasket remnants can be removed by soaking them in cellulose thinners, and then using a scraper. This method is particularly effective for removing traces of gaskets that have been sealed with jointing compound.

Gasket sealing compound is effective for use on joints where oil might leak under pressure, for example on main bearing housing gaskets, and at the sump gasket joints. It is worth buying a tube before you start re-assembly.

ES16. The oil pump fitted to your engine will either be of a rotor or vane type. If the car has covered a considerable mileage (say, more than 50,000 miles), it is advisable to fit a new pump anyway. The wear can be checked accurately, though. Take off the end plate (either pump type) and place a straight edge across the face. Measure the gap between the lower edge of the straight edge, and the end of the rotor, using a feeler gauge. This measurement must not exceed 0.005 in. (0.1270 mm.). On rotor type pumps, check also the clearance between the inner and outer rotors – no more than 0.006 in. (0.15 mm.) is permissible – and the clearance between the outer rotor and the pump body, which should not exceed 0.010 in. (0.25 mm.).

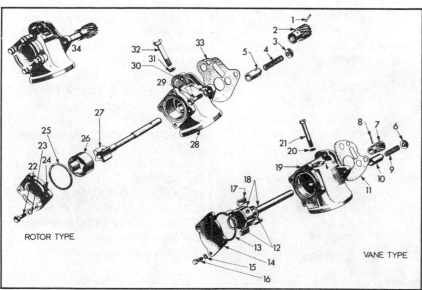

ROTOR TYPE

VANE TYPE

1 Locking pin
2 Oil pump drive gear
3 Oil pressure relief valve retainer
4 Relief valve spring
5 Relief valve plunger
6 Oil pressure relief valve retainer
7 Oil pump drive gear
8 Locking pin
9 Relief valve spring
10 Relief valve plunger
11 Gasket
12 Spacer
13 Oil pump cover sealing ring
14 Cover
15 Spring washer
16 Bolt
17 Rotor blade
18 Rotor and shaft assembly
19 Pump assembly
20 Spring washer
21 Bolt
22 Bolt
23 Spring washer
24 Cover
25 Sealing ring
26 Rotor
27 Rotor shaft
28 Pump body
29 Bolt
30 Spring washer
31 Spring washer
32 Securing bolt
33 Gasket
34 Complete pump assembly

The old bearing shells are hooked out of their locations using a small screwdriver, and the new shells can then be fitted, making sure that they sit squarely, and that there is no grit or oil BEHIND the shells, as they are seated, or tight spots could result. Make sure that your hands are clean for this operation.

ES17.   On vane type pumps, measure the clearances between the tip of the extended rotor blade and the pump body – max. 0.010 in. (0.25 mm.), and between the recessed rotor blade and the pump body – max. 0.005 in. (0.1270 mm). Measure also the gap between rotor blade and adjacent spacer – max. 0.005 in. (0.1270 mm.).

Introduce a little clean engine oil to the pump (of either type), prior to re-fitting, to provide initial lubrication.

ES19.   Fit the crankshaft thrust washers, slotted side outwards, at either side of the centre main bearing mounting, and holding them in position with a dab of engine oil. It is always advisable to fit new thrust washers during a major engine overhaul. With the upper main bearing shells fitted into their housings in the cylinder block, spread a little fresh engine oil over each bearing surface, then sit the crankshaft into position. Measure the crankshaft end float, by placing a feeler gauge between the thrust washer and the centre journal flange. The permitted float is 0.003 to 0.011 in. (0.08 to 0.28 mm.).

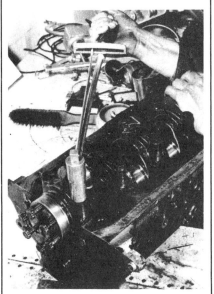

ES18.   Make sure that all the oilways are clean – particularly those in the crankshaft, after a re-grind. Use a short length of soft wire for this job, to push through all sludge and swarf.

ES20.   The lower main bearing shells can now be fitted into their caps, and each lubricated before fitting to the engine. Tighten the cap retaining bolts, a little at a time, to 55 to 60 lb.ft (pre cross-flow Cortinas, and Mark II Escorts) or 65 to 70 lb.ft. (cross-flow Cortinas, and Mark I Escorts). Make sure that the crank revolves freely at each stage.

ES21.   If, as with this Escort, the pistons are worn beyond the re-ringing limits described earlier, new pistons are required. To separate each old piston from its connecting rod, take out both gudgeon pin circlips, and push the pin out, using a drift. We used a car floor mat, resting on the vice, to protect the new pistons while the gudgeon pins were removed and re-fitted.

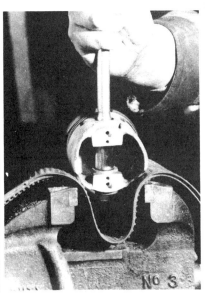

203

ES22. Make sure that the 'Front' mark on the connecting rod, and the arrow on the piston crown are facing the same way, before fitting them together. The job is easier if the piston is heated in a bowl of warm water for a few minutes, to expand the aluminium, and allow the gudgeon pin to enter more easily. Push the pin home, and fit two new circlips, ensuring that they sit correctly in their grooves.

ES24. A piston ring compressor is needed when fitting the pistons into the cylinder block. Use plenty of engine oil, to lubricate the pistons and cylinder walls. Insert the pistons into cylinders numbers 1 and 4.

ES23. Most pistons are supplied with their rings already gapped to suit the oversize cylinders, but check with the fitting instructions supplied with the pistons.

Before fitting the pistons, make sure that the oil control ring expander ends are touching, but not overlapping. Turn the rails and expander, if necessary, so that the gaps are spaced at 120° intervals around each piston. Check also that the top compression rings have their gaps on opposite sides of the piston.

ES25. Turn the cylinder block upside down, and fit the big-end bearing caps to the connecting rods just inserted, having fitted the bearing shells. Coat the shells with clean engine oil before fitting the caps to the engine.

Tighten the bearing cap bolts to 20 to 25 lb.ft. (Mark I Cortinas), 25 to 30 lb.ft. (pre cross-flow Mark II Cortinas), and 30 to 35 lb.ft. (cross-flow Cortinas IIs, and Escorts). Rotate the crankshaft to make sure that there are no tight spots, then repeat these operations for cylinders 2 and 3.

204

ES26. The old oil seal can be drifted from the rear main bearing housing, then a new seal fitted, using a length of softwood and a hammer. Drive the new seal into position as far as it will go, employing the old seal, positioned on top of the new one, as a 'cushion'.

ES27. Oil the rear end of the crankshaft and the lip of the oil seal, then re-fit the housing, complete with the seal. Use a little jointing compound at the ends of the gasket. The housing should centre itself, as it is fitted. Check visually that there is equal clearance all round, between the crankshaft flange and the oil seal, then tighten the bolts, re-checking the alignment afterwards.

ES28. Fit the camshaft timing sprocket to the shaft, temporarily, and align the timing mark so that it is opposite the one on the crankshaft gear. Remove the sprocket, then assemble the new timing chain over the camshaft and crankshaft sprockets, finally re-fitting the assembly to the engine. The timing marks, and the centres of the camshaft and crankshaft, should all be in line. Tighten the camshaft sprocket retaining bolts (12 to 15 lb.ft., for all models except Escort Mark II, 13 to 15 lb.ft.), and tap the locking tabs home. Re-fit the timing chain tensioner assembly (5 to 7 lb.ft.), turning the spring-loaded eccentric back from its free position, so that it bears on the pad, which in turn applies pressure to the chain.

ES29. Re-fit the concave oil thrower to the nose of the crankshaft, over the Woodruff key, so that the dish faces outwards.

ES30.   Take out the old oil seal, and fit a new one to the timing chain cover, making sure that it is pressed in squarely (push it in, using a vice, with the old seal or a wooden block as a spacer). Place the cover loosely in position on the engine, having oiled the lip of the seal. Apply more oil to the mating surface on the crankshaft pulley, then fit this to the crankshaft, so that it centralises the timing chain cover. A little jointing compound should be used at the ends of the gasket.

Re-fit the cover bolts, tightening them, a little at a time, in a diagonal sequence, to 5 to 7 lb.ft. Make sure that the cover is still sitting centrally, on completion. Re-fit the crankshaft pulley bolt, and tighten it to 24 to 28 lb.ft.

ES31.   The oil pick-up pipe can now be re-fitted, using sealing compound where the pipe fits into the cylinder block. Don't forget to fit the support bracket bolt, and make sure that the filter is clear of obstruction. On pre cross-flow engines, the oil pipe is screwed to the cylinder block, with a locking tab to hold it in place.

ES32.   Having cleaned all the gasket faces with cellulose thinners, apply a little sealing compound to the flange surfaces, then fit the sump gasket side sections first, followed by the end strips, so that they overlap the side sections at both ends. Re-fit the sump, taking care not to disturb the gasket, and tighten the bolts, a little at a time, to 6 to 8/9 lb.ft., in two stages.

ES33.   The distributor can now be replaced. To achieve initial timing, if this has been 'lost', turn the engine until the timing marks on the crankshaft pulley and engine block align, with no. 1 piston at top dead centre on the compression stroke – i.e. both valves would be closed, if fitted. Since the valves are not fitted, check instead by reference to the cam follower positions. Fit the distributor so that, when it is fully home, the rotor arm points to the number 1 plug lead contact in the distributor cap. Check that the contact points are just about to open, in this position, and tighten the retaining bolt. It should be stressed that this only gives INITIAL ignition timing, and the setting will need checking precisely with a timing light, when the engine is back in the car.

The flywheel can now be re-fitted, locking the camshaft while the bolts are tightened, as described previously. Tighten the bolts to 45 to 50 lb.ft. for hexagonal types, and 50 to 55 lb.ft. for bi-hexagonal bolts.

The cylinder head can be re-fitted, as described in the 'Cylinder Head Overhaul' section, and the clutch components, as described in the 'Gearbox Out/Clutch Change' section.

The remaining engine ancillaries can be re-fitted now, or when the engine is back in the vehicle. Re-fitting the engine to the car is a reversal of the removal operations, except that great care should be taken when lining up the gearbox shaft with the clutch plate. It sometimes helps to twist the engine from side to side a little, to engage the splines.

Engine bay stripdown

If you are restoring a car, it makes sense to give the engine compartment a clean-up and respray, so that its appearance matches the rest of the car. The first step is to get it clean, and then remove all the electrical and other components which are attached around the engine bay.

Even if you give the engine and its compartment a de-greasing treatment and rinse, before the engine is removed, as described previously, there will still be pockets of grease and dirt which are easier to reach when there is no engine in the way!

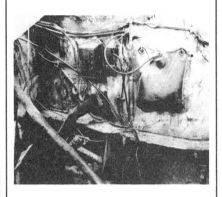

EBS1. The engine compartment on this Cortina was still decidedly grubby, despite initial de-greasing and rinsing.

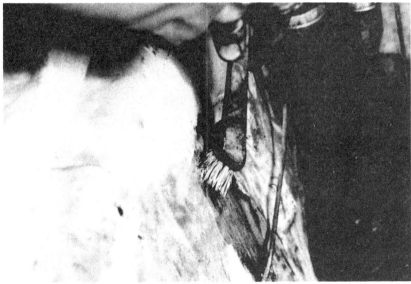

EBS2. Using a bowl of paraffin and a stiff washing-up brush, soak the remaining dirt and grease, wiping off with clean rag, until the original paint colour begins to emerge.

EBS3. Remove all ancillaries from the 'walls' of the engine bay, including the ignition coil, electrical regulator/cut-out box, and brake and clutch master cylinders, and unclip the wiring looms, so that they can be pulled clear.

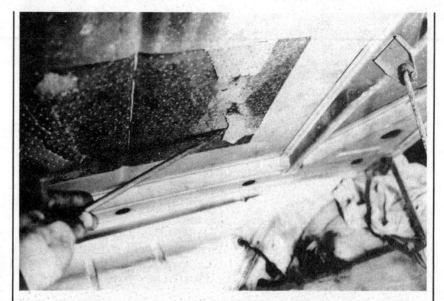

When the engine compartment has been cleaned, and stripped of ancillaries, the paintwork can be rubbed down and sprayed as for the exterior bodywork. Before applying the primer/undercoat, wipe the surface of the areas to be painted with rag dipped in cellulose thinners, to make sure that all traces of grease have been removed.

Gearbox out/clutch change

Removing the gearbox and changing worn clutch components is not a difficult job on Cortinas and Escorts; indeed, compared with many cars, it is very straightforward. There is a reasonable amount of room around the engine and gearbox, which helps when it comes to reaching the bell housing bolts, and so on. The principles are the same for either model; the gearbox is withdrawn from below the vehicle, with the front of the car raised on axle stands or, preferably, ramps (NEVER a

jack), or with the car over a pit.

With the exception of some column change Mark I Cortinas, which 'officially' require the use of a 'setting' gauge when re-fitting the column gearchange linkage, no special tools are needed for the job, except a clutch alignment tool. However, this is easily constructed, using a short length of dowel and a few turns of masking or insulating tape. As already mentioned, you will need to beg, borrow or hire a pair of car ramps – the higher the better – to give sufficient clearance for the gearbox to come out from below the car. A torque wrench is also desirable, for tightening the clutch retaining bolts.

The main stripdown procedures are similar between Cortina and Escort models, but there are some differences, notably with regard to the gearchange linkages, and the method of clutch operation. Hydraulics are employed on the Cortinas, and some of the fast Escorts, while cables are fitted to the 'family' Escorts.

In view of the differences between the models, it is best to look at a typical gearbox out/clutch overhaul operation for each model, to highlight the variations required in working techniques. On all cars, disconnect the battery before you

start work, to avoid the possibility of an accidental short circuit.

Cortina

There are several variations in the gearchange mechanisms you may encounter, but all of them need to be disconnected from the gearbox, to enable the unit to be removed for attention or replacement, or for access to the clutch. Starting with the Mk I Cortinas, there are four different types of column change linkage, a 'direct' floor change mechanism, and a remote control floor change system, as fitted to the GTs. On Mark II Cortinas, there are four basic types; a column change system, a 'direct' floor change, and two remote control floor changes. The first was used on GTs until October, 1968, and from then on, a standardised remote control gearchange was fitted to all models.

For full details of the various mechanisms, their setting up and adjustment, reference should be made to the relevant *Haynes Owners' Workshop Manual,* or the Ford publication relating specifically to your model.

The following notes should help with the disconnection and re-installation of the gearchange linkages, to enable the gearbox to be removed/re-fitted.

Direct gearchange

CCO1. The easiest set-up to deal with is the 'direct change' type. Take out the securing screws, then lift away the rubber gaiter. Unscrew the domed nut holding the gear lever, then lift the gear lever assembly away, complete. Make sure that the retaining pin doesn't fall out of the lever and get lost. Keep the lever assembly in a safe, clean place.

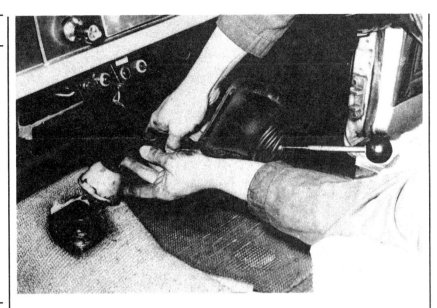

Remote control gearchange

On Mark Is and IIs with remote control gearchanges, the first job is to move the front seats as far back as they will go, giving more room to work around the gear lever area.

Mark I

CCO2. The remote control gearchange assembly, as used on Mark I GT models, looks like this. The remote change housing has to come off to allow the gearbox to be removed.

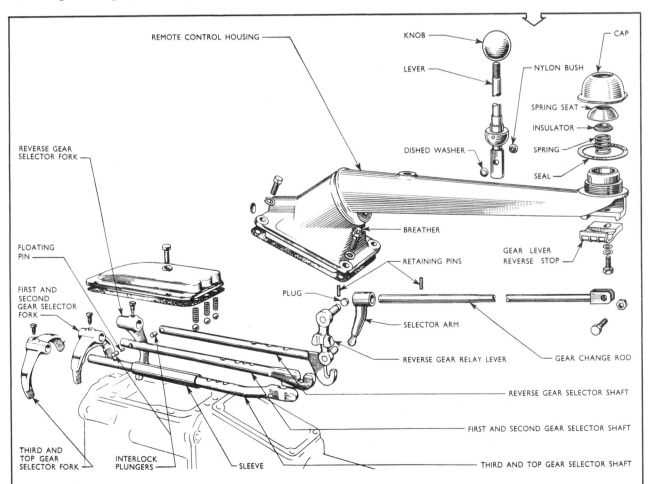

REMOTE CONTROL HOUSING

KNOB

CAP

LEVER

NYLON BUSH

SPRING SEAT

INSULATOR

DISHED WASHER

SPRING

SEAL

REVERSE GEAR SELECTOR FORK

BREATHER

GEAR LEVER REVERSE STOP

FLOATING PIN

RETAINING PINS

FIRST AND SECOND GEAR SELECTOR FORK

PLUG

SELECTOR ARM

REVERSE GEAR RELAY LEVER

GEAR CHANGE ROD

REVERSE GEAR SELECTOR SHAFT

FIRST AND SECOND GEAR SELECTOR SHAFT

THIRD AND TOP GEAR SELECTOR FORK

INTERLOCK PLUNGERS

SLEEVE

THIRD AND TOP GEAR SELECTOR SHAFT

On remote gearchange Mark Is, first remove the console screws and nut in the centre of the parcel shelf, and the two countersunk screws from the rear of the console. Unscrew the gear lever knob, then lift the console upwards at the rear, to clear the gear lever. Pull the console to the rear, and right, taking care not to disconnect the wiring to the instruments. Next, take out the two screws holding the console attachment bracket, at the rear of the draught excluder retaining plate. Pull the carpet away from the remote control housing. Now take out the remaining four screws holding the draught excluder retainer. With the gear lever in 'neutral', move the draught excluder out of the way. This gives access to the four bolts holding the remote control housing to the top of the gearbox rear extension; remove these, with their spring washers. (The left-hand, rear bolt, is a breather, which should be free from obstruction, and should be replaced in its original position). The remote control assembly, complete with the gasket and draught excluder, can now be taken out.

The handbrake secondary

lever should now be unhooked from the lower end of the relay lever, and disconnected from the eyelet on the gearbox cross-member.

CCO3.   Before re-fitting the remote control assembly, it is advisable to check the adjustment of the reverse stop, although in practice, it should seldom need to be altered. The reverse stop, at the gear lever end of the remote control linkage, is located in a slot, and retained by a single bolt. This should be slackened if adjustment is needed. To check the adjustment, the gear lever should be held against the reverse stop, and the clearance checked between the selector arm and the reverse gear relay lever, at the gearbox end of the assembly. Adjustment is quite easy; place a 0.020 in. feeler gauge across the lugs on the reverse gear relay lever, then move the selector arm across so that it just touches the feeler gauge. The reverse stop, with its bolt loosened, is then positioned in its slot so that the end of the gear lever just touches the stop. Tighten the stop bolt and re-check the clearance.

On re-assembly, fit a new gasket to the remote control housing on the rear gearbox extension. Make sure that the gears are in neutral. Lift the gear lever – against it spring – over the reverse stop in the remote control housing. Holding the lever in this position, engage the selector arm in the recess (slot) in the reverse gear relay lever, and fit the assembly to the rear gearbox extension. Make sure that the relay lever connects with the reverse gear selector shaft. With the remote control assembly held in this position, fit the four securing bolts and washers, with the 'breather' bolt re-fitted to the left-hand, rear position. Tighten the bolts evenly, in diagonal sequence, a little at a time, before releasing the gear lever. Fit the rubber draught excluder over the remote control assembly, locating its centre in the groove in the remote control housing arm.

Mark II

Two types of remote control gearchange were fitted to Mark II models, although the methods of disconnecting them for gearbox removal are the same. Remove

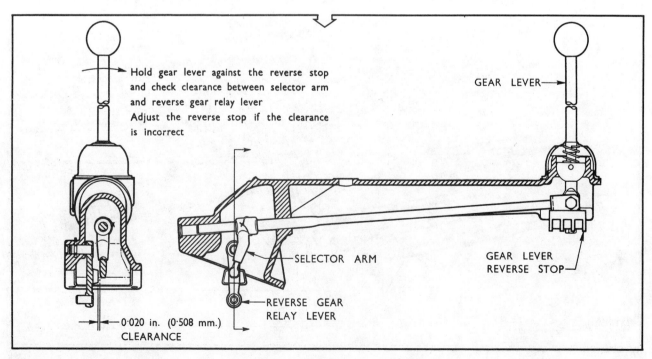

Hold gear lever against the reverse stop and check clearance between selector arm and reverse gear relay lever
Adjust the reverse stop if the clearance is incorrect

0·020 in. (0·508 mm.) CLEARANCE

GEAR LEVER

GEAR LEVER REVERSE STOP

SELECTOR ARM

REVERSE GEAR RELAY LEVER

the gear lever knob, then (where fitted) take out the four screws holding the centre floor console, and lift this clear. Lift out the carpet, then withdraw the screws holding the metal ring and rubber gaiter to the floor, and lift these off. Now unscrew the gear lever turret cover, and take out the cover and the gear lever. On later models, take off the circlip at the base of the gear lever; this holds the lever spring in compression. Bend back the locking tab from the plastic dome nut, and unscrew it, to release the gear lever.

On re-fitting, the reverse stop can be adjusted if necessary, to give correct engagement of reverse gear. The stop is in the extension housing, below the gear lever. If the stop is out of adjustment, unscrew the nut, and turn the adjuster in two turns or so. Hold the gear lever towards the reverse position, and unscrew

the adjuster until reverse gear engages without excessive lever travel, and without hitting the forward gear selector tabs. When all is well, tighten the locknut.

Column change

Mark I

As already mentioned, four types of column change mechanism were employed on the Mark I Cortina, each requiring differing methods of disconnection. Reference should be made to the relevant Ford technical publications for full details of each system.

It appears that the cable-operated type of column gearchange is the one you are most likely to encounter. The cables have adjustment nuts at their gearbox ends, and these are

disturbed when removing the cables from the gearbox. A Ford special tool (P.7115) is the 'official' implement for setting up the cable adjustment on re-assembly. Unless you have this tool, and assuming that adjustment is correct before you dismantle the system, an alternative is to count the 'number of threads' exposed on each of the cables, making a note, and ensuring that, on re-assembly, the cables go back in *exactly* the same position. Final adjustment can then be made, if necessary, by 'trial and error'.

CCO4. The cable-operated column gearchange on Mark I Cortinas has three cables running from the gearchange lever end of the system to the gearbox top, where the cables attach to the selector shafts.

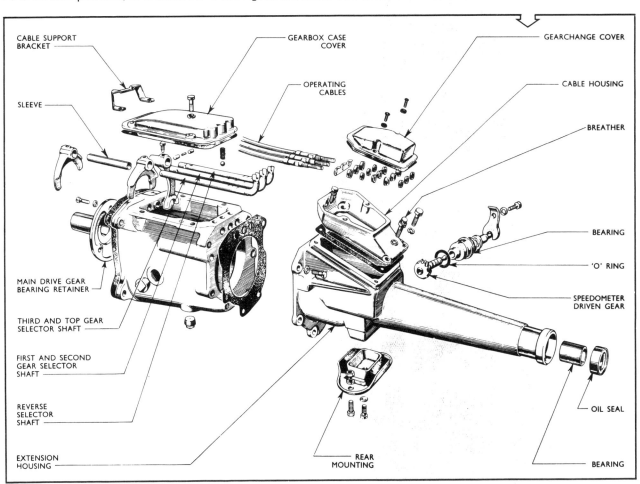

To disconnect the cables from the gearbox, the tail end of the gearbox has to be lowered slightly (onto a trolley jack, for example), having disconnected the propeller shaft, the exhaust pipe to manifold connection, and the gearbox cross-member, and having drained the gearbox oil. Remove the inspection plate from the transmission tunnel. Take off the cable abutment housing top cover, and its gasket. Now withdraw the two bolts holding the cable bracket to the gearbox. Next, take out the four bolts holding the cable abutment housing to the top of the gearbox; the left-hand, rear bolt is a breather, which should be clean.

Remove the gearchange cable collar nuts, and their locknuts, keeping these all together. Now lift off the cable abutment housing, guiding the cables away from their respective selector shafts, and placing the housing and cables to the side of the gearbox.

When re-fitting, if necessary, screw the front collar nuts and lock nuts forward as far as they will go. With the gears in neutral, fit the abutment housing to the gearbox, so that the rear of the housing is clear of the gearchange shaft fork ends, and making sure that the threaded cable ends enter the forks. With the cable nuts and locknuts in their original positions, as noted during dismantling, and tightened, the cable abutment housing can be securely bolted to the gearbox. Adjustment, if necessary, can be made with the gearbox raised and bolted back in its normal position.

Mark II

CCO5. *The column gearchange system fitted to Mark II Cortinas (and some Mark Is) has a system of rods and levers connecting the gear lever to the gearbox.*

To disconnect the steering column gearchange mechanism on Mark II Cortinas, first take off the gearbox inspection panel, on the transmission tunnel. Now separate the lower end of the gear change (selector) rod from the gear selector cross-shaft lever, by taking off the spring clip. Disconnect the cross-shaft from the pivot (mounted on the gearbox casing), by withdrawing its retaining clip, two flat washers, and a waved washer. The gate selector lever, on top of the gearbox, can now be disconnected from the gate selector rod, by taking out the retaining circlip.

The stripdown

Apart from the differences in gearchange mechanisms just described, the remainder of the gearbox out/clutch overhaul procedures are similar for all Cortinas. On completion of the job, on Mark I cars, the clearance between the end of the slave cylinder pushrod and the clutch release arm should be set to $^1/_{10}$ in. (2.5 mm.), while holding the pushrod stationary with a spanner, on the flats on its centre section.

We carried out this overhaul on a pre cross-flow Mark II

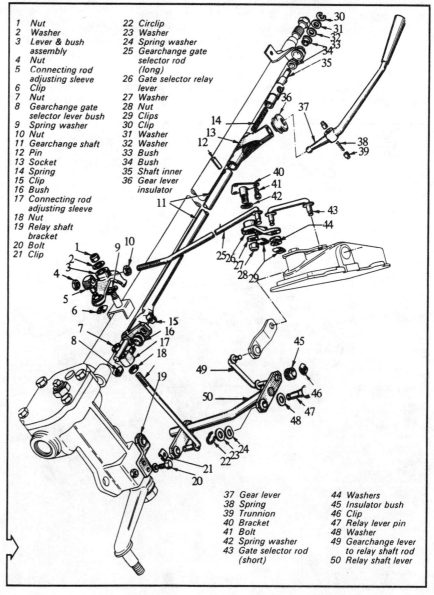

1 Nut
2 Washer
3 Lever & bush assembly
4 Nut
5 Connecting rod adjusting sleeve
6 Clip
7 Nut
8 Gearchange gate selector lever bush
9 Spring washer
10 Nut
11 Gearchange shaft
12 Pin
13 Socket
14 Spring
15 Clip
16 Bush
17 Connecting rod adjusting sleeve
18 Nut
19 Relay shaft bracket
20 Bolt
21 Clip
22 Circlip
23 Washer
24 Spring washer
25 Gearchange gate selector rod (long)
26 Gate selector relay lever
27 Washer
28 Nut
29 Clips
30 Clip
31 Washer
32 Washer
33 Bush
34 Bush
35 Shaft inner
36 Gear lever insulator
37 Gear lever
38 Spring
39 Trunnion
40 Bracket
41 Bolt
42 Spring washer
43 Gate selector rod (short)
44 Washers
45 Insulator bush
46 Clip
47 Relay lever pin
48 Washer
49 Gearchange lever to relay shaft rod
50 Relay shaft lever

which had been suffering from severe clutch slip; the job was straightforward.

It is a good idea to wear an old hat when working underneath the engine and gearbox. These components are inevitably oily, and a hat will help keep you clean.

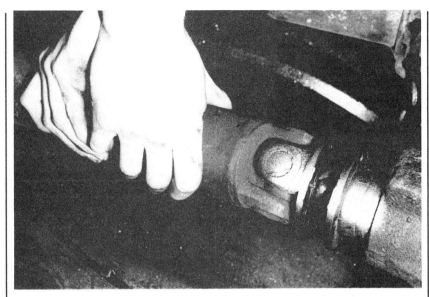

CCO6. Separate the propeller shaft from the differential by removing the four bolts; mark the flanges with paint for easy re-fitting in the same position, otherwise imbalance problems can result.

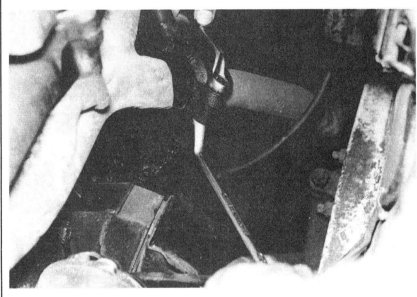

CCO7. Loosen the exhaust pipe to manifold joint by slackening the two retaining nuts/bolts. There is no need to take the clip right off. It is also advisable to release the top hose (drain the coolant first) and carburettor linkages, to allow the engine to drop.

CCO8. The clutch slave cylinder must be separated from the bell housing; compress the circlip and slide the cylinder forwards, away from the gearbox. Don't disconnect the hydraulic fluid pipe. Withdraw the push rod and circlip, and keep them in a safe place.

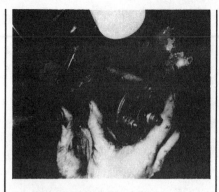

CCO9. The starter motor must come out; simply detach the main cable, and the two retaining bolts. Take out all the upper bell housing bolts – they are all easy to reach. Leave the lower bolts loosely in position, until later.

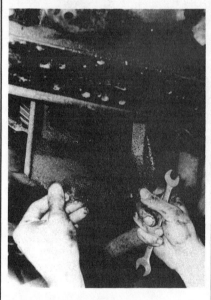

CCO10. Withdraw the engine splash shield and flywheel dust cover, at the back of the engine. A good soaking in paraffin is usually needed, to clean them up.

At this point it is a good idea to disconnect the reversing light cables (if fitted) from the switch at back of the gearbox. The speedometer cable also needs to be disconnected from the gearbox, by releasing the single clamp bolt and bracket. Tuck the cable out of the way, beneath the vehicle.

CCO11. Place a trolley jack, topped by a stout, wide piece of wood, under the back of the sump, and remove the gearbox cross-shaft. If you can place an extra support under the gearbox, to take the weight, so much the better. Keep clear of the area immediately below the gearbox – it might drop suddenly, and you could also get the dregs of the gearbox oil all over you, as the back of the box is lowered.

CCO12. Place a length of wood on top of the cross-member, then carefully lower the gearbox/engine assembly to meet it. The remaining lower bell housing bolts can now be withdrawn, and the gearbox lifted out. An assistant is handy, at this stage, to help take the weight of the gearbox – to avoid the weight hanging on the first motion shaft.

CCO13. Take out the bolts securing the clutch assembly to the flywheel; you may need to wedge the flywheel to stop it turning, as the bolts are loosened. Slacken them in a diagonal sequence, a little at a time, then remove the bolts and lift off the clutch cover assembly, and the clutch driven plate.

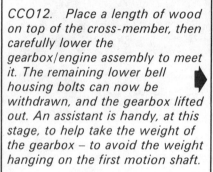
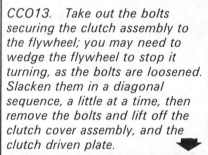

CCO14. Unfortunately, the clutch had been slipping on its rivets for some time, and both the pressure plate and the flywheel were deeply scored. The flywheel therefore had to come off. Slacken the bolts evenly, a little at a time, in diagonal sequence. By using two ring spanners as shown, the flywheel can be prevented from turning as the bolts are loosened.

CCO15. Take great care as the flywheel comes off – it is very heavy.

CCO16. We had intended to renew the clutch anyway, but the flywheel too needed replacing (very expensive) or re-facing. We took the flywheel to a local engineering firm, who skimmed the flywheel surface smooth, at a fraction of the cost of a new item.

It is not always possible to have a flywheel skimmed – for example if heat build-up has been severe, the friction surface of the flywheel will be deeply cracked, in which case it should be replaced. However, there is sufficient metal in the flywheel for grooves caused by 'rivet erosion' to be skimmed off, without adversely affecting the balancing properties of the flywheel. It helps the engineering firm (and saves you money) if you can remove the flywheel dowels before presenting it to them for re-facing. The dowels can be removed by trapping each in turn in a vice, with the dowel surfaces protected by aluminium strips, placed in the vice jaws. Careful 'side to side' twisting of the flywheel will encourage the dowels to move.

On return of the flywheel from the engineering shop, tap the dowels back in place, using a soft-faced hammer.

CCO17. The flywheel can now be replaced, after checking the state of the 'pilot' bearing in the centre of the crankshaft. Hook this out and replace it, unless it is in perfect condition. Apply a LITTLE high melting point or PBC grease to it. We used a length of wood, wedged against the dowels, to stop the flywheel from turning, as the bolts were tightened. The correct torque is 45 to 50 lb.ft., for hexagonal bolts, or 50 to 55 lb.ft., if bi-hexagonal bolts are fitted. Tighten in two stages.

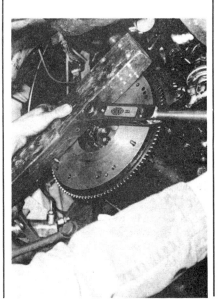

215

CCO18. The new clutch driven plate (it is marked 'flywheel side') and cover assembly can now be positioned on the flywheel, screwing in the bolts just finger-tight. It is always best to replace all three clutch components – driven plate, cover assembly and release bearing – rather than just the obviously worn parts. This can save an untimely repeat performance!

We made a clutch aligning tool from an old valve grinding stick, but a short length of dowel would do equally well, or a round socket bar. Wrap the dowel or bar with several turns of masking or insulating tape, at appropriate distances from one end, so that the rod is a snug fit in the crankshaft pilot bearing, and the splined boss of the clutch driven plate. Align the rod so that the boss of the driven plate is exactly central within the cover plate, then tighten the bolts, in diagonal sequence, a little at a time, to the required torque of 12 to 15 lb.ft. Check constantly that the driven plate is still central, and re-check on completion.

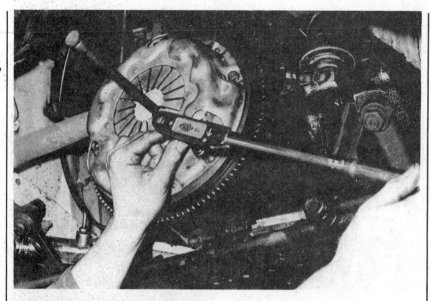

CCO20. We used an $^{11}/_{16}$ in. AF socket and a two legged puller, locked in a vice, to separate the bearing from the housing.

The gearbox and ancillaries can then be re-fitted to the car. Sometimes, the gearbox shaft will not align with the splines in the centre of the clutch driven plate, to begin with. Engage a gear, then try again, turning the tailshaft of the gearbox as it is pushed into place. It is of course much easier if you have an assistant, to help take the weight of the gearbox.

On floor change models which don't have a locking tab on the gear lever's plastic dome nut, apply a little thread locking compound, on re-fitting the nut.

Escort

The general procedures for removing an Escort gearbox and overhauling the clutch are similar to those for the Cortina. None of the Escorts were column change models, however, and, while certain of the fast Escorts (for example Mark I RS 1600 and Mexico models) had hydraulically operated clutches, the 'mainstream' versions all featured cable operation. For specific information on the clutch systems employed in the 'fast' Escorts, consult the appropriate *Haynes Owners' Workshop Manual* relating to the model.

The photograph sequence shows the steps necessary on a

CCO19. Now unhook the release bearing and its housing from the operating lever in the gearbox. The bearing must be pressed from its housing.

CCO21. Use a larger socket or similar spacer to apply pressure ONLY to the inner shoulder of the new bearing, when pressing into position. The assembly can then be fitted to the gearbox.

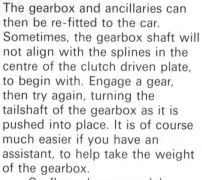

typical Escort gearbox out/clutch overhaul job. To avoid unnecessary repetition, reference has been made, where appropriate, to the 'Cortina' clutch overhaul section, since many of the steps are identical for both models.

ECO1. Inside the car, detach the gear lever gaiter from the floor, and withdraw the circlip from the base of the lever, releasing the spring tension. Bend back the locking tabs (this is very tedious), then loosen the plastic dome nut, using an adjustable spanner or a self-grip wrench. Mind your fingers on the sharp edges of the locking tabs. Finally, withdraw the lever assembly from the car.

ECO3. The rear propeller shaft flange should be marked with a dab of paint, as with Cortina models, to ensure correct re-assembly.

ECO2. On Mark II Escorts of 1300cc and above, there is a central propeller shaft mounting. Release the two bolts securing the mounting to the underbody.

ECO4. Take care as the propeller shaft is withdrawn from the gearbox, for, since there is no drain plug, the gearbox cannot be emptied of oil before you start. Therefore, gear oil will trickle out of the gearbox tailshaft. Keep clear of it, and place a tray below, in which to catch the oil.

217

ECO5. Disconnect the clutch cable from the release arm – simply unhook it – and from the bell housing.

The starter motor, bell housing bolts, speedometer drive and exhaust pipe disconnections are made in exactly the same way as for the Cortina models (please refer to the 'Cortina' clutch overhaul section). It is advisable at this stage to slacken the engine mounting bolts a little, to allow the engine and gearbox to drop at the rear without straining the mountings. It is a good idea also to disconnect the carburettor linkages and the top hose, draining the coolant before taking off the top hose.

If desired, as an alternative to having the engine 'propped up' from below, the weight of the engine can be taken, at the back, by employing a plank of wood, rested across the inner wing tops, and cushioned by clean rags, with a strong rope suspended from the plank and around the engine. This will then take the weight of the engine, while the gearbox is out, leaving the trolley jack free to use as an additional support, and to jack the engine/gearbox assembly back into position when the time comes.

The clutch assembly is removed and re-fitted to the flywheel in exactly the same manner as for the Cortinas, and the flywheel is removed, if necessary, in the same way. The torque recommendations for the clutch to flywheel bolts, and for the flywheel retaining bolts, are identical to Cortina models. Reference should therefore be made to the 'Cortina' clutch overhaul section for full details.

ECO7. Always check that the crankshaft pilot bearing is in good condition, replacing it if necessary. Apply a little high melting point, or PBC grease before re-fitting the clutch assembly. ➡

ECO6. With a support in place beneath the rear of the engine (a trolley jack is useful for this), take out the four bolts holding the gearbox cross-member to the car floor. (There is no need to remove the large central bolt and mounting rubber, unless you are swapping gearboxes, in which case the central bolt will need to be released, so that the cross-member can be fitted to the replacement gearbox. Tighten the central bolt to approximately 40 lb. ft.).

The gearbox can now be lowered at the rear, and separated from the engine by removing the last of the bell housing bolts.

ECO8. As with the Cortinas, there is no need to buy a special tool for centralising the clutch driven plate; a length of wooden dowel, suitably wrapped with masking tape to suit the internal diameters of the crankshaft pilot bearing, and the clutch (driven plate) splined hub, is all that is necessary for perfect alignment. Never touch the friction surface of the new clutch plate with greasy hands; always use a piece of clean rag or paper when gripping it.

ECO9. Having tightened the clutch assembly bolts, check again that the dowel, and therefore the driven plate, are perfectly central within the clutch assembly. Otherwise, the gearbox input shaft will never go in!

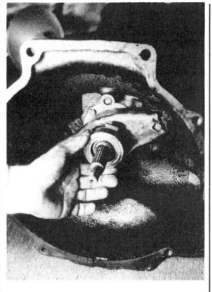

ECO10. The release bearing should be replaced as a matter of course at each clutch change. The bearing unhooks from the release arm, and can be pushed from its retaining hub using a socket spanner or short piece of tube, as for the Cortina models. The new bearing can be pushed onto the hub in a similar fashion. On re-fitting to the gearbox, with the release arm already in the bell housing, fit the bearing to it, making sure that the tags on the release arm engage correctly with the hooked ends of the release bearing assembly. Smear the clutch release arm pivot post with a little high melting point, or 'PBC' grease.

Gearbox overhaul?

There are occasions where it is worthwhile stripping and overhauling a gearbox. For example if a car is particularly old or rare, or where there may be one, simple, specific fault to deal with. Generally speaking, though, it is unusual for one fault – for example jumping out of gear, or bearing rumble – to occur in isolation. Such problems are usually symptoms of overall wear within the gearbox.

It is therefore advisable to replace ALL bearings and synchromesh assemblies while the gearbox is stripped, or you may well find that, having replaced just one item, another fails very shortly afterwards. The problem then arises that the cost of individual gearbox parts is normally prohibitive. From past experience with overhauling Ford (and other) gearboxes, the cost of replacing more than two or three individual components is usually far more than the cost of a complete, reconditioned 'exchange' gearbox, which of course also carries a guarantee.

If you know that your gearbox has perhaps just one isolated problem, it may be worthwhile stripping it to replace the worn components, and full details of dismantling and rebuilding procedures are included in the relevant *Haynes Owners' Workshop Manual* relating to your model.

If, on the other hand, your gearbox is generally worn, with several known faults (normally whining or rumbling, slipping out of gear or lack of synchromesh on one or more gears), it is more cost-effective to buy an 'exchange' gearbox.

Fortunately, reconditioned Ford gearboxes are plentiful in supply, even for the older Cortina models, and there are several suppliers. This is good news too, for the competition keeps the prices comparatively low!

Propeller shaft

The propeller shaft on Mark I and II Cortinas, and on 1100cc Escorts, is a one-piece, tubular unit, with a universal joint at either end.

On 1300cc Escorts, the shaft is divided, with a central, rubber

insulated bearing, which is bolted to the vehicle's floor.

On 1600cc Escorts, an additional, constant velocity, joint is fitted to the two-piece propeller shaft, just behind the centre bearing.

On the Cortina models, the universal joints are held in place with circlips, and these are easily dismantled for replacement of worn universal joint bearings. The same is true of the early Escorts, but later models have 'staked' type joints, which require the use of special kits for their overhaul.

To check for wear in the universal joints, grasp both halves of each joint, and attempt to rotate them in opposite directions. If movement is felt, wear is present. It usually makes itself known when driving the vehicle, and is indicated by vibration, by 'clonks', or by looseness in the transmission take-up. It is also worth checking the rear gearbox mountings, if such symptoms are present, for softness here can cause similar problems, and a 'shimmying' under deceleration.

Overhaul

One-piece shaft

The propeller shafts which have their universal joints retained by circlips are dismantled quite easily. A vice, a torque wrench and a pair of circlip pliers are useful, but not essential. 'Staked' type joints *can* be overhauled, contrary to popular belief, but a special kit is needed, containing the 'setting' tools to do the job. Full instructions are provided with the kits, which are available from most motor accessory shops.

PS1. The propeller shafts fitted to the Cortinas and 1100cc Escorts are the 'traditional' one-piece type. On early Cortina Mark Is, grease nipples were fitted, so that the universal joints could be lubricated. On later models, these were omitted.

Having removed the propeller shaft from the car (four bolts secure the shaft to the differential flange), wire brush the universal joints, to remove all dirt and grease. Extract the circlips from the joints, using a pair of 'internal' circlip pliers, or a small screwdriver and a pair of long-nosed pliers. If the circlips are reluctant to move, tap the bearing face resting on top of the spider, using a mallet, to ease the pressure on the circlip.

PS2. If you don't have a vice, one way to remove the bearing cups and needle rollers is to hold the propeller shaft in one hand, and tap the yoke at each bearing, using a soft-faced hammer. Once the bearings start to emerge, they can be encouraged out of the trunnions by gripping them with a pair of pliers or grips.

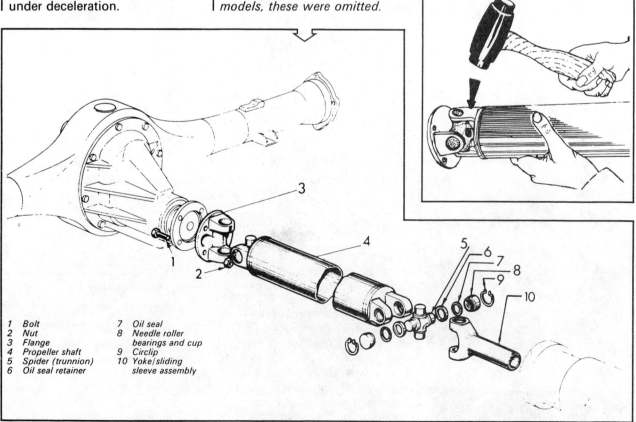

1 Bolt	7 Oil seal
2 Nut	8 Needle roller
3 Flange	bearings and cup
4 Propeller shaft	9 Circlip
5 Spider (trunnion)	10 Yoke/sliding
6 Oil seal retainer	sleeve assembly

A less hazardous method, if you have a vice, is to use two socket spanners. One needs to be of sufficient diameter to accommodate the bearing cup, and the other, to have a diameter just smaller than that of the bearing cup. Sandwich the universal joint in the vice, between the two sockets, making sure that the sockets and bearings are all in line. As the vice is tightened, the smaller socket will force the opposite bearing cup to partially emerge from the yoke. It can then be withdrawn as before.

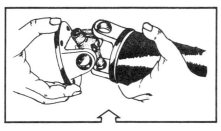

PS3. Once the bearing cups are free, the spiders can be extracted from their yokes by twisting them clear.

Clean out the yokes and spider journals until spotlessly clean, then fit new oil seals and retainers on the journals.

Place the spider on the shaft yoke, and fit the needle rollers in the bearing races, using a little lithium based grease to hold them. Fill each bearing cup about one third full with the same type of grease, then fit the bearing cups to the spiders, preferably squeezing them home with a vice, or tapping them in, if no vice is available.

Finally, replace the circlips, having checked that the bearings are sitting 'squarely' in their housings.

Two-piece shaft

PS4. The 1300cc Escorts have two-piece propeller shafts, like this. Vibration in this system could be due to a worn centre bearing, or sloppy universal joint bearings.

To remove a two-piece propeller shaft, the rear flange is unbolted, as for the one-piece type, but, in addition, the central bearing must be released from the bodywork, after taking out the two supporting bolts, and their washers. Note the positions of the 'U' shaped packing washers found under the centre bearing bolts; these control the angle between the two halves of the shaft, and should always be re-fitted in exactly the same positions.

The universal joints, if retained by circlips, are dismantled as described for the 'one-piece' shaft. However, if the central bearing needs attention, this can be separated from the shaft for the worn components to be replaced.

Before dismantling, mark the relative positions of the two sections of the propshaft, so that they are re-assembled with the same alignment.

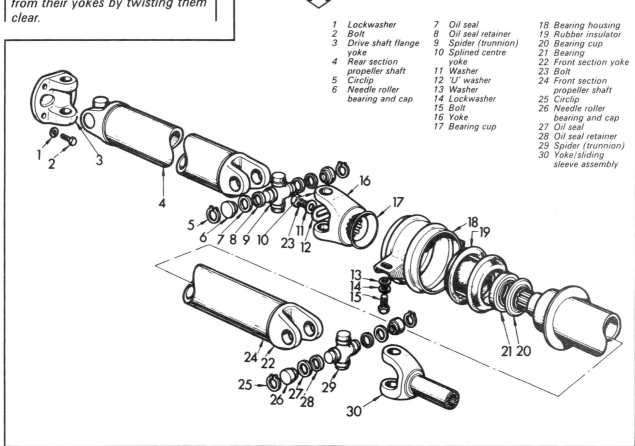

1 Lockwasher
2 Bolt
3 Drive shaft flange yoke
4 Rear section propeller shaft
5 Circlip
6 Needle roller bearing and cap
7 Oil seal
8 Oil seal retainer
9 Spider (trunnion)
10 Splined centre yoke
11 Washer
12 'U' washer
13 Washer
14 Lockwasher
15 Bolt
16 Yoke
17 Bearing cup
18 Bearing housing
19 Rubber insulator
20 Bearing cup
21 Bearing
22 Front section yoke
23 Bolt
24 Front section propeller shaft
25 Circlip
26 Needle roller bearing and cap
27 Oil seal
28 Oil seal retainer
29 Spider (trunnion)
30 Yoke/sliding sleeve assembly

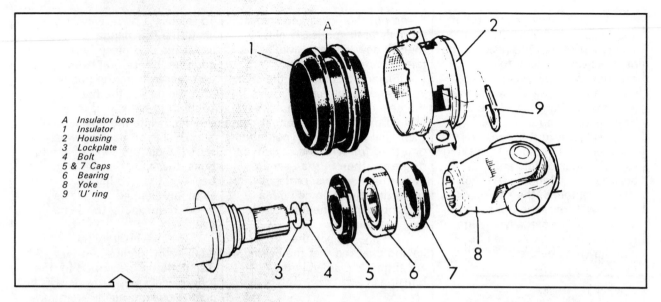

A   Insulator boss
1   Insulator
2   Housing
3   Lockplate
4   Bolt
5 & 7 Caps
6   Bearing
8   Yoke
9   'U' ring

PS5.   The centre bearing consists of these components; dismantling them is not difficult.

To dismantle the bearing assembly, start by knocking back the lock tab, and slackening the bolt (4). The 'U' shaped spacer (9) can now be withdrawn. The rear yoke (8) can be pulled away from the splined end of the front section of the shaft, leaving the centre bolt and washer attached to the front section.

The bearing housing (2), with its rubber insulator (1) can now be slid off the shaft. Bend back the six retaining tabs on the housing, and take off the rubber insulator.

The bearing (6) and its protective caps (5 and 7) can now be levered from the splined section of the shaft, using two long screwdrivers, or tyre levers, if a puller is not available.

Fill the area between the new bearing and its caps with grease, to Ford spec. S - MIC - 4515A.

The bearing can be *carefully* drifted onto the splined section of the shaft, using a soft-faced hammer, and a length of pipe or similar, with a diameter approximately equal to that of the bearing's inner rim.

Fit the rubber insulator to its

housing, making sure that the boss on the insulator is at the top of the housing, and that it will be adjacent to the car's underbody, when the propshaft is re-fitted. When all is well in this respect, bend back the locking tabs, and slide the housing and insulator assembly onto the shaft, over the bearing.

Make sure that the alignment marks, made prior to dismantling, are in line, and slide the splined section of the shaft into the rear yoke. Place the 'U' spacer under the centre bolt, with the spacer's smooth surface facing the front end of the propshaft. The centre bolt should be tightened to 28 lb.ft., and the locking tab bent over to hold it.

If the shaft is of the type with the constant velocity joint incorporated into it, it is important that the vehicle is raised under the rear bodywork, so that the rear axle hangs down, and is not supporting the weight of the car, when re-fitting the shaft to the vehicle. The 'wings' of the centre bearing housing should be pulled towards the front of the car, so that the centre bearing and the front part of the shaft move together, until the constant velocity joint bears against the rear of the centre bearing. Hold the bearing in this position, and tighten the bolts securing the bearing assembly to

the car, to a torque of 13 to 17 lb.ft. The same torque should be used on the centre bearing bolts of cars without the constant velocity joint.

Rear axle

The rear axles on Cortina models, Mark I Escorts and some Mark IIs are similar in design, with the differential bolted to the axle casing from the front. This 'Timken' type unit is identified by the ring of bolts around the forward circumference of the differential housing. Some Mark II Escorts have a 'Salisbury' type rear axle, in which the differential forms an integral part of the assembly, and on these cars, the axle has to be removed in order to change the differential.

The amount of work which can be done to either type of axle on a practical, d-i-y basis is limited, due to the need for special tools and gauges when overhauling an axle unit. The 'normal' jobs which can be undertaken at home include the changing of a complete differential unit, on the 'Timken' type axles, changing a front pinion oil seal, and withdrawing the axle half-shafts, to deal with bearing or oil seal problems.

222

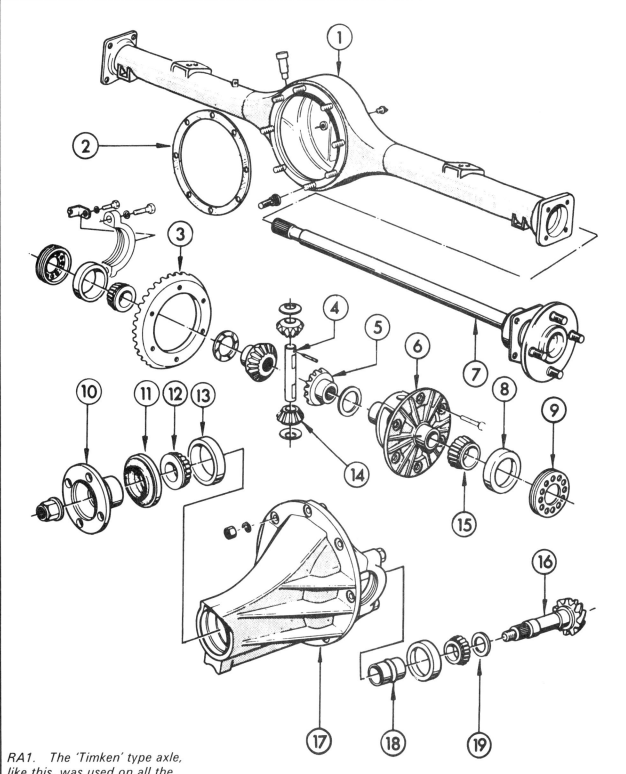

RA1. The 'Timken' type axle, like this, was used on all the Cortina Mark I and II models, all the Escort Mark Is and some of the Mark IIs. The ring of bolts around the differential carrier identifies this type.

1	Rear axle housing	6	Differential case
2	Gasket	7	Half shaft
3	Crown wheel	8	Taper roller
4	Differential pinion		bearing outer race
	gear shaft	9	Adjusting nut
5	Differential side	10	Drive pinion
	gear		flange

11	Oil seal	15	Inner race with
12	Inner race with		taper rollers
	taper rollers	16	Drive pinion
13	Taper roller	17	Differential carrier
	bearing outer race	18	Collapsible spacer,
14	Differential pinion		drive pinion
	gear	19	Drive pinion shim

223

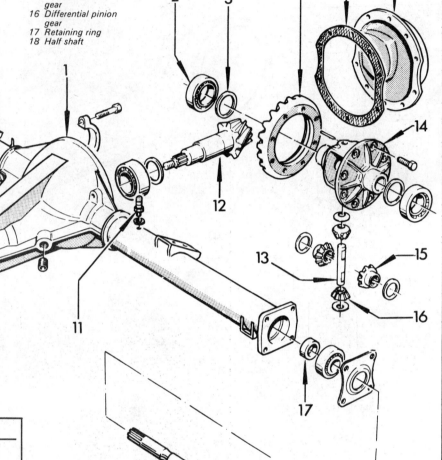

RA2. The 'Salisbury' axle, used on some Mark II Escorts, has an 'integral' differential case, and the axle has to be removed from the car for repairs to be carried out on it.

1 Rear axle housing
2 Differential case taper roller bearing
3 Shim
4 Crown wheel
5 Gasket
6 Cover
7 Drive pinion flange
8 Oil seal
9 Drive pinion taper roller bearing
10 Collapsible spacer
11 Vent valve
12 Drive pinion
13 Differential pinion gear shaft
14 Differential case
15 Differential side gear
16 Differential pinion gear
17 Retaining ring
18 Half shaft

Rear axle removal

Either type of axle is removed from the car after supporting the vehicle underneath its bodywork at the rear. The propeller shaft, the main brake pipe union, handbrake cable, the anti-roll bar clamp plates (where fitted) shock absorber plates and rear spring 'U' bolts and plates are then disconnected from the axle, leaving it free to be removed. This is straightforward, although it helps to have an assistant handy, to help take the weight of the unit, as it is lifted out. On re-fitting, the rear spring 'U' bolts should be tightened to 20 to 25 lb.ft. (18 to 27 lb.ft., Mark II Escorts), once the full weight of the car is on its suspension again.

Further details on separating the suspension units from the axle are included in the 'Rear Suspension' section. The brakes will need bleeding, on completion, to expel all air from the system.

Pinion oil seal

The pinion oil seal at the front of the axle casing (item no. 11 in diagram RA1, no. 8 in diagram RA2.) can be replaced on a d-i-y basis, but it is ESSENTIAL that the differential bearing pre-load is correct on re-assembly. This is determined by the tightness of the pinion flange retaining nut. Provided that this nut is tightened to its original position on re-assembly, the correct

pre-load will be maintained. There are various ways of achieving this, but probably the easiest, in practical terms, is to scribe a line between the pinion flange and the nut, before dismantling, tightening the nut to this point again on re-fitting. An alternative is to remove the wheels and brake drums (to reduce drag), then attach a length of cord to a spring balance, with the other end of the cord wrapped around the pinion flange. Rotate the flange by pulling on the cord, and make a note of the force reading required to rotate the flange, as measured by the spring balance. This is the bearing pre-load figure, which should be matched on re-fitting the nut. The self-locking flange nut can be re-used up to six times, unless it offers little resistance when removing it, in which case it should be renewed anyway. If fitting a new flange nut, you will of course be obliged to use the rather more complicated method, just described, of determining pre-load, rather than by the 'alignment marks' method.

Start by disconnecting the propeller shaft, then scribe the alignment marks, or determine the pre-load by the spring balance method.

The pinion flange must be held in place as the flange nut is undone, since the nut will be tight. To do this, either fit two old bolts into two of the pinion flange holes, and wedge the flange with a long bar, or drill two holes in a length of flat steel bar, bolting this to the flange and holding it still while the flange nut is undone.

Having taken off the flange (and the dust deflector behind it, where fitted), the oil seal can then be 'tipped' out of its housing by carefully drifting one side of the seal inwards, and pulling on the opposite side of the seal, as it emerges from the housing. The new seal can then be gently tapped into position, using a length of pipe (preferably brass or copper) of suitable diameter, or a large socket spanner. The face of the seal, when fitted, should be flush with the differential housing. Avoid hitting the pinion during this operation.

On re-assembly, first tighten the nut until the pinion end float just disappears, rotate the pinion to settle the bearing, and then tighten the flange nut, a FRACTION of a turn at a time, to the marks made previously, AND NO MORE. If you over-tighten the nut, the collapsible spacer, behind the pinion bearing, will be compressed, and the bearing will

then have to be removed in order to fit a new spacer! The pre-load reading on your spring balance, if used, should be between 12 and 18 lb.

Half shaft removal

The half shafts will need to be removed from the axle case to deal with worn outer (wheel) bearings, or leaking oil seals, or in order to remove and re-fit the differential, on 'Timken' types.

Worn half shaft bearings usually make themselves known by a 'ticking' or droning noise, most noticeable during cornering.

On all models except the Mark I Cortinas, the oil seals and half shaft bearings are combined. For all models, new bearings cannot easily be pressed onto the half shaft, since a minimum pressure of 1200 lbs. is needed for the bearing, and up to around 1500 lbs. for the bearing retainer. Therefore if a bearing does need to be changed, the best course is to remove the half shaft from the vehicle yourself, then have the bearing removed, and the new one fitted, by an engineering company, or a Ford dealer, who will have the necessary press to do the job. The bearing retainer collar has to be cut through with a chisel, without damaging the half shaft, to allow the bearing to be withdrawn from the shaft.

RA3. Start by removing the brake drum from the offending side. We also took off the brake shoes, to avoid them getting damaged.

225

RA4. The four bolts securing the bearing retaining plate can now be released, using a socket spanner and extension bar, guided through the holes in the axle shaft flange.

RA5. The axle shaft must now be pulled out of the axle. On later cars, it is impossible to drain the axle oil, since there is no drain plug fitted. On these models, jack the side of the car being worked on rather higher than the opposite side. That way, the oil will stay inside the axle! This 'slide hammer' was made from pieces of scrap found in the garage. However, it is sometimes possible to remove the axle shaft by bolting the wheel back on, and tapping the inside of the wheel on alternate sides, using a block of wood.

On re-assembly, tighten the bearing retainer bolts to 18 lb.ft. (Mark I Cortinas), 15 to 18 lb.ft. (Mark II Cortina, Mark I Escort, and Mark II Escort with 'Timken' axle), or 20 to 24 lb.ft (Mark II Escort with 'Salisbury' axle).

On Cortina Mark I models, once the half shaft is out, the oil seal, contained in the end of the axle tube, can be removed. This can be achieved with a 'claw' type puller, attached to the slide hammer. The claws of the puller need to be located behind the metal rim of the oil seal. Alternatively, it may be possible to lever the old seal out, using a long bar.

Soak the new oil seal in clean engine oil for at least an hour, prior to fitting.

Clean out the housing in the axle case, and apply a little sealing compound to the outer casing of the new seal. Fit the seal in the axle tube, with the lip facing the differential, and gently tap the seal home, using a large socket or a length of copper, brass or plastic tube. Take great care not to damage the inner surface of the oil seal, as the splined half shaft is replaced.

On re-assembly, tighten the bearing retaining plate bolts to 18 lb.ft.

Differential change

If problems are experienced with the differential unit, the complete assembly can be swapped on 'Timken' type axles, and further details on this are given in the 'Modifications' chapter. As with gearboxes, you save little, if anything, in time or money by attempting to overhaul the unit yourself. A reconditioned, exchange unit is the best solution when the original is badly worn. Always make sure, when buying an exchange unit, that the number of teeth on the crownwheel and pinion gears are identical to those on your old unit, or the gearing will be altered . . . that is, unless you are intending to alter the gearing anyway – more about this in the 'Modifications' chapter.

Braking system

The early Mark I Cortinas, and the 1100cc Escorts, have drum brakes all round; other models have disc brakes at the front, with drums at the rear. The Mark II Escorts, and some of the Mark Is, have split circuit brakes (front to back), and a vacuum servo is fitted to the high performance models, Cortina and Escort.

It is vital that scrupulous cleanliness is observed when working on hydraulic systems; even minute specks of grit will ruin cylinder seals and bores.

It is worth considering the use of silicone brake fluid, as supplied by Automec, for example. It is more expensive to buy than conventional fluids, but has a longer service life, and is not hygroscopic. That is to say, it does not absorb water from the atmosphere. One of the benefits of this is that the hydraulic system is less likely to corrode from the inside.

Over the eighteen years of production of the Mark I and II Cortinas, and the rear wheel drive Escorts, detail changes were of

course made to construction of the brake systems. For full information on these, references should be made to the relevant *Haynes Owners' Workshop Manual* relating to your model. Nevertheless, the principles of brake operation remained the same throughout, and d-i-y overhaul is not difficult.

One vital safety point – NEVER attempt to overhaul hydraulic cylinders which have worn or pitted cylinder bores or pistons; only cylinders with perfect bore finishes and piston surfaces are suitable for reconditioning. If, on stripping a cylinder, you find it is internally scored or pitted, or otherwise damaged, fit a new unit, and throw the old one away.

Master cylinder

The master cylinders fitted to the Cortinas, and the early Escorts, are similar in design. On Escorts with dual circuit brakes, a 'tandem' master cylinder is

employed, in conjunction with a 'pressure differential actuator', the function of which is to sense a pressure loss (through a fluid leak, for example) in either of the braking systems, effectively isolating that system and lighting the warning lamp on the facia.

The master cylinder overhauled in these photographs came from a Mark II Cortina, but the basic stripdown sequence applies equally to other models.

The first step in all cases is to remove the cylinder from the car, by separating it at its brake pedal link, under the facia, from the brake pipe(s), and from the servo unit, where fitted.

MC1. *This is the layout of the components comprising the master cylinder, as fitted to Cortina models. The cylinder for single circuit Escort brakes is very similar.*

1 Cap	9 Spring retainer
2 Sealing ring	10 Seal
3 Body	11 Piston
4 Valve seal	12 Circlip
5 Valve stem	13 Push rod
6 Spring washer	14 Bush
7 Valve spacer	15 Dust cover
8 Spring	

227

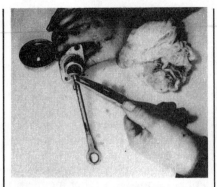

MC2. Having prised off the rubber dust cover, over the pushrod, extract the circlip from the end of the cylinder. A pair of long-nosed pliers can be used.

MC4. Lift the tab securing the piston to the spring retainer, using a small screwdriver.

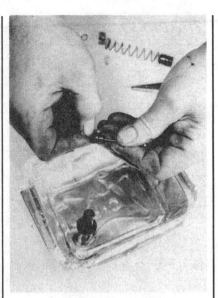

MC6. The valve seal should be removed from the valve, and the piston seal from the piston. Clean all the components in a little fresh brake fluid. 'Chinese takeaway' food containers are ideal trays for holding the brake fluid.

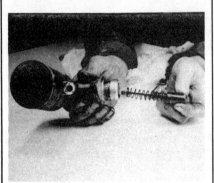

MC3. The internal components of the cylinder are now free to be withdrawn. Pull them out of the cylinder, watching for brake fluid drips, as you do so. TAKE CARE – brake fluid removes paint!

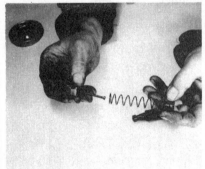

MC5. The spring can now be compressed – carefully – moving the spring retainer to one side, and releasing the valve stem.

MC7. Make sure that there is no grit on your fingers, and replace all the parts supplied in the overhaul kit. Ensure that the piston seal is fitted the correct way round (lips of seal towards closed end of cylinder), and don't stretch it more than necessary when fitting. Re-assemble the valve unit, with the lip of the valve seal towards the closed end of the cylinder, and the convex face of the shim washer abutting the flange on the valve stem.

Dip all parts again in clean brake fluid before re-fitting them to the cylinder. This should be thoroughly cleaned out, using clean rag wrapped around a blunt screwdriver (take care not to score the cylinder bore, and to remove all the rag on completion), and lubricated with a little fresh brake fluid, prior to re-assembly. Make certain that the lip of the piston seal is not bent back as it enters the cylinder.

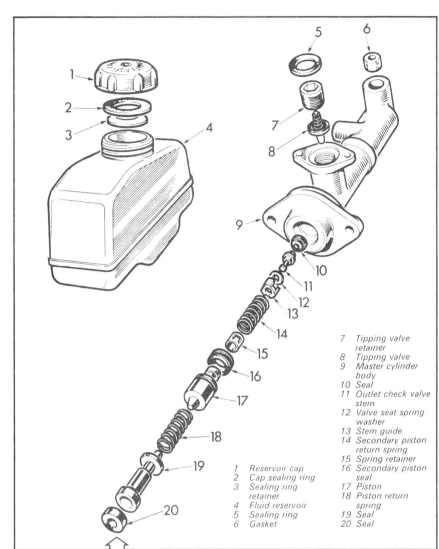

7 Tipping valve
   retainer
8 Tipping valve
9 Master cylinder
   body
10 Seal
11 Outlet check valve
   stem
12 Valve seat spring
   washer
13 Stem guide
14 Secondary piston
   return spring
15 Spring retainer
16 Secondary piston
   seal
17 Piston
18 Piston return
   spring
19 Seal
20 Seal

1 Reservoir cap
2 Cap sealing ring
3 Sealing ring
   retainer
4 Fluid reservoir
5 Sealing ring
6 Gasket

DCO2.   The pad retaining pins
are sometimes reluctant to move,
and it helps to give them a
soaking in penetrating oil, before
you start. Avoid getting oil on the
pads, if you intend to re-use
them.

DCO3.   Use a small punch to
encourage initial movement of
the pins from the caliper body.

MC8.   The Escorts with dual
circuit brakes featured 'tandem'
master cylinders, like this. The
'tipping valve', on top of the
cylinder, is accessible after
removal of the retaining plug
(use a hexagon key), itself
accessible after removal of the
brake fluid reservoir. Replace all
rubber seals, and gaskets, as a
matter of course, if dismantling
the cylinder.

Disc caliper overhaul

The caliper assembly can be
removed from the vehicle,
complete with the brake pads,
after disconnecting the mounting
bolts and the brake fluid pipe.
The calipers on the high
performance Cortinas are of the
'leading' type, fitted at the front
of the discs, while those on the
other Cortinas, and on the
Escorts, are of the 'trailing'
variety, at the back of the discs.
    It is a good idea to cover
your bench or working area with
clean newspaper, to start with,
since penetrating oil and brake
fluid are likely to be spilled
during the initial dismantling
stages.

DCO1.   Start by withdrawing the
pad pin locking clips, using a pair
of long-nosed pliers.

DC04. A small electrical screwdriver, or parallel pin punch, can then be used to push the pins right out of their housings.

DCO7. We were lucky with this caliper, for, although the pistons were dirty, there was no pitting or scoring of them, or the cylinder bores.

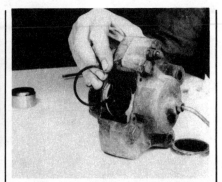

DCO9. NEVER re-use old seals; always fit new. Caliper overhaul kits are cheap, and readily available. Clean the cylinders and the pistons, using clean rag and new brake fluid.

DC05. The pads can now be lifted out of the calipers, for replacement if significantly worn.

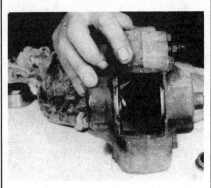

DCO8. With the pistons clear, the rubber sealing rings can be extracted from the cylinders. A small, blunt screwdriver is ideal for this, as it can be used to prise the seal from its groove.

DCO10. Soak the new seals in fresh brake fluid before fitting them, and dip the pistons in fluid just prior to fitting. Always re-fit the pistons to their original bores, and don't separate the two halves of the caliper.

DCO6. The caliper pistons should now be extracted from their cylinders, having taken off the rubber dust covers and their retaining spring clips.

Removal of the pistons can be a little awkward, since there isn't a lot of metal to grip. However, gentle levering from alternate sides, using a large screwdriver, should do the trick. If one or more of the caliper pistons has seized, it can be VERY difficult to remove the pistons. If they have rusted in place, the caliper is scrap anyway, since the cylinder wall and piston will be pitted.

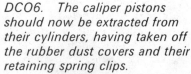

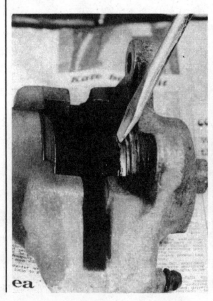

DCO11. Finally, the new dust seals and spring clips can be gently manoeuvred into position. This is a game of patience, as the clips inevitably 'jump' off the dust covers just as you think they are 'home'!

Front drum brakes

Early Mark I Cortinas (to October 1964), and 1100cc Escorts have drum brakes at the front. Inspection and overhaul of the front brake shoes and cylinders is not as straightforward as it might be, since the central hub nut and bearings have to be extracted, in order to remove the brake drum.

The stripdown sequence shown here relates to an Escort Mark I, but the procedures are similar for the Mark I Cortina and Mark II Escort.

FDB3. The castellated nut retainer (Escorts only) can now be taken off.

FDB1. Start by prising off the hub cover, using a large screwdriver. Gentle tapping may be necessary, to encourage the cap to move.

FDB4. The thrust washer and the outer wheel bearing are now extracted, taking care that the bearing is not dropped, or otherwise contaminated by grit.

FDB6. The brakes on this Escort were in a shocking state, with an accumulation of brake lining dust and brake fluid, which had been leaking from the lower cylinder. DON'T inhale the dust from within the brake drums – it contains asbestos and could be DANGEROUS. Use a pair of pliers to compress each spring clip, and turn the steady post through 90 degrees, so that it will pass through the slot in the clip. Put the clips and posts in a safe place.

FDB2. Extract the split-pin using a pair of long-nosed pliers. A few light taps with a hammer, from the opposite side, help.

FDB5. The brake drum assembly, complete with wheel studs, is now lifted off the hub, to expose the brakes.

FDB7. Carefully lift the brake shoes from the operating ends of the cylinders, one at a time, making a note of the spring positions.

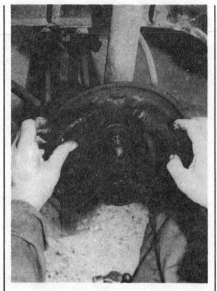

FDB8. Keep the brake shoes in the same relative positions, as they are removed from the car. It helps to lay them on the floor of the garage, for reference when fitting the new shoes.

FDB9. Clean the backplate before proceeding further. Sometimes a wipe with a rag will be sufficient, but in this case, a thorough brushing, using paraffin and a washing-up brush, was necessary. Lay a few sheets of newspaper on the ground, it will help keep the mess to a minimum.

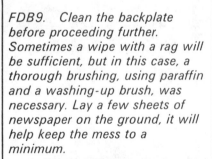

FDB10. Make sure that the manual adjusters are free to rotate. On this Escort, they were very reluctant to move. Use a brake adjuster spanner on the head of the adjuster, gently rocking the adjuster to and fro, while applying penetrating oil to the pivot point. Wipe off all surplus oil on completion.

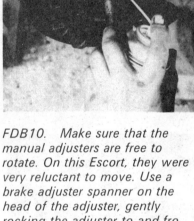

FDB11. Pull back and remove the dust cover from each wheel cylinder.

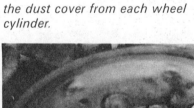

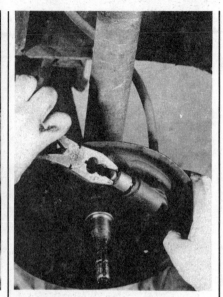

FDB12. Pull the pistons from the cylinders, using a pair of pliers if they are a little tight. If the pistons are seized through rust, buy new cylinders; the pistons and cylinder bores will be damaged.

FDB13. Use a pair of long-nosed pliers to extract the piston spring from the depths of the cylinder, then wipe out the cylinder, and clean the piston and spring, using a little brake fluid on a clean rag.

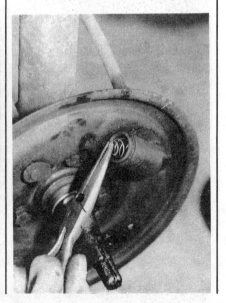

FDB14. Examine the surfaces of the cylinders, visually, and by checking the bore for ridges and pits, with a clean finger. If all is well, wipe out the cylinder again with a clean, dry rag.

If there is the slightest sign of rust, pitting, or scoring within the cylinder, unbolt it and fit a new one.

FDB15. If the pistons and cylinders are in perfect condition, remove the old rubber seals from the pistons, and soak the new seals in clean brake fluid for several minutes, prior to assembly. Dip each piston into the brake fluid, and slide the new seal into position, so that the lip of the seal will face the bottom of the cylinder bore, when the piston is replaced in the cylinder.

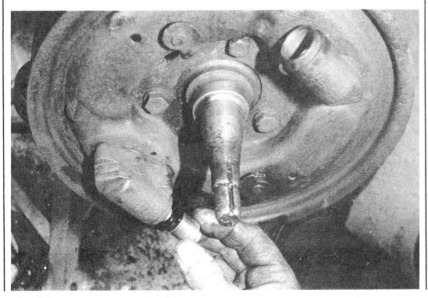

FDB16. NOT forgetting the springs, re-fit the pistons to the cylinders, having lubricated the cylinder bores with a little fresh brake fluid. While 'grimy' fingers are inevitable during this job, it is imperative that dirt and grit are avoided at all costs. Make sure that your hands are free from such contamination during these operations.

Pack the rubber dust covers with the special brake 'sealing' grease provided in the overhaul kit, and fit the dust covers to the cylinders.

FDB17. Fit the new brake shoes, making sure that the springs are in the correct holes, and using a little high melting point grease on the shoe contact points. Re-fit the shoe steady posts and spring clips.

FDB18. Wipe the remains of the old grease from the wheel bearing, and apply a smear of fresh wheel bearing grease (a multi-purpose, lithium based grease is suitable), before re-assembling the brake drum/hub assembly.

FDB19. Rotate the hub to settle the bearings, at the same time tightening the hub nut to 30 lb.ft. (Cortina), or 27 lb.ft. (Escort). Back off the nut between two and two and a half flats (Cortina) or 90 degrees (Escort), then fit a new split pin (having re-fitted the castellated retainer, on Escorts).

Finally, use the two manual adjusters to adjust the brake shoes. Turn the adjusters a quarter of a turn at a time until each wheel is locked, then back off the adjuster one notch, and check that the wheel will rotate without binding. Re-check the adjustment after the car has been driven, and the brake shoes have centralised.

Rear brakes – Cortina

The rear brakes on the Cortina Mark I are operated by a single piston cylinder, which is free to slide on the backplate, or by a double piston cylinder, bolted to the backplate, on GT models. Brake adjustment on Mark I models is by means of a single, square headed manual adjuster, found inboard of the backplate. When completing an overhaul, the rear brakes are adjusted by tightening each adjuster until the wheel locks, then slackening it by two 'clicks', afterwards checking that the wheels are free to revolve.

On Mark II models, the rear brakes have a single piston cylinder each side, incorporating a 'ratchet' self-adjusting mechanism. The cylinder is free to slide on the backplate.

The 'fixed' cylinders on the Mark I GT can be overhauled 'in situ', provided they are in good condition, while for other Cortina models, Marks I and II, it is easier to remove the cylinder from the car for attention.

The cylinders are overhauled by using similar techniques to those illustrated in the 'Front Drum Brakes' section.

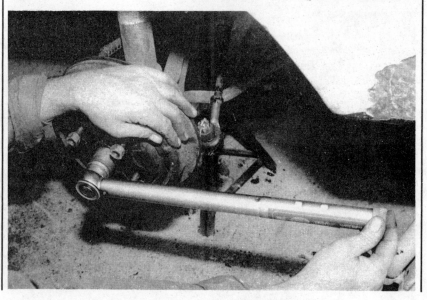

The stripdown described here was carried out on a Mark II Cortina, and illustrates the self-adjusting mechanism, which is frequently found to be seized solid!

RBC1. For this overhaul I chose a car which had been standing, unused, for two years or so. Consequently, the brakes didn't work, and the brake drums were havens for miniature wildlife. The first job was therefore to safely re-house the spiders and beetles, in more natural surroundings, then to slacken each retaining screw and take off the brake drums.

RBC2. The brake shoe steady posts and springs are then removed, using a pair of pliers, or, if you are lucky, your fingers.

RBC3. Lever the brake shoes from their slots, using a screwdriver to start with, if necessary, then 'unhook' the handbrake lever from the upper shoe, as it is withdrawn. The handbrake lever is connected to the self-adjusting mechanism; when the handbrake lever moves, it causes a pivoted arm to move, taking with it the ratchet wheel at the bottom of the cylinder. The rotation of the ratchet wheel in this manner causes the threaded bolt (in which the shoe sits) to effectively 'unwind' from its housing in the cylinder, and push the brake shoe a little nearer the drum. The ratchet wheel remains stationary on the return of the operating lever to its original position. The trouble is that the ratchet wheel/internal bolt often seizes up, with consequent lack of self-adjustment.

RBC4. Behind the backplate, having disconnected the brake fluid pipe, withdraw the retaining clip and clevis pin securing the handbrake cable to the operating lever, and prise the rubber dust cover from the back of the cylinder, using a screwdriver, and taking care not to split the rubber.

RBC5. The cylinder is held to the backplate with two 'horse shoe' shaped clips. Slide the lower one downwards – it may need to be sprayed with penetrating oil, and then tapped to start it moving. The two holes in the legs of the clip engage over two spigots protruding from the other (upper) clip. Therefore you may need to prise the legs of the lower clip outwards a little, to clear the spigots, as it is moved downwards. This can be tricky.

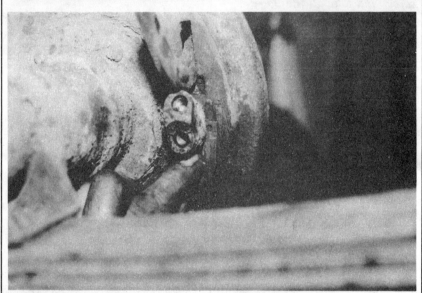

RBC6. Perseverance eventually pays off, and then you can extract the upper half of the clip, upwards. A pair of long-nosed pliers is useful for this operation.

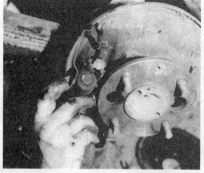

RBC7. The cylinder, complete with self-adjusting mechanism, can now be pulled away from the outside of the backplate.

RBC8. With the cylinder clear of the car, take off the handbrake/self-adjusting lever, for attention later.

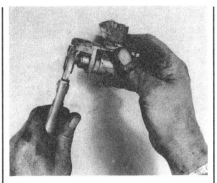

RBC9. Pull off the dust cover retaining clip, and the dust cover.

RBC10. The piston can now be extracted. This one, although reluctant to move at first, was not seized, and gentle rocking with a small pair of grips encouraged it to move. Luckily, the reluctance was due only to a 'soggy' rubber seal, and not to corrosion damage.

RBC11. The old seal was taken off the piston, and the piston then cleaned with a little rag and fresh brake fluid, before a new seal, soaked in brake fluid, was fitted. The piston assembly can then be put aside (in a CLEAN container) while attention is turned to the self-adjusting mechanism.

RBC12. In the case of a seized self-adjuster, the first step is to spray the slot-headed bolt and the ratchet wheel with penetrating oil (keeping it out of the cylinder).

RBC13. Allow the oil to work, then, using a small pair of grips with curved jaws, carefully rotate the ratchet wheel backwards and forwards. Movement should increase at a rapid rate with each turn!

RBC14. Extract the ratchet wheel and bolt from the cylinder, and apply more penetrating oil to the bolt threads, then unscrew the bolt from the ratchet.

RBC15. To prevent the same problem occurring in the future, apply a liberal quantity of Poly Butyl Cuprysil ('PBC') anti-seize protective grease to the threads, and turn the ratchet up and down the bolt several times. PBC grease is heat-resistant, and lubricates for longer than ordinary grease. Finally, wipe off excess grease, and re-fit the assembly to the cylinder.

RBC16. Give the horse shoe shaped cylinder retaining clips, and the handbrake operating lever, a good wire brush, to remove all traces of rust and dirt. Apply a little PBC grease to the points of contact of the cylinder and backplate, also where the clips contact the backplate, and between the mating surfaces of the clips. This will allow the clips to be removed more easily in the future, and the cylinder to slide freely on the backplate, as intended.

RBC17. Finally, apply a little more high temperature or PBC grease to the pivot point on the handbrake/self-adjusting lever, and re-fit to the cylinder, fitting the complete assembly to the car.

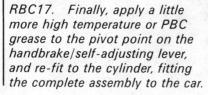

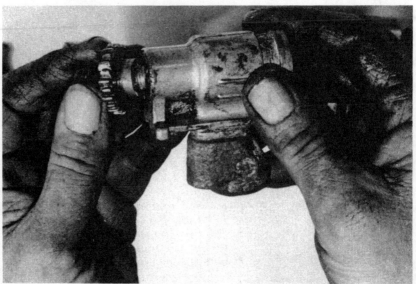

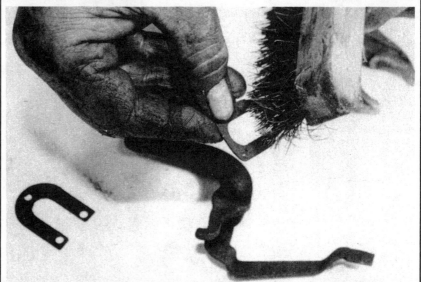

On Mark I Cortinas, there is a mechanical expander unit between the two rear brake shoes, each side of the car, opposite the wheel cylinder. This has two mechanically activated pistons which, when moved by the adjuster square, force the shoes apart and nearer to the drum. It is a good idea to remove the pistons from the unit, and to clean them and the inside of the housing before lightly greasing the mating surfaces (again PBC grease is a longer-term solution), and re-assembling. The adjuster unit simply unbolts from the backplate, for a really thorough cleaning job to be effected.

A similar arrangement is used on the rear of Mark I Escorts. Make sure that, on fitting the rear brake shoes, the shoe return spring with the double set of coils is fitted adjacent to the wheel cylinder.

Rear brakes – Escort I

The rear brakes on Escort Mark Is are very similar in layout to the Cortina Mark I. The wheel cylinder is attached to the backplate by means of twin horse shoe clips, as with the Cortinas.

Removal and overhaul of the cylinder is therefore carried out in exactly the same way. However, unlike the Cortina Mark II system, there is no self-adjusting mechanism. Instead, as with Mark I Cortinas, there is a manual adjuster assembly, at the opposite ends of the brake shoes to the hydraulic cylinder.

RBE1. As with the Cortina Mark Is, a manual adjuster assembly is bolted to the backplate. The mechanically activated pistons should be withdrawn and cleaned, as should the body of the unit. Make sure that the adjuster 'bolt' turns freely in and out, lubricating with penetrating oil and rocking the square headed bolt backwards and forwards, a little at a time, if necessary. Apply a little high melting point or PBC grease to the threads of the bolt and the sliding surfaces of the pistons, prior to re-assembly. The adjuster should then function perfectly for many years to come.

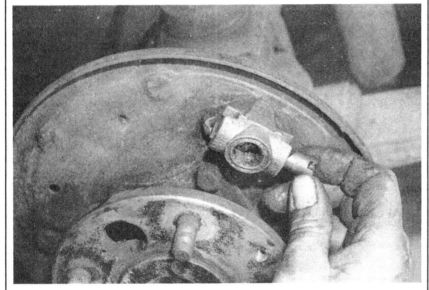

RBE2. Make sure that the spacer plate and its spring clip are transferred from the old brake shoes to the new ones, before fitting them to the vehicle.

RBE3. It is important that, when fitting the brake shoes, the spring with the double set of coils is fitted nearest to the wheel cylinder, and with the longer of the two sets of coils at the bottom.

Rear brakes – Escort II

The rear brakes on Mark II Escorts are operated by a twin piston wheel cylinder, with a spring separating the pistons within the cylinder. The steps required to overhaul the cylinder are similar to those for the cylinders already covered, provided, as always, that the cylinder wall and pistons are in perfect condition.

The self-adjusting mechanism employed on Escort IIs is quite different from that used on the Mark II Cortinas. On the Escorts, the system is operated by the footbrake, rather than by the handbrake, as with the Cortinas.

The mechanism consists of an inter-connecting link (attached at one end to the handbrake operating lever) between the brake shoes, a serrated wheel, and an operating arm, with serrations along one end, which mate with those on the wheel, as shown in diagram *RBE4*. The other end of the operating arm engages in a cut-out in the leading shoe. As the brake lining wears, the non-adjustable clearance 'X' diminishes, as the wheel cylinder piston comes out ever further, to push the shoe closer to the drum. Eventually the gap disappears completely, whereupon further wear causes the brake shoe to exert pressure on the operating arm. This then moves, together with its curved end, against the serrated wheel, by one or two serrations. This has the effect of opening up the gap at 'X' again, and decreasing the distance between the brake lining and the drum.

RBE4. The self-adjusting mechanism on the Escort Mark II models is activated by the footbrake, as described in the text. The gap 'X' varies according to the movement of the operating arm, which effectively keeps pushing the brake shoe out towards the drum, to reduce the clearance between the lining and the drum.

To change the rear brake shoes on Mark II Escorts, the handbrake mechanism must be disconnected from the backplate links, and the 'abutment stop' must be removed from the backplates.

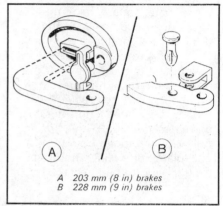

A 203 mm (8 in) brakes
B 228 mm (9 in) brakes

RBE5. On cars with 8 inch diameter brakes, the stop is a bridge piece, held in place by a rubber dust cover; take off the dust cover to release the bridge piece. On cars with 9 inch rear brakes, the abutment stop is a small spacer, secured by a nylon pin; simply lever out the pin to remove the stop.

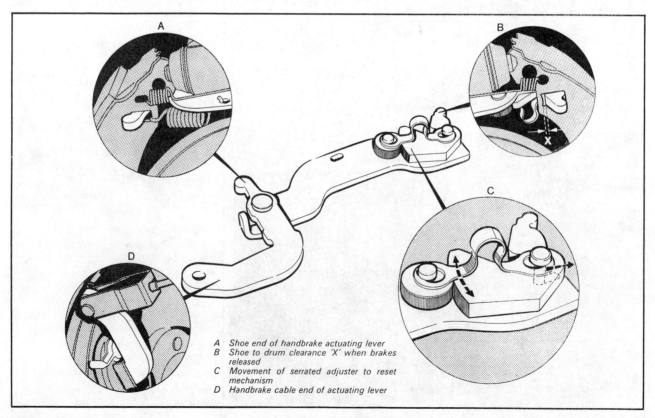

A Shoe end of handbrake actuating lever
B Shoe to drum clearance 'X' when brakes released
C Movement of serrated adjuster to reset mechanism
D Handbrake cable end of actuating lever

RBE6. To remove the rear shoes, start by levering them from their lower supports, detaching the lower return spring.

Carefully lever the leading shoe from the wheel cylinder and self-adjusting arm, and lift the shoe away.

RBE7. Disconnect the trailing shoe from the operating lever, remove the pull-off spring, and detach the shoe from the backplate.

RBE8. Clean the self-adjusting links and the backplate with a small toothbrush. DON'T inhale the dust – it contains ASBESTOS and could be DANGEROUS. Apply a little light oil to the pivots on the self-adjusting mechanism, making sure that ALL excess lubricant is wiped off before re-assembling.

The double-ended wheel cylinder can be overhauled very easily 'in situ'; there's no need to remove the cylinder from the backplate, unless the pistons or the cylinder bore are scored or pitted, or the cylinder has seized. In such cases, the cylinder should be renewed.

On completion of any necessary work on the hydraulics, the brakes can be re-assembled.

When fitting the brake shoes, apply a little high melting point (or PBC) grease to the shoe contact points.

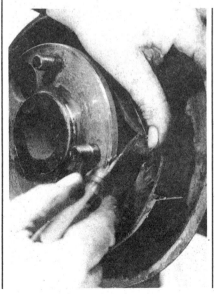

RBE9. Always re-set the automatic adjuster on completion of work on the rear brakes. Using a screwdriver, lever the serrated arm away from the toothed wheel, making sure that the serrated end of the arm then moves towards the backplate, to the limit of the serrations.

With the brake drums replaced (and the hydraulic system bled of air if necessary – more of which later), adjust the brakes to their normal operating position by pumping the brake pedal several times.

Brake pipe renewal

The brake fluid pipes and hoses are, of course, vital to safety, and, as they get older, tend to deteriorate through rust damage (steel piping) and perishing (flexible rubber hoses).

In the case of steel brake pipes, check every inch for traces of rust or other damage. A little surface rust MAY be acceptable – it depends on degree. As a general rule, if rubbing the surface of the pipe with very fine (600 grade) 'wet or dry' paper, used dry, doesn't remove all traces of rust, the pipe MUST be replaced. If pitting is evident, the pipe MUST be changed anyway. Take particular care where the pipes are attached to the underbody, and the rear axle, especially around the supporting clips, where corrosion can lurk unnoticed. 'If in doubt, throw it out' is a good maxim to use when it comes to brake pipes; you can't afford to take chances with brakes.

Flexible rubber hydraulic hoses can be checked by bending the hose tightly through 180 degrees and checking, in a strong light, for evidence of cracking. If ANY cracks appear (they are particularly likely around the ends of the hose), replace the hose.

When removing and re-fitting brake pipes and hoses, ALWAYS use two spanners; one to hold the locknut, and the other to slacken the pipe connection. It is also particularly important to use only close-fitting spanners on

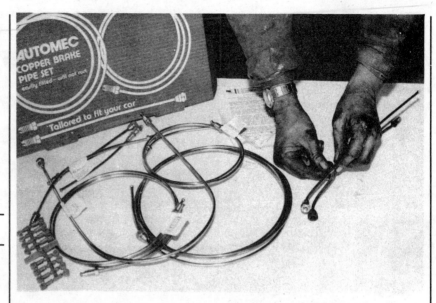

brake pipe connections. These are usually very awkward to release, and a 'loose' spanner will quickly ruin the nut, making it even more difficult to release! Apply penetrating oil to the joints, before you start.

On a car several years old, it is wise to replace ALL the brake pipes in one go, if several are found to be suspect. That way, you will KNOW that the pipes are good, and, if you fit copper pipes, rather than steel, that they will last a very long time.

Brake pipes can be made on a d-i-y basis, using a roll of piping and one of the special 'flaring' tools available on the d-i-y market for the job. If you just have one or two pipes to replace, this is a quick solution.

If, on the other hand, you intend to change all the pipes on the vehicle, it is worth investing in a complete set of copper brake pipes, like those sold by Automec. These pipes come ready labelled, with the correct flares and fittings, and without the need for cutting to length. Such sets are not expensive, and fitting takes very little time; the copper pipes are easy to bend to shape, to match the original pipes. The old pipes are simply unscrewed, and the new ones fitted in their place. Once on the car, they should last for many years; they cannot rust, of course.

BPR1. On any restoration project vehicle, it pays to renew all the brake pipes if you have the slightest doubt about the state of the originals. A set of copper pipes, like these, comes complete with full instructions, pipe support clips, fittings, and even labels attached to each pipe, so that you CAN'T confuse them. Automec supply sets to fit Mark I and II Cortinas and Escorts.

The old pipes can be used as a guide for shaping the new ones.

BPR2. Always use two spanners when releasing pipe connections; one on the pipe connection, and one on the locknut. This is especially important when releasing hoses and pipes from bodywork brackets, otherwise the brackets can break off.

BPR3. Sometimes, things just don't work out, and the brake pipes may prove impossible to separate from, for example, wheel cylinders. The problem is normally due to corrosion between dissimilar metals, (normally steel to aluminium joints) and is made worse by the necessity to use open-ended spanners on brake pipe connections. One answer is to buy a proper brake pipe spanner. This has the ease of access of an open-ended spanner, combined with the grip of a ring spanner, and slips over the pipe, to fit snugly onto the pipe nut. An alternative, if you haven't got such a spanner, and are replacing the brake pipe anyway, is to hacksaw through the pipe, fairly close to the offending joint. A ring spanner can then be guided over the pipe and onto the nut.

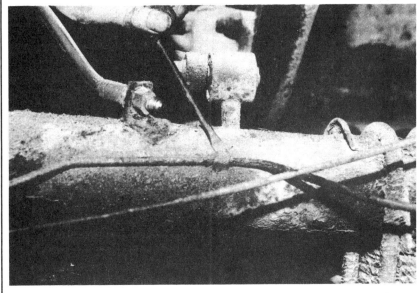

BPR4. It is important not to break any pipe support clips, for example on the rear axle. Gently prise the clips open with a screwdriver . . .

BPR5. . . . then ease the pipe away, directly out of the mouth of the clip, rather than against the side of it. It is amazing how rusty some brake pipes are allowed to become before they are replaced. The rear axle pipe is a favourite for rust, as it collects much of the salt spray that swirls aound the rear wheels.

Brake bleeding

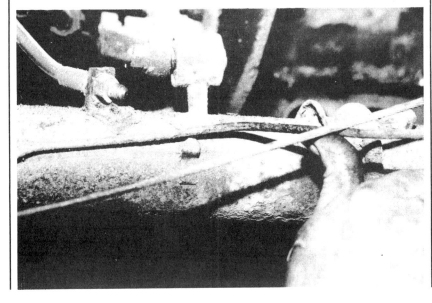

If any part of the hydraulic system has been dismantled, it will be necessary to bleed the brakes of air before they will function correctly. To do this, a length of tube, about a foot or so long (and a close fit on the bleed nipples found at the back

of the backplates on the front brakes, and nearside rear brake), and a jam jar or similar, are needed, plus an assistant, to pump the pedal. If you are working on your own, one of the 'one man' brake bleeding kits, available in motor accessory shops, will be useful.

The basic principles

Having re-assembled the brake system and checked that the breather in the top of the master cylinder cap is clear, fill the cylinder with clean brake fluid. The caps on the three bleed screws now need to be removed, and the screws should be checked to make sure that they are all closed. Clean the area immediately around each bleed screw. Now attach your length of pipe to the front wheel bleed screw on the side of the car nearest to the master cylinder. Place the other end of the tube in the jam jar, into which a little fresh brake fluid, to a depth of about one inch, has been poured. Push the lower end of your pipe below the surface of the fluid, and make sure that it stays there throughout the operation.

Slacken the bleed screw, and ask your assistant to pump the pedal. It should be pumped steadily, down to the floor, and then allowed to return, pausing at the top of the stroke to allow the master cylinder to 'recuperate', then repeating the process. Fluid and air bubbles should emerge from the end of your pipe. After the third 'down' stroke, and while the brake pedal is still held to the floor, close the bleed screw. The pedal can now be allowed to return, and a check can then be made on the level of brake fluid in the master cylinder, topping up as necessary.

The procedure should be repeated until just fluid, with no air bubbles present, emerges from the pipe. At this stage, move on to the opposite front wheel, repeating the procedure, and

finally tackling the single bleed screw at the rear of the car. Try the brake pedal at this point; if it still feels 'spongy', go round the car again, bleeding the air from each part of the circuit once more. This is often necessary, especially where the brake system has been completely drained, and new components fitted. It is wise to rid the system of ALL old fluid anyway, so if any remains in the system, pump it through until fresh fluid emerges at all bleed points.

When topping up the master cylinder between pumping sessions, ALWAYS use NEW brake fluid. Never use fluid that has been pumped through the system, even where it has been allowed to stand for some time. It contains tiny air bubbles, and often particles of dirt as well. It is best disposed of by screwing the lid tightly onto the jam jar, and carefully placing it, upright, in the dustbin. DON'T pour it down a drain, and especially not down a soakaway. Plants and animals are not partial to brake fluid!

If you cannot achieve a 'firm' brake pedal, there is usually a very simple reason. It could be due, for example, to the use of a pipe which is of too large internal diameter to tightly grip the end of the bleed screw. Air can therefore enter the system through the gap, causing sponginess at the pedal. Another problem could be that very little fluid (or, sometimes, none at all!) emerges from the pipe during pumping. Try slackening the bleed screw a little more. If this fails, remove the bleed screw from the cylinder, and make sure that the passageway in the bleed screw, and the aperture in the cylinder into which the screw fits, are clear of dirt. A piece of fine wire will often shift rust, etc, from the bleed screw passageway.

On the other hand, it is possible to release the bleed screw too far, allowing air to enter around the threads. The screw should be undone far enough to allow fluid and air out

in reasonable quantity, but no further.

On cars with vacuum servos, pump the brake pedal a few times prior to bleeding the brakes, to make sure that no vacuum remains in the unit.

Occasionally a car can be a bit of a 'rogue' vehicle when it comes to bleeding brakes, in that it is difficult to achieve a 'firm' pedal, despite all the normal checks. Assuming that the brakes themselves have been assembled correctly, sometimes fitting a longer tube to the bleed screw, and taking this to a 'remote' jam jar, held above the level of the brakes being bled, will do the trick. I know of several Escorts where this has worked, for example. A little more brake fluid is needed, of course, to fill the longer pipe, but this is a small price to pay for making sure that all the air is out of the system.

Don't forget to re-fit the bleed screw caps, on completion of the job.

This method applies to Mark I and II Cortinas, and Mark I Escorts. However, Mark II Escorts, some Mark I Escorts, and export versions of the Cortina Mark II have dual circuit brakes, with a pressure differential valve ('actuator'), which is a 'shuttle' valve, designed to isolate a defective circuit, for example in the event of a fluid leak, and to light the warning lamp on the dashboard. During brake bleeding, the shuttle valve piston must be held in its central position, or the facia warning light may not want to go out!

A tool can be made, using an old screwdriver, and grinding or filing its blade to the dimensions shown in the diagram. Remove the rubber cover from the bottom of the pressure differential warning actuator, and insert the tool into the aperture in the body of the unit, where it will engage in a slot in the larger piston within, drawing it into the central position. It should be maintained here throughout the brake bleeding operation.

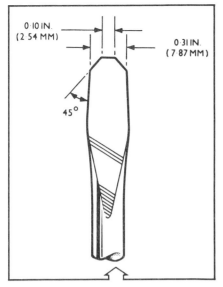

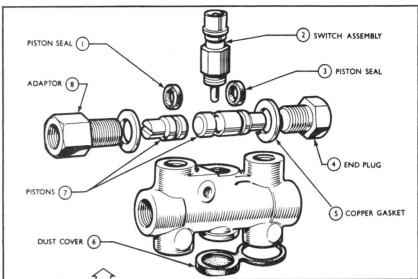

BB1. An old screwdriver can be turned into this useful tool, for centralising the piston on the pressure differential warning actuator, when bleeding the brakes on cars with dual circuit systems.

It is possible to dismantle a pressure differential warning activator unit, but, as can be seen from the diagram, it is a fairly complex, precision piece of machinery, and a stripdown should not be undertaken lightly. Dismantling and overhauling the pressure differential warning actuator is basically similar to dealing with a hydraulic cylinder, and the same attention to cleanliness is needed. In addition, unless the internal metal components are in PERFECT condition, the unit should be replaced. In particular, if scratches or rust are present within the unit, fit a new one. With the unit dismantled, the switch assembly can be tested by connecting the wiring to it, and pressing the plunger against any bare metal on the engine or bodywork. The light should illuminate. The bulb in the warning light can be checked by operating a switch on the dashboard.

BB2. The internal components of the pressure differential warning actuator unit are fairly complex, and great care is needed during overhaul.

Overhaul or renew?

While it is POSSIBLE to overhaul the pressure differential warning actuator unit, just described, and also the vacuum servo units fitted to some models, such jobs are not for the faint hearted, and call for particular attention to, for example, torque settings for the various components in the actuator, and operating clearances in the case of servo units. Full instructions for the overhaul of both items are included in the *Haynes Owners' Workshop Manual* relating to your particular model, should you wish to tackle them. If you are less confident, it would be better to swallow your pride, and buy new units.

Handbrake cables

Handbrake adjustment is normally taken care of by adjustment of

the rear brake shoes, whether this is manual or automatic (depending on the model). However, a separate adjustment is provided on all Cortinas and Escorts, to take account of cable stretch, and to enable the cables to be 'set' when the system has been dismantled. Refer to the *Haynes Owners' Workshop Manual* covering your model, for full details of replacing and adjusting the handbrake cable(s) on your Ford.

Replacement of the cables is fairly straightforward, involving disconnection of the clevis pins and threaded links at the ends of the cables. Renew any worn clevis pins, and apply a little grease to the pins, and to the threads of the new cables, when fitting.

Steering and front suspension

The front suspension on all the cars covered by this book is by MacPherson struts, with coil springs, and integral shock absorbers.

On Mark I and early Mark II Cortinas, a ball joint, incorporated into the steering arm, is attached to the lower end of the

245

suspension unit. The ball bolt of the joint connects the suspension unit to the track control arm, on each side of the vehicle. The track control arm is pivoted at its inner end, on a bolt and rubber bush which attaches it to the cross-member. An anti-roll bar connects the outer end of each track control arm, and is attached to the body, forward of the suspension, through rubber insulated brackets. On later Mark II Cortinas, a standard type ball joint connects the lower end of the suspension unit with the steering and track control arms.

Two adjustable track rods join the steering arms at each side to a transverse rod, which itself inter-connects the steering box drop arm and the idler arm.

The upper MacPherson strut mountings on Mark I Cortinas, and Mark IIs up to August, 1967, incorporate a thrust ball race, fitted in a rubber bush. The bearings can be replaced, but the mounting comes only as a complete assembly. Later cars have a tapered rubber bush bonded to the upper mounting, with no ball race.

Early Mark I Cortinas have six grease points to attend to on the steering joints, but later cars have seven sealed joints, and two more are rubber-bonded joints, requiring no lubrication.

The prime mover in the steering system of the Cortina models is the steering box, of the recirculating ball variety.

Only one adjustment – to the rocker shaft – can be carried out with the box in situ. Any further attentions must be done with the unit removed from the vehicle.

SFS1.   The layout of the steering gear on Mark I and Mark II Cortinas is very similar. All the moving joints are susceptible to wear after a long time in use, and if several joints have a little 'lost motion', the steering can become rather vague.

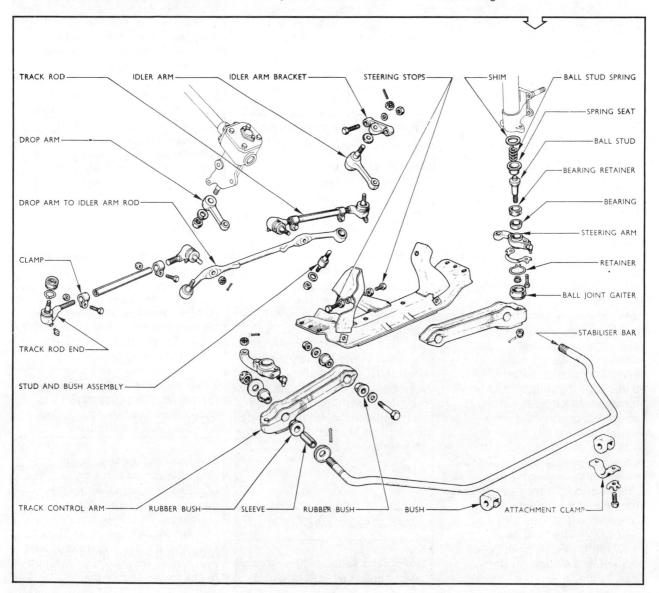

On the Escorts, which have rack and pinion steering, the steering arms at the base of the MacPherson struts connect to track rods, which are themselves linked directly to the steering rack. The lower end of each suspension unit is located by a track control arm. On cars up to September, 1969, there is a compression strut fitted between the outer end of each track control arm and a strengthened mounting on each side member. Later cars have an anti-roll bar linking the outer ends of the track control arms, and secured to the underbody by rubber-insulated brackets on the front member.

SFS2. Later Mark I Escorts, and Mark IIs, have an anti-roll bar forming part of the front suspension, whereas on early Mark Is, compression struts were used.

The steering on Escorts has less inherent free play in it than on Cortinas, since the linkage is more direct, with fewer ball joints and links. Nevertheless, free play can develop in the steering rack/pinion assembly, in the flexible steering column coupling, and in the track rod end (steering rack) ball joints, which can give very uncertain steering.

MacPherson strut overhaul

The condition of the MacPherson strut units is vital to safe motoring, on all Ford Cortinas and Escorts. If, for example, the integral shock absorbers are leaking fluid, the result will be a restless, uncomfortable ride, shaking and uncertain steering, and very poor cornering. Bouncing on each front 'corner' of the car and letting go should see the vehicle settle almost instantly. If oscillations continue, the shock absorber units are suspect. Unfortunately it is

necessary to take the MacPherson strut unit off the vehicle, in order to overhaul it. It is also necessary to compress the main road springs, in order to dismantle the unit. For this job you MUST use proper, safe spring compressors, to hold the springs in a state of compression as you work on the suspension unit. If one of these springs should come loose, it might prove FATAL, so take EXTRA care when compressing or releasing the tension on the springs.

The MacPherson strut units can either be replaced, complete – but this involves removal of the hub assemblies and transferring

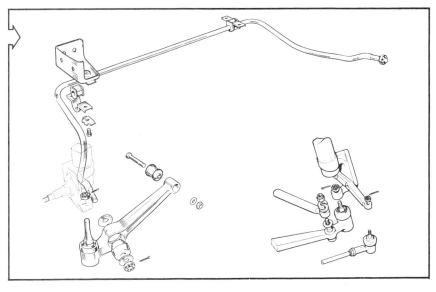

them to the new units – or the 'business' ends of the units only can be renewed. These strut 'inserts' are in effect the shock absorbers, which are screwed into the top of the MacPherson strut units. These are easy to fit, and cheaper to buy than complete suspension legs.

MSO1. The MacPherson strut assembly must be removed from the car (as described in the 'Bodywork' chapter), but first the brake caliper, on disc braked models, can be taken off. Start by knocking back the locking tabs on the main caliper supporting bolts

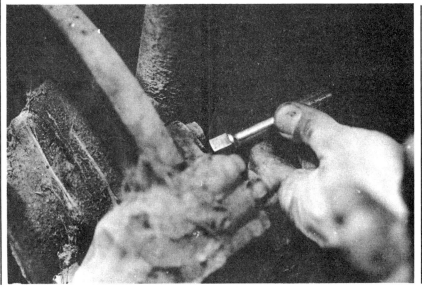

MSO2. Use a ring spanner to slacken the bolts – they may be VERY tight, due to the accumulation of mud and salt in the area. On re-fitting, tighten the bolts to 45 lb.ft. (Cortina Mark I), 45 to 50 lb.ft (Cortina Mark II, and Escorts).

MSO3. With the brake pipes disconnected, the caliper can now be released from the suspension unit, for overhaul, if necessary, as described in the 'Braking System' section.

The suspension leg, complete with coil spring and upper mounting, is now removed from the car, as detailed in the 'Front Wing Change – Cortina' section. The general principles are the same for Cortina or Escort models.

MSO4. On drum brakes models (this is an Escort), the first step in taking out the suspension unit is to remove the brake drum and wheel bearings.

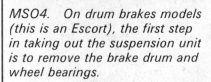

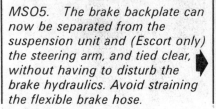

MSO5. The brake backplate can now be separated from the suspension unit and (Escort only) the steering arm, and tied clear, without having to disturb the brake hydraulics. Avoid straining the flexible brake hose.

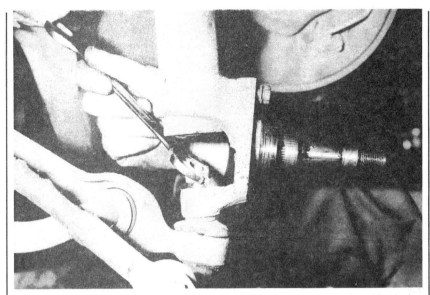

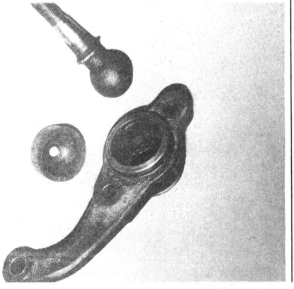

MSO6. On Escorts, the lower end of the suspension unit is secured to the track control arm by a single nut, onto the ball pin bolt from the track control arm. The nut can be released after taking out the split pin. With the upper end of the suspension unit released from the vehicle, by taking out the three securing bolts, the taper joint between the track control arm ball joint and the lower end of the suspension unit can be separated, if necessary using a ball joint separator. It helps to use a trolley jack handle or similar between the top of the anti-roll bar and the lower face of the front cross-member; this gives plenty of leverage with very little effort, and is especially useful when re-fitting the track control arm ball joint to the suspension unit.

MSO7. With the suspension unit out of the car, the ball joint at the outer end of the track control arm can be checked for wear. It makes sense to change the joint, if necessary, while the suspension unit is out of the car. The joints on this Mark II Cortina were in perfect condition.

MSO8. On Mark I and early Mark II Cortinas, the ball pin in the joint at the base of the suspension unit (part of the steering arm assembly) tends to become corroded and pitted in time, like this one, taken from a 1965 estate car. Please refer also to the 'Track Control Arm' section.

MSO9. Before attempting to strip a MacPherson strut unit, the coil spring should be compressed and held in this state, using proper coil spring compressors. It is always safer to use four compressors, equally spaced around the spring. Tighten them, a little at a time, and equally, until the spring is compressed. NEVER put your face above the top of the spring while it is under tension. The latent power in a vehicle's suspension spring is terrific, and could easily kill. Keep children and pets well away from the working area during this operation.

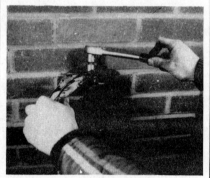

MSO10. When the spring is compressed, grip the upper rebound stop bracket (where fitted) with a pair of grips, or the upper spring seat, to prevent them from turning, while the central nut is released.

MSO12. The dust cover is lifted out – it may still be attached to the spring seat. If the dust cover is damaged, replace it with a new one, to keep dirt and moisture out of the 'works' of the new suspension unit.

MSO13. The coil spring – still in its compressed state, and with the compressors still firmly attached – can now be lifted off the unit. The rebound (bump) stop rubber follows. Place the spring out of harm's way, where it will not be moved until it is time to re-fit it to the car.

MSO11. The upper bearing, and the spring seat and associated washers can now be taken off, noting the correct order for re-assembly.

MSO14. The special nut holding the suspension unit insert in position must now be released. Unless you have the special spanner for the nut, a pipe wrench or similar can be used. New nuts are provided with the inserts, anyway.

MSO18. ALWAYS use strut inserts of reputable quality; Monroe units like these are good examples. Pump the piston rod up and down to its full extent by hand, several times, to 'prime' the unit. Just place the insert gently into the tube . . .

MSO15. The defective shock absorber unit is now simply lifted out of the suspension leg.

MSO16. Treat the suspension leg to a coat or two of rust-resistant paint, while it is out of the vehicle.

MSO17. It pays to treat the inside of the suspension tube with a rust killer, allowing this to 'cure' as directed by the makers, before pouring a few ccs of clean engine oil into the bottom of the tube. This will help keep internal corrosion at bay. A torch is useful for checking the inside of the tube for corrosion.

MSO19. . . . and fit the new nut, tightening it with a large adjustable spanner if you haven't got the correct sized spanner in your tool kit.

MSO20. A new rubber dust cover can then be fitted, to protect the unit for the future.

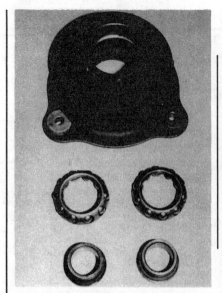

On Cortinas, the track control arm stud nut should be tightened to 30 to 35 lb.ft., and the anti-roll bar end nut to 25 to 30 lb.ft. The track rod end ball joint stud nut, and the brake backplate bolts, require a torque of 18 to 22 lb.ft.

On Escorts, the track control arm ball stud nut should be tightened to 30 to 35 lb.ft. Always use new split pins on the castellated nuts, when re-assembling.

Steering links – Cortina

The steering links and their various joints on Cortinas should be checked very carefully for wear. The easiest way of doing this is to get an assistant to turn the steering wheel to and fro, while you observe relative movement between adjacent components within the system. Even then, worn joints can be difficult to spot until the links are dismantled.

Any of the joints could be found to be worn, and it is best to replace any that display even slight movement of the centre pin in relation to the body of the joint. Since there are many joints within the system, a little wear at

MSO21. *Always check the condition of the upper mounting bearing assembly. A loose upper bearing mounting, or collapsed bearings, will give a clicking noise when travelling over bumps. If your car is a Mark I Cortina, or a Mark II prior to August 1967, the upper bearings suffered from the entry of water, corroding the bearings, and causing stiff steering. Liberally smear the bearings with a lithium-based grease, or PBC grease, prior to re-fitting.*

Another problem with these models can be that the rubber part of the mounting assembly can rub against the spring seat, gradually being destroyed by abrasive grit; replace it if wear is severe. The thrust bearing locknut should be tightened to 45 to 55 lb.ft.

On later Mark II Cortinas, and Escorts, check the condition of the rubber upper mounting, and replace if the rubber is cracked or soft.

MSO22. *The coil spring can now be replaced, and the upper spring seat and bearing components – the piston rod will need to be held (by hand only – NOT with grips or pliers) while the central nut is attached. Screw the nut on securely – but don't yet fully tighten it.* ▶

MSO23. *Finally, the coil spring compressors can be released – evenly, a little at a time, making sure that the spring sits correctly in its seats, top and bottom. The complete suspension leg can then be re-fitted to the car, tightening the three upper bearing securing bolts to 15 to 18 lb.ft. (all models). The centre spindle nut should only be finally tightened when the weight of the vehicle is once again taken by the wheels, which must be in the straight ahead position. Tighten the nut to 28 to 32 lb.ft. (29 to 33 lb.ft., Escort Mark II).*

252

each point soon adds up to a great deal of sloppiness!

Known troublesome areas include the two stud and bush assemblies that link the 'drop arm to idler arm rod' (drag link) with the drop arm, from the steering box, and the idler arm. On Mark I and early Mark II Cortinas, the composite bushes fitted at these two points are made from rubber, with steel outer casings, which are pressed into the holes in the drag link. The rubber part of the bush can become soft, or break up, with obvious consequences on the accuracy and directness of the steering! Later models have nylon inserts at these pivot points, which should also be checked for wear.

It is, of course, important that the wheel bearings are in good condition; play here is easy to confuse with steering gear 'lost motion'.

Reference back to diagram SFS 1., will be helpful in identifying the relative positions of the various components referred to in this section.

SL1.   Start by disconnecting the outer track rod ends from the steering arms, having first loosened the nuts so that they cover the ends of the threads. It is worth investing a few pounds on a proper ball joint separator, since it avoids possible damage which can be caused by the more chancy method of hitting the ball joints and/or steering links with hammers. The ball pin should move in its housing under thumb pressure, without feeling 'loose'.

Move the track rod backwards and forwards on its inner ball joint (at its junction with the drag link) to check for wear. Like the ball pin, it should move smoothly.

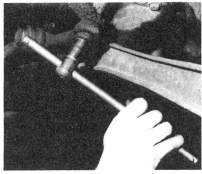

SL2.   Release the nut securing the drag link to the steering box drop arm joint. This is one of the dreaded 'stud and bush' assemblies . . .

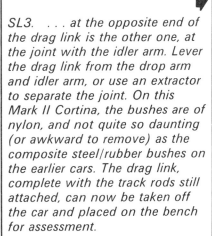

SL3.   . . . at the opposite end of the drag link is the other one, at the joint with the idler arm. Lever the drag link from the drop arm and idler arm, or use an extractor to separate the joint. On this Mark II Cortina, the bushes are of nylon, and not quite so daunting (or awkward to remove) as the composite steel/rubber bushes on the earlier cars. The drag link, complete with the track rods still attached, can now be taken off the car and placed on the bench for assessment.

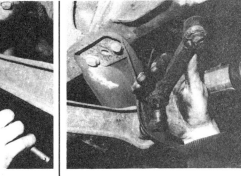

SL4.   While the drag link is off the car, check the operation of the idler arm (relay lever). It should swivel smoothly in its housing, without evidence of free play in the bearing.

The rubber bushes on the Mark I and early Mark II Cortinas can be rather more awkward to deal with. If you haven't got the necessary extractor for pushing out the central bolt, start by releasing the nuts securing the studs, as shown in SL2. The drag link can then be carefully levered away from the drop arm and idler arm, since the rubber in the bushes is normally soft. This leaves you with the threaded sections of the studs to remove from the drop arm and idler arm. This is easy to achieve, having released the upper nut. Place an old socket over each offending stud, followed by the original

253

large washer and nut from the stud. By simply tightening the nut, the stud is pulled out of the arm.

If you are intending to use the old drag link, with new stud and bush assemblies, the remains of the old bushes must first be removed. Start by prising out any rubber remaining in the hole, then, VERY CAREFULLY use a small hacksaw to cut through the metal outer ring of the original bush. Take great care not to damage the 'parent' metal of the drag link, or it could seriously weaken it. If you should cut into the drag link, scrap it and buy a new one.

The remains of the outer casings of the old bushes can now be removed, and the new bushes inserted. Preferably, press them into place, using a socket and a vice, until the outer sleeves are flush with the boss on each end of the rod. If you don't have a vice, the bushes can be carefully tapped home, using a spacer, such as an old socket.

SL5.   The nylon bushes on later Mark II Cortinas can be extracted from the drag link quite easily. Even if the bushes are not too badly worn (and these were quite good) it is probably a good idea to change them anyway, while the system is apart. They are not very expensive fortunately.

There is, of course, no need to remove the pins from the steering box and idler drop arms, with this type of bush. Simply clean off any surface rust, and wipe the pins with a little lithium-based or PBC grease.

On re-assembly. the drag link is installed with the new bushes, and a nylon washer on each side of the drag link, with the heavy steel washer, and finally the securing nut, fitted over the stud.

When re-fitting the drag link to the steering box arm and idler arm, make sure that the steering arms are in the 'straight ahead' position, or else the rubber/nylon bushes will be under constant pressure, and will try to bias the steering to one side or the other. The bushes will also fail prematurely, of course.

If any of the track rod ends are worn (with loose pins and/or split gaiters), accurately measure the distance between the centre of the offending ball joint, and the end of the track rod sleeve, before dismantling. This is likely to be more accurate than counting the number of 'exposed threads' on the track rod, since the new track rod ends are quite likely to be of different construction and dimensions, compared with the originals.

To change a worn track rod end, slacken the clamp bolt on the adjusting sleeve, and unscrew the old ball joint, using penetrating oil if necessary, beforehand. Fit the new joint to give the same measurement (centre of joint to sleeve) as you had originally. When fitting a track rod end, the clamp should be located on the track rod so that the bolt is at the bottom of the clamp, and the head of the pinch bolt faces the drag link (i.e. with the nut towards the rear of

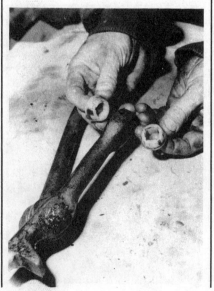

the car).

Always fit new split pins, and preferably new nuts, on re-assembling the steering links and track rods to the vehicle. The correct torque for the ball joint nuts is 18 to 22 lb.ft., and for the steering and idler arm joints, 20 to 25 lb.ft. (Mark I) or 25 to 30 lb.ft. (Mark II).

If you have assembled the track rod ends according to measurements made before dismantling, then *theoretically* the tracking of the front wheels should be okay (assuming that it was correct before you started!). However, after carrying out any work on the steering, it pays to check the tracking, either with one of the d-i-y tracking gauges, available in motor accessory shops, or 'by eye' initially. Another approximate method is to measure the distance between the front wheel rims, at the front and back of each wheel, at points level with the wheel hub centre. If 'approximate' methods are used, it is wise to take the car to a garage or tyre fitting specialist as soon as possible, to have the tracking checked properly.

Should it be obvious that the tracking is out (because the wheels point in or out, for example), slacken the track rod clamps, and rotate the rods (carefully using a pair of grips, if necessary) so that the track rod effectively lengthens or shortens, as necessary. It is important that the track rods are of equal length, so that the steering box is maintained on a 'central' setting, with the front wheels in the 'straight ahead' position. When adjustment is correct, the clamp bolts can be tightened so that the jaws on each clamp are in line with a slot in the track rod. The clamp bolt should be positioned, again, at the bottom of the clamp, with the nut facing the rear of the car. Before finally tightening the clamp bolts, make sure that each track rod end is set correctly, with each ball joint in the centre of its arc of travel (i.e. not set at an angle).

Track rod end change – Escort

The steering system on the Escorts is much simpler than that on the Cortinas. The steering rack operates directly through the track rod ends, to the steering arms connected to the hubs.

Wear still develops, of course, and the hard working track rod ends are one cause of sloppy steering, when worn. Watch each track rod to steering arm joint while an assistant rocks the steering wheel to and fro – wear in the joint will show up in terms of 'lost motion' between the two. If there is ANY free movement here, the joint should be changed. At the same time, it is worth inspecting the condition of the steering rack gaiters. These MUST be in sound condition. If cracks develop in the rubber, oil will come out, and dirt will get in. The inevitable result of this is premature (and rapid) wear in the rack, and MoT failure. Since the track rod ends must be removed in order to change the gaiters, it makes sense to tackle the two jobs together.

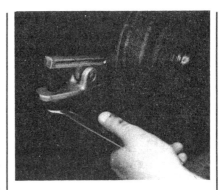

TRE1. Remove the split pin and release the nut on the track rod end, so that it covers the ends of the threads. Then either tap the joint apart, or use a ball joint splitter to separate the joint.

TRE2. The ball joint on this particular Escort was not worn, and so we intended to re-fit it, having changed the steering rack gaiter, which was badly split. Therefore we marked the exact position of the joint on the track rod, so that it could be re-fitted at the same point, to maintain tracking. This method can be used with new track rod ends, provided they are of the same dimensions as the old unit. If not, make a mark on the track rod, and measure the distance from this to the centre of the track rod end, prior to dismantling. Make sure that the centre of the new track rod end is at exactly the same distance from your mark, on fitting.

TRE3. Using a tight-fitting spanner, slacken the locknut on the track rod end; you will need to hold the track rod firmly with a pair of grips, initially.

TRE4.   The track rod end can then be unscrewed by hand.

TRE5.   After slackening the securing clips and pulling off the remains of the old gaiter, fit the new one over the end of the track rod, having wiped the insides of the steering rack, if necessary, with clean rag. Don't forget to slide the larger, inner clip, onto the rack before fitting the gaiter!

TRE6.   Secure the outer end of the gaiter with one of the new clips provided in the kit, then, using a 'flexy' plastic oil bottle, or an oil can with a long spout, top up the gaiter with SAE 90 EP oil. The total capacity of the rack is just $^1/4$ pint. Don't overfill the gaiter, or the internal pressure could be so high that the gaiter could split, if the steering is turned quickly from lock to lock!
    Now tighten the inner clip.

TRE7.   Sometimes difficulty can be experienced when tightening the nut onto the ball pin, due to this turning with the nut. Placing a jack beneath the ball joint helps, and another trick is to place a spare open ended spanner between the nut and the ball joint, as the nut is initially tightened. The extra pressure keeps the ball pin still while the nut is turned. Finally, with the nut tightened to 18 to 22 lb.ft., fit a new split pin.
    If you haven't got a tracking gauge, it is a good idea to have the tracking checked professionally, as soon as possible.

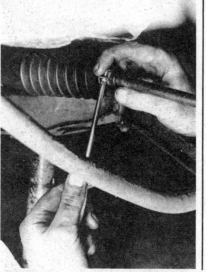

Steering box – Cortina

Steering boxes normally last a very long time, provided that the oil level is kept topped up. However, eventually wear does set in, and the result may then be looseness in the steering, knocking when travelling over rough surfaces, and so on.
    Before removing the unit, make sure first that the problem is not due simply to the bolts holding the unit to the side member being loose. They should be torqued to 25 to 30 lb.ft.
    If the bolts are tight, get an assistant to rock the steering wheel from side to side. Carry out

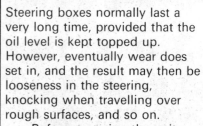

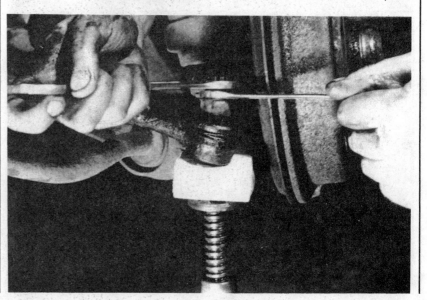

the test first with the wheels in the straight ahead position, and then on almost full lock to each side. A little lost motion detected only in the 'straight ahead' position indicates wear in the worm and/or the nut. However, if free play is evident at all positions, the culprit is probably the rocker shaft bush.

If you are hearing knocking noises on rough surfaces, and the suspension is in good order, the problem should be solved simply by adjusting the rocker shaft – the only adjustment which can be made with the steering box in the car, incidentally.

To check whether adjustment is necessary, the drop arm from the steering box needs to be disconnected from the drag link. Then, with the steering box central (drop arm pointing straight ahead, and parallel to the steering column), a spring balance should be attached to the steering wheel rim (at one of the spoke junctions) and the

force required to turn the wheel, noted. For Mark I models, the reading should be 1 1/4 to 1 1/2 lbs. If it is too low, unbolt the steering box cover, and remove a paper or steel shim. Re-fit the cover, tightening the bolts to 12 to 15 lb.ft, then repeat the test with the spring balance. If the force recorded initially was more than the specified figure, you will need to add shims. As they could prove difficult to obtain, you could fabricate new ones from brown paper.

When the adjustment is correct, re-fit the drag link to the drop arm, and tighten the nut to 20 to 25 lb.ft.

On Mark II cars, the required force, applied at the steering wheel rim, to move the wheel (steering linkage disconnected, as for the Mark I) is 1 3/4 to 2 lbs. Adjustment on the Mark II is by means of a screw and locknut, mounted on the steering box cover. Slacken the adjuster locknut, turn the adjuster screw

until the correct reading is obtained, and then re-tighten the locknut. Double check that the adjustment is still correct. The correct torque for the drag link to drop arm connection on the Mark II is 25 to 30 lb.ft.

If a steering box is badly worn, it must be removed from the vehicle for repairs, or for fitting a reconditioned box. While it is possible to dismantle and rebuild the unit at home, your main problem is going to be obtaining new parts for rebuilding the unit. In addition, some of the operations require presses and reamers, which few of us have access to. Therefore, by far the most practical option is to have your unit professionally rebuilt – for example by Lione (Merton) Ltd. – or exchanged for a reconditioned unit.

SBC1. The steering box and column assembly on Cortina Mark I models looks like this.

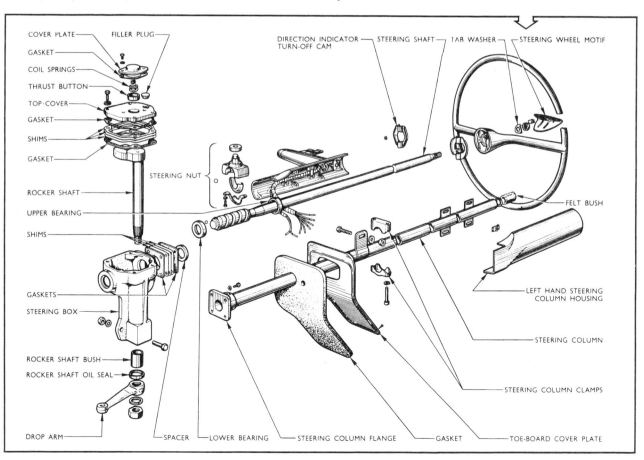

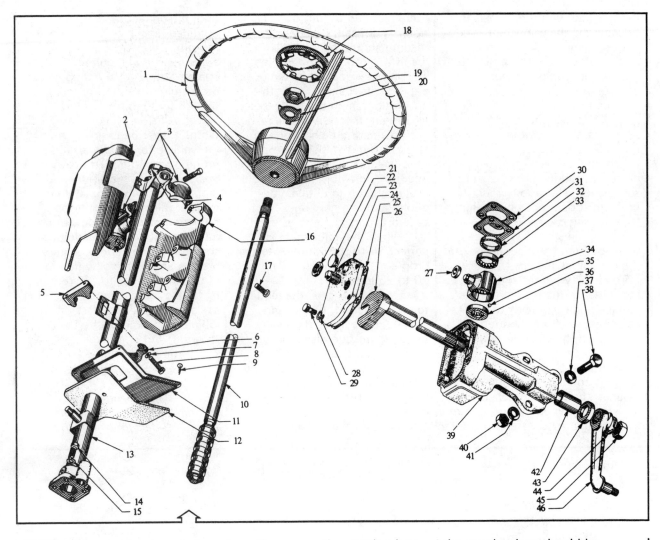

SBC2. The steering box design for the Mark II models is similar to the Mark I, but on the Mark IIs adjustment of the rocker shaft end float is by an adjusting screw and locknut.

1 Steering wheel	25 Gasket
2 Upper cowl	26 Steering gear
3 Control unit	shaft
switch assembly	27 Main worm nut
4 Bush	roller
5 Column clamp	28 Split washer
6 Column clamp	29 Bolt
7 Washer	30 Gasket
8 Screw	31 Shim
9 Screw	32 Seal
10 Inner column	33 Shaft bearing cup
11 Cover plate	34 'Nut' assembly
12 Seal	35 Ball bearing
13 Outer column	36 Shaft bearing cup
14 Bolt	37 Washer
15 Split washer	38 Bolt
16 Lower cowling	39 Steering gear
17 Bolt	body
18 Centre motif	40 Nut
19 Nut	41 Washer
20 Tab washer	42 Bush
21 Nut	43 Seal
22 Plug	44 Split washer
23 Threaded plug	45 Nut
24 Cover plate	46 Steering gear arm

To remove the steering box, disconnect the battery, then the steering wheel must be removed, by taking off the central securing nut and tapping the wheel free with a soft-faced hammer, or 'pulling' it off with a puller, with the front wheels in the 'straight ahead' position. The column shroud and securing bracket bolts inside the car are then taken out, along with any rubber gaskets.

On column change models, the pin securing the gearchange tube to the gearchange housing must be removed from under the bonnet, then, from inside the car, withdraw the gearchange lever/tube assembly. At the bottom of the column, take out the bolts securing the gearchange housing to the steering box, and tie the linkage to one side.

Under the front of the car,

the steering box should be separated from the steering linkage – either by taking the drop arm off the steering box shaft (a near impossibility with the unit still in the car), or by separating the drop arm from the drag link. The three bolts holding the steering box to the side member can then be released, and the steering box removed from the vehicle. On all but left-hand drive 1600E and GT versions, the unit can be withdrawn from below the car. On these models, however, the box and column assembly must be removed through the top of the engine compartment, having first removed the clutch slave cylinder, and the air cleaner.

If it is necessary to remove the indicator cancelling mechanism cam, first turn the

drop arm until it is in the 'straight ahead' position, then make a note of the position of the cam on the splines at the top of the column, before tapping it off.

With the unit out of the car, the drop arm can be taken off the steering box shaft. Various methods can be tried, including wedges, pullers, and so on. Hammering is risky, and could damage the soft casing of the unit, if you miss! One possible answer is to heat the arm, then pour oil around the splines, leaving it to cool overnight. Hopefully, in the morning, a sharp hammer blow will then spring it off.

If you should decide to dismantle the steering box, full details of the stripdown sequence are given in the *Haynes Owners' Workshop Manuals* covering the Cortina models. Take great care not to lose or damage components when they are removed, especially the shim washers and ball bearings.

SBC3. Take particular care of the shim washers as they are withdrawn, keep them in a safe, clean container.

SBC4. One job that is easy to carry out at home is replacement of the felt bush in the outer column. Simply lever it out, and push a new bush in, having first soaked it in engine oil.

SBC5. The lower steering box shaft oil seal can also be replaced at home; make sure that it is not damaged on the splines, as it is carefully drifted home. The lips of the seal should face inwards. If you cannot find a suitable length of pipe for drifting the seal into place, use an ordinary drift, tapping gently, a little at a time, around the edge of the seal.

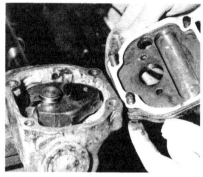

SBC6. Make sure that the gasket is sound, and in position, before re-fitting the steering box lid.

SBC7. With the lid in place, the thrust button, with its two concentric springs and cover plate, can be re-fitted.

On re-assembly of the unit to the car, tighten the securing bolts to 25 to 30 lb.ft., having made sure that there is a flat washer under each bolt and nut head, and the drop arm to drag link connection should be tightened to 20 to 25 lb.ft. (Mark I) and to 25 to 30 lb.ft. (Mark II). The correct torque for the drop arm securing nut is 60 to 70 lb.ft. (Mark I) and 60 to 80 lb.ft. for the Mark II. The steering wheel nut should be tightened to 20 to 25 lb.ft., making sure that it is in the 'straight ahead' position, in line with the wheels, first. Bend up the lock tab after tightening the nut.

Finally, top up the steering box with SAE 90 EP oil, to the bottom of the filler plug aperture.

Steering rack change – Escort

When wear develops in the steering rack assembly, it can be replaced very easily. D-i-y overhaul of the rack and pinion assembly is not a practical proposition. A rack will normally develop excessive free play, or roughness, or both. If the car has been driven for very long with a split rack gaiter, the chances are that water and grit have entered and wrecked the mating surfaces within, anyway.

With 'exchange' steering racks readily available at reasonable prices, and with steering racks normally lasting for anything up to 100,000 miles (or sometimes more), the most cost-effective solution to a worn rack assembly is to fit a reconditioned unit.

SRC1. Start by pulling out the split pins, then slackening the nuts, on the track rod ends, having first raised the car and secured it 'airborne' on safe axle stands.

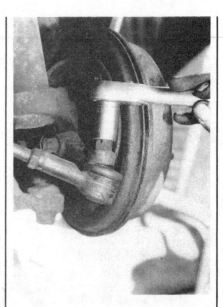

SRC2. Use a ball joint splitter to separate the joints, leaving the nuts covering the outer ends of the threads, for protection – especially important if you intend to re-use the track rod ends on the new rack.

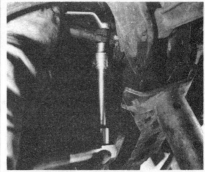

SRC3. Release the clamp bolt at the flexible fabric joint – if the fabric joint is worn, it should be replaced. Therefore, leave it attached to the rack, and disconnect it at the clamp joint to the steering column, above the fabric unit. It will then come off the car with the rack.

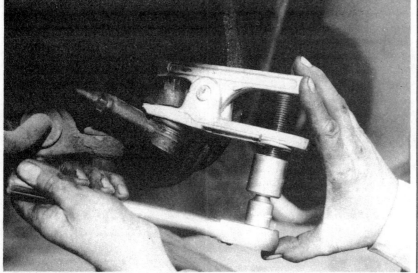

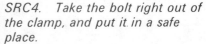

SRC4. Take the bolt right out of the clamp, and put it in a safe place.

SRC5.   Knock back the locking tabs on the rack supporting bolts, at the front cross-member. A short socket extension bar is useful for this.

SRC6.   The four bolts can now be released from the cross-member – take care that the rack doesn't fall on top of you as you take out the last bolts.

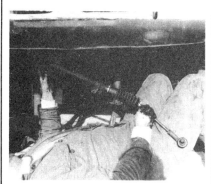

SRC7.   Guide the rack away from below the front of the car.

SRC8.   Fitting the new rack is a reversal of the dismantling operations. First fit the track rod ends to the rack, using the same measuring techniques described in the 'Track Rod End Change' section. It is of course an ideal opportunity to fit new track rod ends, if the old ones are worn. Use new split-pins, after tightening the track rod end nuts to 18 to 22 lb.ft.

Check that the wheels and the steering rack are in the 'straight ahead' position before fitting the rack, with the distances between the track rod end centres and the rack body equal on both sides. Make sure that the fabric coupling is not strained when fitting the rack assembly, and don't tighten the coupling clamp bolts until the rack mounting bolts have been

tightened to 12 to 15 lb.ft. (Mark I), or 15 to 18 lb.ft (Mark II), and the locking tabs have been knocked over.

If the fabric coupling appears to be under tension, simply slide it a little further onto the splines on the steering column, before tightening the clamp bolts.

Anti-roll bar (front)

The bushes around each of the anti-roll bar mountings deteriorate as they get older, and it is important that they should be replaced before they become too badly worn.

Cortina and Escort

ARB1.   The anti-roll bar (stabiliser bar) is attached as shown to the track control arm and to the front underbody. The bar for a Mark II Cortina is shown, although the set-up is very similar on the Mark I Cortina, and the Escorts.

1	Split pin	7	Stop washer
2	Castellated nut	8	Stabiliser bar
3	Washer	9	Bush
4	Insulator	10	Clamp
5	Insulator	11	Tab washer
6	Sleeve	12	Bolt

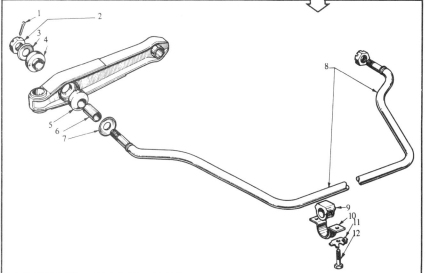

The bushes in the two clamps at the front mountings of the anti-roll bar are easily replaced. Jack the front of the car, placing blocks beneath the front wheels. Lower the jack until the wheels are touching the blocks, but with the car's weight still taken by the jack. Insert axle stands under the front cross-member, to maintain this position.

Take out the two bolts holding each of the two clamps on the front mountings, after knocking back the locking tabs. The rubber bushes have slits in them, to enable them to be removed over the anti-roll bar. Prise these out, and fit new bushes, with the slits in them facing the front of the vehicle. Re-fit the clamps and bolts, and, with the weight of the car back on the wheels, tighten the bolts to 15 to 18 lb.ft., locking them with new tabs. It is worthwhile, if possible, replacing the original bolts with stainless steel ones, to avoid rust problems in the future.

To change the bushes at each end of the anti-roll bar, the complete assembly must be removed from the car. It is advisable to compress the coil springs ('in situ'), with proper compressors, placed equidistantly around the springs, before starting work – you will therefore need at least two sets of spring compressors.

First remove the front attachment point clamps and bushes, as just described, then take off the split pins, nuts, large washers and bushes from the ends of the bar. The anti-roll bar is then free to be removed, from the front of the vehicle. The forward bushes, sleeves and large washers can be taken from the bar once it is clear of the vehicle.

When fitting the new bushes, which may be of rubber (early cars) or plastic (later models), first place a large washer on each end of the bar, followed by a sleeve and bush at each end. Fit the bar through the holes in the track control arm, and assemble the rear bushes, large washers

and nuts. If the bushes are difficult to insert into the track control arm, smear them with a little washing-up liquid, to help them slide into place; make sure they are fully home. If the anti-roll bar ends are reluctant to pull in sufficiently, to go back into their respective holes in the track control arms, loop a stout cord around the ends of the bar, and use a screwdriver, tourniquet fashion, to pull the ends together sufficiently to slip them through the holes. Take great care that the cord doesn't slip towards the front of the car, during this operation.

Tighten the nuts only finger-tight, initially. When the car is back on its wheels, tighten the nuts on the ends of the anti-roll bar to 25 to 30 lb.ft., then fit new split pins.

Compression struts

Early (pre September 1969) Escorts had compression struts, rather than an anti-roll bar, at the front. To remove these, first take out the nut holding the front end of each compression strut to the track control arms, and then lift off the recessed washer and nylon washer. At the back of each compression strut, take out the single nut (securing the strut to the mounting bracket on the body side member), followed by the dished washer and rubber bush – note which way round these are fitted.

The rear end of the strut can now be released from its mounting bracket, and the remaining rubber bush and dished washer taken out, again noting their respective positions, for re-assembly. The strut can now be taken from the vehicle.

When re-fitting the strut, always fit a new nylon washer on either side of the compression

strut, at the track control arm stud. When the strut has been fitted, and the car is back on its wheels, tighten the single nut at the rear of the compression strut to 25 to 30 lb.ft., and the nut holding the strut to the track control arm to 35 to 40 lb.ft.

Track control arms

The coil spring on the side being worked on should be compressed 'in situ', using proper coil spring compressors, before work commences. Jack and support the car under the front cross-member, so that the weight is off the track control arms. Take out the split pin, nut, washer and outer bush from the end of the anti-roll bar.

On Mark I and early Mark II Cortinas, take out the split pin and castellated nut from the lower suspension ball joint, at the foot of the MacPherson strut, and, with a suitable puller, extract the bolt from the tapered hole in the outer end of the control arm. On later Cortinas, the three bolts (and on Escorts, the single nut) are simply released from the lower ball joint, and the track control arm can then be levered down, away from the suspension leg. On the later Mark II Cortinas, there is then a single nut holding the mounting cup (for the suspension leg) in place. The only snag with the later Cortinas, and the Escorts is that when the outer ball joint is worn, the new joint comes as part of a complete new track control arm assembly, which of course is more expensive than a normal ball joint.

The inner end of the track control arm can then be unbolted from the cross-member, and the track control arm can be extracted, around the end of the anti-roll bar. Its removal is made easier if you have already taken

the anti-roll bar from the car, of course.

On the Mark I, and early Mark II Cortinas, the track control arm ball joint (as illustrated in photograph *MSO8.* in the 'MacPherson Strut Overhaul' section), located at the bottom of the suspension leg, can be dismantled, after disconnecting the track rod end ball joint from the steering arm. The rubber gaiter and its retaining ring can then be taken off, and the two bolts holding the steering arm to the suspension leg can be removed. If the surfaces of the ball are rusty or scored (water often gets in and hastens their demise), replace them. The end float in the new joint must be checked when re-assembling; to do this, fit the ball stud spring seat, and the ball stud, but not the spring. Re-fit the steering arm and bearing assembly, and tighten the two bolts. Now a dial gauge *should* be used to measure the end float in the joint. However, if you have no dial gauge, a threaded rod can be used instead. Insert this into the hole in the steering arm, with a flat bar held to the rod by two nuts, so that the bar just makes light contact with the end of the ball joint stud. Push the ball stud inwards, and use a spacer and feeler gauges to measure the distance between the end of the ball joint stud and the flat bar. Pull the stud outwards, and measure the distance again. The difference (the movement, or end float) should be between 0.009 in. and 0.025 in. Adjust the shims (up to a maximum of three), if necessary, to achieve the correct end float. Don't forget to re-fit the spring to the assembly. On rebuilding, pack the ball joint and assembly and its gaiter with lithium-based grease containing molybdenum disulphide, for long-term protection. Tighten the track control arm ball joint nut to 30 to 35 lb.ft., and the steering arm to track rod end ball joint to 18 to 22 lb.ft., on completion of the job.

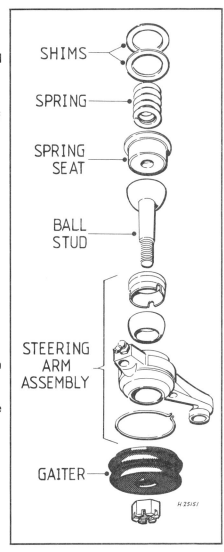

TCA1. *The track control arm ball joint fitted on Mark I and early Mark II Cortinas consists of these components. When checking the end float on the ball stud, a threaded rod can be inserted into the (extreme right-hand, in this diagram) hole in the steering arm, and a flat bar attached, as described in the text.*

If new rubber bushes are being fitted, use a little washing-up liquid to help them slide into place. Fit the inner end of the track control arm to the cross-member, and fit the bolt from the front. Fit the flat washer and self-locking nut to the pivot bolt, and tighten it to 30 lb.ft.

The anti-roll bar can now be re-fitted through the track control arm, with its bushes correctly seated, and the nut tightened to 25 to 30 lb.ft.

Idler arm – Cortina

If wear occurs in the idler arm joint, on Cortina models, it should be renewed as an assembly.

The track rod ends should be disconnected from the drag link, then the drag link from the idler arm. The two bolts securing the idler bracket assembly to the vehicle's side member can then be taken out. The idler arm pivot bolt must now be pressed out of the tapered hole in the bracket. New stud and bush assemblies can be fitted to the idler arm rod as described in the 'Steering Links' section, so that the outer sleeves are flush with the boss on each end of the rod.

To complete the rebuild, fit the idler arm pivot bolt in the tapered hole in the idler bracket, and fit a new split pin, after tightening the nut to 25 to 30 lb.ft. (Mark I) or 35 lb.ft. (Mark II). The ball joint stud nuts should be tightened to 20 to 25 lb.ft. (Mark I) or to 25 to 30 lb.ft. (Mark II). The idler arm bracket to car body bolts should be tightened to 25 to 30 lb.ft.

Rear suspension

With the exception of early Cortina Lotus models, which used coil springs at the back, the rear suspension employed on Cortinas and Escorts is strictly conventional, with leaf springs and telescopic shock absorbers (on saloons and Escort estate cars), and lever arm shock absorbers (on Cortina estate cars).

Mark I Escorts, from September 1973, and Mark IIs have anti-roll bars at the rear, and Cortina GT models have rear radius arms to help locate the rear axle. The rubber bushes holding these refinements need regular checks, and the bushes should be replaced if soft, but these extra fitments do not seriously complicate the system, as far as restoration is concerned.

As with most suspension overhauls, the various nuts and bolts loosened when working on the springs and shock absorbers should only be fully tightened once the car is on its wheels again.

Shock absorbers – Cortina

Telescopic rear shock absorbers are fitted to the Cortina saloons, and lever arm units to the estate cars.

If the car bounces more than it should at the rear, or if leaks are evident from the bodies of the shock absorbers, they should be replaced. On lever arm types, leaks from the seals are evidenced by signs of fluid around the operating arm joint, where it attaches to the main body of the unit.

SAC1. The rear shock absorbers on Mark I and II Cortina saloons are easily changed. From inside the boot, hold the top of the piston ($^1/4$ inch AF spanner) while the locknut and main securing nut are removed, followed by the large dished washer, the rubber bush and (where fitted) a second dished washer. Underneath the car, release the nut, lockwasher and bolt that hold the shock absorber to the axle. The shock absorber can now be removed from the car, then the remaining rubber bush and steel washer lifted off the piston rod.

When re-fitting, make sure that the lips of the steel washers face the adjacent rubber bushes. Tighten the lower mounting nut and bolt to 40 to 45 lb.ft (Mark I and II) and the main nut on the top mounting to 25 to 30 lb.ft. (Mark I) or 15 to 20 lb.ft. (Mark II). As many shock absorbers don't have spanner flats on the piston rods, and it will damage the rod to use a pair of grips, get a helper to hold the upper section of the shock absorber, from below the car, while the top nut is tightened.

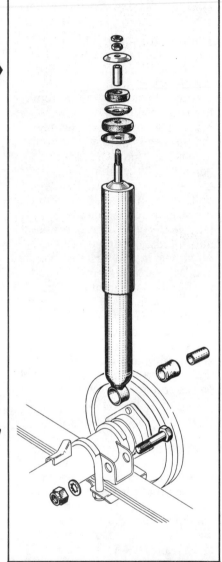

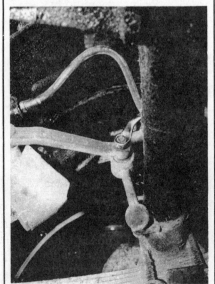

SAC2. The Cortina estates have lever arm type shock absorbers. Both units on this vehicle were past their best, but it is always best to change shock absorbers in pairs, anyway. The first step in changing them is to release the joints at each side between the shock absorber operating arms and the rubber-bushed links, connecting them to the rear axle. If the bushes in these links are soft, replace the links. First slacken the nuts so that they cover the ends of the threads on the link studs.

SAC3. A ball joint splitter can then be used to separate the joints.

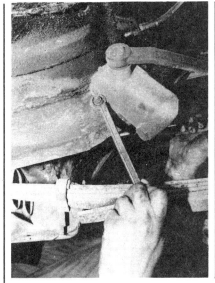

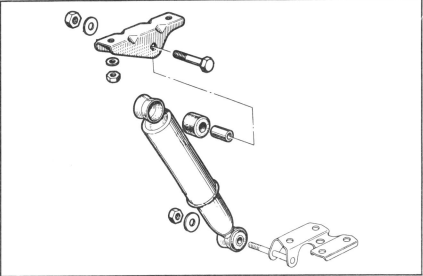

SAC4. The main body of each shock absorber can now be released from the car's 'chassis' by taking out the two mounting bolts. A ring spanner will be needed, to hold the bolt heads on the wheel arch side of the body side member, and another one to release the nuts, facing the centre of the car.

Shock absorbers – Escort

The shock absorbers fitted to Escorts are all telescopic units. The mountings vary according to the model, as shown in the illustrations.

SAE1. Early Escort Mark Is have mountings like this; the upper through-bolt needs to be withdrawn to allow the unit to come away at the top. The lower end is then simply pulled or tapped off the mounting plate spigot. The bushes in the eye of the shock absorber can be difficult to remove, although they can sometimes be pushed out, using an old socket as a guide.

SAE2. Later Escort Mark Is have a cross-member joining the top shock absorber links, below the car. The cross-member has to be lowered from the car body to allow the shock absorber through-bolt to be withdrawn.

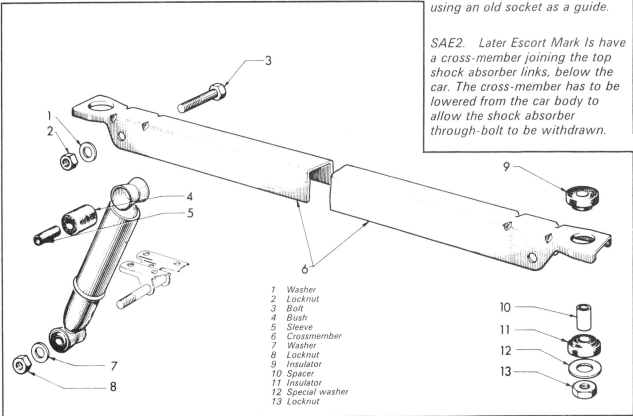

1   Washer
2   Locknut
3   Bolt
4   Bush
5   Sleeve
6   Crossmember
7   Washer
8   Locknut
9   Insulator
10 Spacer
11 Insulator
12 Special washer
13 Locknut

SAE3. On later Mark I Escorts, slacken the upper shock absorber through-bolts, followed by the cross-member mounting bolts. The cross-member can then be lowered to permit the through-bolts to be released.

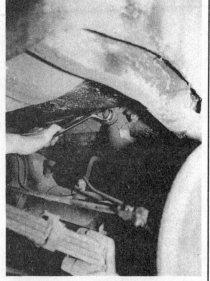

SAE4. At the lower end of the shock absorber, simply release the nut and pull the unit off the mounting plate spigot.

Tighten the bolts holding the cross-member to the car to 15 to 18 lb.ft., and the shock absorber mounting bolts to 25 to 30 lb.ft.

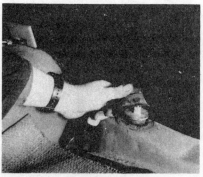

SAE5. To change the shock absorbers on a Mark II Escort, start in the boot, by taking off the protective covering from the shock absorber top mounting.

SAE6. Release the locknut, then the securing nut, and take these off, followed by the flat washer and bush.

SAE7. Underneath the car, remove the nut holding the unit to the spigot at the spring 'U' bolt retaining plate. The shock absorber can then be released from under the vehicle. On fitting shock absorbers to the vehicle, tighten the lower fixing nut to 25 to 31 lb.ft. (27 to 33 lb.ft., for vans), and the upper mounting securing nut to 15 to 21 lb.ft. (9 to 12 lb.ft., for vans), with the upper locknut requiring a torque of 12 to 15 lb.ft.

To test telescopic shock absorbers, once off the car, alternately compress and stretch the units; resistance throughout each stroke should be firm and uniform. On lever arm type units, move the arm up and down fully several times. If resistance is erratic, there may be a fault within the unit, or it could just require topping up. If it *does* need topping up, however, the chances are that fluid has leaked from the unit, so it could be defective anyway. Lever arm shock absorbers should be filled very slowly, with shock absorber oil, with the unit upright, and while moving the arm slowly up and down through the full length of its stroke, to expel air.

Always prime new units, telescopic or lever arm types, prior to fitting, by manually moving the shock absorber through the full length of its operating stroke, several times.

Rear spring change

The principles apply equally to Cortina and Escort models. Start by raising the rear of the car as high as possible, with the front wheels chocked, and support the bodywork securely with axle stands, in this position. Place a trolley jack under the differential, to take the weight of the axle once the springs are removed. Don't raise the jack so high that the springs are flattened, but just enough to take the full weight of the axle, with the springs fully extended.

The photographs depict the job on a Mark II Escort estate, but the procedures apply to all models.

Escorts built after September, 1973 have an anti-roll bar at the rear, and this must be disconnected before removing the rear springs. First take off the nuts and bolts holding each end of the anti-roll bar to the bodywork, noting which way round the bolts are fitted. Take out the two bolts holding each clamp to the axle tube, then slacken the locknuts at the end of each bush housing, and unscrew the bushes from the bar, followed by the locknuts. The rubber mounting bushes can now be slid off the bar. Refit in the reverse order, but make sure that, when replacing the end bush housing, the centre line of the bush is 10.45 ± 0.097 in. (265.5 ± 2.5 mm.) from the centre line of the transverse section of the bar, as shown in diagram RSC8. To fit new bushes to the anti-roll bar, a suitable sized length of pipe or an old socket can be used, to press the bushes in or out, using a little washing-up liquid as a lubricant. When assembled, the voids in the bush must be vertical to the centre line of the bar.

Notes on variations between models, and a full list of the torque settings required for the rear suspension on all models, follow the photograph stripdown sequence.

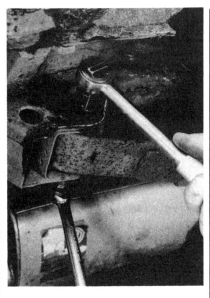

RSC1.   To remove a spring, start by releasing the nut and through-bolt at the front end of the spring.

RSC2.   Leaving the nut screwed onto the bolt a few turns, to protect the threads, use a soft-faced hammer to start the bolt moving out of the spring eye and the bodywork mounts. A small drift may be needed to drive the bolt right out.

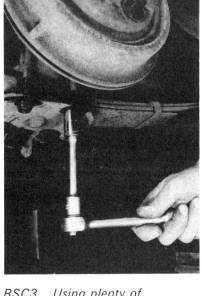

RSC3.   Using plenty of penetrating oil around the nuts, release the 'U' bolts from the spring/shock absorber mounting plate. Release the lower shock absorber mounting bolt, to allow the plate to be twisted out of the way as the 'U' bolts are withdrawn.

RSC4.   Pull the 'U' bolts upwards and clear. Take off the upper axle bump stops, where fitted, with the 'U' bolts. (That coil spring in the background isn't a standard fitting, incidentally, but a towing aid, to assist the car's own suspension, when heavily laden at the rear).

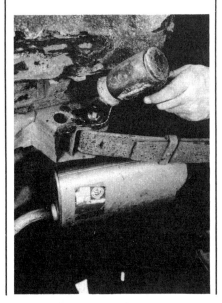

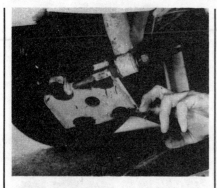

RSC5. The spring/shock absorber mounting plate can now be twisted downwards, and out of the spring's exit path.

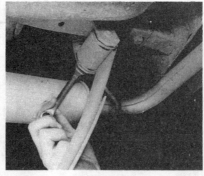

RSC6. The front end of the spring should now be lowered to the floor, and the rear link disconnected. The spring can then be lifted away.

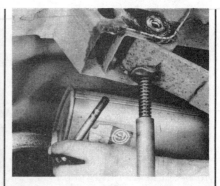

RSC7. When re-fitting the spring, especially if working on your own, it helps to use a 'bottle' jack under the front end of the spring, which can then be carefully eased back into position so that the front bolt can be re-fitted. These bolts can suffer from corrosion, and it is a good idea to fit stainless steel bolts here, to avoid the problem in future. A smear of PBC grease will also help to prevent seizure.

RSC8. If fitting new end bushes to the anti-roll bar on late model Escorts, check that the dimension between the centre line of the end bush and the centre line of the transverse bar is as shown.

265·5±2·5mm
(10·45±0·097in)

On all models covered by this book, the rear ends of the springs are held by combined shackle bolt and plate assemblies. The rubber bushes fitting over the shackle bolts, into the apertures in the body, should be checked very carefully for cracks or softness, and replaced if doubtful. GT and 1600E versions of the Cortina have radius arms fitted between the axle and the bodywork; simply removing the bolts and bushes frees them from the car.

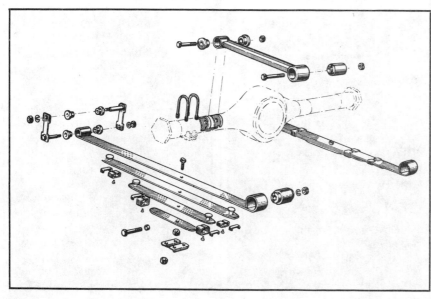

RSC9. This rear suspension layout applies to a Mark I Cortina GT, but (with the exception of the radius arms which are peculiar to the sports models) is typical of all the cars covered by this book.

When working on the nearside rear spring on the Mark II Cortina saloon, the spare wheel will need to be removed from the boot, and rubber grommet in the spare wheel well taken out, in order to get to the shackle assembly.

The correct torque settings for the rear suspension are:

MARK I CORTINA: Spring front hanger, 30 lb.ft.; spring rear shackle, 15 lb.ft.; spring 'U' bolts, 20 to 25 lb.ft.; radius arm to body (GT), 50 lb.ft.; radius arm to axle casing (GT), 25 lb.ft.

MARK II CORTINA: Spring front hanger, 25 to 30 lb.ft.; spring rear shackle, 12 to 15 lb.ft; spring 'U' bolts, 20 to 25 lb.ft; radius arm to body (GT and 1600E), 45 to 50 lb.ft.; radius arm to axle (GT and 1600E), 22 to 27 lb.ft.

MARK I ESCORT: Spring front hanger, 22 to 27 lb.ft.; spring rear shackle, 12 to 15 lb.ft.; spring 'U' bolts, 20 to 25 lb.ft.

MARK II ESCORT: Spring front hanger, 52 to 66 lb.ft.; spring rear shackle, 19 to 23 lb.ft.; spring 'U' bolts, 18 to 27 lb.ft.; anti-roll bar to axle bolts, 29 to 37 lb.ft.; anti-roll bar to body bolts, 44 to 52 lb.ft.; anti-roll bar end bush locknuts, 44 to 59 lb.ft. In the case of the Escort II, before tightening the nuts securing the anti-roll bar and bushes to the body, the weight of the car must be on the wheels, and the rear of the vehicle loaded so that the rear spring eye centres are in line with (i.e. at the same height as) the centre of the axle tube.

All the other nuts and bolts should only be fully tightened to the recommended torque settings when the weight of the vehicle is again taken by the wheels.

Notes on carburettors

There were many different types of carburettor fitted to the Cortinas and Escorts during their production lives, as listed in Appendix 3 at the end of this book. Full details of maintenance, tuning and stripdown procedures for each individual type are included in the *Haynes Owners' Workshop Manual* relating to each model.

Although the carburettors are of varying types and construction, there are several common features and points to note during restoration.

If your restoration project vehicle has been laid up for a long time, it is likely that dirt will have settled and solidified within the carburettor, and at the very least, a stripdown and clean-up operation would be beneficial. Even if the car has been used regularly, dirt tends to accumulate in the float chamber and it is worth cleaning this out before it lodges in a jet and stops the engine.

Before embarking on stripping the carburettor, however, it is worth cleaning the exterior of the unit, to rid it of surplus grime. This lessens the chance of grit entering, and makes handling the carburettor a lot more pleasant. The most effective way of cleaning the outside of a carburettor is probably to use one of the special sprays made for the job. Available in aerosol cans, these sprays dissolve fuel stains, grease deposits and grime within seconds, without the need for scrubbing the carburettor body with a brush. Alternatively, you could use a little cellulose thinners, on a rag, but only use it in small doses, and make sure that it doesn't contact plastic or rubber components, or the car's paintwork.

With the carburettor externally clean, take off the float chamber lid and clean out all 'mud' from the bottom, using a small screwdriver as a scoop, and small quantities of petrol, on a rag, for final cleaning. The aerosol carburettor cleaner can then be used for cleaning out all the jets (a small nozzle is provided for this purpose), also to give the internal passageways of the carburettor a 'rinse', and to blow away tiny particles of grit.

Check sideways movement of each of the main operating spindles – particularly the throttle spindle – it should be minimal, or it indicates signs of wear on the spindle and/or the carburettor body. If wear is severe, air leaks can result, with 'flat spots' and poor performance, often combined with heavy fuel consumption. It is possible to have the carburettor body drilled out and re-bushed, and for a new spindle to be fitted. This is likely to be cheaper than buying a new carburettor; carburettor specialists and engineering companies can tackle such jobs.

It is a good idea to replace all the gaskets and the float chamber needle valve assembly as a matter of course while the carburettor is in bits. These parts are not expensive, and fitting them will pay dividends in terms of reduced fuel consumption and better running.

When re-fitting the carburettor, make sure that the flange face, where it bolts onto the inlet manifold, and the matching face on the manifold, are perfectly flat – this can be checked with a straightedge, such as a steel rule. If the flange is not perfectly flat (and it is usually the carburettor face which is warped, possibly due to over-tightening in the past), it will give erratic running (particularly on tickover), and poor performance. It can be ground true, using a scrap, flat sheet of glass (the thicker the better), and a little fine valve grinding paste. Spread the paste onto the glass, and rub the flange against the paste, firmly, in a circular motion. Check frequently, and, when the appearance of the flange is a uniform grey, with no 'low' areas, wipe off the remnants of the paste, using a rag dipped in clean paraffin, and re-check the flange with a straightedge. If

all is well, re-fit the carburettor, but make sure that the bolts are tightened evenly, a little at a time, and don't overtighten them.

Finally, apply a little engine oil to all pivot points on the carburettor, and, prior to re-connecting the control cables, make sure that they move freely. A sticking cable will cause high fuel consumption, and make the car difficult to drive smoothly. If a cable is particularly reluctant to move, tie the free end to the top of the (open) bonnet, and drip light oil, followed by a little engine oil, down the cable, between the inner and outer casings. A small funnel can be made from modelling clay or similar, to hold the oil, if it proves difficult to 'trickle' in.

You should then have a smooth, clean, efficient and economical carburettor, which will last a long time before it again needs attention.

NOC1.   The carburettors fitted to the 'family' versions of the Mark I Cortina are single choke, downdraught units. Check for wear in the spindles, and failure of the diaphragms in the economy device and accelerator pump. This is the carburettor fitted to the 1200cc cars; the units on the 1500cc models have minor differences, but are basically similar.

NOC2.   The GT versions of the Mark I Cortina have a twin choke, downdraught Weber DCD carburettor. Check for wear on the throttle spindles, and make sure that all the jets are clean. Mark II GTs up to September, 1967 have a similar unit; later Mark II GTs have a different Weber DFM twin choke carburettor.

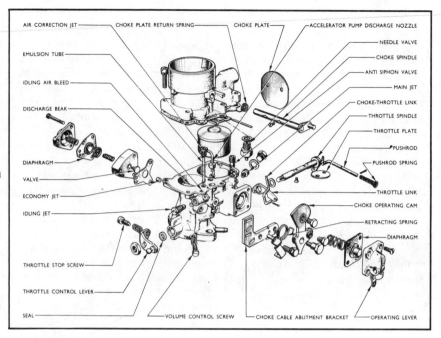

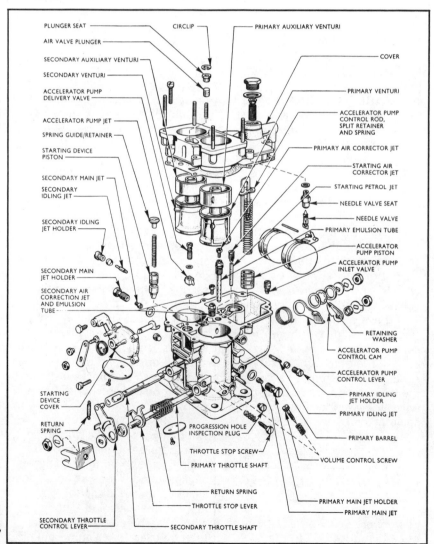

NOC3. The Ford carburettor fitted to the Mark II differs slightly from the units on the Mark I cars, but the wear points to check are the same; notably the spindles and the accelerator pump. This is a manual choke version; some cars have automatic chokes.

1 Air cleaner retaining bracket
2 Choke control lever
3 Spring
4 Choke plate
5 Choke spindle
6 Plate to spindle retaining screws
7 Screw
8 Cable clamp-top
9 Cable clamp-bottom
10 Nut
11 Bracket
12 Choke control rod
13 Pump discharge ball weight
14 Discharge ball valve
15 ?
16 Spring
17 Fast idle cam
18 Screw
19 Screw
20 Throttle lever & spindle assembly
21 Plate retaining screws
22 Throttle plate
23 Spring
24 Throttle stop screw
25 Pump control lever
26 Spring
27 Idling mixture adjustment needle
28 Accelerator pump link to lever rod
29 Washer
30 Spring
31 Screw
32 Overflow pipe
33 Screw
34 Adaptor
35 Carburettor top cover
36 Washer
37 Filter
38 Needle valve
39 Gasket
40 Main metering jet
41 Float pivot pin
42 Float
43 Carburettor body
44 Screw
45 Diaphragm return spring
46 Accelerator pump diaphragm
47 Accelerator pump cover
48 Actuating lever pivot pin
49 Actuating lever
50 Air cleaner bracket retaining pin

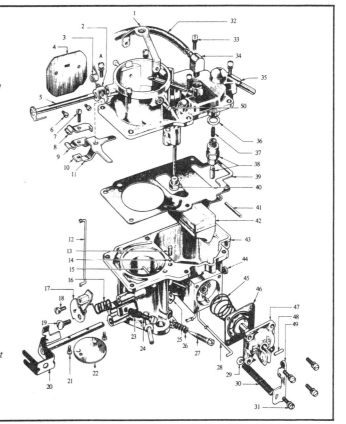

NOC4. The Escorts also use a single choke downdraught carburettor; this is a typical unit. Some versions (like this one) have an automatic choke, while some have a manual choke. The same wear check points apply as to Cortina units.

1 Air cleaner bracket
2 Choke spindle
3 Choke plate
4 Screw
5 Clip
6 Gasket
7 Choke control rod
8 Gasket
9 Screw
10 Vacuum piston
11 Screw
12 Bi-metallic spring anchor
13 Vacuum piston/spring link
14 Automatic choke housing cover
15 Bi-metallic spring
16 Fast idle rod
17 Pump discharge ball weight
18 Pump discharge ball
20 Bush
21 Washer
22 Screw
23 Shakeproof washer
24 Throttle lever and spindle assembly
25 Plate retaining screw
26 Throttle plate
27 Spring
28 Throttle stop screw
29 Fast idle cam
30 Spindle
31 Auto-choke housing
32 Bracket
33 Screw
34 Main metering jet tube
35 Overflow pipe
36 Screw
37 Adaptor
38 Carburettor cover assembly
39 Air filter bracket retaining pin
40 Washer
41 Filter
42 Needle valve assembly
43 Gasket
44 Main metering jet
45 Float pivot spindle
46 Float
47 Carburettor body
48 Screw
49 Diaphragm return spring
50 Diaphragm
51 Accelerator pump cover
52 Lever pivot pin
53 Accelerator pump actuating lever
54 Spring
55 Idling mixture adjustment screw
56 Pump to lever rod
57 Spring retaining washer
58 Spring
59 Screw
60 Screw

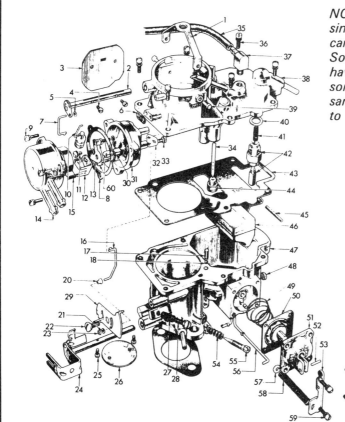

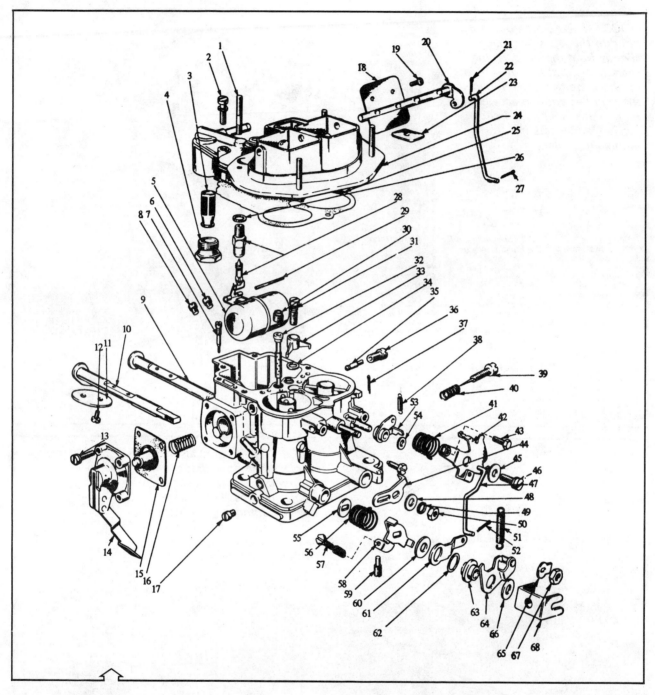

NOC5.   The fast Escorts used various carburettors; this is the Weber 32/36 DGV unit as fitted to the Mexico. Check the spindles and accelerator pump diaphragm as for all the carburettors.

1   Stud
2   Screw
3   Gauze filter element
4   Plug
5   Float
6   Main metering jet
7   Accelerator pump blanking needle
8   Main metering jet
9   Spindle
10 Spindle
11 Throttle plate or butterfly valve
12 Screw
13 Screw
14 Accelerator pump cover
15 Diaphragm
16 Diaphragm return spring
17 Plug
18 Choke spindle plate
19 Plate retaining screw
20 Choke spindle
21 Split pin
22 Choke actuating arm
23 Dust seal
24 Carburettor top cover
25 Gasket
26 Washer
27 Split pin
28 Needle valve
29 Float pivot spindle
30 Starting air adjusting jet
31 Accelerator pump discharge valve
32 Starting jet
33 Pump discharge nozzle
34 Gasket
35 Secondary idling jet
36 Idling jet holder
37 Split pin
38 Spring
39 Volume control screw
40 Spring
41 Spring
42 Choke control lever
43 Bolt
44 Throttle stop lever
45 Washer
46 Screw
47 Fast idle rod
48 Washer
49 Spring washer
50 Nut
51 Spring
52 Split pin
53 Choke relay lever
54 Nylon washer
55 Slotted washer
56 Spring
57 Idling adjustment lever screw
58 Idling adjustment lever
59 Adjuster
60 Spacer
61 Choke/throttle interconnecting fast idle lever
62 Washer
63 Bush
64 Throttle control lever
65 Tab washer
66 Washer
67 Nut
68 Throttle lever assembly

272

6 Electrical Components

Wiring

It is vital that the electrical wiring in your car is in good condition, for an accidental short-circuit could easily lead to a serious fire, in a matter of seconds. For the same reason, ALWAYS disconnect the battery before working on any of the car's electrical components, or the wiring.

Complete wiring diagrams covering each model are included in the relevant *Haynes Owners' Workshop Manual,* together with details of the colours used for each circuit.

The overall state of the wiring looms in your vehicle will normally be apparent from a brief inspection. However, it pays to check each section very carefully, making sure that, in particular, the insulation is sound, and that the connections are good. Start your inspection under the bonnet, then, using a torch, under the facia, and inside the car, moving on to look closely at the wiring in the boot. If the wiring itself is sound, but the connections to the individual components are suspect, rectification is relatively straightforward. A variety of electrical connectors are available at most car accessory shops, together with soldering equipment, and tools for cutting the wires and for crimping the various cable connectors onto them.

EC1. An electrical set like this contains a crimping tool and a large number of different connectors. This is particularly useful if you are not good at soldering!

EC2. If you are good at soldering, a small gas torch, a little flux, a soldering iron and some bullet type connectors are all you need to deal with poor connections. A small electrical soldering iron can be used as an alternative to the large type shown here, but heat penetration is less.

273

If the wiring itself is generally in poor shape, one alternative is to find another model like yours in a breaker's yard, and extract the wiring, complete, from it. Then lay the new wiring in position next to the old loom, and disconnect the old wires, one at a time, connecting the new wires in their place. This is, of course, a long-winded process, but it works, and is cheap. Another option is to purchase a complete *new* wiring assembly, ready made for your car. You then know that the wiring should last for a very long time.

In many cases, the poor section of wiring can be confined to a specific area. For example, on one Mark I Cortina I know of, the under-dash wiring had suffered from fire damage, while the rest of the car and its wiring had escaped unscathed. The owner simply cut the complete damaged section out, and spliced in a replacement 'partial loom' from a scrap vehicle.

Care must be taken during these operations, of course, and in particular, attention should be paid to the electrical capacity of the cables used (more about this in the 'Fuses' section), the security of any new connections made, and to the use of grommets at all points where the wires pass through metal bulkheads, and so on.

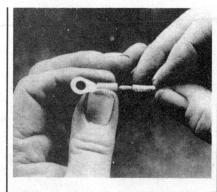

EC4. Make sure that any connections you fit are properly insulated from surrounding metal, and that the length of wire bared is sufficient only to JUST fit fully into the connector. If you trim the wire's insulation back too far, there is the possibility that there will be a gap in the insulation, between the new connector and the wire's own insulator covering. If the wire is live, and this touches earth – problems begin!

Troubles can often arise simply through connections being dirty, especially where they have been exposed to moisture, or where the car has been standing idle for some time. If you have problems with components operating erratically, yet the wiring looks in good shape, try separating each connection, and cleaning the joints. A little fine 'wet or dry'

paper, used dry, followed by a wipe and a squirt of water dispellant spray, usually works wonders in such cases. Make sure too that the plug/socket connector blocks used at the bulkhead between the engine compartment and the car's interior, are pushed fully home, and that the connector pins and sockets are clean.

The plastic covered wiring used on Cortinas and Escorts usually looks grubby after a few years in service, as it gets covered in grease, oil and dirt – especially in the under-bonnet areas, of course. A little paraffin on a rag will help to shift most of the grime. This leaves the wiring looking clean, but dull. To bring back the shine, use one of the plastic cleaner/polishes available for interior trim; it will restore an 'as new' look to the wiring.

Fuses

Cortinas dating from before October, 1968 did not have a fusebox, with the result that, should there be an electrical malfunction, the wiring will go up in smoke. Fortunately it is fairly straightforward to protect the circuits by fitting a fusebox (seven fuse type – part number 70AG 14A067BB) from an Escort. If you should wish to

EC3. Use rubber grommets at every point where wires pass through metal. If fitting new, and perhaps non-standard headlamp bowls, for example, these are often supplied without grommets. Buy suitable new items to do the job and replace any soft or cracked grommets around the rest of the vehicle, at the same time. It's worth the effort to avoid the possibility of an electrical fire.

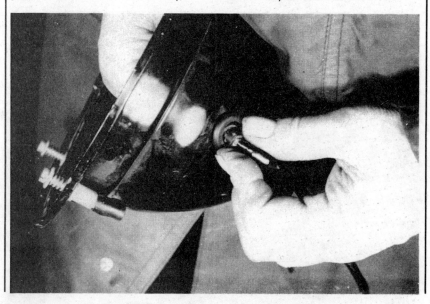

protect the lighting circuits only, a six fuse fusebox (part no. 3024E 14A067A) from an early Escort can be used. It is also possible, of course, to update your early Escort, which has protection only for the lighting circuits, and fit a 'full protection' seven circuit fusebox from a later car.

Mount the fusebox at a point convenient to the main loom, and out of the way, yet where it can be reached reasonably easily in order to change a fuse. The area under the dashboard, on the driver's side of the car, meets all these requirements. There should be few problems in wiring the box, and the two diagrams show the respective connections to make for the Mark I and Mark II Cortinas.

If, when fitting, you encounter bunches of cables of the same colour, and are unsure which cable relates to which circuit, a 12 volt test light will show which wire goes where. Connect the test light between the end of the wire and a good earth, and switch on the various components one at a time, until

the bulb lights. Repeat the test on all the cables. Once you have established which circuit is which, it helps to label the wires with a little masking tape, marked appropriately.

Disconnect the battery while work is proceeding, for safety, so that no wires are accidentally shorted to earth.

On completion of the wiring, bind the new cables using wiring tape, or proprietary vehicle wiring conduit, for a neat, safe job.

If you are fitting any extra accessories to your car, ALWAYS make sure that the circuit is fused – either by taking the circuit through an existing fusebox connection with extra capacity, or by incorporating a separate line fuse into the circuit.

It is important that the wiring you install – when fitting a fusebox or when carrying out any cable work – is up to the job, and capable of handling the power in a particular circuit. For side and tail lights, ignition circuits, and low-powered accessories, 14/0.012 cable is sufficient (that is, 14 strands, each of 0.012 in. diameter), this has a capacity of 7

amps. For the main charging circuit, and high powered accessories (auxiliary lights, and so on), 28/0.012 cable is required, with a capacity of 14 amps. Main battery feed circuits need 44/0.012 cable, with a 22 amp capacity.

Often these days, wire is sold in metric units, in which, for example, the equivalent to 14/0.012 cable is 14/0.30 (14 strands, each of 0.30 mm. diameter).

The heavy lines in the diagrams indicate the new wiring needed for fitting the fusebox; the dotted lines show the existing wiring to be disconnected. The colour codes employed are: BL = Blue, R = Red, BK – Black, V = White, G = Green, PK = Pink, BR = Brown, Y = Yellow and P = Purple.

F1. The early Cortina Mark I circuitry, when fitted with the seven fuse fusebox, looks like this. It is desirable to use the same colours for the new wiring as in the existing circuits. This greatly helps any future wire tracing operations.

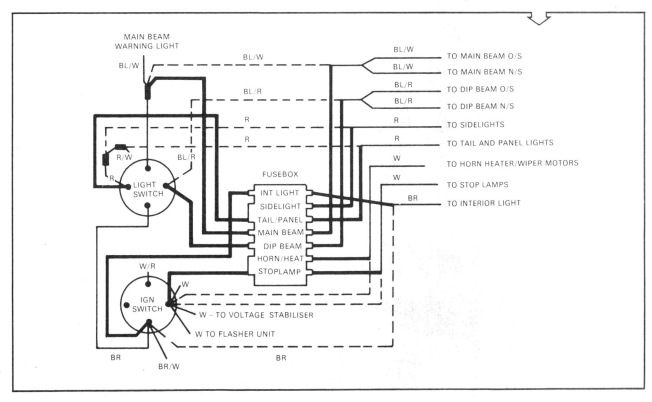

F2.   The later Mark I models, from 1964 onwards, vary slightly in their wiring, and the new connections necessary for fitting the fusebox are as shown.

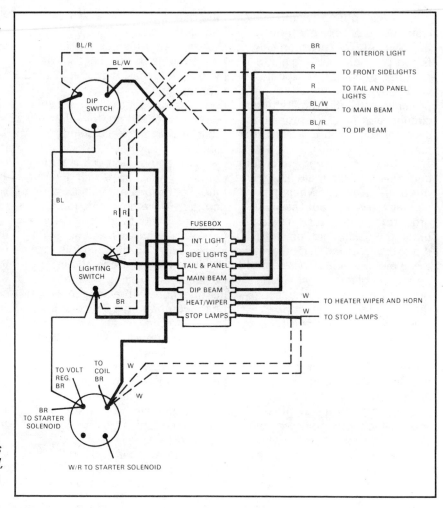

F3.   The Cortina Mark II circuits are wired like this; on this model, the dipswitch is mounted on the steering column.

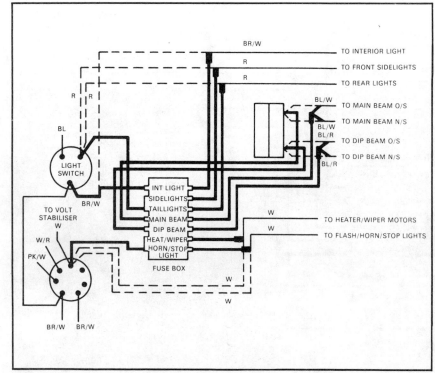

Distributor

If the distributor on your car is worn, the result will be erratic running and high fuel consumption, combined with a lack of power. It therefore pays to take a close look at the unit fitted to your engine, and find out what sort of state it's in.

There is no need to remove the distributor from the engine to examine it. However, if you do take it out, release it at the main securing bolt, rather than at the clamp bolt, and note the position of the rotor arm, so that the unit can be re-fitted at exactly the same point. This will retain the basic ignition timing. However, it is always best to check the timing after any work on the distributor – including just changing the contact points. Even a small

variation in the contact points gap will affect the ignition timing.

D1.   This is the Autolite distributor, as fitted to the Mark II Cortina, and is typical of the type of unit used on Cortinas and Escorts covered by this book. The first check to make on the condition of the distributor is to rock the main shaft from side to side at the top. If there is appreciable play, the shaft assembly will need to be replaced. In this case, probably the most practical answer is to obtain a complete replacement unit.

It is always possible to use a distributor from a later model, if your original unit is badly worn, and you have difficulty in obtaining the 'correct' type replacement unit for your vehicle. For example, if your car is a Cortina Mark I, the distributor from a Mark II can be used.

1	Rotor arm	15	Spring
2	Oil pad	16	Vacuum advance
3	Spring clip		retard unit
4	Mechanical	17	Skew gear
	advance & cam		retaining pin
	assembly	18	Clamp plate
5	Flyweight tension	19	Nut
	spring	20	'O' ring oil seal
6	Circlip	21	Bolt & washer
7	Flyweight	22	Distributor body
8	Stop	23	Washer
9	Action plate &	24	Washer
	main shaft	25	Lower C.B. plate
10	Shim retaining	26	Upper contact
	bolt		breaker plate
11	Wave washer	27	Capacitor
12	Thrust washer	28	Distributor cap
13	Skew gear	29	Contact breaker
14	Stop		assembly

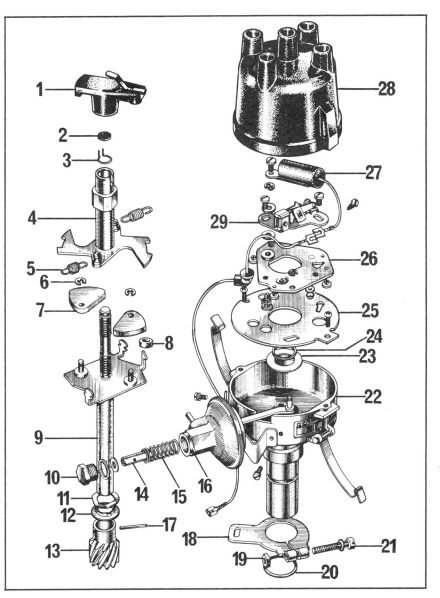

D2.   With the distributor cap and rotor arm removed, the next step is to loosen (there's no need to remove it) the screw holding the wires from the condenser and the coil.

D3.   The condenser is simply unscrewed from the base plate. If the history of the condenser is unknown, and particularly if the car has been laid up for a long time, it is best to invest in a new unit. These are not expensive, and are easy to obtain. A defective condenser gives erratic running, and poor starting.

D4.   The contact points can be removed next, after taking out the two securing screws. Again, unless the points are nearly new, it is good policy to replace them. The ignition system should then be on top form when re-assembled.

D5.   The main baseplate is released from the distributor body by taking out the two screws on opposite sides of the unit, but, before it can be lifted off . . .

D6.   . . . the circlip holding the vacuum advance mechanism attachment pin must be released; a tiny screwdriver is ideal for prising it out. Take care not to lose the clip.

D7.   The complete baseplate assembly can now be lifted clear of the distributor body.

D8. The flyweights in the base of the distributor should be free to move, and should spring back into their normal position if gently pulled out and released.

D9. Spray penetrating oil around the weights and pivots if their operation seems sluggish. This is especially likely if the car has been unused for several years.

D10. Once the pivots move freely again, apply a little engine oil, for long-term lubrication.

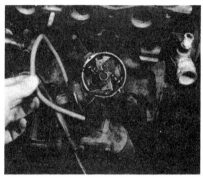

D11. To test if the vacuum advance diaphragm is intact, fix a short length of rubber tube onto the pipe stub on the diaphragm capsule, and suck at the open end of the tube. If all is well, the advance mechanism pull-rod will move under suction.

D12. On re-assembly. apply a little high melting point grease to the surface of the cam, and to the sliding surfaces on the base plates.

D13. Apply a few drops of engine oil to the felt pad in the centre of the distributor shaft, before re-fitting the rotor arm.

D14. Fit a new set of contact points, wiping the faces of the points with a clean rag, beforehand.

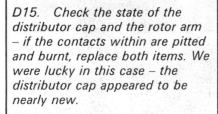

D15. Check the state of the distributor cap and the rotor arm – if the contacts within are pitted and burnt, replace both items. We were lucky in this case – the distributor cap appeared to be nearly new.

Charging system

The Cortinas and early Escorts were fitted with dynamos, while alternators may be found on some Escorts up to October, 1973, and all Escorts after that date had them as a standard fitting.

Whether a dynamo or alternator is fitted, new brushes can be fitted on a d-i-y basis. The diode pack, on alternators, can be replaced at home, too. The extent beyond this, to which an overhaul is worth doing is governed by the extent of wear present in your unit. If, for example, a dynamo is generally worn, with rough bearings, badly worn commutator and signs of molten metal within, it is better to exchange it for a reconditioned unit, which carries a guarantee. If, on the other hand, just the brushes are worn, but the bearings and other components are in good condition, It is obviously worthwhile fitting a new set of brushes, to give new life to the unit.

The same general comments apply to alternators; brushes can be changed fairly easily, as a rule, whether the unit is a Lucas, Bosch or Femsa one. In the case of Bosch units, a soldering iron will be needed to remove the old brushes and solder on the new ones. Further replacements depend on how keen, and how handy with a soldering iron you are. Changing the brushes, cleaning the slip rings and possibly changing a diode pack is about as far as most people would wish to go, and many people wouldn't even go this far, for great care is needed when assembling the pack to the alternator; if too much heat is used when soldering, the diodes will be ruined. Always use a heat sink, therefore (a pair of pliers can be used for this, by attaching them between the heat source

and the diode, and holding their handles together with an elastic band, while the connection is made).

As with dynamos, if serious problems are present within the unit, probably the cheapest and most effective course of action is to buy an exchange reconditioned unit. Exchange electrical units are readily available, and the prices are reasonable, for reputable re-manufactured units.

CS1. The Lucas ACR alternator consists of these main components. To change the brushes, unscrew and remove the rear cover (12), then, making a note of the cable connections, take out the screws and withdraw the brushes from the brushgear/regulator assembly (1). Take care not to lose the brush anti-rattle spring(s). The minimum length for the brushes is 8mm. Take off the brush box, after removing the two $1/4$ inch AF screws, and clean all dust from the brush recesses, and the box. Using a clean rag dipped in methylated spirits, clean the faces of the slip rings, and re-assemble the unit, when dry.

1	Brushgear and regulator assembly	7	Pulley
2	Rectifier pack	8	Fan
3	Stator	9	12 pole rotor
4	Ball race bearing	10	Slip ring
5	Ball race bearing	11	Slip ring end bracket
6	Drive end bracket	12	Cover

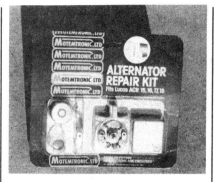

CS2. If you are keen on electrical work, kits like this one are available from motor accessory shops for d-i-y alternator overhaul, and contain all the necessary parts.

The brush box on Femsa alternators is held by a single screw. With the cable to the box disconnected, take out the screw and withdraw the box. Take out the brushes, and clean the housing, before re-assembling. The minimum permissible length for the brushes is 7mm.

On Bosch alternators, remove the brush box after taking out the two securing screws. Use a soldering iron to disconnect the old brushes, and solder in the new ones, if necessary. Clean the brush box, and make sure that the new brushes are a comfortable, sliding fit in the box. When re-assembling, the brush box must be held against brush spring pressure.

Always re-connect the alternator before starting the engine.

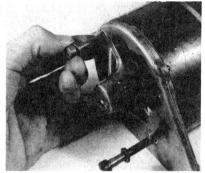

CS3. To dismantle a dynamo, the first step is to take out the two long screws which pass right through the unit at each side.

CS4. The end plate can then be lifted clear; it may be necessary to tap the sides of the plate very gently, with a soft-faced hammer, to free them.

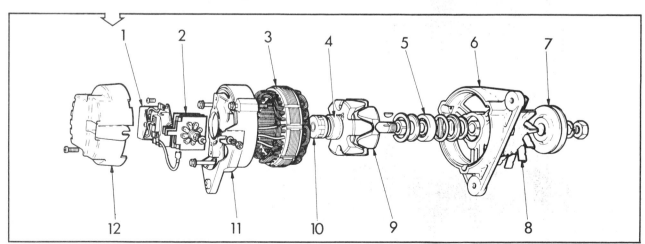

CS5. The armature assembly, complete with the front bearing and end plate, can be carefully withdrawn. The pulley had already been removed from this unit, by releasing the end nut (use a slim spanner, behind the fan assembly, to prevent the shaft from turning as the nut is undone). It is not normally necessary to remove the pulley unless, as in this case, it is damaged, and needs to be changed, or unless you wish to remove the end plate. Spin the end plate on its bearings to check for roughness, and rock it from side to side for evidence of excessive wear in the bearings. Check that the dynamo is clean within, before re-fitting the armature and the front end plate assembly.

CS6. The commutator can be cleaned, evenly, with fine glass paper, unless badly worn, in which case it will need to be 'skimmed' on a lathe. Wipe all swarf and abrasives from the surface, then use a tiny screwdriver blade or similar tool for cleaning out the grooves between the commutator segments. If the commutator has been skimmed, use the end of a hacksaw blade to 'undercut' the segment grooves by $^1/32$nd inch.

CS7. A little engine oil, applied from an oil can to the front plate bearing, helps to preserve the bearing.

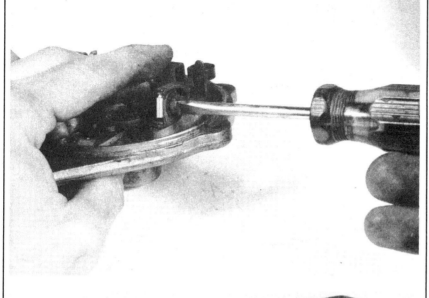

CS8.   The brushes should be checked, and, if worn down to a length approaching $^1/4$ inch, should be replaced. If worn, unscrew the old brushes from their holders, clean out all dust, and fit new brushes. These are readily available, and comparatively cheap. Make sure that the brushes slide freely in their holders.

CS9.   Before re-fitting the end plate, complete with brushes, to the dynamo, pull the brushes away from the centre of the end plate. Now hook the end of each brush spring, under tension, over the edge of the brush holder. This will allow the brushes to stay in this position, wedged by the springs, and to fit easily over the edges of the commutator, on re-assembly of the end plate to the dynamo. Apply a few drops of engine oil to the inside of the bearing in the end plate, then re-fit the assembly to the dynamo.

CS10.   With the end plate re-fitted, unhook the brush springs with a screwdriver, and position the springs so that they are applying pressure directly on the brushes, towards the commutator.

The same general principles can be applied to fitting new brushes to a starter motor, but in this case the brushes are soldered in place. Check the condition of the drive gear pinion teeth whenever the starter motor is removed; if badly worn, the teeth will ruin the mating teeth on the starter ring gear.

7 Interior and Trim

Whether you tackle work on the interior of your car before you put it on the road, or afterwards, on a 'running restoration' basis, it is an important part of the job. After all, it is the inside of the car that you see when you are driving it, and by which the restoration is largely judged by your passengers.

It is appreciated that not everybody is good at upholstery work. In addition, unless you have an 'industrial' type, heavy duty sewing machine, the amount of work you can do is limited anyway. For these reasons it is often better to do as much of the *initial* work as possible yourself, for example removing seats and perhaps stripping the damaged coverings, then welding up broken frames, etc., before taking the components to a professional vehicle upholsterer for the necessary material renewal, re-stitching and rebuilding.

Interior dismantling

You may not need to take out all the trim from your car, but, even if you do, there are no problems. Taking it out is easy; but take care if you intend to re-use, for example, door aperture sealing rubbers, for they will not stand a

great deal of tugging. The same comment also applies to trim panels and most of the interior coverings; they need treating with respect if they are to survive and look good.

ID1.   Door aperture trims can be removed for re-use by VERY carefully prising them away from the bodywork, using a screwdriver, initially, then gently pulling them away by hand. Keep them in a dry, clean place. If they are sound but faded, they can be painted with an upholstery paint designed for use on pvc materials.

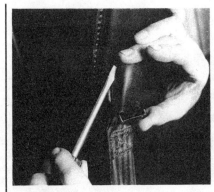

ID2.   Prise off the seat belt mounting covers, using a screwdriver, and taking care not to make a hole in the trim material on the door pillar, as you do so.

ID3. The seat belt mounting can now be unscrewed from the pillar; keep the fixing bolt and all the washers together, and clearly labelled for future reference.

ID4. The door pillar trim panels can now be carefully peeled away from the bodywork; don't rush this job, or the plastic may tear.

ID5. Similarly, the lower mounting can be released. Wrap up the seat belts, and put them away safely in boxes.

ID6. Prise the carpet away from the inner sill, and keep this, even if tatty. It can be used later as a pattern, if you intend to make your own carpets. Even if you are planning to buy a proprietary set of carpets for your car, the new sections are sometimes found to be cut with a lot of material to spare, in which case the original piece of carpet can be used as a guide for trimming the new section down to size.

ID7. On estate cars, take out the screws securing the wheel arch covers; these may be tight, but penetrating oil and perseverance usually pay off.

ID8. Once the retaining band is clear, the wheel arch cover can be prised away from the inner flange, using a screwdriver. Again, take care not to hole the material, if you intend to use it again.

ID9. With all the trim removed, use soap and water, initially, to rid it of surface grime. The easiest way to do this is to lay all the washable trim items on the ground, and work round them, using a small scrubbing brush and warm water, containing washing-up liquid. When clean, go round again using clean water, and finally dry each item carefully. Try to make sure that water doesn't reach hardboard door panels, and so on. Items such as the door panels can then be given another clean, to rid them of ingrained dirt, using an upholstery cleaner. The seats can be dealt with separately.

ID10. There are many different types of upholstery cleaner on the market. One of the most effective types is still the 'brush-on' sort. Coat the entire seat surface, and allow the cleaner to work.

ID11. If necessary, use a small brush to work the cleaner into the dirt.

ID12. Wipe the seat over with a damp rag, and repeat the procedure if the seat is still dirty. Finally, dry with a soft cloth. Keep as much moisture as possible away from the stitching between the seat panels.

ID13. An alternative to the brush-on type is a spray-on cleaner. The foam is very effective at cleaning grime from the seats.

ID14. After cleaning as described, the surface of the seat may be spotless, yet dull. A gloss spray like this will restore the shiny 'as new' look. It can be used on most plastic trim around the car.

ID15. Attention to detail always pays off, and the silver-finish air vent trims on the dashboard, which often lose their shine, can be brought back to life using a little aluminium finish paint. Two coats are usually needed, following a light rub down with 600 grade 'wet or dry' paper, used dry.

ID16. It is always possible to improve the trim quality on your Ford by fitting interior trim from a more 'upmarket' model than your own. The Cortina estate car featured in the 'Respray' section of the bodywork chapter was a 'De Luxe' car, and had no full floor covering for the load area. This grubby but sound mat was bought from a local vehicle dismantler (it came from a scrapped 'Super' version), then cleaned, using a strong solution of washing-up liquid in hot water, and using a small stiff brush to deal with the worst dirt. It was then rinsed and dried.

ID17. Unfortunately, the colour of the 'new' mat was blue, whereas the rest of the trim on the project estate car was black. We therefore used 'PVC paint' for changing its colour. After one coat, it looked good; after two, it looked indistinguishable from new. The brush marks disappeared and the mat had a glossy, uniform surface, which matched the colour of the door panels.

ID18.   The same paint was used on the rear load compartment side panels. These were also from the scrapped 'Super' estate, and blue. However, within minutes, they were a glossy black, and ready to fit into their future home.

The panels from the scrapped 'Super' were in much better condition than the original hardboard items fitted to the 'De Luxe' car, and the overall effect was very pleasing, once the 'new' panels were cleaned and painted. Similar 'upgrading' can be carried out on any of the Fords covered by this book. By using trim and upholstery fittings from a model higher up the range, it is possible to build a more comfortable car. Perhaps purists would argue that the car's originality is being affected, but on the other hand, if the original upholstery is scruffy, and the vehicle is to be used as everyday transport, rather than strictly for 'concours' events only, such improvements are well worthwhile.

Seat dismantling

Rebuilding a car seat is one job that is difficult to tackle at home, unless you have heavy duty, industrial type sewing machinery. In addition, unless you are skilled at working with upholstery, or at least needlework, it is, with the best will in the world, quite likely that you will end up with a very unprofessional looking seat. Therefore if the seats in your Ford are well past their best, with sagging springs, broken frames and torn coverings, it would be better to enlist the help of a professional for the parts of the job you *cannot* do yourself – usually making the new panels or complete coverings – having done basic preparation and repair work yourself, beforehand.

An alternative is to scour local vehicle dismantlers' yards for cars the same as yours, but with better seats. This can be a good solution to the problem, *provided* you can find a seat in good condition.

To illustrate the sort of preliminary work that most people can tackle on seats, at home, Mr. Peter Exley, who has had many years of experience in rebuilding motor car interiors – and particularly on Fords – showed me how to dismantle Escort and Cortina seats, in preparation for repair and re-covering.

The seats on Cortinas and Escorts are simply unbolted from the vehicle floor/cross-member, respectively, to remove them from the vehicle, as shown in the 'Sills and Floor – Escort' section of the bodywork chapter. If the captive nuts should break away – for example those mounted inaccessibly in the Escort seat mounting cross-member – threaded rivets, or steel (NOT rubber) anchor nuts, or cavity wall fixings can be used to secure the seat when re-fitting.

Although I have split the dismantling procedures between Escort and Cortina, to show the differences, the basic stripdown technique applies to either model. Therefore it is worth reading both sections before starting work.

Escort seat dismantling

ESD1.   The driver's seat is usually the worst in the car, since it gets more use, and this Escort seat was no exception! From on top it looked shabby in the extreme, with splits in the covers and sagging all over. The whole frame had a 'flexible' feel to it, and when driving the car, it was more a case of sitting in the seat, than on it, since the bottom of the seat simply disappeared down to floor level!

ESD2.   With the seat turned upside down, the reasons for the lack of support became clearer. Quite simply the bottom of the seat, with its springs, had collapsed. There was just nothing left to support the driver but the car floor (and on this particular car, that wasn't in much better condition than the seat!).

ESD3.   Start dismantling by unscrewing the seat tipping mechanism release trigger and its plastic surround.

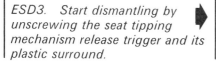

ESD4.   The 'hog rings' along the lower front edge of the seat can be extracted with a pair of side cutters. Put all the hog rings and clips taken from the seat into small boxes or jars; label them and keep them somewhere safe, so that they can go, with the seat, to the upholsterer. Some of them may have to be re-used when the seat is re-assembled.

ESD5.   Using a screwdriver or spiked tool, release the trim clips around the perimeter of the material, at the underside of the seat.

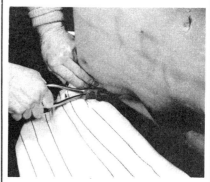

ESD6. The seat base cover can then be pulled back, to allow the release of remaining clips, using a pair of side cutters.

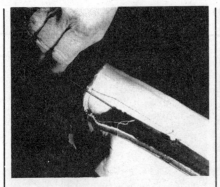

ESD7.   The pocketed wires on the underside of the seat covering can now be withdrawn.

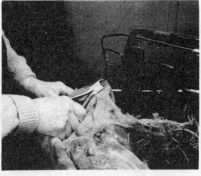

ESD9.   The hessian, the foam and the wire base assembly virtually fell apart as the final clips were released from the sprung base on this seat.

ESD11.   An inspection of the frame at this stage also revealed that the rear cross-member was no longer attached to the side rails, and welding would be needed to repair the frame at these points.

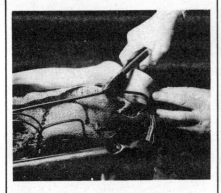

ESD8.   The next stage is to release the hessian cover from the sprung base. Again, the side cutters are useful. Start at the front edge, and work around the perimeter.

ESD10.   As the wired foam and hessian 'assembly' was lifted clear of the base, it was clear that the centre 'zig zag' ('snake wire') springs forming part of the sprung base were broken, giving no support to any driver!

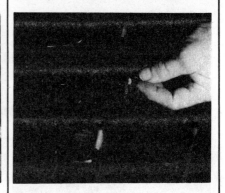

ESD12.   The broken sections of the centre 'zig zag' springs should be carefully extracted from the sprung base. Start by using a pair of pliers to ease the 'rolled' metal clips away from the front edge of the frame. The zig zag springs perform a 'U' turn at this point, continuing downwards at the front to meet the fixed frame rail. Save the clips for use at re-assembly; you may not easily be able to buy new ones.

ESD13.   To separate the end of the spring from the fixed front frame cross-member, use a wide screwdriver blade to gently ease the metal clamp apart.

ESD14. The hooked end of the spring can then be guided out of the clamp.

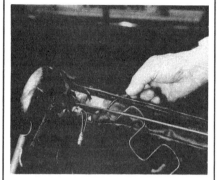

ESD15. The spring can then be angled to release the rear end from the fixing holes in the frame cross-member, at the back of the seat.

ESD16. The two coiled 'balance springs', one on either side of the seat frame, should be examined. These springs often break, and their mounting seats can part company with the main seat frame, as this one had. This type of spring is found in domestic furniture, and old household chairs can be a source of replacements. ▼

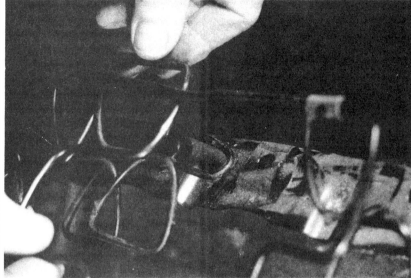

ESD17. To release the balance springs, 'unwind' the rolled clips, using a pair of pliers or side cutters. This spring had broken in half.

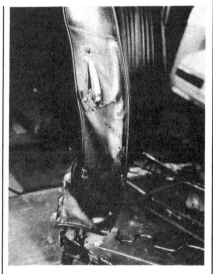

ESD18. With the base stripped of all the broken bits (which didn't leave a lot!), the backrest ⬆ assembly remained to be tackled. In fact, most of the material was intact, except for the badly holed outer side panel, which is always exposed to more wear than the other backrest sections.

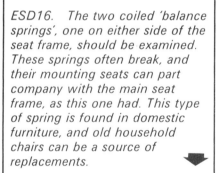

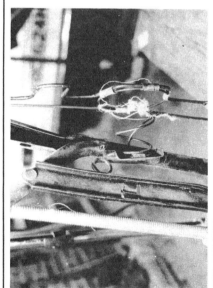

ESD19. Since this section was to be replaced anyway, it can be separated from the rest of the seat by VERY CAREFULLY ◀ slicing the stitches with a sharp ◀ knife, pulling the material outwards, and away from the seat frame as you proceed. The remaining backrest covering can then be very gently eased away from the seat.

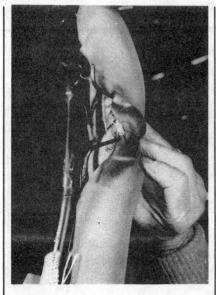

ESD20. With the backrest covering out of the way, carefully examine the rest of the frame, in particular checking the side support extensions. They are often broken away from the main frame, like this.

Having stripped the seat, the next problem is going to be obtaining replacements for the broken zig-zag springs. Unless your upholsterer has some in stock (it's always worth asking), the easiest answer is to buy the scruffiest seat you can find, from a vehicle dismantler, and extract

the necessary spring(s). It is usually the centre springs which break, while the outer ones are normally intact. Therefore even in a really rough seat there should be some that you can use as replacements for yours.

Cortina seat dismantling

Before we moved on to repairing the broken seat frame on the Escort, Mr. Exley gave a close inspection to a Cortina seat which had *appeared* to be in sound condition, with the exception of a tear in one of the backrest panels. However, closer inspection, prior to dismantling, led to the discovery that the rear frame cross-member had fractured, since it was pushing against the covering material at a very strange angle! Therefore the decision was taken to strip the seat, and to investigate.

Although the Cortina seats are of different construction to those used in the Escort (having a thick foam base sandwiched between the lower sprung section and the cover material, without the 'wired' seat base layer used in the Escort), they are dismantled in the same way. Therefore, as with the Escort seats, start by releasing the anchor clips around the frame perimeter.

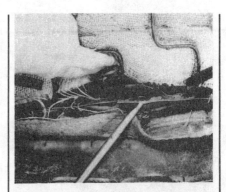

CSD1. With the base cover separated from the frame around the edges, the condition of the frame is easier to assess. On this seat, gently levering against the rear frame cross-member with a screwdriver revealed movement of several inches in each direction. The frame was completely severed at this point.

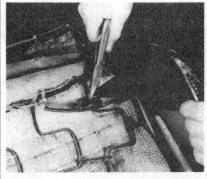

CSD2. To enable the seat to be taken apart, the 'wrap around' sections of the cover material, at each side, need to be released from the base springs, using a pair of side cutters to take out the metal clips.

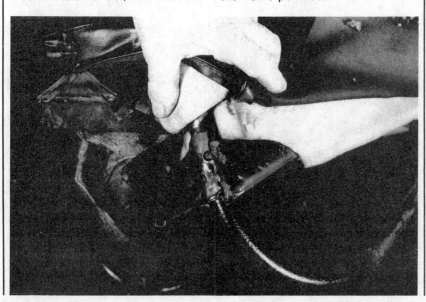

CSD3. The cover material can now be carefully pulled up at the rear edges; we found that the frame cross-member had also broken away from the seat's upright side support.

292

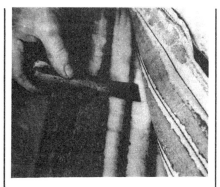

CSD4. Separate the seat base cover from the foam within, encouraging it with a flat bladed scraper, but taking care not to damage the cover material or the foam base.

CSD5. The foam base can be lifted away from the seat frame, leaving the hessian matting. Both the foam and matting were in good condition on this seat, luckily.

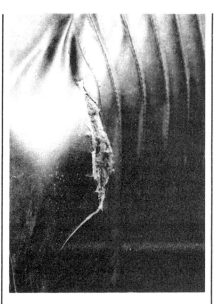

CSD6. This backrest side panel had an ugly split, but the rest of the seat cover was in perfect condition.

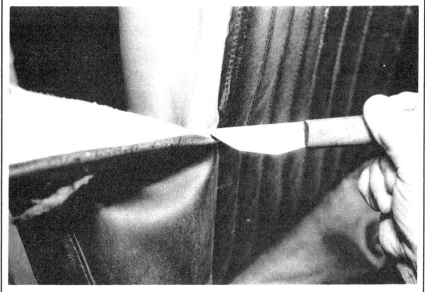

CSD7. Use a sharp knife to separate the damaged section from the rest of the seat. Take care to cut ONLY the stitches, and not the material of the adjacent panel.

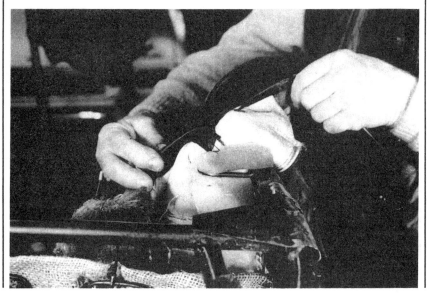

CSD8. The remaining sections of the backrest cover can now be peeled back more easily, taking care not to exert too much pressure on the stitching or sound material. The cover has to be removed – at least partially – from the frame, to allow repairs to be carried out to the frame.

The hessian cover can now be taken off the sprung base. NEVER leave material on the seat close to where welding or brazing is to take place.

293

Seat frame repairs

Repairs to the seat frames –
Escort or Cortina – should be
made by welding or secure
brazing. It is always helpful to
have an assistant on hand, to
help hold the seat frame sections
together while they are being
welded, for example.

*SFR1. The first step is to bring
the broken sections of the frame
back into line, prior to clamping
them into position with a
self-grip wrench.*

*SFR2. It is vital that secure
joints are made, or you will soon
have to strip the seat again for a
repeat operation. Make sure that
the weld penetration is sufficient
to hold the frame together; if in
doubt, repeat the weld along the
back of the joint.*

*SFR3. The corner joints are, of
course, critical in providing a
rigid seat frame. Make sure that
the frame members are correctly
positioned, prior to welding, and
that the weld is strong.*

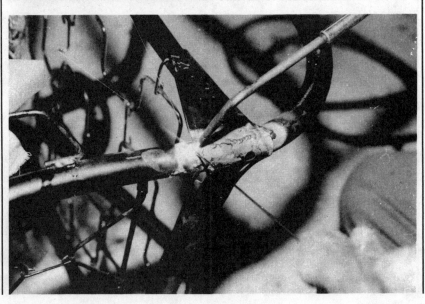

When the metal has cooled
sufficiently, the frame can be
treated with an anti-rust paint,
and allowed to dry. The seat,
complete with its covers,
damaged sections, frames, and
anchor clips, can then be
transported to the upholsterer, for
repairs to the cover material. It is
best to ask the upholsterer to
reassemble the seat, so that the
material can be correctly
tensioned and lined up on the
frames.

Obviously it is a good idea to
talk to your upholsterer before
you start stripping the seat
yourself; some may prefer to take
on the whole job. However, most
will be quite happy for you to do
the preliminary work, especially if
they are very busy. It saves them
time, and you money, of course.
In addition, at least you will have
the knowledge that *part* of the
work was your own.

Of course you may be lucky
and not need to strip the seats;
sometimes there are just small
blemishes on the surfaces of the
material. Small tears in upholstery
can be dealt with using one of
the special glues available, or, for
slightly larger areas, patching kits
can be bought. Often a small
piece of 'spare' trim can be cut
from overlapping edges
underneath the seat, for example,
to make good a small hole on the
outside of the seat.

294

Rear seat removal

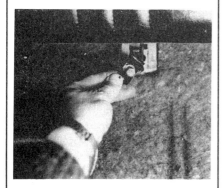

RSR1. Having released the seat base by taking out the single securing screw at the lower front edge, take out the two bolts holding the lower edge of the backrest to the bodywork.

RSR2. With the securing screws at the top of the backrest released from the parcel shelf, the seat unit can be pulled forward at one side, and taken from the car.

The rear seats on estate car models are released from the vehicle by unbolting them from the floor and side panels.

Carpet fitting

Complete carpet sets are available for all the Fords covered by this book. They are pre-shaped (although admittedly some need a little trimming to make them fit perfectly!) and are relatively inexpensive. Therefore, unless you are particularly keen, there is no point in constructing your own carpet set; it will certainly cost you as much, if not more, to buy the carpet and cut it to shape yourself, and of course it will take far longer.

Fitting the carpets is not difficult, but it will probably take longer than you think since the seats, sill kick plates and sometimes seat belt mountings have to be taken out. If you are carrying out a complete rebuild, fitting the carpets should be one of the final jobs, or they may accumulate dust, or oil before the car is ready for the road!

It is a good idea to apply a layer of underfelt to the floor below the main carpet. This helps insulate the car and keep road and mechanical noise down. It is also worthwhile fitting one of the generally available soundproofing kits before you install the carpets; these usually include extra, sound-insulating felt. It is, of course, essential that you cure all water leaks to the car's interior, before fitting underfelt or carpets, or these will hold moisture against the floor and eventually rust will develop.

CF1. Start by removing all dust from the floor. The quickest way to do this is to 'borrow' the domestic vacuum cleaner. If you are not permitted, by your 'house rules' to borrow such equipment for automotive work, a small, soft brush and a dust pan will do the job.

CF2. Offer up the carpet sections to their respective positions BEFORE applying glue to them, to make sure that they fit perfectly. You may find that minor trimming operations are needed to ensure a good fit. ➡

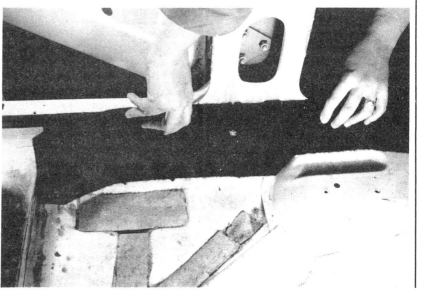

CF3. *Use a good quality waterproof adhesive to stick the carpet in place on vertical panels, such as the sills.*

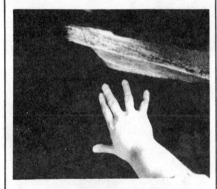

CF4. *The main floor sections of the carpet usually need to be pushed into all the corners, initially, to spread them out. Carpet securing clips, screwed to the floor, are available if necessary to keep the carpets in place. This is particularly important around the control pedal area, where the carpets must not be permitted to interfere with the operation of the pedals.*

Headlining

Removing and re-fitting a headlining can be a traumatic experience, so it is probably best left to experienced upholsterers. However, if you are enthusiastic, it *can* be done at home, but you should be aware that it is extremely difficult to get the lining back into the car and free from wrinkles.

Ideally, the windscreen and rear window should be removed; on two door Cortinas, it may be easier to remove the rear side windows, too. It is *possible* to do the job with the glass in place, but rather more difficult, since the headlining material tucks into the rubber window seal at each end, and can be easily torn in trying to remove or re-fit it.

The headlining is supported on 'listing rails', attached at each end to the body side frames. The rails should be eased very carefully from the side frames, having first released the lining from all windows and door aperture trim strips – a blunt screwdriver is useful for this. At the front end, detach the two spring clips (where fitted) holding the listing rail to the front panel. Take care not to lose the nylon sockets on the ends of the listing rails.

If you are fitting a new headlining, number the old listing rails before removing them from the material, and make sure that they are fitted to the new lining so that they fit back into the car in their original positions, since they vary slightly in length and shape. It is important that, when fitted, the listing rails are central, and free to move in the headlining sleeves, with an equal amount of material hanging from each end.

Unless you are particularly good at sewing, it would be best to let an experienced person make the new headlining, although it is *possible* to make your own from the appropriate material, using the original as a pattern.

The new headlining should be stuck at the rear window aperture, using an impact adhesive, having first pulled the material so that it is free from creases. The headlining should then be stuck in position above the windscreen in a similar manner, followed by the remaining edges of the lining. It will be necessary to slit the corners of the headlining at front and back, at either side of the windscreen and rear window, to ensure a crease-free fit, but make sure that the slits are not visible – they must not extend beyond the edges of the rubber seals.

Any excess headlining material can be cut off level with the edge of the screen and window apertures, where it is covered by rubber window seals. Where the headlining is covered by serrated finisher strips, allow enough material to overlap the edge of the aperture, before trimming.

Even if you don't need to change the headlining, you may need to gain access to the area behind it, for example if fitting a roof-mounted radio aerial, or for running a cable around it. Fitting a cable into the centre part of the roof area – as in fitting a roof aerial – is best tackled in two operations, using a flexible curtain wire. First thread it up the screen pillar, with the cable attached, then peel back the headlining in the front corner, so that the curtain wire and the cable can be 're-routed' across the roof panel's front box member.

8 Modifications

Fords have always been modified by their owners, either to make them go faster and handle better, or to make them look different, to stand out from similar models, or just to make them more comfortable.

The Cortinas and Escorts are no exception, and there are almost limitless possibilities to the range of modifications you can make to your car.

Increasingly, of course, as the cars get older, they get scarcer, and so the range of products available for the older models gradually shrinks. Therefore, there are obviously more tuning and other components available for altering the Escorts than there are for the early Cortina models. The Escorts, with their rallying and racing tradition, have always inspired 'performance' tuning and many today are still being modified – even the Mark I cars – to make them go faster.

That doesn't mean to say that you cannot improve the performance, safety and comfort of the Cortinas, for tuning and other 'upgrading' parts are still readily available from many firms for these models. It has to be said though that nowadays the emphasis on the Cortina models is heading more towards 'originality', as the cars increasingly become 'collectable'.

Nevertheless there are many ways in which these Fords – Cortinas and Escorts – can be improved, without losing any of their character, and this is very good news if, for example you use your car for everyday use. In these circumstances the sacrifice of a little originality in return for improved performance, safety and comfort may be considered worthwhile. It all depends on how you, as an individual owner, view your car.

The subject of modifications to Cortinas and Escorts would, of course, fill several books, let along a single chapter. However the aim here is to give you an idea of the sort of modifications which can be carried out on your model, on a d-i-y basis.

Power units

There are a number of ways to increase the performance of your Ford, and one of the easiest is to simply swap the engine for a larger or more powerful unit. Fortunately, this is comparatively straightforward. For example, the engines fitted to the pre cross-flow Cortinas can be swapped directly between models of varying engine size. It is worth bearing in mind, although it needn't make life complicated, that the engines fitted to Mark I Cortinas have their flywheels held on with four bolts, whereas those on the 1500cc Mark II and the later cross-flow engines are secured by six bolts. Provided you use the 'new' engine complete with its flywheel, all should be well.

Identification of the pre cross-flow engines is not difficult, for the 1200cc units have '109E' stamped on the block, as do the Classic/Capri engines of the same era, while the 1500cc Mark I engines have '120E' stamped on them; Mark II versions (as also used in the Corsair) are marked '2731'. All except the Classic/Capri engines have similar cylinder heads.

The later, cross-flow engines can also be interchanged, provided the engine is from the same model; that is from Cortina to Cortina, or Escort to Escort. It is very easy to uprate an Escort so that, for example, a 1300 engine can be fitted to an 1100, or a 1600 engine to a 1300, without having to alter engine mounts and so on. The cross-flow Cortina 1300 can similarly be uprated to a 1600 by a straightforward engine change.

M1. One of the easiest ways to gain more power is simply to change your engine for a larger unit from the same range.

It is possible to fit a cross-flow Cortina engine to an Escort or vice versa, but the sumps are different. The Cortina Mark IIs have the deep portion of their sumps at the front, to clear the steering links, mounted well back in the engine bay. The Escorts, Capris and Mark III Cortinas using the same engines have the deep part of the sump at the rear, to clear the forward-mounted steering rack. Therefore, to effect a swap, the sump from your original engine will have to be used, together with the oil pipes, and the dipstick, with its tube. When swapping the oil return pipe, take care not to push it in too far, or it will cut off the oilway. A hole will be needed to accommodate the new dipstick tube and dipstick; there is a 'pilot' hole already in the cylinder block at the appropriate point, One of the project Cortinas for this book had obviously already been the subject of an 'Escort' engine swap, for it had two dipsticks! The redundant hole could be plugged, of course.

If you prefer to retain your original cylinder block, you could uprate your engine, say, from 1100cc to 1300cc by changing the crankshaft and connecting rods. The 1100cc rods are stamped with the number '2733E', while 1300cc items have '2735E' stamped on them.

At a quick glance, the 1100 and 1300cc power units appear the same. However, the 1600cc engines are about two inches taller, which helps identification.

M2. Alternative power units can often be found in breakers' yards; This Cortina, apart from having many good trim items and body panels, also had a 1600GT engine, in good condition. In 'open' yards like this one, it is sometimes possible to hear the engine running before you buy it, which is useful.

Of course, swapping engines almost certainly means that you will be buying secondhand. This can be okay, but there are risks, of course, especially when you cannot actually hear the engine running. This often applies in the case of breakers' yards, where the engine will already be out of the vehicle, in many cases.

Another possibility is that you may be able to buy the engine you need through advertisements in the local newspapers. There may be someone living near you who is breaking a car, which perhaps has accident damage, but which nevertheless has a good engine.

It is always sensible to examine the engine carefully before you buy – in particular look at the state of the oil, the general condition of the unit (has it been blowing oil out all over the top of the engine, due to worn pistons/rings/cylinder bores, for example?) and inside the rocker cover. However, unless you can actually drive the car, or actually strip and examine the unit, neither of which are usually practical, you will be taking some risk.

When you get the engine home, you can either fit it and 'try' it, which sometimes works out all right, or you can take off at least the cylinder head, and overhaul it, also the oil pump, and the sump, to check the bearings and crankshaft, carrying out re-ringing and perhaps a re-bore if necessary. If you do just fit the engine without any close inspection, don't hold your hopes too high . . . you may be disappointed. At the very least, in any case, you should use fresh engine oil and fit a new filter before you run the engine.

When fitting any 'non original' unit to your car, always try to get the ancillaries with the engine, and fit the whole assembly. This includes the distributor and carburettor, both of which are matched to engine size and type, and, if possible, the radiator. In addition, on GT types, try to obtain the correct exhaust system for the engine.

Before you attempt to fit a powerful V6 engine into a Mark I Cortina originally designed for a 1200cc engine (for example), it is worth considering the practical consequences. AND the likely insurance premium. To make the car safe, the brakes and suspension will need to be uprated considerably to handle the extra power. This is not impossible, of course, but considerable time and money will be needed to make the project a safe machine, rather than a lethal projectile which will travel very quickly, but which is less inclined to go round corners, or to stop!

Insurance companies have traditionally taken rather a dim view of altering the vehicle manufacturers' specifications. However, it is ESSENTIAL that you advise them of any modifications made, for if you don't, and then have an accident, you could well be considered to be uninsured, effectively, with disastrous results, especially if you have damaged someone else's property or killed or injured another person. While an insurance company may settle for just a modest premium increase for moving, say, from 1200 to 1500cc, the premium could get VERY expensive if you move up from 1200cc to 3 litres. You will almost certainly need an 'Engineer's Report' on the car's condition, together with full details of all the alterations made.

Tuning

The alternative to fitting a different engine is to improve the one you already have. Again, since you own a Ford, you are fortunate in that there are so many different tuning parts available specifically for uprating Fords. From carburettors to camshafts, cylinder heads to exhaust systems, there is an almost limitless supply of parts to make Fords move more quickly! The specialist motoring magazines dealing with performance motoring, for example *Cars and Car Conversions* and *Hot Car*, to name just two, carry advertisements every month from firms who can supply every imaginable tuning accessory. It is always worth talking to your local motor accessory shops, to enquire about tuning accessories; many of the owners and managers are keen to help, and have a lot of knowledge themselves about the equipment needed to uprate your car to different levels of performance.

With any engine, harnessing its potential performance is only possible if the 'breathing' is correct. Therefore the carburation, ports and manifolds need to be modified, if necessary, to smooth the gas flow, and to make the most of each cc of fuel mixture, as it passes through the engine.

T1. Standard air filters seldom allow the optimum quantity of air into the engine, and there are a wide range of different filters available for Fords, which not only work more efficiently, but which look smart, too.

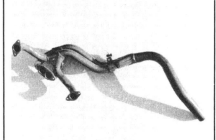

T2. A carefully designed exhaust manifold can make a world of difference to an engine, even without any other modifications. It is not being over-optimistic to expect a power increase of around 10 per cent by fitting a 4 into 2 into 1 manifold like this.

Even if your car is one of the earliest 1200cc Mark I Cortinas, tuning parts are still available. For example, Janspeed, of Salisbury, a well respected and long-established tuning firm, can still supply exhaust manifolds, modified cylinder heads (to three different stages of tune), and Weber carburettor kits for these early cars, and of course the later cross-flow Cortinas. They also supply these items, as well as complete 'straight through' exhaust systems for the Escorts, from 1100cc models to RS2000s. Competition parts are also available for enthusiasts. In these days when many firms are not interested in supplying parts for the older models, it is good to know that some companies still cater for enthusiasts of vehicles which are now obsolete.

If you intend keeping your car for a long time, and particularly if you use it every day, it is worth spending some money to improve the performance. The fitting of a matched carburettor, cylinder head and manifolding will improve the car's pulling power, acceleration AND fuel economy, for a properly tuned engine will make more efficient use of the fuel it burns.

Of course, further stages of tune are also possible, by fitting high performance camshafts, and so on. Head skimming is not a good idea, on the cross-flow engines, since the combustion chambers are formed within the piston crowns, and any reduction in clearance between the piston top and the cylinder head will result in violent contact with the valves, giving severe loss of compression (and valves and pistons!), rather than the desired increase in compression, and power.

Before deciding to extract more power from your engine, it is sensible to make sure that it is in good shape to start with. Certainly if it is already beginning to burn oil, and perhaps is low on compression, with a rattling camshaft, you should think carefully before you buy tuning components. Trying to improve

the motor's ailing performance by bolting on expensive goodies is only going to hasten its already imminent demise. Far better to spend some money now on overhauling the engine, then when it has been fully run in, consider 'go faster' parts.

Tuning engines properly is an art, and it is always helpful to talk to experts (and other owners) with experience before spending a lot of money on parts which may be of little real benefit for the sort of use you give your car. There are quite a few fast Fords on the road which would be ideal on a race track, but which are awful to drive in town traffic, where they spend most of their time. Therefore it is quite possible to 'over tune' an engine by going for maximum possible power, without considering other factors, such as low speed torque. As an example, rushing out and buying the 'wildest' camshaft you can find could give you a car with a lot of power at high revs, but no pull at low speeds, which can make it very difficult to drive in traffic.

If you are simply looking for a modest improvement in power and economy, without loss in flexibility, this can be achieved just by bolting on a performance carburettor/air cleaner assembly, and by fitting a modified manifold/exhaust system. A modified cylinder head would be the next stage, with improved gas flow, and probably larger valves. Beyond these relatively straightforward 'bolt on' items, come camshaft changes, and so on. The first few extra horsepower are fairly easy to attain, but further improvements need a lot more work, and, usually, a lot more money too.

If you are really interested in making your Ford move faster, it is worth buying one of the many books available which deal specifically with tuning engines.

You should, of course, notify your insurance company of any modifications which have been made to your engine.

Gearboxes

If fitting a more powerful engine from the same model range, it pays where possible to fit the matching gearbox, with a new clutch if necessary, at the same time. At least you will then be sure that the gearbox is capable of carrying the extra power, rather than, for example, trying to mate a powerful engine with a gearbox designed for a family model. It will probably fit, and work for a while, but, if you use the extra power, it won't last very long. In addition, the ratios chosen for the gearboxes on the fast models are deliberately 'close', to match the performance characteristics of the engine; full details of the ratios used in each gearbox are given in Appendix 3, at the back of this book.

It is possible to swap gearboxes about between different Ford models, and again, the range of permutations and combinations is vast. However, as a general guide, the gearboxes used in the Cortinas are basically interchangeable, but gear lever positions will obviously vary, for example between 'long lever' Mark I Cortinas and later, remote change gearboxes. As an example the gearboxes fitted to late Mark II Cortinas can be fitted to earlier cars, subject to rearranging the mounting supports, and the need to modify or change the gear lever, to avoid it coming into contact with the handbrake, where this is floor-mounted.

The gearboxes are also interchangeable between most Escort cross-flow models, but, as already mentioned, in any case it is best to use the gearbox originally matched with the engine you are using.

Another point to watch is that the gearboxes fitted to the Escorts have integral bell housings, except for the Mexico, whereas those fitted to Cortinas have separate bell housings.

The best way of making sure that a particular gearbox will fit is by physical inspection and measurement. Look particularly at the pattern of the bolts around the bell housing, and length and diameter of the first motion shaft, and the number of splines on this.

Differential change

If you have changed the engine on your car for a more powerful unit, or even if you simply need to alter the overall gearing to take account of the vehicle's use, there are a wide variety of differential ratios to choose from. The various ratios used in the Cortinas and Escorts are listed in Appendix 3, at the back of this book, and they allow for various compromises between acceleration, cruising speed, fuel economy and ultimate top speed. Generally speaking, the higher the power of the engine, the higher the back axle ratio (and therefore the lower the number) can be. The higher the ratio, the slower the engine will need to turn for a given road speed. Therefore, if you use your car a lot for high speed cruising, and less for town work, a higher ratio differential will give you more relaxed cruising, longer engine life and lower petrol consumption, even if you retain the original engine. On the other hand, if your vehicle is used almost entirely in town traffic, a high ratio differential will be a nuisance, calling for more gear changing than is necessary, and making the car less 'flexible'. A lower ratio differential will give improved acceleration and easier driving around town, but make the engine increasingly fussy as the speed rises, and will lower the ultimate maximum speed attainable.

Of course there are occasions when you can deliberately alter the characteristics of the car by

fitting a more powerful engine and *not* changing the final drive ratio.

It is possible that you could be fitting a more powerful engine to cope with towing, or for carrying heavy loads, for example, and in that case it may be preferable to leave the original ratio fitted, rather than 'uprating' the differential to a higher ratio unit. For example, my own brother has recently uprated his Escort van from standard 1300cc to 1600cc 'GT' specification, primarily to cope with regular towing of a heavily laden trailer. Rather than fit the higher ratio 3.545:1 differential, as fitted to the 1600cc cars to 'match' the higher power output from the new engine, he retained the relatively low standard 1300cc van axle ratio, of 4.125:1. The vehicle is now a superb towing machine, and when lightly laden, has terrific acceleration. The potential top speed may be a little lower, but this is rather academic anyway in daily use.

The best compromise ratio for your vehicle really depends on what sort of motoring you normally do.

It should be borne in mind that changing the differential ratio will alter the speedometer

readings, unless the appropriate speedometer drive gear ratio is also fitted, or the speedometer is recalibrated.

To change a differential is quite easy on the 'Timken' type axles. Before you start, make sure that you have a new differential case gasket and a supply of fresh axle oil, with which to fill the unit on completion of the job. You will also need a differential unit, of course. If you intend to fit a second-hand unit, Appendix 3 lists the ratios fitted to each model, together with the number of teeth on the crown wheel and pinion, for each ratio. If you are unsure which axle is fitted to a particular vehicle, or to double check that you are buying the ratio you need, simply count the number of teeth on each gear wheel, and compare it with the list.

The same working procedures apply, of course, if you are simply replacing a worn out differential with a new one of the same ratio.

Start by pulling the axle shafts from each side of the differential casing, as described in the 'Rear Axle' section of the 'Mechanical Components' chapter, under 'Half Shaft Removal'.

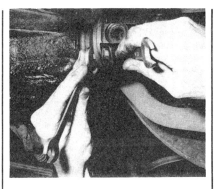

DC1. With the half shafts clear, release the four bolts (or nuts and bolts, as on this Cortina) holding the propeller shaft to the front flange on the differential.

DC2. The nuts around the perimeter of the differential casing are now released; take care that the differential assembly doesn't drop as the last nuts are taken off. More often than not, however, it will need to be prised away from the axle casing.

DC3. This is a new differential unit, and therefore spotlessly clean. If you are buying a second-hand unit, and removing it from a vehicle yourself, take a large carrier bag with you, so that the assembly can be kept clean until it is fitted. Always check that there is no grit or dust in the 'works' immediately prior to fitting the unit.

DC4. Fit a new gasket to the axle casing, having cleaned the flange with a little cellulose thinners on a rag. Fit the new unit very carefully, then tighten the bolts, to 18 lb.ft. (Cortina Mark I), 15 to 18 lb.ft. (Cortina Mark II and Escort Mark I), or 26 to 30 lb.ft. (Escort Mark II), and re-fit the half shafts. Finally, fill the axle with 2 pints (1.1 litres) SAE 90 EP hypoid gear oil.

Before leaving the subject of transmissions, it is worth mentioning another 'modification' which may be of interest to Escort owners. On cars with two-piece propeller shafts, the centre and universal joint bearings eventually wear, and can give nasty vibrations through the floor. As an alternative to overhauling all five joints, a single piece propeller shaft can be fitted from an 1100cc model.

Exhaust system

I have already mentioned that modified exhaust manifolds and complete systems are available, particularly for the Escorts. However another aspect of modifying exhaust systems relates to keeping the early cars on the road. While systems for the Cortina saloons are still available, those for the Mark I automatic estate cars, for example, are 'no longer available', which can mean problems, especially if the car is in everyday use. If you have trouble in locating the 'correct' system for your car, it is worth visiting your local exhaust centre and talking to them. Most of

them will be only too pleased to help try to find an alternative system or individual pipe to help you out, provided that you don't call on them at a busy time.

Indeed, many such centres will construct a system and fit it, out of parts originally designed for other (normally later) models.

Returning to the case of the Mark I automatic estate, an ordinary saloon system can be used, provided that the main pipe is cut two inches in front of the forward exhaust box, leaving the flange in place, then 'reversed', so that what was the forward box is now at the rear. This sort of modification can be made to many cars; there are few limits to ingenuity when it comes to making up exhaust systems. However, ALWAYS take care if welding a system, and NEVER weld near to a fuel line or fuel tank.

Another problem which can be encountered concerns 'GT' Escorts, with the 4 into 2 into 1 exhaust manifolds, which can be prone to cracking at the joint of the number 1 and number 4 pipes; under the triangular reinforcing plate. Taking off the reinforcing plate and re-setting the pipes, before welding the plate back in position, normally cures the trouble, although it is difficult to ensure that the pipe from number 1 cylinder doesn't

move in the process.

If you are keeping your car for a long time, and are fed up with changing the standard mild steel exhaust system every two or three years, it would be worth investing in a complete stainless steel system. These can be made to the pattern of your original system on older cars, and are available 'off the shelf' for the later models; there are several suppliers around the country. Stainless steel systems are, of course, more expensive than standard items, but last indefinitely, and the investment is worthwhile, long-term.

Electrics

I have already covered the fitting of fuses to the early cars, in the 'Electrical Components' chapter. This 'modification' is one of the most important you can make to your car, for it could literally save it from disappearing in a cloud of smoke.

There are a wide range of electrical accessories which can be fitted to Cortinas and Escorts, ranging from driving lamps to electronic ignition systems.

E1. An electronic ignition system is useful for keeping the car in tune for far longer than with a normal ignition system. On types where the contact points are used as 'triggers' for the system, the points will last a lot longer, and will not become burnt and pitted, as with a conventional ignition system. On 'contactless' types, the physical limitations of the mechanical contact breaker are dispensed with, to give more accurate ignition timing, particularly at speed.

On some engines, for example the BDA units fitted to the RS1600 Escorts, where the distributor is far from accessible, an electronic ignition system can save a lot of time and frustration in setting contact points.

E2. Auxiliary driving lamps are available, together with heavy duty mounting brackets, and they can make the front of the car look imposing, apart from being a valuable driving aid at night.

There are many small, yet useful modifications which can be made to the electrical systems originally fitted to these Fords.

A safety-related improvement concerns the column mounted stalks fitted to the Mark I

Cortinas. These were not as robust as the units fitted on later models, and can break. The later type stalks, as fitted to the Mark II Cortina, and the Escort, have identical functions, but different connections. Connector blocks were employed on Mark I Cortinas, while plug-in connectors were fitted to Mark II models. However, the problem can be overcome by cutting the wires on the 'new' unit just before they enter the connector, and by fitting a household type connector block to link the original wiring to the new unit. The different angle of the stalk used on the later cars can be amended by placing it in the vice, between aluminium protector plates, and *gently* bending it to the shape of the original arm.

Another useful tip is that the door switches for the courtesy light as fitted to Escorts, which are prone to breaking, can be replaced with the type fitted to later Cortinas, under Finis code 1595734. The wire will need a 1/4 inch female 'push-on' type connector to be fitted, to allow connection to the later type of switch.

An easy alteration to the lighting system is to replace the separate bulb variety of headlamps with sealed beam units, or indeed, to do the reverse swap if required.

Bodywork and wheels

Bodywork modifications can be made to Cortinas and Escorts, and in fact there are many 'styling kits' available for the Escorts, in particular. Just one word of caution, regarding the early cars; the more the bodywork is modified, the more difficult it will be to revert the car to 'standard' if you ever wanted to sell it as a 'collector's car', for example. While this may not matter if you intend to keep the vehicle anyway, it may be worth thinking about. The value of a car which has modified bodywork will, generally, be lower than that of an 'original' vehicle.

It is possible to fit laminated windscreens to any of the Fords covered by this book, and the extra expense is worthwhile if you are going to keep the car for a long time.

If you have a two-door Escort with opening rear side windows, and are experiencing problems with the security of the glass, there is an easy answer. If you don't mind losing the facility of being able to open the rear windows, the fixed type from a 'lower' trim level model can be fitted, complete with the rubbers. This also makes the car a little more thief-proof, of course.

The choice of alternative wheels for your Ford is extremely wide. It pays to buy good quality wheels, and it is essential that when fitted, the new wheels and tyres, if wider than the originals, do not hit the bodywork, brake lines or suspension/steering components under full lock or 'rough road' conditions. Before parting with your cash, survey the market and talk to the wheel suppliers – they will be able to advise you on specific fitting problems.

BAW1. Wide wheel arch flares can be purchased for Escorts and Cortinas, normally to be used in conjunction with fitting wide wheels and tyres. In fact, if you fit wide wheels, you MUST make sure that the bodywork covers them. Take care when fitting such wing extensions, to make sure that the edges are fully blended in with the original contours of the bodywork, or the overall visual effect will be lost. Airdams and spoilers are also available for most Cortina and Escort models.

BAW2. Wheels and wheel spacers are available in a variety of types. If fitting wheel spacers, always ask the advice of the suppliers, since extra load will be imposed on the wheel bearings, proportional to the increase in the distance between the wheel and the hub.

BAW3. It is useful if you are able to 'offer up' a wheel of the type you intend to buy, to the vehicle. You can then be sure that the pitch circle diameter (the diameter of an imaginary circle drawn through the centres of the hub studs) of the wheel matches that of the studs on your car, and also get an idea whether the wheel is likely to protrude beyond the bodywork.

There are a huge number of small but useful modifications one can make to the bodywork on a Ford during a restoration project. It is, of course, impossible to list all of them, but a few examples of the sort of modifications possible should be helpful.

If the kickplates on your Mark I Cortina are looking a little scruffy, they can be replaced by the later, plastic type, with moulded edges. These are a direct replacement for the earlier items, are longer-lasting, and easier to keep clean.

Another simple but effective improvement which can be made on the Mark I Cortina concerns the clips attaching the bright trim strips to the bodywork. The originals can be replaced with plastic clips as used on later Fords – Finis code 1432241 – these are slightly wider than the originals, but modification is straightforward; a small round file can be used to ease out the holes, if necessary. Where the trim holes are too large, a non-rusting (brass) nut and bolt can be used to attach the trim with.

On cars which have 'fixed position' sun visors (that is, which don't swivel to cover the driver's and passenger's door windows), it is a simple matter to fit an extra visor above each

door, fastening it to the double skinning with self-tapping screws. If you do a lot of north-south driving on motorways, this can be a very worthwhile modification.

A problem which affects most Cortinas and Escorts is the age-hardening of the outer door window glass weatherstrip seals. These become brittle, and trap grit in their old age, which of course scratches the window glasses. When fitting new weatherstrips, try soaking them in Waxoyl or similar wax for a few days prior to fitting – this should help to keep them supple. Wipe off all excess wax before fitting, of course.

Suspension

Uprated springs and shock absorbers can make a great deal of difference to the handling of your car. Stiffer springs and firmer shock absorbers will usually improve cornering, at the expense of ride comfort, so talk to the supplier before you buy, and explain what you are aiming for. Some shock absorbers, such as Woodhead's sophisticated twin-tube 'Gasglide' units make considerable improvements to ride and handling. They are only a little more expensive than standard units, too, so are a worthwhile investment.

If you have fitted a larger, heavier engine to your car, you may be obliged to fit heavy duty front springs, to cope with the extra weight. If you use your Ford for carrying heavy loads, and particularly if it is used for towing, spring assisters or auxiliary springs can be fitted, to preserve the original suspension, and to help keep the vehicle from riding too low at the rear. Alternatively, heavy duty rear springs could be fitted, as direct replacements for the original items.

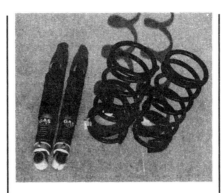

S1. There are an enormous variety of uprated shock absorbers and springs available for improving roadholding. Most normally affect ride quality to some extent, and the result is therefore usually a compromise. Talk to your supplier about the type of use the car receives, and he will be able to advise you on the best units to fit for that particular application.

S2. More for competition work than road use, this strut bolts between the upper suspension mounts on Escorts, to cut down flexing of the bodywork when driving in severe conditions.

Brakes

Your brakes need to be improved if you have uprated the power output from your own engine, or have fitted a more powerful unit. This can be quite easy, if expensive. For example, if you have simply fitted a larger engine from a more powerful model in the same range, swapping your existing braking system for one as fitted to the faster model, (and overhauling it as a matter of course before fitting), is the answer. If your car has drum brakes and you increase the engine's power, you should think in terms of fitting discs at the front. Unfortunately this will also mean changing the suspension legs to accommodate the discs and hub assemblies.

Contrary to popular belief, fitting a brake servo unit will *not* make the brakes more effective, it will simply reduce the pedal pressure required to slow the car. It is a useful aid, but not an improver of the braking efficiency of the car, in itself. The same applies to fitting harder 'competition' brake pads and linings. These will probably be more resistant to 'fade' than ordinary types, when under prolonged or hard use, but the braking effort required may well be increased. Again, the use of such items, in isolation, will not help very much, but will be more useful as part of a properly planned, co-ordinated braking system re-vamping.

Take care, too, if you are swapping brake assemblies from one model to another. For instance, if you attempt to fit larger brakes from a more powerful car in another model range, they may not physically fit onto your vehicle.

With brakes, more than any other of the car's systems, modifications must be made VERY carefully, and with due regard to all the possibilities. Talk to the Club(s) catering for your model, and to as many people as possible who have tried similar conversions – you will then learn about many of the possible snags. Finally, if in doubt about uprating brakes to this extent, don't attempt it yourself. Take the car to a tuning specialist with experience in this field. Far better to pay to have the job done, than to risk lives with inadequate or unsafe brakes.

There are, of course, less drastic modifications which can be made to brakes, and one concerns the handbrake on early Cortina automatic estate cars with the dash-mounted handbrake levers. Since the cables are 'no longer available' for this model, it is worth modifying the system to accept normal saloon replacement cables, which are around 2 inches shorter. Heavy steel links can be used to bridge the gap, and similar modifications can be made to other models where cables may be increasingly difficult to obtain.

Instruments

Driving can be made more enjoyable by having a set of instruments to keep one up to date with what is happening under the bonnet. Supplementary instruments can be fitted to the non sports models, and among the dials generally available, tachometer, coolant temperature, oil pressure, vacuum, voltmeter and ammeter gauges are probably the most useful. If you are enthusiastic, it is also possible to obtain oil temperature gauges, ambient temperature indicators, and so on. It depends just how much information you need.

Another instrument I find particularly useful is an 'Icelert'; this is fitted to the outside of the car, and, when the temperature dips, a light flashes as it approaches freezing point. The intensity of the flashes increases as the temperature drops still further, and the warning light stays on continuously when the temperature is below freezing. If travelling long distances in winter it can give early warning of a temperature change between areas, also of changing weather conditions, and the possibility of ice on the road.

There are other instruments one can fit, of varying degrees of usefulness. I must confess to once having fitted an aeroplane's altimeter to my car, which was perhaps not the most essential of gauges, but nevertheless very entertaining when crossing the Alps, and when visiting the Lake District and Scottish Highlands! It had the dual role of acting as a barometer, as the pressure changed, provided you knew what height you were at!

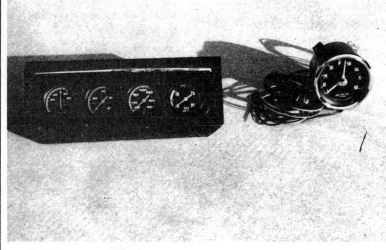

11. Sets of four gauges, complete with a neat mounting bracket, all the necessary sender units, and full instructions for fitting, can be bought at reasonable prices from most motor accessory shops. A tachometer (rev counter) is rather more expensive, but nevertheless useful – it could help prolong your engine life, as could the other instruments, provided you take notice of what they are trying to tell you!

Security

It is a sad fact that if you restore a vehicle to a high standard, it can increasingly become a target for car thieves. Although the vehicles are sometimes recovered, they are usually damaged, if not wrecked, by thoughtless joyriders (or those with malicious intent from the outset), so it pays to secure your car as well as you can.

The fairly basic door locks fitted as standard equipment can be supplemented by the use of extra, high security locks, such as those made by Safeways Security Products, of 10, Grange Mount, Birkenhead, Merseyside, L43 4XW. These are fairly unobtrusive yet could act as a deterrent in themselves. It is also possible to fit extra locks to the bonnet and boot, and to equip the car with a comprehensive alarm system and ignition immobiliser.

A cheap deterrent is to have the windows and screen permanently marked with the registration number of your vehicle. To change the vehicle's identity is then far more difficult, since all the glass will need to be changed, and this would probably be enough to deter most thieves.

Hopefully, of course, your car will not be stolen, but, if it is, the results can be horrifying. I have been involved with recovering several 'classic' cars which have been stolen and dumped, and the wicked way in which some of them have

deliberately been torn apart by the vandals who stole them is sickening. In many cases, there is little left to salvage or rebuild. Take care of your Ford.

General

It is impossible to list all the possible modifications which can be made to Cortinas and Escorts.

In many cases, ingenuity and common sense will suggest ways and means of improving your car, often with very little outlay.

It is usually possible to use parts fitted to other Fords – for example the Mark I Cortinas have floorpans, running gear and door trims, etc., similar to the Corsair (at least up to V4 engined cars). Many Fords use the same basic components, and a trip round a breakers' yard will usually yield all sorts of interchangeable parts, and ideas for useful modifications. At the same time, there is no reason why parts from other makes of car cannot be used successfully. As examples, door aperture trims from Mini vans can be used on Mark I Cortinas, and trim clips from Austin A35s can be used to secure the rear trims in estate car models!

With a little careful thought and time spent in experimentation, a great deal of pleasure can be derived from improving your Ford; in most cases this can be done without altering its basic character.

Appendices

1 Workshop Procedures – Safety First

Professional motor mechanics are trained in safe working procedures, whereas the onus is on you, the home mechanic, to find them out for yourself and act upon them. However enthusiastic you may be about getting on with the job in hand, do take the time to ensure that your safety is not put at risk. A moment's lack of attention can result in an accident, as can failure to observe certain elementary precautions.

There will always be new ways of having accidents, and the following points do not pretend to be a comprehensive list of all dangers; they are intended rather to make you aware of the risks and to encourage a safety-conscious approach to all work you carry out on your vehicle.

Be sure to consult the suppliers of any materials and equipment you may use, and to obtain and read carefully operating and health and safety instructions that they may supply.

Essential DOs and DON'Ts

DON'T rely on a single jack when working underneath the vehicle. Always use reliable additional means of support, such as axle stands, securely placed under a part of the vehicle that you know will not give way.

DON'T attempt to loosen or tighten high-torque nuts (e.g. wheel hub nuts) while the vehicle is on a jack; it may be pulled off.

DON'T start the engine without first ascertaining that the transmission is in neutral (or 'Park' where applicable) and the parking brake applied.

DON'T suddenly remove the filler cap from a hot cooling system – cover it with a cloth and release the pressure gradually first, or you may get scalded by escaping coolant.

DON'T attempt to drain oil, automatic transmission fluid, or coolant until you are sure it has cooled sufficiently to avoid scalding you.

DON'T grasp any part of the engine, exhaust or catalytic converter without first ascertaining that it is sufficiently cool to avoid burning you.

DON'T allow brake fluid or antifreeze to contact vehicle paintwork.

DON'T syphon toxic liquids such as fuel, brake fluid or antifreeze by mouth, or allow them to remain on your skin.

DON'T inhale dust – it may be injurious to health (see Asbestos below).

DON'T allow any spilt oil or grease to remain on the floor – wipe it up straight away, before someone slips on it.

DON'T use ill-fitting spanners or other tools which may slip and cause injury.

DON'T attempt to lift a heavy component which may be beyond your capability – get assistance.

DON'T rush to finish a job, or take unverified short cuts.

DON'T allow children or animals in or around an unattended vehicle.

DON'T park vehicles with catalytic converters over combustible materials such as dry grass, oil rags, etc., if the engine has recently been run. As catalytic converters reach extremely high temperatures, any such materials in close proximity may ignite.

DON'T run vehicles equipped with catalytic converters without the exhaust system heat shields fitted.

DO wear eye protection when using power tools such as an electric drill, sander, bench grinder, etc., and when working under the vehicle.

DO use a barrier cream on your hands prior to undertaking dirty jobs – it will protect your skin from infection as well as making the dirt easier to remove afterwards; but make sure your hands aren't left slippery. Note

that long-term contact with used engine oil can be a health hazard.

DO keep loose clothing (cuffs, tie, etc.) and long hair well out of the way of moving mechanical parts.

DO remove rings, wrist watch, etc., before working on the vehicle – especially the electrical system.

DO ensure that any lifting tackle used has a safe working load rating adequate for the job, and is used precisely as recommended by the manufacturer.

DO keep your work area tidy – it is only too easy to fall over articles left lying around.

DO get someone to check periodically that all is well, when working alone on the vehicle.

DO carry out work in a logical sequence and check that everything is correctly assembled and tightened afterwards.

DO remember that your vehicle's safety affects that of yourself and others. If in doubt on any point, get specialist advice.

IF, in spite of following these precautions, you are unfortunate enough to injure yourself, seek medical attention as soon as possible.

Fire

Remember at all times that petrol (gasoline) is highly inflammable. Never smoke, or have any kind of naked flame around, when working on the vehicle. But the risk does not end there – a spark caused by an electrical short-circuit, by two metal surfaces contacting each other, by a central heating boiler in the garage 'firing up', or even by static electricity built up in your body under certain conditions, can ignite petrol vapour, which in a confined space is highly explosive.

Always disconnect the battery earth (ground) terminal before working on any part of the fuel system, and never risk spilling fuel on to a hot engine or exhaust.

It is recommended that a fire extinguisher of a type suitable for fuel and electrical fires is kept handy in the garage or workplace at all times. Never try to extinguish a fuel or electrical fire with water.

Fumes

Certain fumes are highly toxic and can quickly cause unconsciousness and even death if inhaled to any extent. Petrol (gasoline) vapour comes into this category, as do the vapours from certain solvents such as trichloroethylene and those from many adhesives. Any draining or pouring of such volatile fluids should be done in a well-ventilated area.

When using cleaning fluids and solvents, read the instructions carefully. Never use any materials from unmarked containers – they may give off poisonous vapours.

Never run the engine of a motor vehicle in an enclosed space such as a garage. Exhaust fumes contain carbon monoxide which is extremely poisonous. If you need to run the engine, always do so in the open air or at least have the rear of the vehicle outside the workplace.

If you are fortunate enough to have the use of an inspection pit, never drain or pour petrol, and never run the engine, while the vehicle is standing over it; the fumes, being heavier than air, will concentrate in the pit with possibly lethal results.

The battery

Never cause a spark, or allow a naked light, near the vehicle battery. It will normally be giving off a certain amount of hydrogen gas, which is highly explosive.

Always disconnect the battery earth (ground) terminal before working on the fuel or electrical systems.

If possible, loosen the filler plugs or cover when charging the battery from an external source. Do not charge at an excessive rate or the battery may burst.

Take care when topping up and when carrying the battery. The acid electrolyte, even when diluted, is very corrosive and should not be allowed to contact the eyes or skin.

If you ever need to prepare electrolyte yourself, always add the acid slowly to the water, and never the other way round. Protect against splashes by wearing rubber gloves and goggles.

Mains electricity

When using an electric power tool, inspection light, etc., which works from the mains, always ensure that the appliance is correctly connected to its plug and that, where necessary, it is properly earthed (grounded). Do not use such appliances in damp conditions and, again, beware of creating a spark or applying excessive heat in the vicinity of fuel or fuel vapour.

Also, before using any mains powered electrical equipment, take one more simple precaution – use an RCD (Residual Current Device) circuit breaker. Then, if there is a short, the RCD circuit breaker minimises the risk of electrocution by instantly cutting the power supply. Buy from any electrical store or DIY centre. RCDs fit simply into your electrical socket before plugging in your electrical equipment.

Ignition HT voltage

A severe electric shock can result from touching certain parts of the ignition system, such as the HT leads, when the engine is running or being cranked,

309

particularly if components are damp or the insulation is defective. Where an electronic ignition system is fitted, the HT voltage is much higher and could prove fatal. Consult your handbook or main dealer if in any doubt. Risk of injury while working on running engines, e.g. adjusting the timing, can arise if the operator touches a high voltage lead and pulls his hand away on to a projection or revolving part. On some vehicles the voltage used in the ignition system is so high that it can cause injury or death by electrocution.

Welding and bodywork repairs

It is so useful to be able to weld when carrying out restoration work, and yet there is a good deal that could go dangerously wrong for the uninformed – in fact more than could be covered here. **For safety's sake** you are strongly recommended to seek tuition, in whatever branch of welding you wish to use, from your local evening institute or adult education classes. In addition, all of the information and instructional material produced by the suppliers of materials and equipment you will be using must be studied carefully. You may have to ask your stockist for some of this printed material if it is not made available at the time of purchase.

In addition, it is strongly recommended that *The Car Bodywork Repair Manual*, published by Haynes, is purchased and studied before carrying out any welding or bodywork repairs. Consisting of 292 pages, around 1,000 illustrations and written by Lindsay Porter, the author of this book, *The Car Bodywork Repair Manual* picks the brains of specialists from a variety of fields, and covers arc, MIG and 'gas' welding, panel beating and

accident repair, rust repair and treatment, paint spraying, glass-fibre work, filler, lead loading, interiors and much more besides. Alongside a number of projects, the book describes in detail how to carry out each of the techniques involved in car bodywork repair, with safety notes where necessary. As such, it is the ideal complement to this book.

Compressed gas cylinders

There are serious hazards associated with the storage and handling of gas cylinders and fittings, and standard precautions should be strictly observed in dealing with them. Ensure that cylinders are stored in safe conditions, properly maintained and always handled with special care, and make constant efforts to eliminate the possibility of leakage, fire and explosion.

The cylinder gases that are commonly used are oxygen, acetylene and liquid petroleum gas (LPG). Safety requirements for all three gases are: Cylinders must be stored in a fire resistant, dry and well-ventilated space, away from any source of heat or ignition and protected from ice, snow or direct sunlight. Valves of cylinders in store must always be kept uppermost and closed, even when the cylinder is empty. Cylinders should be handled with care and only by personnel who are reliable, adequately informed and fully aware of all associated hazards. Damaged or leaking cylinders should be promptly taken outside into the open air, and the supplier and fire authorities should be notified immediately. No one should approach a gas cylinder store with a naked light or cigarette. Care should be taken to avoid striking or dropping cylinders, or knocking them together. Cylinders should never be used as rollers. One cylinder should

never be filled from another. Every care must be taken to avoid accidental damage to cylinder valves. Valves must be operated without haste, never fully opened hard back against the back stop (so that other users know the valve is open) and never wrenched shut but turned just securely enough to stop the gas. Before removing or loosening any outlet connections, caps or plugs, a check should be made that the valves are closed. When carrying cylinders, close all valves and appliance taps, and extinguish naked flames, including pilot jets, before disconnecting them. When reconnecting, ensure that all connections and washers are clean and in good condition, and do not overtighten them. Immediately a cylinder becomes empty, close its valve.

Safety requirements for acetylene: Cylinders must always be stored and used in the upright position. If a cylinder becomes heated accidentally or becomes hot because of excessive backfiring, immediately shut the valve, detach the regulator, take the cylinder out of doors well away from the building, immerse it in, or continuously spray it with, water, open the valve and allow the gas to escape until the cylinder is empty. If necessary, notify the emergency fire service without delay.

Safety requirements for oxygen are: No oil or grease should be used on valves or fittings. Cylinders with convex bases should be used in a stand or held securely to a wall.

Safety requirements for LPG are: The store must be kept free of combustible material, corrosive material and cylinders of oxygen.

Cylinders should only ever be carried upright, securely strapped down, preferably in an open vehicle or with windows open. Carry the suppliers' safety data with you. In the event of an

accident, notify the Police and Fire Services and hand the safety data to them.

Dangerous liquids and gases

Because of inflammable gas given off by batteries when on charge, care should be taken to avoid sparking by switching off the power supply before charger leads are connected or disconnected. Battery terminals should be shielded, since a battery contains energy and a spark can be caused by any conductor which touches its terminals or exposed connecting straps.

When internal combustion engines are operated inside buildings, the exhaust fumes must be properly discharged to the open air. Petroleum spirit or mixture must be contained in metal cans which should be kept in a store. In any area where battery charging or the testing of fuel injection systems is carried out there must be good ventilation, and no sources of ignition. Inspection pits often present serious hazards. They should be of adequate length to allow safe access and exit while a car is in position. If there is an inspection pit, petrol may enter it. Since petrol vapour is heavier than air it will remain there and be a hazard if there is any source of ignition. All sources of ignition must therefore be excluded.

Work with plastics

Work with plastic materials brings additional hazards into workshops. Many of the materials used (polymers, resins, adhesives and materials acting as catalysts and accelerators) readily produce very dangerous situations in the form of poisonous fumes, skin irritants, risk of fire and explosions. Do not allow resin or 2-pack

adhesive hardener, or that supplied with filler or 2-pack stopper to come into contact with skin or eyes. Read carefully the safety notes supplied on the tin, tube or packaging.

Jacks and axle stands

Special care should be taken when any type of lifting equipment is used. NEVER even consider working under your car using only a jack to support the weight of it. Lifting jacks are for raising vehicles not supporting them, and must be replaced by adequate supports before any work is begun on the vehicle. Axle stands are available from many discount stores, and all auto parts stores. These stands are absolutely essential if you plan to work under your car. Simple triangular stands (fixed or adjustable) will suit almost all of your working situations. Drive-on ramps are very limiting because of their design and size.

When jacking the car from the front, leave the gearbox in neutral and the brake off until you have placed the axle stands under the frame. Make sure that the car is on level ground first! Then put the car into gear and/or engage the handbrake and lower the jack. Obviously, DO NOT put the car in gear if you plan to turn over the engine! Leaving the brake on, or leaving the car in gear while jacking the front of the car will necessarily cause the jack to tip (unless a good quality trolley jack with wheels is being used). This is unavoidable when jacking the car on one side, and the use of the handbrake in this case is recommended. If the car is older and if it shows signs of weakening at the jack tubes while using the factory jack, it is best to purchase a good scissors jack or hydraulic jack – preferably trolley-type (depending on your budget).

Workshop safety – summary

1 Always have a fire extinguisher at arm's length whenever welding or when working on the fuel system – under the car, or under the bonnet.
2 NEVER use a naked flame near the petrol tank.
3 Keep your inspection lamp FAR AWAY from any source of dripping petrol (gasoline); for example, while removing the fuel pump.
4 NEVER use petrol (gasoline) to clean parts. Use paraffin (kerosene) or white (mineral) spirit.
5 NO SMOKING!

If you do have a fire, DON'T PANIC. Use the extinguisher effectively by directing it at the base of the fire.

Paint spraying

NEVER use 2-pack, isocyanate-based paints in the home environment or home workshop. Ask your supplier if you are not sure which is which. If you have use of a professional booth, wear an air-fed mask. Wear a charcoal face mask when spraying other paints, and maintain ventilation to the spray area. Concentrated fumes are dangerous!

Spray fumes, thinners and paint are highly inflammable. Keep away from naked flames or sparks.

Paint spraying safety is too large a subject for this book. See Lindsay Porter's *The Car Bodywork Repair Manual* (Haynes) for further information.

Fluoroelastomers – *Most Important! Please Read This Section!*

Many synthetic rubber-like

materials used in motor cars contain substances known as fluoroelastomers (containing fluorine). These are commonly used for oil seals, wiring and cabling, bearing surfaces, gaskets, diaphragms, hoses and 'O' rings. If they are subjected to temperatures greater than 315°C, they will decompose and can be potentially hazardous. Fluoroelastomer materials will show physical signs of decomposition under such conditions in the form of charring of black sticky masses. Some decomposition may occur at temperatures above 200°C, and it is obvious that when a car has been in a fire or has been dismantled with the assistance of a cutting torch or blow torch, the fluoroelastomers can decompose in the manner indicated above.

In the presence of any water or humidity, including atmospheric moisture, the by-products caused by fluoroelastomers being heated can be extremely dangerous.

According to the Health and Safety Executive, 'Skin contact with this liquid or decomposition residues can cause painful and penetrating burns. Permanent irreversible skin and tissue damage can occur.' Damage can also be caused to eyes or by the inhalation of fumes created as fluoroelastomers are burned or heated.

If you are in the vicinity of a vehicle fire or a place where a vehicle is being cut up with cutting equipment, the Health and Safety Executive recommend the following action:

1   Assume, unless you know otherwise that seals, gaskets and 'O' rings, hoses, wiring and cabling, bearing surfaces and diaphragms are fluoroelastomers.
2   Inform firefighters of the presence of fluoroelastomers and toxic and corrosive fume hazards when they arrive.
3   All personnel not wearing breathing apparatus must leave the immediate area of a fire.

After fires or exposure to high temperatures:
1   Do not touch blackened or charred seals or equipment.
2   Allow all burnt or decomposed fluoroelastomer materials to cool down before inspection, investigation, tear-down or removal.
3   Preferably, don't handle parts containing decomposed fluoroelastomers, but if you must, wear goggles and PVC (polyvinyl chloride) or neoprene protective gloves whilst doing so. Never handle such parts unless they are completely cool.
4   Contaminated parts, residues, materials and clothing, including protective clothing and gloves, should be disposed of by an approved contractor to landfill, or by incineration according to national or local regulations. Original seals, gaskets and 'O' rings, along with contaminated material, must not be burned locally.

Symptoms and clinical findings of exposures:
A   Skin/eye contact:
Symptoms may be apparent immediately after contact, or there may be considerable delay following exposure. Do not assume that a lack of immediate symptoms means there has been no damage; delays of minutes in treatment can have severe consequences:
1   Dull throbbing ache.
2   Severe and persistent pain.
3   Black discoloration under nails (skin contact).
4   Severe, persistent and penetrating burns.
5   Skin swelling and redness.
6   Blistering.
7   Sometimes pain without visible change.
B   Inhalation (breathing) – immediate:
1   Coughing.
2   Choking.
3   Chills lasting one or two hours after exposure.
4   Irritation.
C   Inhalation (breathing) – delays of one to two days or more:
1   Fever.
2   Cough.
3   Chest tightness.
4   Pulmonary oedema (congestion).
5   Bronchial pneumonia.

FIRST AID
A   Skin contact:
1   Remove contaminated clothing immediately.
2   Irrigate affected skin with copious amounts of cold water   or lime water (saturated calcium hydroxide solution) for 15   to 60 minutes. Obtain medical assistance urgently.
B   Inhalation:
Remove to fresh air and obtain medical supportive treatment immediately. Treat for pulmonary oedema.
C   Eye contact:
Wash/irrigate eyes immediately with water followed by normal saline for 30 to 60 minutes. Obtain immediate medical attention.

2 Tools and Working Facilities

Introduction

A selection of good tools is a fundamental requirement for anyone contemplating the maintenance and repair of a motor vehicle. For the owner who does not possess any, their purchase will prove a considerable expense, offsetting some of the savings made by doing-it-yourself. However, provided that the tools purchased are of good quality, they will last for many years and prove an extremely worthwhile investment.

To help the average owner to decide which tools are needed to carry out the various tasks detailed in this manual, we have compiled three lists of tools under the following headings: Maintenance and minor repair, Repair and overhaul, and Special. The newcomer to practical mechanics should start off with the 'Maintenance and minor repair' tool kit and confine himself to the simpler jobs around the vehicle. Then, as his confidence and experience grows, he can undertake more difficult tasks, buying extra tools as, and when, they are needed. In this way a 'Maintenance and minor repair' tool kit can be built up into a 'Repair and overhaul' tool kit over a considerable period of time without any major cash outlays. The experienced do-it-yourselfer will have a tool kit good enough for most repairs and overhaul procedures and will add tools from the 'Special' category when he feels the expense is justified by the amount of use these tools will be put to.

Maintenance and minor repair tool kit

The tools given in this list should really be considered as a minimum requirement if routine maintenance, servicing and minor repair operations are to be undertaken.

Ideally purchase sets of open-ended and ring spanners, covering similar size ranges. That way, you will have the correct tools for loosening nuts from bolts having the same head size, for example, since you will have at least two spanners of the same size.

Alternatively, a set of combination spanners (ring one end, open-ended the other), give the advantages of both types of spanner. Although more expensive than open-ended spanners, combination spanners can often help you out in tight situations, by gripping the nut better than an open-ender.

Combination spanners – $^3/8$, $^7/16$, $^1/2$, $^9/16$, $^5/8$, $^{11}/16$, $^3/4$, $^{13}/16$, $^7/8$, $^{15}/16$ in. AF.
Combination spanners – 8, 9, 10, 11, 12, 13, 14, 15, 17, 19 mm.

Adjustable spanner – 9 inch
Engine sump/gearbox/rear axle drain plug key (where applicable)
Spark plug spanner (with rubber insert)
Spark plug gap adjustment tool
Set of feeler gauges
Brake adjuster spanner (where applicable)
Brake bleed nipple spanner
Screwdriver – 4 in. long x $^1/4$ in. dia. (plain)
Screwdriver – 4 in. long x $^1/4$ in. dia. (crosshead)
Combination pliers – 6 inch
Hacksaw, junior
Tyre pump
Tyre pressure gauge
Grease gun (where applicable)
Oil can
Fine emery cloth (1 sheet)
Wire brush (small)
Funnel (medium size)

Repair and overhaul tool kit

These tools are virtually essential for anyone undertaking any major repairs to a motor vehicle, and are additional to those given in the Basic list. Included in this list is a comprehensive set of sockets. Although these are expensive they will be found invaluable as they are so versatile – particularly if various drives are included in the set. We recommend the $1/2$ square-drive type, as this can be used with most proprietary torque wrenches. If you cannot afford a socket set, even bought piecemeal, then inexpensive tubular box spanners are a useful alternative.

The tools in this list will occasionally need to be supplemented by tools from the Special list.

Sockets (or box spanners) to cover range in previous list
Reversible ratchet drive (for use with sockets)
Extension piece, 10 inch (for use with sockets)
Universal joint (for use with sockets)
Torque wrench (for use with sockets)
'Mole' wrench – 8 inch
Ball pein hammer
Soft-faced hammer, plastic or rubber
Screwdriver – 6 in. long x $5/16$ in. dia (plain)
Screwdriver – 2 in. long x $5/16$ in. square (plain)
Screwdriver – $1^1/2$ in. long x $1/4$ in. dia. (crosshead)
Screwdriver – 3 in. long x $1/8$ in. dia. (electrician's)
Pliers – electrician's side cutters
Pliers – needle noses
Pliers – circlip (internal and external)
Cold chisel – $1/2$ inch
Scriber (this can be made by grinding the end of a broken hacksaw blade)
Scraper (This can be made by flattening and sharpening one end of a piece of copper pipe)
Centre punch
Pin punch
Hacksaw
Valve grinding tool
Steel rule/straightedge
Allen keys
Selection of files
Wire brush (large)
Axle stands
Jack (strong scissor or hydraulic type)

Special tools

The tools in this list are those which are not used regularly, are expensive to buy, or which need to be used in accordance with their manufacturer's instructions. Unless relatively difficult mechanical jobs are undertaken frequently, it will not be economic to buy many of these tools. Where this is the case, you could consider clubbing together with friends (or a motorists' club) to make a joint purchase, or borrowing the tools against a deposit from a local garage or tool hire specialist.

The following list contains only those tools and instruments freely available to the public, and not those special tools produced by the vehicle manufacturer specially for its dealer network.

Valve spring compressor
Piston ring compressor
Ball joint separator
Universal hub/bearing puller
Impact screwdriver
Micrometer and/or vernier gauge
Carburettor flow balancing device (where applicable)
Dial gauge
Stroboscopic timing light
Dwell angle meter/tachometer
Universal electrical multi-meter
Cylinder compression gauge
Lifting tackle
Trolley jack
Light with extension lead
Rivet gun

Buying tools

Tool factors can be a good source of implements, due to the extensive ranges which they normally stock. On the other hand, accessory shops usually offer excellent quality goods, often at discount prices, so it pays to shop around.

The old maxim "Buy the best tools you can afford" is a good general rule to go by, since cheap tools are seldom good value, especially in the long run. Conversely, it isn't always true that the MOST expensive tools are best. There are plenty of good tools available at reasonable prices, and the shop manager or proprietor will usually be very helpful in giving advice on the best tools for particular jobs.

Care and maintenance of tools

Having purchased a reasonable tool kit, it is necessary to keep the tools in a clean and serviceable condition. After use, always wipe off any dirt, grease and metal particles using a clean, dry cloth, before putting the tools away. Never leave them lying around after they have been used. A simple tool rack on the garage or workshop wall, for items such as screwdrivers and pliers is a good idea. Store all normal spanners and sockets in a metal box. Any measuring instruments, gauges, meters etc., must be carefully stored where they cannot be damaged or become rusty.

Take a little care when the tools are used. Hammer heads inevitably become marked and

screwdrivers lose the keen edge on their blades from time-to-time. A little timely attention with emery cloth or a file will soon restore items like this to a good serviceable finish.

twist drills, is virtually essential for fitting accessories such as wing mirrors and reversing lights.

Last, but not least, always

keep a supply of old newspapers and clean, lint-free rags available, and try to keep any working areas as clean as possible.

Working facilities

Not to be forgotten when discussing tools, is the workshop itself. If anything more than routine maintenance is to be carried out, some form of suitable working area becomes essential.

It is appreciated that many an owner mechanic is forced by circumstance to remove an engine or similar item, without the benefit of a garage or workshop. Having done this, any repairs should always be done under the cover of a roof, if feasible.

Wherever possible, any dismantling should be done on a clean flat workbench or table at a suitable working height.

Any workbench needs a vice: one with a jaw opening of 4 in. (100mm) is suitable for most jobs. As mentioned previously, some clean, dry storage space is also required for tools, as well as the lubricants, cleaning fluids, touch-up paints and so on which soon become necessary.

Another item which may be required, and which has a much more general usage, is an electric drill with a chuck capacity of at least $5/16$ in. (8mm). This, together with a good range of

Spanner jaw gap comparison table

AF size	Actual size	Nearest metric size	Metric size in ins.
4BA	0.248in.	7mm.	0.276in.
2BA	0.320in.	8mm.	0.315in.
$7/16$in.	0.440in.	11mm.	0.413in.
$1/2$in.	0.500in.	13mm.	0.510in.
$9/16$in.	0.560in.	14mm.	0.550in.
$5/8$in.	0.630in.	16mm.	0.630in.
$11/16$in.	0.690in.	18mm.	0.710in.
$3/4$in.	0.760in.	19mm.	0.750in.
$13/16$in.	0.820in.	21mm.	0.830in.
$7/8$in.	0.880in.	22mm.	0.870in.
$15/16$in.	0.940in.	24mm.	0.945in.
1in.	1.000in.	26mm.	1.020in.

Whitworth size	Actual size	Nearest AF size	AF Actual size
$3/16$in.	0.450in.	$7/16$in.	0.440in.
$1/4$in.	0.530in.	$1/2$in.	0.500in.
$5/16$in.	0.604in.	$9/16$in	0.560in.
$3/8$in.	0.720in.	$11/16$in.	0.690in.
$7/16$in.	0.830in.	$13/16$in.	0.820in.
$1/2$in.	0.930in.	$7/8$in.	0.880in.
$9/16$in.	1.020in.	1in.	1.010in.

Whitworth size	Actual size	Nearest Metric size	Metric size in ins
$3/16$in.	0.450in.	12mm.	0.470in.
$1/4$in.	0.530in.	14mm.	0.550in.
$5/16$in.	0.604in.	15mm.	0.590in.
$3/8$in.	0.720in.	18mm.	0.710in.
$7/16$in.	0.830in.	21mm.	0.830in.
$1/2$in.	0.930in.	24mm.	0.945in.
$9/16$in.	1.020in.	26mm.	1.020in.

3 Specifications

Engines

Note: Units used in this section have been standardised to provide ready comparison between models.

All engines are four cylinder, in-line units.

Cortina I 1200

Type	Overhead valve (pushrod), indirect flow cylinder head
Capacity	1198 cc (73.09 cu.in.)
Bore	80.96 mm (3.1875 in.)
Stroke	58.17 mm (2.290 in.)
Compression ratio	HC – until October, 1964 – 8.7:1
	HC – October, 1964 on – 9.0:1
	LC – 7.3:1
Max. power (net)	HC – until October, 1964 – 48.5 bhp @ 4,800 rpm
	HC – October, 1964 on – 50 bhp @ 5,000 rpm
	LC – 46 bhp @ 4,800 rpm
Max. torque (net)	HC – until October, 1964 – 63 lb.ft. (8.71 kg.m.) @ 2,700 rpm
	HC – October, 1964 on – 69 lb.ft. (9.54 kg.m.) @ 2,700 rpm
	LC – 60 lb.ft. (8.30 kg.m.) @ 2,700 rpm
Compression pressure at cranking speed	HC – until October, 1964 – 175 psi
	HC – October, 1964 on – 179 psi
	LC – 145 psi

Cortina I 1500

Type	Overhead valve (pushrod), indirect flow cylinder head
Capacity	1498 cc (91.43 cu.in.) or 1500 cc (91.54 cu.in.), for later 1966 cars only
Bore	80.96 mm (3.1875 in.)

Stroke	72.75 mm (2.864 in.) or 72.82 mm (2.867 in.), for later 1966 cars only
Compression ratio	HC – until October, 1964 – 8.3:1
	HC – October, 1964 on – 9.0:1
	LC – 7.0:1
	GT – 9.0:1
Max. power (net)	HC – until October, 1964 – 59.5 bhp @ 4,600 rpm
	HC – October, 1964 on – 61 bhp @ 4,700 rpm
	LC – 56 bhp @ 4,700 rpm
	GT – 78 bhp @ 5,200 rpm
Max. torque (net)	HC – until October, 1964 – 81.5 lb.ft. (11.27 kg.m.) @ 2,300 rpm
	HC – October, 1964 on – 83 lb.ft. (11.48 kg.m.) @ 2,500 rpm
	LC – 77.5 lb.ft. (10.72 kg.m.) @ 2,700 rpm
	GT – 91 lb.ft. (12.58 kg.m.) @ 3,600 rpm
Compression pressure at cranking speed	HC – until October, 1964 – 173 psi
	HC – October, 1964 on – 179 psi
	LC – 144 psi
	GT – 179 psi

Cortina II 1300 (Non cross-flow)

Type	Overhead valve (pushrod), indirect flow cylinder head
Capacity	1297 cc (79.17 cu.in.)
Bore	80.97 mm (3.1878 in.)
Stroke	62.99 mm (2.480 in.)
Compression ratio	HC – 9.0:1
	LC – 7.5:1
Max. power (net)	HC – 53.5 bhp @ 5,000 rpm
	LC – 52.0 bhp @ 5,000 rpm
Max. torque (net)	HC – 70.5 lb.ft. (9.74 kg.m.) @ 2,750 rpm
	LC – 67 lb.ft. (9.26 kg.m.) @ 2,500 rpm
Compression pressure at cranking speed	HC – 175 psi
	LC – 155 psi

Cortina II 1500 (Non cross-flow)

Type	Overhead valve (pushrod), indirect flow cylinder head
Capacity	1500cc (91.54 cu.in.)
Bore	80.97 mm (3.1878 in.)
Stroke	72.82 mm (2.867 in.)
Compression ratio	HC – 9.0:1
	LC – 7.5:1
	GT – 9.0:1
Max. power (net)	HC – 61.5 bhp @ 4,700 rpm
	LC – 57.5 bhp @ 4,700 rpm
	GT – 78 bhp @ 5,200 rpm
Max. torque (net)	HC – 83.5 lb.ft. (11.54 kg.m.) @ 2,500 rpm
	LC – 80 lb.ft. (11.06 kg.m.) @ 2,700 rpm
	GT – 91 lb.ft. (12.58 kg.m.) @ 3,600 rpm
Compression pressure at cranking speed	HC – 185 psi
	LC – 155 psi
	GT – 185 psi

Cortina I/II Lotus

Type	Twin overhead camshaft, chain driven
Capacity	1558 cc (95.07 cu.in.)
Bore	82.55 mm (3.250 in.)
Stroke	72.75 mm (2.867 in.)
Compression ratio	9.5:1
Max. power (net)	Until late 1966 – 105 bhp @ 5,500 rpm
	Late 1966 on – 109.5 bhp @ 6,000 rpm
Max. torque (net)	Until late 1966 – 108 lb.ft. (14.93 kg.m.) @ 4,000 rpm
	Late 1966 on – 106.5 lb.ft. (14.72 kg.m.) @ 4,500 rpm
Compression pressure at cranking speed	170 psi

Cortina II 1300 (Cross-flow)

Type	Overhead valve (pushrod), cross-flow cylinder head
Capacity	1298cc (79.20 cu.in.)
Bore	80.978 mm (3.1881 in.)
Stroke	62.99 mm (2.480 in.)
Compression ratio	HC – 9.0:1
	LC – 8.0:1
Max. power (net)	HC – 57.5 bhp @ 5,000 rpm
	LC – 53.5 bhp @ 5,000 rpm
Max. torque (net)	HC – 71.5 lb.ft. (9.75 kg.m.) @ 2,500 rpm
	LC – 68 lb.ft. (9.40 kg.m.) @ 2,500 rpm
Compression pressure at cranking speed	HC – 168 psi
	LC – 157 psi

Cortina II 1600 (Cross-flow)

Type	Overhead valve (pushrod), cross-flow cylinder head
Capacity	1599 cc (97.58 cu.in.)
Bore	80.978 mm (3.1881 in).
Stroke	77.62 mm (3.056 in.)
Compression ratio	HC – 9.0:1
	LC – 8.0:1
	GT/1600E – 9.0:1
Max. power (net)	HC – 71 bhp @ 5,000 rpm
	LC – 69.5 bhp @ 5,000 rpm
	GT/1600E – 88 bhp @ 5,400 rpm
Max. torque (net)	HC – 91.5 lb.ft. (12.58 kg.m.) @ 2,500 rpm
	LC – 87 lb.ft. (12.03 kg.m.) @ 2,500 rpm
	GT/1600E – 96 lb.ft. (13.27 kg.m.) @ 3,600 rpm
Compression pressure at cranking speed	HC – 188 psi
	LC – 170 psi
	GT/1600E – 188 psi

Escort I 1100

Type	Overhead valve (pushrod), cross-flow cylinder head
Capacity	1098 cc (67.0 cu.in.)
Bore	80.978 mm (3.1881 in.)
Stroke	53.29 mm (2.098 in.)
Compression ratio	HC – 9.0:1
	LC – 8.0:1
Max. power (net)	HC – until September, 1970 – 45 bhp @ 5,500 rpm
	HC – September, 1970 on – 48 bhp @ 5,500 rpm
	LC – until September, 1970 – 42.5 bhp @ 5,500 rpm
	LC – September, 1970 on – 44 bhp @ 5,500 rpm
Max. torque (net)	HC – 54 lb.ft. (7.47 kg.m.) @ 3,000 rpm
	LC – 50 lb.ft. (6.91 kg.m.) @ 3,000 rpm
Compression pressure at cranking speed	HC – 165 psi
	LC – 154 psi

Escort I 1300

Type	Overhead valve (pushrod), cross-flow cylinder head
Capacity	1298 cc (79.21 cu.in.)
Bore	80.978 mm (3.1881 in.)
Stroke	62.99 mm (2.480 in.)
Compression ratio	HC – 9.0:1
	LC – 8.0:1
	GT – 9.2:1
Max. power (net)	HC – until September, 1970 – 52 bhp @ 5,000 rpm
	HC – September, 1970 on – 57 bhp @ 5,000 rpm
	LC – until September, 1970 – 49 bhp @ 5,000 rpm
	LC – September, 1970 on – 54 bhp @ 5,000 rpm
	GT – until September, 1970 – 64 bhp @ 6,000 rpm
	GT – September, 1970 on – 72 bhp @ 6,000 rpm
Max. torque (net)	HC – 67 lb.ft. (9.26 kg.m.) @ 2,500 rpm
	LC – 63 lb.ft. (8.71 kg.m.) @ 2,500 rpm
	GT – 70 lb.ft. (9.68 kg.m.) @ 4,300 rpm
Compression pressure at cranking speed	HC/GT – 168 psi
	LC – 157 psi

Note: 1300GT specifications also apply to Sport and 1300E models.

Escort I Twin Cam

Type	Lotus, with chain-driven, double overhead camshaft cylinder head
Capacity	1558 cc (95.07 cu.in.)
Bore	82.55 mm (3.250 in.)
Stroke	72.75 mm (2.867 in.)
Compression ratio	9.5:1
Max. power (net)	109.5 bhp @ 6,000 rpm
Max. torque (net)	106.5 lb.ft. (14.72 kg.m.)
Compression pressure: at cranking speed	185 psi

Escort I RS 1600

Type	Cosworth, with 16 valve cylinder head and belt driven, twin overhead camshafts
Capacity	1601 cc (97.70 cu.in.)
Bore	80.993 mm (3.1887 in.)
Stroke	77.724 mm (3.060 in.)
Compression ratio	10.0:1
Max. power (net)	115 bhp @ 6,000 rpm
Max. torque (net)	112 lb.ft. (15.48 kg.m.) @ 4,000 rpm

Escort I Mexico

Type	Overhead valve (pushrod), cross-flow cylinder head
Capacity	1599 cc (97.58 cu.in.)
Bore	80.978 mm (3.1881 in.)
Stroke	77.62 mm (3.056 in.)
Compression ratio	9.0:1
Max. power (net)	86 bhp @ 5,500 rpm
Max. torque (net)	92 lb.ft. (12.72 kg.m.) @ 4,000 rpm
Compression pressure at cranking speed	188 psi

Escort I RS 2000

Type	Belt-driven, overhead camshaft
Capacity	1993 cc (121.62 cu.in.)
Bore	90.82 mm (3.576 in.)
Stroke	76.95 mm (3.03 in.)
Compression ratio	9.2:1
Max. power (net)	100 bhp @ 5,700 rpm
Max. torque	108 lb.ft. (14.93 kg.m.) @ 3,500 rpm
Compression pressure at cranking speed	142 to 170 psi

Escort II 1.1

Type	Overhead valve (pushrod), cross-flow cylinder head
Capacity	1098 cc (67.0 cu.in.)
Bore	80.978 mm (3.1881 in.)
Stroke	53.29 mm (2.098 in.)
Compression ratio	HC – 9.0:1
	LC – 8.0:1
	2v (GT – France/Italy) 9.0:1
	Popular – 9.0:1
Max. power (net)	HC – 48 bhp @ 5,500 rpm
	LC – 44 bhp @ 5,500 rpm
	2v (GT) – 57 bhp @ 5,500 rpm
	Popular – 41 bhp @ 5,300 rpm

Max. torque (net)	HC – 54 lb.ft. (7.47 kg.m.) @ 3,000 rpm
	LC – 52 lb.ft. (7.19 kg.m.) @ 3,000 rpm
	2v (GT) – 56 lb.ft. (7.74 kg.m.) @ 4,000 rpm
	Popular – 50 lb.ft. (6.91 kg.m.) @ 3,000 rpm
Compression pressure at cranking speed	
	HC – 142 to 170 psi
	LC – 128 to 156 psi
	2v (GT) – 142 to 170 psi

Escort II 1.3

Type	Overhead valve (pushrod), cross-flow cylinder head
Capacity	1298 cc (79.21 cu.in.)
Bore	80.978 mm (3.1881 in.)
Stroke	62.99 mm (2.480 in.)
Compression ratio	HC – 9.0:1
	LC – 8.0:1
	Sport/Ghia – 9.0:1
Max. power (net)	HC – 57 bhp @ 5,500 rpm
	LC – 54 bhp @ 5,500 rpm
	Sport/Ghia – 70 bhp @ 5,500 rpm
Max. torque (net)	HC – 67 lb.ft. (9.26 kg.m.) @ 3,000 rpm
	LC – 63 lb.ft. (8.71 kg.m.) @ 3,000 rpm
	Sport/Ghia – 68 lb.ft. (9.40 kg.m.) @ 4,000 rpm
Compression pressure at cranking speed	
	HC – 142 to 170 psi
	LC – 128 to 156 psi
	Sport/Ghia 142 to 170 psi

Escort II 1.6 Sport/Ghia

Type	Overhead valve (pushrod), cross-flow cylinder head
Capacity	1599 cc (97.58 cu.in.)
Bore	80.978 mm (3.1881 in.)
Stroke	77.62 mm (3.056 in.)
Compression ratio	9.0:1
Max. power (net)	84 bhp @ 5,500 rpm
Max. torque (net)	92 lb.ft. (13.55 kg.m.) @ 4,000 rpm
Compression pressure at cranking speed	
	142 to 170 psi

Escort II RS 1800

Type	Cosworth, with 16 valve cylinder head and twin, belt-driven, overhead camshafts
Capacity	1840 cc (112.28 cu.in.)
Bore	86.75 mm (3.415 in.)
Stroke	77.62 mm (3.056 in.)
Compression ratio	9.0:1
Max. power (net)	115 bhp @ 6,000 rpm
Max. torque (net)	120 lb.ft. (16.59 kg.m.) @ 4,000 rpm

Escort II RS Mexico

Type	Belt-driven, overhead camshaft
Capacity	1593 cc (97.21 cu.in.)
Bore	87.67 mm (3.452 in.)
Stroke	66.0 mm (2.598 in.)
Compression ratio	9.2:1
Max. power (net)	95 bhp @ 5,750 rpm
Max. torque (net)	92 lb.ft. (12.72 kg.m.) @ 4,000 rpm
Compression pressure at cranking speed	142 to 170 psi

Escort II RS 2000

Type	Belt-driven, overhead camshaft
Capacity	1993 cc (121.62 cu.in.)
Bore	90.82 mm (3.576 in.)
Stroke	76.95 mm (3.03 in.)
Compression ratio	9.2:1
Max. power (net)	110 bhp @ 5,500 rpm
Max. torque (net)	119 lb.ft. (16.45 kg.m.) @ 4,000 rpm
Compression pressure at cranking speed	142 to 170 psi

Transmission – Cortina

Gearbox ratios:

(All models have four speed, all synchromesh gearboxes).

Cortina I

	Cortina I 1200 and 1500 (inc.GT)	Cortina I Lotus to Oct.65	Oct.65 on	Cortina I 1500 Automatic
Reverse	3.963:1	2.810:1	3.324:1	2.094:1
First	3.543:1	2.500:1	2.972:1	2.393:1
Second	2.396:1	1.640:1	2.010:1	1.450:1
Third	1.412:1	1.230:1	1.397:1	
Top	1.000:1	1.000:1	1.000:1	1.000:1

Cortina II

	Cortina II 1300, 1500, 1600 and 1500GT (to Jan.67)	Cortina II 1500GT/1600GT, (from Jan.67), Lotus
Reverse	3.963:1	3.324:1
First	3.543:1	2.972:1
Second	2.396:1	2.010:1
Third	1.412:1	1.397:1
Top	1.000:1	1.000:1

Rear axle ratios

(All models have semi-floating, banjo casing axle with hypoid final drive).

Cortina I: 1200	4.125:1
1500	3.900:1 (4.125:1 optional)
Estate 1200	4.444:1
Estate 1500	3.900:1 or 4.125:1
GT/Lotus	3.900:1 (3.777:1, 4.125:1, 4.444:1 optional)
Cortina II: 1300	4.125:1 (4.444:1 optional)
1500/1600	3.900:1 (4.125:1 optional)
1500GT to Sept.67	3.900:1
1600GT from Sept.67	3.777:1
Pinion/Crown wheel, number of teeth	4.444:1 – 9/40
	4.125: 1 – 8/33
	3.900:1 – 10/39
	3.777:1 – 9/34

Transmission – Escort

Gearbox ratios

(All models have four speed, all synchromesh gearboxes).

Escort I	1100/1300	GT	TC/RS/Mexico	RS2000	Automatic
Reverse	4.235:1	3.867:1	3.324:1	3.660:1	2.094:1
First	3.656:1	3.337:1	2.972:1	3.651:1	2.393:1
Second	2.185:1	1.995:1	2.010:1	1.968:1	1.450:1
Third	1.425:1	1.418:1	1.397:1	1.368:1	
Top	1.000:1	1.000:1	1.000:1	1.000:1	1.000:1
Escort II	**1.1/1.3**	**1.3 Ghia/Sport and 1.6 cars**	**Mexico/ RS2000**	**RS1800**	**Automatic**
Reverse	4.235:1	3.867:1	3.660:1	3.37:1	2.111:1
First	3.656:1	3.337:1	3.651:1	3.36:1	2.474:1
Second	2.185:1	1.995:1	1.968:1	1.81:1	1.474:1
Third	1.425:1	1.418:1	1.368:1	1.26:1	1.000:1
Top	1.000:1	1.000:1	1.000:1	1.00:1	1.000:1

Rear axle ratios

(All models have semi-floating, banjo casing axle with hypoid final drive).

Escort I	Until Sept.70	Sept.70 on
1100 manual	3.900:1 (3.777:1 optional)	3.900:1 (4.125:1 optional)
1100 automatic	4.125:1	
1300 manual/GT	3.777:1 (4.125:1 optional)	3.900:1 (4.125:1 optional)
1300 automatic	4.125:1 (3.777:1 optional)	3.900:1 (4.125:1 optional)
TC/RS1600/Mexico	3.777:1	3.777:1
RS2000		3.545:1
Estates/vans, 1100	4.444:1 (4.125:1 optional)	4.444:1 (4.125:1 optional)
Estates/vans, 1300	4.125:1 (3.777:1 optional)	4.125:1 (3.777:1 optional)
Pinion/crown wheel, number of teeth	4.444:1 – 9/40	
	4.125:1 – 8/33	
	3.900:1 – 10/39	
	3.777:1 – 9/34	
	3.545:1 – 11/39	

Escort II

Timken axles (identifiable by 'bolt-on' differential);

Saloons 1.1 HC	4.125:1 (4.444:1 optional)
1.1 HC, with 12 in. wheels	3.889:1
1.1 LC	3.889:1 (4.444:1 optional)
1.1 Economy – 12 in. wheels and radial tyres	3.777:1
1.1 Economy – 12 in. wheels and cross-ply tyres, or 13 in. wheels	3.889:1
1.3 LC	3.889:1 (4.125:1 optional)
1.3 HC	3.889:1 (4.444:1 and 4.125:1 optional)
1.3 GT	4.125:1 (4.444:1 optional)
1.6	3.545:1

Vans
Standard

1.1	4.125:1 (4.444:1 optional)
1.1 Economy – 12 inch wheels	3.777:1
1.1 Economy – 13 inch wheels	3.889:1
1.3	4.125:1
Heavy duty	
1.3	4.125:1 (4.444:1 optional)

Salisbury axles (identifiable by 'integral' differential):

1.1	4.111:1 (4.444:1 optional)
1.1 GT	4.444:1
1.3	3.889:1 (4.111:1 optional)
1.3 GT	4.111:1 (4.444:1 optional)
Mexico, RS1800, RS2000	3.545:1

Pinion/crown wheel, number of teeth:

4.444:1	– 9/40
4.125:1	– 8/33
3.889:1	– 9/35
3.777:1	– 9/34
3.545:1	– 11/39

Fuel system

Cortina I

Carburettor(s)	**1198 cc**	**1498 cc**	**1498 cc GT**	**Lotus**
Make	Solex	Zenith	Weber	Twin Weber
Type	Single choke, downdraught	Single choke, downdraught	Twin choke, downdraught	Twin choke, side draught
Model	B30 PSEI-2	33VN2	28/36 DCD 16/18, 1963/64 28/36 DCD 22, 1965/66	40 DCOE/18

Fuel pump – all models – mechanical, diaphragm type.

Cortina II

Non cross-flow Carburettor	**1297 cc**	**1500 cc**	**1500 cc auto**	**1500 cc GT**
Make	Ford	Ford	Ford	Weber
Type	Single choke, downdraught	Single choke, downdraught	Single choke, downdraught	Twin choke, downdraught
Standard, no.	C6BH-9510-A	C6BH-9510-B	C6BH-9510-C	28/36 DCD 23
Emission, no.	C6BH-9510-D	C6BH-9510-E	C6BH-9510-F	28/36 DCD38

Cross-flow

Carburettor	1298 cc	1298 cc auto	1599 cc	1599 cc auto
Make	Ford	Ford	Ford	Ford
Type	single choke, downdraught	single choke, downdraught	single choke, downdraught	single choke downdraught
Standard, no.	C7BH-9510-A	C7BH-9510-C	C7BH-9510-B	C7BH-9510-D
Emission, no.			C7BH-9510-A	C7BH-9510-B

GT/Lotus

Carburettor(s)		GT		Lotus
Make		Weber		Twin Weber
Type		Twin choke, downdraught		Twin choke, side draught
Standard, no.		32-DFM		40 DCOE/31
Emission, no.		32-DFD		

Fuel pump – all models – mechanical, diaphragm type

Escort I

Carburettor	1100	1100 autochoke	1300 to Sept. 70	1300 autochoke to Sept. 70	1300 Sept.70 on	1300 autochoke Sept.70 on
Make	Ford	Ford	Ford	Ford	Ford	Ford
Type	Single choke, downdraught	Single choke, downdraught	Single choke, downdraught	Single choke, downdraught	Single choke, downdraught	Single choke downdraught
Standard, no.	C7AH-A	C7AH-C	C7AH-B	C7AH-D	711W 9510 BVB	711W 9510 CAB
Emission, no.	C7AH-E	C7AH-G				

Carburettor(s)	**Twin Cam**	**1300GT**	**RS1600**	**Mexico**
Make	Twin Weber	Weber	Twin Weber or Dell'orto	Weber
Type	Twin choke, side draught	Twin choke, downdraught	Twin choke, side draught	Twin choke downdraught
Model no.	40DCOE 48	32 DFE (to Sept.70) DGV-HA (Sept.70 on)	40 DCOE 48 40 DHLAE	32/36 DGV-FA

Fuel pump – all models – mechanical, diaphragm type

Escort II

Carburettor	1.1/1.3	1.3 Sport/ Ghia	1.6 Sport/ Ghia	RS1800	RS Mexico	RS2000
Make	Ford	Weber	Weber	Weber	Weber	Weber
Type	Single	Twin choke	Twin choke	Twin choke	Twin choke	Twin choke
Model	GPD	32/36 DGV	32/36 DGV	32/36 DGAV	32/36 DGV	32/36 DGAV

(Note: From mid 1975, Ford progressively introduced their 'Sonic Idle' ('Bypass') carburettor to 1.1 and 1.3 litre models, and all the "Popular" versions, introduced in July, 1975, were fitted with this unit. From May, 1976, all the Ford carburettors used were 'Sonic Idle' types, and all had 'tamperproof' mixture control screws.)

Fuel pump – all models – mechanical, diaphragm type.

Ignition system

Cortina I	Spark plug type	Plug gap	Contact points gap
All except GT	Champion N5/ Autolite AG32	0.023 to 0.028 in.	0.014 to 0.016 in.
GT	Champion N4/ Autolite AG22	0.023 to 0.028 in.	0.014 to 0.016 in.
Lotus 1963/4	Lodge 2HLN	0.023 to 0.028 in.	0.014 to 0.016 in.
1965/6	Champion N4/ Autolite AG22	0.023 to 0.028 in.	0.014 to 0.016 in.

	Spark plug type	Plug gap	Contact points gap
Cortina II			
1300/1500 (non cross-flow)	Champion N5/ Autolite AG32	0.020 to 0.024 in.	0.025 in.
GT (non cross-flow)	Champion N4/ Autolite AG22	0.023 to 0.028 in.	0.025 in.
All cross-flow models, and Lotus	Champion N4/ Autolite AG22	0.023 to 0.028 in.	0.025 in.

Firing Order All Cortinas, 1-2-4-3, except Lotus versions, 1-3-4-2.

	Spark plug type	Plug gap	Contact points gap
Escort I			
1100/1300	Champion N4/ Autolite AG22	0.023 in.	0.025 in.
Twin Cam	Champion N4/ Autolite AG22	0.023 in.	0.014 to 0.016 in.
RS1600	Motorcraft AG12	0.019 in.	0.014 to 0.016 in.
Mexico	Champion N4/ Autolite AG22	0.023 in.	0.025 in.
RS2000	Motorcraft BF32	0.023 in.	Bosch 0.018 in. Motorcraft 0.025 in.
Escort II			
All except GTs/RS2000	Motorcraft AGR22	0.025 in	0.022 to 0.028 in.
GT models	Motorcraft AG12	0.025 in.	0.022 to 0.028 in.
RS2000	Motorcraft BF32	0.030 in.	Bosch 0.016 to 0.020 in. Motorcraft 0.025 in.

Firing order All Escorts 1-2-4-3, except Twin Cam and RS2000. 1-3-4-2.

Steering

	Type	Ratio	Turning circle
Cortina I	Recirculating ball	15.0:1 (Std.) 13.4:1 (GT)	34 feet
Cortina II	Recirculating ball	16.4:1	30 feet
Escort I	Rack and pinion	16.4:1 or 16.6:1 (To Sept. 1970) 17.5:1 (Sept. 1970 on)	29 feet
Escort II	Rack and pinion	17.9:1	29 feet

Suspension

Cortina I/II

Front MacPherson struts, with coil springs, integral shock absorbers, and anti-roll bar.

Rear Semi-elliptical leaf springs, with telescopic shock absorbers (saloons) or lever arm shock absorbers (estate cars). Early Lotus models (up to September, 1965) have rear coil springs with 'A' brackets. Later Lotus models, and Mark I GTs, from October, 1964, have radius arms (trailing links) locating the rear axle.

Escort I

Front MacPherson struts, with coil springs and integral shock absorbers. Early cars (up to October, 1969) have compression strut/track control arm lower location; anti-roll bar fitted to later cars. TC, RS 1600, Mexico and RS 2000 have uprated front suspension, with anti-roll bar.

Rear	Semi-elliptic leaf springs, with inclined, telescopic shock absorbers, until October, 1973; later cars had vertical rear shock absorbers, and a rear anti-roll bar. Twin Cams, RS 1600s, Mexicos, RS 2000s and early GTs had twin radius rods locating rear axle.
Escort II	
Front	MacPherson struts with coil springs and integral shock absorbers; anti-roll bar.
Rear	Semi-elliptic leaf springs, with vertically mounted, telescopic rear shock absorbers. Sport, RS 1800, Mexico and RS 2000 models have uprated rear springs and axle location rods.

Brakes

Cortina I
Up to Oct. 1964, except GT/Lotus

Front	8 x 1.75 in. drums (9 in. on 'Super'; optional on De Luxe)
Rear	8 x 1.5 in. drums

Oct. 1964 on, except GT/Lotus

Front	9.5 in. discs
Rear	8 x 1.5 in. drums

GT and Lotus

Front	9.5 in discs
Rear	9 x 1.75 in. drums (with vacuum servo on Lotus)

Cortina II
Up to Sept. 1967, except GT/1600E and Lotus

Front	9.5 in. discs
Rear	8.0 x 1.5 in. drums

1500GT

Front	9.5 in. discs
Rear	9 x 1.75 in. drums

Sept. 1967 on, except GT/1600E and Lotus

Front	9.625 in. discs
Rear	8 x 1.5 in. drums

GT/1600E/Lotus

Front	9.625 inch discs
Rear	9 x 1.75 in. drums (with vacuum servo)

(Note: Late Mark II GTs, 1600Es and estate cars, fitted with dual circuit brakes – split front/rear – all have vacuum servo. Dual circuit brakes were an optional extra on U.K. models, and fitted as standard on export models).

Escort I
1100

Front	8 x 1.5 in. drums (Optional; 8.6 in. discs/servo)
Rear	8 x 1.5 in. drums

1100 estate and 6 cwt. van (with manual gearbox), and 1300 saloons

Front	8 x 1.75 in. drums
Rear	8 x 1.5 in. drums

1300 estate, 6 cwt. van (with auto gearbox), all 8 cwt vans, and 1300 GT

Front	8.6 in. discs
Rear	8 x 1.75 in. drums

Twin Cam/RS1600/Mexico

Front	9.625 in. discs
Rear	9 x 1.75 in. drums

RS2000

Front	9.625 in. discs
Rear	8 x 1.5 in. drums

(Note: Vacuum servo on 1300 estate and GT, TC, RS 1600, Mexico and RS 2000).

Escort II
1.1
Front 8 x 1.75 in. drums
Rear 8 x 1.5 in. drums
1.3
Front 9.625 in. discs
Rear 8 x 1.5 in. drums

1.3/1.6 Sport/Ghia
Front 9.625 in. discs
Rear 9.0 x 1.75 in. drums
RS1800/Mexico/RS2000
Front 9.625 in. discs
Rear 9 x 1.75 in. drums

Wheels and tyres

	Wheels	Tyres
Cortina I		
All except GT/Lotus	4J x 13	5.20 x 13 (5.60 x 13 optional)
GT	4J x 13	5.60 x 13
Lotus	5½J x 13	6.00 x 13 speed type
Cortina II		
All cars to Sept. 1967, except Lotus	4J x 13	5.20 x 13, 5.60 x 13 (1500 saloons, GTs)
Sept. 1967 on; De Luxe saloons, with cross-ply tyres	4J x 13	5.60 x 13
GT, Estate cars, and Super saloon, with cross-ply or radial tyres, and De Luxe cars with radial tyres	4½J x 13	5.60 x 13 (1600 saloon), 6.00 x 13 (estate cars), or 165 x 13 (any model with radials)
1600E	5½J x 13	165 x 13 radial
Lotus	5½J x 13	165 x 13 radial
Escort I		
1100, 1300	3.5C x 12	5.50 x 12 (155 x 12 optional)
GT (optional on 1100 and 1300 saloon)	4.5C x 12	155 x 12
1100 and 1300 vans and estate cars	4.5C x 12	5.50 x 12 (6 cwt. vans), 6.00 x 12 (8 cwt. vans, and estate cars)
TC, RS1600, Mexico, RS2000	5½J x 13 (later options 6 and 7 in.)	165SR 13 (175 or 185/70 on wider rims)
Escort II		
All except Ghias/Sports and faster versions	4½J x 13 (drum-braked cars, 4½J x 12)	155SR 13 (or 155SR12)
Ghia/Sport	5J x 13	155SR 13 (175/70SR 13, Sport)
RS1800/Mexico	5½J x 13	175/70SR 13
RS2000	6J x 13 (5½J on later, 'base' version)	175/70SR 13

Electrics

Cortina I 12 volt, positive earth system
Battery capacity Standard, 38 amp/hr.; Cold climate, 51 amp/hr
Dynamo output Standard, Lucas C40, 22 amps; Cold climate, C40 L, 25 amps

Cortina II		
Battery capacity	12 volt, negative earth system	
Dynamo output	Standard, 38 amp/hr.; Cold climate, 57 amp/hr	
	Standard, Lucas C40, 22 amps; Cold climate, C40 L, 25 amps	

Escort I
Battery capacity — 12 volt, negative earth system
1100 – 32 amp/hr
1100 export – 38 amp/hr
1300/TC – 38 amp/hr
Cold climate – 53 amp/hr
Dynamo output — Standard, Lucas C40, 22 amps; Cold climate, C40 L, 25 amps
Alternator output — Lucas 16 ACR, 34 amps
(Note – alternators were optional until October, 1973, and standard equipment from then on).
Batteries, fast versions
Twin Cam/RS1600/Mexico — Standard, 38 amp/hr.; Cold climate, 57 amp/hr
Charging equipment, fast versions
Twin Cam — Lucas C40 L dynamo (25 amps), then Lucas 15 ACR alternator (28 amps), then 17 ACR alternator (35 amps)
RS 1600 — Lucas 17 ACR (35 amps)
Mexico — Lucas 15 ACR (28 amps), then 17 ACR (35 amps)
RS 2000 — Lucas 17 ACR (35 amps)

Escort II
Battery capacities — 12 volt, negative earth system
38, 44, or 55 amp/hr
Alternators — Bosch; 28, 35 or 55 amps
Femsa; 32 amps
Lucas; 15 ACR (28 amps), 17 ACR (35 amps) or 18 ACR (43 amps)

Performance

These figures give an *average* guide to the sort of performance to expect from a particular model. It is impossible to list figures for *every* variation of Cortina and Escort produced, and allowance should therefore be made for minor variations in engine specification, gearbox and differential ratios, and so on, all of which affect acceleration, maximum speed and fuel consumption figures. The figures quoted represent *true* speeds, as opposed to those recorded by the vehicles' speedometers, since these are almost invariably optimistic. It is therefore quite possible, for example, that your car will reach an *indicated* 60 mph more quickly than these figures suggest, but it is also probable that at this speed, the speedo will be recording up to around 4 mph too fast! However, it is impossible to generalise, and each instrument varies.

	0-60 MPH (seconds)	MAX. speed (mph)	Overall MPG (approx.)
Cortina I			
1200 – to Sept. 1964	25	78	30 to 35
1200 – Sept. 1964 on	22.5	78	30 to 35
1500	21	85	30 to 35
1500 GT	13.2	95	26 to 28
Lotus	8	107	20 to 25
Cortina II			
1300	21.5	80	30
1500	24	83	30
1500 GT	13.8	95	26 to 28
1300 cross-flow	19	84	30
1600 cross-flow	16	90	30
1600 GT/E	12.5	95	26 to 28
Lotus	9	107	20 to 25

Escort I/II

1100 – Mark I to Sept. 1970, and			
Mark II Popular	20	78	35 to 40
1100 – Mark I/II, Sept. 1970 on	19	80	35 to 40
1300 – Mark I, to Sept. 1970 and			
Mark II Popular	16.5	85	35 to 40
1300 – Mark I/II, Sept. 1970 on	15.5	89	35 to 40
1300 GT – to Sept.1970	13	93	35
1300 GT/E/Sport, Sept. 1970 on	12.5	95	35
1600	12	97	30 to 35
TC	8.5	110+	20 to 25
RS 1600	8.3	110+	22 to 28
Mexico Mark I	10.5	100+	25 to 30
RS 2000 Mark I	9	110	26 to 28
RS 1800 Mark I	9	115	26 to 28
RS 2000 Mark II	8	110	26 to 28
RS Mexico Mark II	10	100	25 to 30

Dimensions – saloons

	Length	**Width**	**Height**
Cortina I	14 ft. 2½in.	5 ft 3 in.	4 ft. 9 in
Cortina II	14 ft. 2 in.	5 ft. 5¼in.	4 ft 8½in
Escort I	13 ft. 0½in.	5 ft. 2 in.	4 ft. 5 in.
Escort II	13 ft. 0½in.	5 ft. 0 ½ in.	4 ft. 5¾in.
Escort II RS 2000	13 ft. 7in.	5 ft. 0½in.	4 ft. 5¾in.

4 Production Modifications

Full details of the changes made through the production life of the Cortina and Escort Mark I and II models are included in the 'Heritage' Chapters, 1 and 2. However the main changes made to the models are summarised here, for easy reference

Cortina

1962
September. Original Cortina introduced, with 1198cc, three main crankshaft bearing engine. 'Consul' on bonnet.

October. Four door version introduced.

1963
January. Five main bearing, 1498cc engine optional on De Luxe, standard on Super models, which also had bigger brakes, better trim and chrome body trims. Lotus version introduced, with 1558 cc, 105 bhp, twin overhead camshaft engine.

March. Estate car versions introduced, with exterior wood trim on Super versions.

April. GT introduced; two or four door, with 78 bhp version of 1498cc engine. Uprated suspension, disc front brakes, remote gearchange and extra instrumentation all standard.

September. Circular speedometer fitted in place of strip type.

December. Automatic transmission optional on 1498cc cars.

1964
July. Lotus versions altered; aluminium panels replaced by steel, Ford gearbox used in place of Lotus unit, split propeller shaft fitted.

September. Facelift to range; full-width, close mesh grille fitted, Aeroflow ventilation and front disc brakes now standard. Seats and trim revised. 'Cortina' on bonnet and boot. More power from higher compression ratio.

1965
September. Standard version of saloon discontinued, also column gearchange option, and wood trims on Super estate cars. Coil springs replaced by half elliptics on Lotus. Opening quarter lights replaced by fixed glass types on all models. GT has larger disc calipers and self-adjusting rear brakes. Lotus now has close-ratio gearbox from Corsair 2000E.

1966	
September.	Mark I Cortina saloon discontinued.
November.	Mark I Cortina estate discontinued.
September.	Mark II Cortina saloons introduced, with 1297cc or 1500cc engines; both have five bearing crankshafts. Optional column gearchange/bench type front seat. New, 'boxy' bodywork based on same floor pan as Mark I models. Automatic transmission optional on 1297cc cars.
1967	
January.	GT gear ratios improved.
February.	Estate car versions introduced.
March.	Lotus version introduced.
August.	Cross-flow engines of 1298cc or 1599cc replace earlier 1300 and 1500 units. Super has GT style remote control gearchange.
September.	1600E model announced, with GT engine and running gear, and luxury interior fittings, including walnut facia and door cappings.
October.	Interior changes to Lotus version, including centre console mounting for clock. Carpets and vinyl facia now standard on De Luxe.
1968	
October.	All models have remote gearchange. Reclining seats optional. 'FORD' appears on bonnet and boot.
1970	
July.	Lotus version discontinued.
August.	1600E discontinued. Mark III Cortina models introduced.
September.	All Mark II models discontinued.

Escort

1967	
November.	Escort production commenced.
1968	
January.	Escort saloon range introduced, with 1098cc or 1298cc cross-flow engines, in basic, De Luxe and Super versions. Twin Cam, with 1558cc, double overhead camshaft Lotus engine, also introduced.
March.	Estate versions introduced.
May.	Automatic transmission optional on all saloons.
October.	Safety and comfort features improved; e.g. breakaway door handles, colour-coded trim. GT/Super models have 'wood grain' effect on facia.
1969	
May.	Super version of estate car introduced.
August.	Automatic option no longer available on 1100.
October.	Suspension uprated. Four door saloons introduced.
1970	
January.	RS 1600, from 'Advanced Vehicle Operations' announced.
April.	Escort GT estate car introduced.
May.	RS 1600 available, with 1601cc, 16 valve, double overhead camshaft, Cosworth developed engine fitted.
September.	Model specifications changed, 1100 and 1300 engines uprated, designations changed to 'L' and 'XL'.
November.	Escort Mexico announced, with 1600 GT, overhead valve, cross-flow engine.
1971	
June.	Twin Cam discontinued.
July.	Clubman Pack available for RS 1600 and Mexico models.
October.	Escort Sport introduced, with 1300 GT engine, flared wheel arches. More spartan trim than GT model. Clubman Pack available for RS 1600 and Mexico models.

1972
August. Two speed wipers and hazard flashers introduced for 1973 models.
October. RS 1600 now has aluminium engine; performance unchanged.
1973
March. 1300E introduced. Similar 'luxury' concept to 1600E Cortina, with 1300 GT engine, close ratio gearbox, and high quality interior fittings.
June. RS 2000 introduced, with 1993cc 'Pinto' overhead camshaft engine, producing 100 bhp.
October. Suspension modifications, including vertical rear shock absorber mountings, and rear anti-roll bar, also designed to help locate rear axle.
November. GT discontinued.
1974
April. Four door version of 1300E introduced.
1975
January. New Escort (Escort Mark II) announced in Europe, in 1.1, 1.3 and 1.6 litre form. New estate models have same bodywork as Mark I models, from rear door pillar backwards. Designations now 'L', 'GL', 'Ghia', above the basic model. 1.3 and 1.6 litre 'Sport' models also available. 16 valve, RS 1800 announced.
March. New Escorts available. Mark II RS 2000 announced, with 1993cc Pinto engine.
June. RS 1800 available, with 1840cc, twin overhead camshaft BDA engine.
July. Escort Popular and Popular Plus models introduced; more basic than other versions, but at lower prices. 'L' cars gain 13 inch wheels, disc brakes at front, reclining seats and bright trim mouldings. 'GL' cars now have sports 13 inch wheels and body mouldings.
1976
February. All 1100 cars fitted with 'economy' engine, of lower power output.
1977
January. RS 1800 discontinued.
September. Traditional oval 'Ford' badge appears on bodywork, and engine size depicted on bootlid. Rear wash/wipe system standard on 'GL' estate cars; optional on others.
October. Suspension modifications include single leaf rear spring, smaller diameter anti-roll bar, revised shock absorber ratings.
1978
September. Range revised. New features include soft feel steering wheel (not Sport and RS cars), and wider offset wheels. Radial tyres fitted on Popular and basic estate models, carpeting on Popular saloons, and heated rear screen on Popular Plus. 'L' cars have square headlights and sports wheels. 'GL' models have different trim, and radio as standard. Mexico discontinued. RS 2000 now available as standard model, with Mexico trim and steel wheels, or RS 2000 Custom, with alloy wheels and more elaborate trim.
1979
April. Basic estate has brake warning light and carpet.
September. Popular models and basic estate cars now have hazard lights and inertia reel seat belts.
October. Linnet 'Special Edition' model introduced, based on 1300 Popular Plus.
December. Escort Harrier introduced, based on 1600 Sport.
1980
May Escort Goldcrest introduced, based on 1.3L and 1.6L four door models.

5 Identify your car

It is always useful to be able to identify your car in terms of the engine fitted, bodywork, paint colours, trim and so on, or at least be able to find out what the original specifications were for your vehicle, in these respects.

Fortunately, the Fords covered by this book carry a detailed vehicle identification plate, found under the bonnet, on the driver's side of the engine bay. This can make these Fords easier to identify precisely than most other makes of vehicle, *provided* you are able to translate the various codes employed. While the exact details shown on each plate have altered over the years, the following model by model translation of the plates and the codes used on them, should help you identify what sort of Ford you are dealing with!

As far as the author is aware, the complete information to enable you to do this has not been published previously in one volume.

Cortina Mark I

Ford designations

1198cc; 113E = right hand drive.
114E = left hand drive.

1498cc; 118E = right hand drive.
119E = left hand drive.
Lotus; 125E = right hand drive.

Vehicle/chassis number
Shown on plate on battery side of engine compartment.
Models to January, 1965
The vehicle number is prefixed by four characters:
One letter, denoting assembly plant;
Z = Dagenham.
Two figures, denoting body and gearchange type;
71 = 2 door Standard, floor change.
72 = 4 door Standard, floor change.
73 = 2 door De Luxe, column change.
74 = 2 door De Luxe, floor change, or Cortina Lotus.
75 = 4 Door De Luxe, column change.
76 = 4 door De Luxe, floor change.
77 = 2 door GT.
78 = 4 door GT.
81 = 2 door Super, column change.
82 = 2 door Super, floor change.
83 = 4 door Super, column change.
84 = 4 door Super, floor change.
86 = Estate car De Luxe, column change.
87 = Estate car De Luxe, floor change.

88 = Estate car Super, column change.
89 = Estate car Super, floor change.
One letter, denoting year of manufacture;
B = 1962.
C = 1963.
D = 1964.
Models from January, 1965:
A new type of plate was employed as shown:

IYC1. This plate identifies the car to which it belongs as being a right hand drive model, with a 1498 cc, high compression engine and automatic transmission, with a standard (3.900:1) axle ratio, having Dove Grey/Condor Grey seats, black floor coverings, and Aqua Blue paintwork. It also identifies the car as being built in Britain, at Dagenham, as a De Luxe estate car, in April, 1965! That's a lot of information for a little plate, achieved by the use of code letters and numbers, explained next. . .

334

The relevant translations of the codes used in the identification plates are:

Drive:
1 = right hand drive.
2 = left hand drive.

Engine:
1 = 1198 cc, high compression.
2 = 1198 cc, low compression.
3 = 1498 cc, high compression.
4 = 1498 cc, low compression.
5 = 1498 cc, GT.

Trans (i.e. gearbox)
1 = floor change.
2 = column change.
3 = automatic.
4 = remote control floor change.

Axle (i.e. rear axle ratio)
S = Standard ratio (1198cc saloons, 4.125:1, 1498cc saloons and estate cars, 3.900:1; 1198cc estate cars, 4.444:1).
1 = 4.444:1
2 = 4.125:1

Trim
Each car has a trim code number, consisting of a letter, followed by a three figure number, denoting the colours of the seats and floor coverings, and the dates applicable to the particular code. Note that where two colours are given for the seat coverings, the first given applies to the seat face, the second, to the seat border. The application of the various trim combinations between models was rather complex, so, for clarity and ease of identification, the codes are listed in numerical order, with model designations shown as appropriate. Sadly, it is very unlikely that Ford dealers will be able to supply trim from stock for these early codes, nowadays.

Trim code No.	Seat colour(s) and seat face material: (P = PVC, L = Leather, C = Cloth)	Floor covering colour	Dates used
Standard Cortina Saloon			
A459	Atlas Grey, P	Black	Sep.62 – Aug.63
A460	Sierra Beige, P	Black	Sep.62 – Aug.63
A461	Kingston Blue, P	Black	Sep.62 – Oct.64
A462	Elm Green, P	Black	Sep.62 – Aug.63
A463	Ravenna Red, P	Black	Sep.62 – Oct.65
A464	Platinum/Atlas Grey, P	Black	Sep.62 – Mar.63
A465	Platinum/Atlas Grey, L	Black	Sep.62 – Aug.63
A466	Javelin Bronze/Sierra Beige, L	Beechwood Brown	Sep.62 – Aug.63
A467	Javelin Bronze/Sierra Beige, P	Beechwood Brown	Sep.62 – Mar.63
A468	Shearwater Blue/Kingston Blue, P	Kingston Blue	Sep.62 – Mar.63
A469	Shearwater Blue/Kingston Blue, L	Kingston Blue	Sep.62 – Aug.63
A470	Peru Green/Elm Green, L	Fir Green	Sep.62 – Aug.63
A471	Peru Green/Elm Green, P	Fir Green	Sep.62 – Mar.63
A472	Ravenna Red, P	Black	Sep.62 – Aug.63
A473	Ravenna Red, L	Black	Sep.62 – Aug.63
A474	Grey 'Fern'/Brummel Grey, C	Black	Sep.62 – Aug.63
A475	Beige 'Fern'/Thaxted Beige, C	Beechwood Brown	Sep.62 – Aug.63
A476	Blue 'Fern'/Azure Blue, C	Kingston Blue	Sep.62 – Aug.63
A477	Green 'Fern'/Pastel Green, C	Fir Green	Sep.62 – Aug.63
A476	Red 'Fern'/Ravenna Red, C	Black	Sep.62 – Aug.63
Cortina De Luxe estate			
A537	Platinum Grey/Atlas Grey, L	Black	Mar.63 – Aug.63
A538	Platinum Grey/Atlas Grey, P	Black	March 1963 only
A539	Grey 'Fern'/Brummel Grey, C	Black	Mar.63 – Aug.63
A540	Shearwater Blue/Kingston Blue, L	Kingston Blue	Mar.63 – Aug.63
A541	Shearwater Blue/Kingston Blue, P	Kingston Blue	March 1963 only
A542	Blue 'Fern'/Azure Blue, C	Kingston Blue	Mar.63 – Aug.63
A543	Peru Green/Elm Green, L	Fir Green	Mar.63 – Aug.63
A544	Peru Green/Elm Green, P	Fir Green	March 1963 only
A545	Green 'Fern'/Pastel Green, C	Fir Green	Mar.63 – Aug.63
A546	Javelin Bronze/Sierra Beige, L	Beechwood Brown	Mar.63 – Aug.63
A547	Javelin Bronze/Sierra Beige, P	Beechwood Brown	March 1963 only
A548	Beige 'Fern'/Thaxted Beige, C	Beechwood Brown	Mar.63 – Aug.63
A549	Ravenna Red, L	Black	Mar.63 – Aug.63
A550	Ravenna Red, P	Black	Mar.63 – Aug.63
A551	Red 'Fern'/Ravenna Red, C	Black	Mar.63 – Aug.63

Trim code No.	Seat colour(s) and seat face material: (P = PVC, C = Cloth)	Floor covering colour	Dates used
Cortina Super saloon			
A582	Atlas Grey/Platinum Grey, P	Black	Nov.62 – Aug.63
A583	Kingston Blue/Shearwater Blue, P	Kingston Blue	Nov.62 – Aug.63
A584	Elm Green/Peru Green, P	Fir Green	Nov.62 – Aug.63
A585	Sierra Beige/Javelin Bronze, P	Beechwood Brown	Nov.62 – Aug.63
A586	Ravenna Red, P	Black	Nov.62 – Aug.63
A587	Grey 'Saran'/Platinum Grey, C	Black	Nov.62 – Aug.63
A588	Blue 'Saran'/Shearwater Blue, C	Kingston Blue	Nov.62 – Aug.63
A589	Green 'Saran'/Peru Green, C	Fir Green	Nov.62 – Aug.63
A678	Beige 'Saran'/Javelin Bronze. C	Beechwood Brown	Nov.62 – Aug.63
A679	Red 'Saran'/Ravenna Red, C	Black	Nov.62 – Aug.63
Cortina Super estate			
A740	Atlas Grey/Platinum Grey, P	Black	Mar.63 – Aug.63
A741	Kingston Blue/Shearwater Blue, P	Kingston Blue	Mar.63 – Aug.63
A742	Elm Green/Peru Green, P	Fir Green	Mar.63 – Aug.63
A743	Sierra Beige/Javelin Bronze, P	Beechwood Brown	Mar.63 – Aug.63
A744	Ravenna Red, P	Black	Mar.63 – Aug.63
A745	Grey 'Saran'/Platinum Grey, C	Black	Mar.63 – Aug.63
A746	Blue 'Saran'/Shearwater Blue, C	Kingston Blue	Mar.63 – Aug.63
A747	Green 'Saran'/Peru Green, C	Fir Green	Mar.63 – Aug.63
A748	Beige 'Saran'/Javelin Bronze, C	Beechwood Brown	Mar.63 – Aug.63
A749	Red 'Saran'/Ravenna Red, C	Black	Mar.63 – Aug.63
Cortina De Luxe saloon			
A775	Platinum Grey 'Thai Silk'/Atlas Grey, P	Black	Feb.63 – Aug.63
A776	Javelin Bronze 'Thai Silk'/Sierra Beige, P	Beechwood Brown	Feb.63 – Aug.63
A777	Shearwater Blue 'Thai Silk'/Kingston Blue, P	Kingston Blue	Feb.63 – Aug.63
A778	Peru Green 'Thai Silk'/Elm Green, P	Fir Green	Feb.63 – Aug.63
Cortina De Luxe Estate			
A779	Platinum Grey 'Thai Silk'/Atlas Grey, P	Black	Mar.63 – Aug.63
A780	Shearwater Blue 'Thai Silk'/Kingston Blue, P	Kingston Blue	Mar.63 – Aug.63
A781	Peru Green 'Thai Silk'/Elm Green, P	Fir Green	Mar.63 – Aug.63
A782	Javelin Bronze 'Thai Silk'/Sierra Beige, P	Beechwood Brown	Mar.63 – Aug.63
Cortina GT			
A825	Brummel Grey, P	Black	Apr.63 – Oct.64
A826	Kingston Blue, P	Kingston Blue	Apr.63 – Oct.64
A827	Elm Green, P	Fir Green	Apr.63 – Aug.63
A828	Ravenna Red, P	Black	Apr.63 – Oct.63
Cortina Lotus			
A875	Black, P	Black	Mar.63 – Oct.64
Cortina GT (Home Market)			
A876	Sierra Beige, P	Beechwood Brown	Aug.63 – Oct.64
A877	Sierra Beige, P	Beechwood Brown	Aug.63 – Oct.64
Standard Cortina saloon			
A879	Elm Green, P	Black	Aug.63 – Oct.64
Cortina De Luxe saloon			
A881	Pewter Grey 'Thai Silk'/Atlas Grey, P	Black	Aug.63 – Oct.64
A882	Grey 'Fern'/Brummel Grey, C	Black	Aug.63 – Oct.64
A883	Lucerne Blue 'Thai Silk'/Kingston Blue, P	Kingston Blue	Aug.63 – Oct.64
A884	Blue 'Fern'/Azure Blue, C	Kingston Blue	Aug.63 – Oct.64

Trim code No.	Seat colour(s) and seat face material: (P = PVC, C = Cloth)	Floor covering colour	Dates used
A885	Peru Green 'Thai Silk'/Elm Green, P	Fir Green	Aug.63 – Oct.64
A886	Green 'Fern'/Pastel Green, C	Fir Green	Aug.63 – Oct.64
A887	Ravenna Red, P	Black	Aug.63 – Oct.64
A888	Red 'Fern'/Ravenna Red, C	Black	Aug.63 – Oct.64
Cortina De Luxe estate			
A889	Pewter Grey 'Thai Silk'/Atlas Grey, P	Black	Aug.63 – Oct.64
A890	Grey 'Fern'/Brummel Grey, C	Black	Aug.63 – Oct.64
A891	Lucerne Blue 'Thai Silk'/Kingston Blue, P	Kingston Blue	Aug.63 – Oct.64
A892	Blue 'Fern'/Azure Blue, Rayon cloth	Kingston Blue	Aug.63 – Oct.64
A893	Peru Green 'Thai Silk'/Elm Green, P	Fir Green	Aug.63 – Oct.64
A894	Green 'Fern'/Pastel Green, C	Fir Green	Aug.63 – Oct.64
A895	Ravenna Red, P	Black	Aug.63 – Oct.64
A896	Red 'Fern'/Ravenna Red, C	Black	Aug.63 – Oct.64
Cortina Super saloon			
A897	Atlas Grey/Pewter Grey, P	Black	Aug.63 – Oct.64
A898	Grey 'Saran'/Pewter Grey, C	Black	Aug.63 – Oct.64
A899	Kingston Blue/Lucerne Blue, P	Kingston Blue	Aug.63 – Oct.64
A900	Blue 'Saran'/Lucerne Blue, C	Kingston Blue	Aug.63 – Oct.64
A901	Elm Green/Peru Green, P	Fir Green	Aug.63 – Oct.64
A902	Green 'Saran'/Peru Green, C	Fir Green	Aug.63 – Oct.64
A903	Ravenna Red, P	Black	Aug.63 – Oct.64
A904	Red 'Saran'/Ravenna Red, Rayon cloth	Black	Aug.63 – Oct.64
Cortina Super estate			
A905	Atlas Grey/Pewter Grey, P	Black	Aug.63 – Oct.64
A906	Grey 'Saran'/Pewter Grey, C	Black	Aug.63 – Oct.64
A907	Kingston Blue/Lucerne Blue, P	Kingston Blue	Aug.63 – Oct.64
A908	Blue 'Saran'/Lucerne Blue, C	Kingston Blue	Aug.63 – Oct.64
A909	Elm Green/Peru Green, P	Fir Green	Aug.63 – Oct.64
A910	Green 'Saran'/Peru Green, C	Fir Green	Aug.63 – Oct.64
A911	Ravenna Red, P	Black	Aug.63 – Oct.64
A912	Red 'Saran'/Ravenna Red, C	Black	Aug.63 – Oct.64
Cortina GT (Home Market)			
A913	Black, P	Black	Aug.63 – Oct.64
A917	Elm Green, P	Fir Green	Aug.63 – Oct.64
Cortina De Luxe saloon			
A918	Kashmir Beige 'Thai Silk'/Sierra Beige, P	Beechwood Brown	Aug.63 – Oct.64
A919	Beige 'Fern'/Thaxted Beige, C	Beechwood Brown	Aug.63 – Oct.64
Cortina De Luxe estate			
A920	Kashmir Beige 'Thai Silk'/Sierra Beige, P	Beechwood Brown	Aug.63 – Oct.64
A921	Beige 'Fern'/Thaxted Beige, C	Beechwood Brown	Aug.63 – Oct.64
Cortina Super saloon			
A922	Sierra Beige/Kashmir Beige, P	Beechwood Brown	Aug.63 – Oct.64
A923	Beige 'Saran'/Kashmir Beige, C	Beechwood Brown	Aug.63 – Oct.64
Cortina Super estate			
A924	Sierra Beige/Kashmir Beige, P	Beechwood Brown	Aug.63 – Oct.64
A925	Beige 'Saran'/Kashmir Beige, Rayon cloth	Beechwood Brown	Aug.63 – Oct.64

Trim code No.	Seat colour(s) and seat face material: (P = PVC, C = Cloth)	Floor covering colour	Dates used
Cortina Super GT (Export model)			
B021	Black, P	Black	Oct.63 – Oct.64
B022	Atlas Grey/Pewter Grey, P	Black	Oct.63 – Oct.64
B023	Kingston Blue/Lucerne Blue, P	Kingston Blue	Oct.63 – Oct.64
B024	Elm Green/Peru Green, P	Fir Green	Oct.63 – Oct.64
B025	Sierra Beige/Kashmir Beige, P	Beechwood Brown	Oct.63 – Oct.64
B026	Ravenna Red, P	Black	Oct.63 – Oct.64
B027	Grey 'Saran'/Pewter Grey, C	Black	Oct.63 – Oct.64
B028	Blue 'Saran'/Lucerne Blue, C	Kingston Blue	Oct.63 – Oct.64
B029	Green 'Saran'/Peru Green, C	Fir Green	Oct.63 – Oct.64
B030	Beige 'Saran'/Kashmir Beige, C	Beechwood Brown	Oct.63 – Oct.64
B031	Red 'Saran'/Ravenna Red, C	Black	Oct.63 – Oct.64
B032	Grey 'Saran'/Black, C	Black	Oct.63 – Oct.64
Cortina De Luxe saloon			
B098	Condor Grey 'Curzon'/Condor Grey, C	Black	Oct.64 – Oct.65
B099	Teal Blue 'Curzon'/Teal Blue, C	Kingston Blue	Oct.64 – Oct.65
B100	Forest Green 'Curzon'/Forest Green, C	Fir Green	Oct.64 – Oct.65
Cortina De Luxe estate			
B101	Condor Grey 'Curzon'/Condor Grey, C	Black	Oct.64 – Oct.65
B102	Teal Blue 'Curzon'/Teal Blue, C	Kingston Blue	Oct.64 – Oct.65
Standard Cortina saloon			
B104	Teal Blue, P	Black	Oct.64 – Oct.65
Cortina De Luxe saloon			
B111	Ravenna Red, P	Black	Oct.64 – Oct.65
Cortina De Luxe estate			
B116	Ravenna Red, P	Black	Oct.64 – Oct.65
Cortina Super saloon			
B129	Ravenna Red, P	Black	Oct.64 – Oct.65
Cortina Super estate			
B134	Ravenna Red, P	Black	Oct.64 – Oct.65
Cortina GT (Home market)			
B135	Black, P	Black	Oct.64 – Oct.65
B136	Condor Grey, P	Black	Oct.64 – Oct.65
B137	Teal Blue, P	Teal Blue	Oct.64 – Oct.65
B138	Forest Green, P	Fir Green	Oct.64 – Oct.65
B139	Brushwood Beige, P	Beechwood Brown	Oct.64 – Oct.65
B140	Ravenna Red, P	Black	Oct.64 – Oct.65
Cortina Super GT (Export markets)			
B141	Black, P	Black	Oct.64 – Oct.65
B146	Ravenna Red, P	Black	Oct.64 – Oct.65
Cortina De Luxe saloon (Bench seats)			
B153	Ravenna Red, P	Black	Oct.64 – Oct.65
Cortina De Luxe estate (Bench seats)			
B158	Ravenna Red, P	Black	Oct.64 – Oct.65

Trim code No.	Seat colour(s) and seat face material: (P = PVC, C = Cloth)	Floor covering colour	Dates used
Cortina Super saloon (Bench seats)			
B171	Ravenna Red, P	Black	Oct.64 – Oct.65
Cortina Super estate (Bench seats)			
B176	Ravenna Red, P	Black	Oct.64 – Oct.65
Cortina De Luxe estate			
B202	Forest Green 'Curzon'/Forest Green, C	Fir Green	Oct.64 – Oct.65
Cortina De Luxe saloon (Bench seats)			
B203	Condor Grey 'Curzon'/Condor Grey, C	Black	Oct.64 – Oct.65
B204	Teal Blue 'Curzon'/Teal Blue, Nylon cloth	Kingston Blue	Oct.64 – Oct.65
B205	Forest Green 'Curzon'/Forest Green, C	Fir Green	Oct.64 – Oct.65
Cortina De Luxe estate (Bench seats)			
B206	Condor Grey 'Curzon'/Condor Grey, C	Black	Oct.64 – Oct.65
B207	Teal Blue 'Curzon'/Teal Blue, C	Kingston Blue	Oct.64 – Oct.65
B208	Forest Green 'Curzon'/Forest Green, C	Fir Green	Oct.64 – Oct.65
Cortina Super saloon			
B209	Condor Grey 'Curzon'/Condor Grey, C	Black	Oct.64 – Oct.65
B210	Teal Blue 'Curzon'/Teal Blue, C	Teal Blue	Oct.64 – Oct.65
B211	Forest Green 'Curzon'/Forest Green, C	Fir Green	Oct.64 – Oct.65
B212	Brushwood Beige 'Curzon'/Brushwood Beige, C	Beechwood Brown	Oct.64 – Oct.65
Cortina Super estate			
B213	Condor Grey 'Curzon'/Condor Grey, C	Black	Oct.64 – Oct.65
Cortina GT (Home market; with carpets)			
B267	Condor Grey 'Curzon'/Condor Grey, C	Black	Oct.64 – Oct.65
Cortina De Luxe saloon			
B268	Dove Grey/Condor Grey, P	Black	Oct.64 – Oct.65
B269	Delta Blue/Teal Blue, P	Kingston Blue	Oct.64 – Oct.65
B270	Arras Green/Forest Green, P	Fir Green	Oct.64 – Oct.65
Cortina Super estate			
B271	Teal Blue 'Curzon'/Teal Blue, C	Teal Blue	Oct.64 – Oct.65
Cortina De Luxe estate			
B272	Dove Grey/Condor Grey, P	Black	Oct.64 – Oct.65
B273	Delta Blue/Teal Blue, P	Kingston Blue	Oct.64 – Oct.65
B274	Arras Green/Forest Green, P	Fir Green	Oct.64 – Oct.65
Cortina Super estate			
B275	Forest Green 'Curzon'/Forest Green, C	Fir Green	Oct.64 – Oct.65
Cortina Super saloon			
B276	Condor Grey/Dove Grey, P	Black	Oct.64 – Oct.65
B277	Teal Blue/Delta Blue, P	Teal Blue	Oct.64 – Oct.65
B278	Forest Green/Arras Green, P	Fir Green	Oct.64 – Oct.65
B279	Brushwood Beige/Luxor Beige, P	Beechwood Brown	Oct.64 – Oct.65
Cortina Super estate			
B280	Condor Grey/Dove Grey, P	Black	Oct.64 – Oct.65
B281	Teal Blue/Delta Blue, P	Teal Blue	Oct.64 – Oct.65
B282	Forest Green/Arras Green, P	Fir Green	Oct.64 – Oct.65
B283	Brushwood Beige/Luxor Beige, P	Beechwood Brown	Oct.64 – Oct.65

Trim code No.	Seat colour(s) and seat face material: (P = PVC, C = Cloth)	Floor covering colour	Dates used
Cortina Super GT (Export model; with carpets)			
B284	Condor Grey/Dove Grey, P	Black	Oct.64 – Oct.65
B285	Teal Blue/Delta Blue, P	Teal Blue	Oct.64 – Oct.65
B286	Forest Green/Arras Green, P	Fir Green	Oct.64 – Oct.65
B287	Brushwood Beige/Luxor Beige, P	Beechwood Brown	Oct.64 – Oct.65
Cortina De Luxe (Bench seats)			
B288	Dove Grey/Condor Grey, P	Black	Oct.64 – Oct.65
B289	Delta Blue/Teal Blue, P	Kingston Blue	Oct.64 – Oct.65
B290	Arras Green/Forest Green, P	Fir Green	Oct.64 – Oct.65
Cortina Super estate			
B291	Brushwood Beige 'Curzon'/Luxor Beige, C	Beechwood Brown	Oct.64 – Oct.65
Cortina De Luxe estate (Bench seats)			
B292	Dove Grey/Condor Grey, P	Black	Oct.64 – Oct.65
B293	Delta Blue/Teal Blue, P	Kingston Blue	Oct.64 – Oct.65
B294	Arras Green/Forest Green, P	Fir Green	Oct.64 – Oct.65
Cortina Super saloon (Bench seats)			
B295	Condor Grey 'Curzon'/Condor Grey, C	Black	Oct.64 – Oct.65
B296	Condor Grey/Dove Grey, P	Black	Oct.64 – Oct.65
B297	Teal Blue/Delta Blue, P	Teal Blue	Oct.64 – Oct.65
B298	Forest Green/Arras Green, P	Fir Green	Oct.64 – Oct.65
B299	Brushwood Beige/Luxor Beige, P	Beechwood Brown	Oct.64 – Oct.65
Cortina Super estate (Bench seats)			
B300	Condor Grey/Dove Grey, P	Black	Oct.64 – Oct.65
B301	Teal Blue/Delta Blue, P	Teal Blue	Oct.64 – Oct.65
B302	Forest Green/Arras Green, P	Fir Green	Oct.64 – Oct.65
B303	Brushwood Beige/Luxor Beige, P	Beechwood Brown	Oct.64 – Oct.65
Cortina Lotus			
B304	Black, P	Black	Oct.64 – Oct.65
Cortina Super saloon (Bench seats)			
B305	Teal Blue 'Curzon'/Teal Blue, C	Teal Blue	Oct.64 – Oct.65
B306	Forest Green 'Curzon'/Forest Green, C	Fir Green	Oct.64 – Oct.65
B307	Brushwood Beige 'Curzon'/Brushwood Beige, C	Beechwood Brown	Oct.64 – Oct.65
Cortina Super estate (Bench seats)			
B308	Condor Grey 'Curzon'/Condor Grey, C	Black	Oct.64 – Oct.65
B309	Teal Blue 'Curzon'/ Teal Blue, C	Teal Blue	Oct.64 – Oct.65
B310	Forest Green 'Curzon'/Forest Green, C	Fir Green	Oct.64 – Oct.65
B311	Brushwood Beige 'Curzon'/Brushwood Beige, C	Beechwood Brown	Oct.64 – Oct.65
Cortina Super GT (Export model; with carpets)			
B312	Condor Grey 'Curzon'/Condor Grey, C	Black	Oct.64 – Oct.65
B313	Teal Blue, 'Curzon'/Teal Blue, C	Teal Blue	Oct.64 – Oct.65
B314	Forest Green 'Curzon'/Forest Green, C	Fir Green	Oct.64 – Oct.65
B315	Brushwood Beige 'Curzon'/Brushwood Beige, C	Beechwood Brown	Oct.64 – Oct.65
Cortina GT (Home market; with carpets)			
B334	Teal Blue 'Curzon'/Teal Blue, C	Teal Blue	Oct.64 – Oct.65
B335	Forest Green 'Curzon'/Forest Green, C	Fir Green	Oct.64 – Oct.65
B336	Brushwood Beige 'Curzon'/Brushwood Beige, C	Beechwood Brown	Oct.64 – Oct.65

Trim code No.	Seat colour(s) and seat face material: (P = PVC, C = Cloth)	Floor covering colour	Dates used
Cortina De Luxe saloon			
B393	Ravenna Red, P	Black	Oct.65 – Sep.66
B394	Aqua Medium, P	Aqua	Oct.65 – Sep.66
B395	Forest Green, P	Fir Green	Oct.65 – Sep.66
B396	Silver Mink Medium, P	Black	Oct.65 – Sep.66
Cortina De Luxe estate			
B397	Ravenna Red, P	Black	Oct.65 – Sep.66
B398	Aqua Medium, P	Aqua	Oct.65 – Sep.66
B399	Forest Green, P	Fir Green	Oct.65 – Sep.66
B400	Silver Mink, Medium, P	Black	Oct.65 – Sep.66
Cortina Super saloon			
B401	Black, P	Black	Oct.65 – Sep.66
B402	Ravenna Red, P	Black	Sep.65 – Sep.66
B403	Aqua Medium, P	Aqua	Oct.65 – Sep.66
B404	Forest Green, P	Fir Green	Oct.65 – Sep.66
Cortina Super estate			
B405	Black, P	Black	Oct.65 – Sep.66
B406	Ravenna Red, P	Black	Oct.65 – Sep.66
B407	Aqua Medium, P	Aqua	Oct.65 – Sep.66
B408	Forest Green, P	Fir Green	Oct.65 – Sep.66
Cortina Lotus			
B409	Black, P	Black	Oct.65 – Sep.66
Cortina GT (With carpets)			
B409	Black, P	Black	Oct.65 – Sep.66
B410	Aqua Medium, P	Aqua	Oct.65 – Sep.66
B411	Forest Green, P	Fir Green	Oct.65 – Sep.66
B412	Ravenna Red, P	Black	Oct.65 – Sep.66
Standard Cortina saloon			
B413	Ravenna Red, P	Black	Oct.65 – Sep.66
B414	Aqua Medium, P	Black	Oct.65 – Sep.66
Cortina De Luxe saloon (Bench seats)			
B511	Ravenna Red, P	Black	Oct.65 – Sep.66
B512	Aqua Medium, P	Aqua	Oct.65 – Sep.66
B518	Forest Green, P	Fir Green	Oct.65 – Sep.66
B519	Silver Mink Medium, P	Black	Oct.65 – Sep.66
Cortina De Luxe estate (Bench seats)			
B520	Ravenna Red, P	Black	Oct.65 – Sep.66
B521	Aqua Medium, P	Aqua	Oct.65 – Sep.66
B522	Forest Green, P	Fir Green	Oct.65 – Sep.66
B523	Silver Mink Medium, P	Black	Oct.65 – Sep.66
Cortina Super (Bench seats)			
B524	Black, P	Black	Oct.65 – Sep.66
B525	Ravenna Red, P	Black	Oct.65 – Sep.66
B526	Aqua Medium, P	Aqua	Oct.65 – Sep.66
B527	Forest Green, P	Fir Green	Oct.65 – Sep.66

Trim code No.	Seat colour(s) and seat face material: (P = PVC, C = Cloth)	Floor covering colour	Dates used
Cortina Super estate (Bench seats)			
B528	Black, P	Black	Oct.65 – Sep.66
B529	Ravenna Red, P	Black	Oct.65 – Sep.66
B530	Aqua Medium, P	Aqua	Oct.65 – Sep.66
B531	Forest Green, P	Fir Green	Oct.65 – Sep.66
Cortina GT (With carpets)			
B549	Black, C	Black	Oct.65 – Sep.66
B550	Aqua, C	Aqua	Oct.65 – Sep.66
B551	Forest Green, C	Fir Green	Oct.65 – Sep.66
B552	Ravenna Red, C	Black	Oct.65 – Sep.66
Cortina Super saloon (Export model; with bench seats)			
B553	Black, C	Black	Oct.65 – Sep.66
B554	Aqua, C	Aqua	Oct.65 – Sep.66
B555	Forest Green, C	Fir Green	Oct.65 – Sep.66
B556	Ravenna Red, C	Black	Oct.65 – Sep.66
Cortina Super saloon (Export model)			
B557	Black, C	Black	Oct.65 – Sep.66
B558	Aqua, C	Aqua	Oct.65 – Sep.66
B559	Forest Green, C	Fir Green	Oct.65 – Sep.66
B560	Ravenna Red, C	Black	Oct.65 – Sep.66
Cortina Super estate (Export model, with bench seats)			
B561	Black, C	Black	Oct.65 – Sep.66
B562	Aqua, C	Aqua	Oct.65 – Sep.66
B563	Forest Green C,	Fir Green	Oct.65 – Sep.66
B564	Ravenna Red, C	Black	Oct.65 – Sep.66
Cortina Super estate (Export model)			
B565	Black, C	Black	Oct.65 – Sep.66
B566	Aqua, C	Aqua	Oct.65 – Sep.66
B567	Forest Green, C	Fir Green	Oct.65 – Sep.66
B568	Ravenna Red, C	Black	Oct.65 – Sep.66
Cortina De Luxe saloon (Export model; bench seats)			
B569	Aqua, C	Aqua	Oct.65 – Sep.66
B570	Silver Mink, C	Black	Oct.65 – Sep.66
B571	Forest Green, C	Fir Green	Oct.65 – Sep.66
B572	Ravenna Red, C	Black	Oct.65 – Sep.66
Cortina De Luxe saloon (Export model)			
B573	Aqua, C	Aqua	Oct.65 – Sep.66
B574	Silver Mink, C	Black	Oct.65 – Sep.66
B575	Forest Green, C	Fir Green	Oct.65 – Sep.66
B576	Ravenna Red, C	Black	Oct.65 – Sep.66

Trim code No.	Seat colour(s) and seat face material: (P = PVC, C = Cloth)	Floor covering colour	Dates used
Cortina De Luxe estate (Export model; bench seats)			
B577	Aqua, C	Aqua	Oct.65 – Sep.66
B578	Silver Mink, C	Black	Oct.65 – Sep.66
B579	Forest Green, C	Fir Green	Oct.65 – Sep.66
B580	Ravenna Red, C	Black	Oct.65 – Sep.66
Cortina De Luxe estate (Export model)			
B581	Aqua, C	Aqua	Oct.65 – Sep.66
B582	Silver Mink, C	Black	Oct.65 – Sep.66
B583	Forest Green, C	Fir Green	Oct.65 – Sep.66
B584	Ravenna Red, C	Black	Oct.65 – Sep.66
Standard Cortina saloon			
B590	Silver Mink, P	Black	Oct.65 – Sep.65
Cortina De Luxe saloon (Bench seats)			
B592	Black, C	Black	Oct.65 – Sep.66
Cortina De Luxe saloon			
B593	Black, C	Black	Oct.65 – Sep.66
Cortina De Luxe estate (Bench seats)			
B594	Black, C	Black	Oct.65 – Sep.66
Cortina De Luxe estate			
B595	Black, C	Black	Oct.65 – Sep.66
Standard Cortina saloon			
B596	Ravenna Red, P	Black	September, 1966
B597	Aqua, medium, P	Aqua	September, 1966
B598	Silver Mink medium, P	Silver Mink	September, 1966

NOTE: Of the colours listed, the following have a metallic finish; Platinum Grey, Javelin Bronze, Shearwater Blue, Peru Green.

SVC. Ref
Denotes date of manufacture, in the case of a vehicle shipped unassembled for assembly in another country.

Vehicle number
This consists of:
Two letters;
First letter denotes country of origin (or in which assembled); B = Britain
Second letter denotes assembly plant; A = Dagenham.
Two figures;
Body and gearchange type (as for 1962 – 1964 cars; please see previous list).
Two letters; Year and month of manufacture (or date of assembly abroad).
The codes shown in the table apply to all Cortina and Escort Marks I and II built between 1965 and 1980.

Ford Year and Month Codes from Vehicle Identification Plate, Used from Jan. 1965 on.

Reg Letter	C	D	E/F	F/G	G/H	H/J	J/K	K/L	L/M	M/N	N/P	P/R	R/S	S/T	T/V	V/W
Year built	1965	1966	1967	1968	1969	1970	1971	1972	1973	1974	1975	1976	1977	1978	1979	1980
Month built:																
January	EJ	FL	GC	HB	JJ	KL	LC	MB	NJ	PL	RC	SB	TJ	UL	WC	AB
February	EU	FY	GK	HR	JU	KY	LK	MR	NU	PY	RK	SR	TU	UY	WK	AR
March	EM	FS	GD	HA	JM	KS	LD	MA	NM	PS	RD	SA	TM	US	WD	AA
April	EP	FT	GE	HG	JP	KT	LE	MG	NP	PT	RE	SG	TP	UT	WE	AG
May	EB	FJ	GL	HC	JB	KJ	LL	MC	NB	PJ	RL	SC	TB	UJ	WL	AC
June	ER	FU	GY	HK	JR	KU	LY	MK	NR	PU	RY	SK	TR	UU	WY	AK
July	EA	FM	GS	HD	JA	KM	LS	MD	NA	PM	RS	SD	TA	UM	WS	AD
August	EG	FP	GT	HE	JG	KP	LT	ME	NG	PP	RT	SE	TG	UP	WT	AE
September	EC	FB	GJ	HL	JC	KB	LJ	ML	NC	PB	RJ	SL	TC	UB	WJ	AL
October	EK	FR	GU	HY	JK	KR	LU	MY	NK	PR	RU	SY	TK	UR	WU	AY
November	ED	FA	GM	HS	JD	KA	LM	MS	ND	PA	RM	SS	TD	UA	WM	AS
December	EE	FG	GP	HT	JE	KG	LP	MT	NE	PG	RP	ST	TE	UG	WP	AT

Five figures;
Vehicle identification number, unique to the vehicle

Paint code
Note: This code includes colours used prior to January, 1965 and shown before that date on the separate Trim Identification Plate.

A	=	Savoy Black
M	=	Ambassador Blue
AH	=	Sunburst Yellow
AN	=	Monza Red
AP	=	Cirrus White
AQ	=	Morocco Beige
AR	=	Pompadour Blue
AS	=	Lichen Green
AU	=	Smoke Grey
AV	=	Shark Blue
AX	=	Vulcan Grey
AZ	=	Imperial Maroon
BA	=	Ermine White
BC	=	Lime Green
BH	=	Caribbean Turquoise
BL	=	Ascot Grey
BM	=	Windsor Grey
BP	=	Panama Yellow
BR	=	Goodwood Green
BS	=	Monaco Red
BT	=	Aqua Blue
BU	=	Platinum Grey
BY	=	Light Blue (Glacier Blue)
BZ	=	Spruce Green
CA	=	Sable
CB	=	Midnight Blue
CD	=	Lombard Grey
CF	=	Alcuda Blue
CG	=	Malibu Gold

Cortina Mark II

Ford designations

3014E	=	1300 De Luxe, 2 and 4 door saloon and estate car.
3016E	=	1500 De Luxe and Super, 2 and 4 door saloon and estate car; 1500 GT, 2 and 4 door saloon;
3018E	=	1600 De Luxe and Super, 2 and 4 door saloon and estate car; 1600 GT, 2 and 4 door saloon; 1600E 4 door saloon.
3020E	=	Cortina Lotus, 2 door saloon

Vehicle identification
A plate generally similar to that used on the Cortina Mark I was employed; details as for Mark I, except for codings altered as follows:

Drive

R/1	=	right hand drive.
L/2	=	left hand drive.

Engine

A	=	1297 cc, high compression (with low compression distributor)
B	=	1297 cc, low compression.
C	=	1297 cc, high compression (with normal distributor).
D	=	1500 cc, high compression (with low compression distributor).
E	=	1500 cc, low compression.
F	=	1500 cc, high compression (with normal distributor).
G	=	1500 cc, high compression, GT.
H	=	1558 cc, Lotus.
J/S	=	1298 cc, high compression (cross-flow).
K/T	=	1298 cc, low compression (cross-flow).
L/U	=	1599 cc, high compression (cross-flow).
M/W	=	1599 cc, low compression.
N/X	=	1599 cc, high compression, GT.
P/Y	=	1558cc, Lotus.

Trans (i.e. gearbox)

A/1	=	floor change.
B/2	=	column change.
C/3	=	automatic.

Axle (i.e. rear axle ratio)

A/2	=	3.900:1
A/J	=	3.889:1
B/4	=	4.125:1
C/5	=	4.444:1
D/9	=	3.777:1

Trim

As with the Mark I Cortinas, the Mark IIs each have a trim code number, consisting of a letter, followed by a three figure number, denoting the colours of the seats and floor coverings, and the dates applicable to the particular code. Where two colours are given for the seat coverings, the first applies to the seat face, the second, to the seat border. The application of the various trim combinations between models was rather complex, so for clarity and ease of identification, the codes are listed in numerical order, with model designations shown as appropriate.

Trim code No.	Seat colour(s) and seat face material: (P = PVC, C = Cloth)	Floor covering colour	Dates used
Standard Cortina saloon			
B596	Ravenna Red, P	Black	Sep.66 – Aug.67
B597	Aqua – medium, P	Black	Sep.66 – Aug.67
B598	Silver Mink – medium, P	Black	Sep.66 – Aug.67
Cortina De Luxe saloon			
B599	Ravenna Red, P	Black	Sep.66 – Aug.67
B600	Aqua – medium, P	Aqua	Sep.66 – Aug.67
B601	Forest Green, P	Fir Green	Sep.66 – Aug.67
B602	Silver Mink – medium, P	Black	Sep.66 – Aug.67
Cortina De Luxe saloon (Bench seats)			
B603	Ravenna Red, P	Black	Sep.66 – Aug.67
B604	Aqua – medium, P	Aqua	Sep.66 – Aug.67
B605	Forest Green, P	Fir Green	Sep.66 – Aug.67
B606	Silver Mink medium, P	Black	Sep.66 – Aug.67
Cortina De Luxe estate			
B607	Ravenna Red, P	Black	Sep.66 – Aug.67
B608	Aqua – medium, P	Aqua	Sep.66 – Aug.67
B609	Forest Green, P	Fir Green	Sep.66 – Aug.67
B610	Silver Mink – medium, P	Black	Sep.66 – Aug.67
Cortina De Luxe estate (Bench seats)			
B611	Ravenna Red, P	Black	Sep.66 – Aug.67
B612	Aqua – medium, P	Aqua	Sep.66 – Aug.67
B613	Forest Green, P	Fir Green	Sep.66 – Aug.67
B614	Silver Mink – medium, P	Black	Sep.66 – Aug.67
Cortina Super saloon			
B615	Black, P	Black	Sep.66 – Aug.67
B616	Ravenna Red, P	Black	Sep.66 – Aug.67
B617	Aqua – medium, P	Aqua	Sep.66 – Aug.67
B618	Forest Green, P	Fir Green	Sep.66 – Aug.67
Cortina Super saloon (Bench seats)			
B619	Black, P	Black	Sep.66 – Aug.67
B620	Ravenna Red, P	Black	Sep.66 – Aug.67
B621	Aqua – medium, P	Aqua	Sep.66 – Aug.67
B622	Forest Green, P	Fir Green	Sep.66 – Aug.67
Cortina Super estate			
B623	Black, P	Black	Sep.66 – Aug.67
B624	Ravenna Red, P	Black	Sep.66 – Aug.67
B625	Aqua – medium, P	Aqua	Sep.66 – Aug.67
B626	Forest Green, P	Fir Green	Sep.66 – Aug.67

Trim code No.	Seat colour(s) and seat face material: (P = PVC, C = Cloth)	Floor covering colour	Dates used
Cortina Super estate (Bench seats)			
B627	Black, P	Black	Sep.66 – Aug.67
B628	Ravenna Red, P	Black	Sep.66 – Aug.67
B629	Aqua – medium, P	Aqua	Sep.66 – Aug.67
B630	Forest Green, P	Fir Green	Sep.66 – Aug.67
Cortina GT saloon			
B631	Black, P	Black	Sep.66 – Aug.67
B632	Ravenna Red, P	Black	Sep.66 – Aug.67
B633	Aqua – medium P	Aqua	Sep.66 – Aug.67
B634	Forest Green, P	Fir Green	Sep.66 – Aug.67
Cortina De Luxe saloon			
B635	Ravenna Red, C	Black	Sep.66 – Aug.67
B636	Aqua – medium, C	Aqua	Sep.66 – Aug.67
B637	Forest Green, C	Fir Green	Sep.66 – Aug.67
B638	Silver Mink – medium, C	Black	Sep.66 – Aug.67
Cortina De Luxe saloon (Bench seats)			
B639	Ravenna Red, C	Black	Sep.66 – Aug.67
B640	Aqua – medium, C	Aqua	Sep.66 – Aug.67
B641	Forest Green, C	Fir Green	Sep.66 – Aug.67
B642	Silver Mink – medium, C	Black	Sep.66 – Aug.67
Cortina De Luxe estate			
B643	Ravenna Red, C	Black	Sep.66 – Aug.67
B644	Aqua – medium, C	Aqua	Sep.66 – Aug.67
B645	Forest Green, C	Fir Green	Sep.66 – Aug.67
B646	Silver Mink – medium, C	Black	Sep.66 – Aug.67
Cortina De Luxe estate (Bench seats)			
B647	Ravenna Red, C	Black	Sep.66 – Aug.67
B648	Aqua – medium, C	Aqua	Sep.66 – Aug.67
B649	Forest Green, C	Fir Green	Sep.66 – Aug.67
B650	Silver Mink – medium, C	Black	Sep.66 – Aug.67
Cortina Super saloon			
B651	Black, C	Black	Sep.66 – Aug.67
B652	Ravenna Red, C	Black	Sep.66 – Aug.67
B653	Aqua – medium, C	Aqua	Sep.66 – Aug.67
B654	Forest Green, C	Fir Green	Sep.66 – Aug.67
Cortina Super saloon (Bench seats)			
B655	Black, C	Black	Sep.66 – Aug.67
B656	Ravenna Red, C	Black	Sep.66 – Aug.67
B657	Aqua – medium, C	Aqua	Sep.66 – Aug.67
B658	Forest Green, C	Fir Green	Sep.66 – Aug.67
Cortina Super estate			
B659	Black, C	Black	Sep.66 – Aug.67
B660	Ravenna Red C	Black	Sep.66 – Aug.67
B661	Aqua – medium, C	Aqua	Sep.66 – Aug.67
B662	Forest Green, C	Fir Green	Sep.66 – Aug.67

Trim code No.	Seat colour(s) and seat face material: (P = PVC, C = Cloth)	Floor covering colour	Dates used
Cortina Super estate (Bench seats)			
B663	Black, C	Black	Sep.66 – Aug.67
B664	Ravenna Red, C	Black	Sep.66 – Aug.67
B665	Aqua – medium, C	Aqua	Sep.66 – Aug.67
B666	Forest Green, C	Fir Green	Sep.66 – Aug.67
Cortina GT saloon			
B667	Black, C	Black	Sep.66 – Aug.67
B668	Ravenna Red, C	Black	Sep.66 – Aug.67
B669	Aqua – medium, C	Aqua	Sep.66 – Aug.67
B670	Forest Green, C	Fir Green	Sep.66 – Aug.67
Cortina De Luxe saloon			
B796	Black, P	Black	Sep.66 – Aug.67
Cortina De Luxe saloon (Bench seats)			
B797	Black, P	Black	Sep.66 – Aug.67
Cortina De Luxe saloon			
B798	Black, C	Black	Sep.66 – Aug.67
Cortina De Luxe saloon (Bench seats)			
B799	Black, C	Black	Sep.66 – Aug.67
Cortina De Luxe estate			
B800	Black, P	Black	Sep.66 – Aug.67
Cortina De Luxe (Bench seats)			
B801	Black, P	Black	Sep.66 – Aug.67
Cortina De Luxe estate			
B802	Black, C	Black	Sep.66 – Aug.67
Cortina De Luxe estate (Bench seats)			
B803	Black, C	Black	Sep.66 – Aug.67
Cortina Super saloon			
B804	Parchment, P	Parchment	Sep.66 – Aug.67
B805	Saddle, P	Saddle	Sep.66 – Aug.67
Cortina Super saloon (Bench seats)			
B806	Parchment, P	Parchment	Sep.66 – Aug.67
B808	Saddle, P	Saddle	Sep.66 – Aug.67
Cortina GT saloon			
B808	Parchment, P	Parchment	Sep.66 – Aug.67
B809	Saddle, P	Saddle	Sep.66 – Aug.67
Cortina Super saloon			
B810	Parchment, C	Parchment	Sep.66 – Aug.67
B811	Saddle, C	Saddle	Sep.66 – Aug.67
Cortina Super saloon (Bench seats)			
B812	Parchment, C	Parchment	Sep.66 – Aug.67
B813	Saddle, C	Saddle	Sep.66 – Aug.67

Trim code No.	Seat colour(s) and seat face material: (P = PVC, C = Cloth)	Floor covering colour	Dates used
Cortina GT saloon			
B814	Parchment, C	Parchment	Sep.66 – Aug.67
B815	Saddle, C	Saddle	Sep.66 – Aug.67
Cortina Super estate			
B816	Parchment, P	Parchment	Sep.66 – Aug.67
B817	Saddle, P	Saddle	Sep.66 – Aug.67
Cortina Super estate (Bench seats)			
B818	Parchment, P	Parchment	Sep.66 – Aug.67
B819	Saddle, P	Saddle	Sep.66 – Aug.67
Cortina Super estate			
B820	Parchment, C	Parchment	Sep.66 – Aug.67
B821	Saddle, C	Saddle	Sep.66 – Aug.67
Cortina Super estate (Bench seats)			
B822	Parchment, C	Parchment	Sep.66 – Aug.67
B823	Saddle, C	Saddle	Sep.66 – Aug.67
Cortina De Luxe saloon (Export model)			
B824	Ravenna Red, P	Black	Dec.66 – Aug.67
B825	Aqua – medium, P	Aqua	Dec.66 – Aug.67
B826	Forest Green, P	Fir Green	Dec.66 – Aug.67
B827	Silver Mink – medium, P	Silver Mink	Dec.66 – Aug.67
B828	Black, P	Black	Dec.66 – Aug.67
B829	Ravenna Red, C	Black	Dec.66 – Aug.67
B830	Aqua – medium, C	Aqua	Dec.66 – Aug.67
B831	Forest Green, C	Fir Green	Dec.66 – Aug.67
B832	Silver Mink – medium, C	Silver Mink	Dec.66 – Aug.67
B833	Black, C	Black	Dec.66 – Aug.67
Cortina De Luxe estate (Export model)			
B834	Ravenna Red, P	Black	Dec.66 – Aug.67
B835	Aqua – medium, P	Aqua	Dec.66 – Aug.67
B836	Forest Green, P	Fir Green	Dec.66 – Aug.67
B837	Silver Mink – medium, P	Silver Mink	Dec.66 – Aug.67
B838	Black, P	Black	Dec.66 – Aug.67
B839	Ravenna Red, C	Black	Dec.66 – Aug.67
B840	Aqua – medium, C	Aqua	Dec.66 – Aug.67
B841	Forest Green, C	Fir Green	Dec.66 – Aug.67
B842	Silver Mink medium, C	Silver Mink	Dec.66 – Aug.67
B843	Black, C	Black	Dec.66 – Aug.67
Standard Cortina saloon			
B959	Black, P	Black	Aug.67 – Oct.68
Cortina De Luxe saloon			
B964	Black, P	Black	Aug.67 – Oct.68
B965	Ravenna Red, P	Black	Aug.67 – Oct.68
B966	Aqua, P	Black	Aug.67 – Oct.68
Cortina De Luxe saloon (Bench seats)			
B967	Black, P	Black	Aug.67 – Oct.68
B968	Ravenna Red, P	Black	Aug.67 – Oct.68
B969	Aqua, P	Black	Aug.67 – Oct.68

Trim code No.	Seat colour(s) and seat face material: (P = PVC, C = Cloth)	Floor covering colour	Dates used
Cortina Super saloon			
B970	Black, P	Black	Aug.67 – Oct.68
B971	Ravenna Red, P	Black	Aug.67 – Oct.68
B972	Aqua, P	Black	Aug.67 – Oct.68
B973	Parchment, P	Black	Aug.67 – Oct.68
B974	Saddle, P	Black	Aug.67 – Oct.68
Cortina Super saloon (Bench seats)			
B975	Black, P	Black	Aug.67 – Oct.68
B976	Ravenna Red, P	Black	Aug.67 – Oct.68
B977	Aqua, P	Black	Aug.67 – Oct.68
B978	Parchment, P	Black	Aug.67 – Oct.68
B979	Saddle, P	Black	Aug.67 – Oct.68
Cortina GT and Lotus			
B980	Black, P	Black	Aug.67 – Oct.68
B981	Ravenna Red, P	Black	Aug.67 – Oct.68
B982	Aqua, P	Black	Aug.67 – Oct.68
B983	Parchment, P	Black	Aug.67 – Oct.68
B984	Saddle, P	Black	Aug.67 – Oct.68
Cortina De Luxe saloon			
B985	Black, C	Black	Aug.67 – May 68
B986	Ravenna Red, C	Black	Aug.67 – May 68
B987	Aqua, C	Black	Aug.67 – May 68
Cortina De Luxe saloon (Bench seats)			
B988	Black, C	Black	Aug.67 – May 68
B989	Ravenna Red, C	Black	Aug.67 – May 68
B990	Aqua, C	Black	Aug.67 – May 68
Cortina Super saloon			
B991	Black, C	Black	Aug.67 – May 68
B992	Ravenna Red, C	Black	Aug.67 – May 68
B993	Aqua, C	Black	Aug.67 – May 68
B994	Parchment, C	Black	Aug.67 – May 68
B995	Saddle, C	Black	Aug.67 – May 68
Cortina Super saloon (Bench seats)			
B996	Black, C	Black	Aug.67 – May 68
B997	Ravenna Red, C	Black	Aug.67 – May 68
B998	Aqua, C	Black	Aug.67 – May 68
B999	Parchment, C	Black	Aug.67 – May 68
C001	Saddle, C	Black	Aug.67 – May 68
Cortina GT and Lotus			
C002	Black, C	Black	Aug.67 – May 68
C003	Ravenna Red, C	Black	Aug.67 – May 68
C004	Aqua, C	Black	Aug.67 – May 68
C005	Parchment, C	Black	Aug.67 – May 68
C006	Saddle, C	Black	Aug.67 – May 68
Cortina De Luxe estate			
C007	Black, P	Black	Aug.67 – Oct.68
C008	Ravenna Red, P	Black	Aug.67 – Oct.68
C009	Aqua, P	Black	Aug.67 – Oct.68

Trim code No.	Seat colour(s) and seat face material: (P = PVC, C = Cloth)	Floor covering colour	Dates used
Cortina De Luxe estate (Bench seats)			
C010	Black, P	Black	Aug.67 – Oct.68
C011	Ravenna Red, P	Black	Aug.67 – Oct.68
C012	Aqua, P	Black	Aug.67 – Oct.68
Cortina Super estate			
C013	Black, P	Black	Aug.67 – Oct.68
C014	Ravenna Red, P	Black	Aug.67 – Oct.68
C015	Aqua/Flecked Grey, P	Black	Aug.67 – Oct.68
C016	Parchment, P	Black	Aug.67 – Oct.68
C017	Saddle, P	Black	Aug.67 – Oct.68
Cortina Super estate (Bench seats)			
C018	Black, P	Black	Aug.67 – Oct.68
C019	Ravenna Red, P	Black	Aug.67 – Oct.68
C020	Aqua, P	Black	Aug.67 – Oct.68
C021	Parchment, P	Black	Aug.67 – Oct.68
C022	Saddle, P	Black	Aug.67 – Oct.68
Cortina De Luxe estate			
C023	Black, C	Black	Aug.67 – May 68
C024	Ravenna Red, C	Black	Aug.67 – May 68
C025	Aqua, C	Black	Aug.67 – May 68
Cortina De Luxe estate (Bench seats)			
C026	Black, C	Black	Aug.67 – May 68
C027	Ravenna Red, C	Black	Aug.67 – May 68
C028	Aqua, C	Black	Aug.67 – May 68
Cortina Super estate			
C029	Black,C	Black	Aug.67 – May 68
C030	Ravenna Red, C	Black	Aug.67 – May 68
C031	Aqua, C	Black	Aug.67 – May 68
C032	Parchment, C	Black	Aug.67 – May 68
C033	Saddle, C	Black	Aug.67 – May 68
Cortina Super estate (Bench seats)			
C034	Black, C	Black	Aug.67 – May 68
C035	Ravenna Red, C	Black	Aug.67 – May 68
C036	Aqua, C	Black	Aug.67 – May 68
C037	Parchment, P	Black	Aug.67 – May 68
C038	Saddle, C	Black	Aug.67 – May 68
Cortina De Luxe saloon (U.S.A.)			
C040	Black, P	Black	Dec.67 – Oct.68
C041	Ravenna Red, P	Black	Dec.67 – Oct.68
C042	Aqua, P	Black	Dec.67 – Oct.68
Cortina De Luxe estate (U.S.A.)			
C043	Black, P	Black	Dec.67 – Oct.68
C044	Ravenna Red, P	Black	Dec.67 – Oct.68
C045	Aqua, P	Black	Dec.67 – Oct.68
Cortina GT and Lotus saloon (U.S.A.)			
C046	Black, P	Black	Dec.67 – Oct.68
C047	Ravenna Red, P	Black	Dec.67 – Oct.68
C048	Aqua, P	Black	Dec.67 – Oct.68
C049	Parchment, P	Black	Dec.67 – Oct.68
C050	Saddle, P	Black	Dec.67 – Oct.68

Trim code No.	Seat colour(s) and seat face material: (P = PVC, C = Cloth)	Floor covering colour	Dates used
Cortina De Luxe saloon (U.S.A.)			
C051	Black, C	Black	Dec.67 – May 68
C052	Ravenna Red, C	Black	Dec.67 – May 68
C053	Aqua, C	Black	Dec.67 – May 68
Cortina De Luxe estate (U.S.A.)			
C054	Black, C	Black	Dec.67 – May 68
C055	Ravenna Red, C	Black	Dec.67 – May 68
C056	Aqua, C	Black	Dec.67 – May 68
Cortina GT and Lotus (U.S.A.)			
C057	Black, C	Black	Dec.67 – May 68
C058	Ravenna Red, C	Black	Dec.67 – May 68
C059	Aqua, C	Black	Dec.67 – May 68
C060	Parchment, C	Black	Dec.67 – May 68
C061	Saddle, C	Black	Dec.67 – May 68

NOTE: Cars with Trim Code numbers B964 – C061 had Flecked Grey/Black Floor Covering until January, 1968.

Standard Cortina saloon			
C062	Ravenna Red, P	Black	Dec.67 – Oct.68
Cortina 1600E saloon			
C084	Black, P	Black	Sep.67 – Oct.68
C085	Ravenna Red, P	Black	Sep.67 – Oct.68
C086	Aqua – medium, P	Black	Sep.67 – Oct.68
C087	Parchment, P	Black	Sep.67 – Oct.68
C088	Saddle, P	Black	Sep.67 – Oct.68
C089	Black, C	Black	Sep.67 – May 68
C090	Ravenna Red, C	Black	Sep.67 – May 68
C091	Aqua – medium, C	Black	Sep.67 – May 68
C092	Saddle, C	Black	Sep.67 – May 68
Cortina De Luxe saloon			
C104	Parchment, P	Black	Dec.67 – Oct.68
Cortina De Luxe saloon (Bench seats)			
C105	Parchment, P	Black	Dec.67 – Oct.68
Cortina De Luxe saloon (U.S.A.)			
C106	Parchment, P	Black	Dec.67 – Oct.68
Cortina De Luxe estate			
C107	Parchment, P	Black	Dec.67 – Oct.68
Cortina De Luxe estate (Bench seats)			
C108	Parchment, P	Black	Dec.67 – Oct.68
Cortina De Luxe estate (U.S.A.)			
C109	Parchment, P	Black	Dec.67 – Oct.68
Cortina De Luxe saloon			
C110	Black, C	Black	May 68 – Oct.68
Cortina De Luxe saloon (Bench seats)			
C111	Black, C	Black	May 68 – Oct.68

Trim code No.	Seat colour(s) and seat face material: (P = PVC, C = Cloth)	Floor covering colour	Dates used
Cortina De Luxe saloon			
C112	Black, C	Black	May 68 – Oct.68
C113	Ravenna Red, C	Black	May 68 – Oct.68
Cortina De Luxe saloon (Bench seats)			
C114	Ravenna Red, C	Black	May 68 – Oct.68
Cortina De Luxe saloon			
C115	Ravenna Red, C	Black	May 68 – Oct.68
C116	Aqua – medium, C	Black	May 68 – Oct.68
Cortina De Luxe saloon (Bench seats)			
C117	Aqua – medium, C	Black	May 68 – Oct.68
Cortina De Luxe saloon			
C118	Aqua – medium, C	Black	May 68 – Oct.68
Cortina De Luxe estate			
C119	Black, C	Black	May 68 – Oct.68
Cortina De Luxe estate (Bench seats)			
C120	Black, C	Black	May 68 – Oct.68
Cortina De Luxe estate			
C121	Black, C	Black	May 68 – Oct.68
C122	Ravenna Red, C	Black	May 68 – Oct.68
Cortina De Luxe estate (Bench seats)			
C123	Ravenna Red, C	Black	May 68 – Oct.68
Cortina De Luxe estate			
C124	Ravenna Red, C	Black	May 68 – Oct.68
C125	Aqua – medium, C	Black	May 68 – Oct.68
Cortina De Luxe estate (Bench seats)			
C126	Aqua – medium, C	Black	May 68 – Oct.68
Cortina De Luxe estate			
C127	Aqua – medium, C	Black	May 68 – Oct.68
Cortina Super saloon			
C128	Black, C	Black	May 68 – Oct.68
Cortina Super saloon (Bench seats)			
C129	Black, C	Black	May 68 – Oct.68
Cortina Super saloon			
C130	Ravenna Red, C	Black	May 68 – Oct.68
Cortina Super saloon (Bench seats)			
C131	Ravenna Red, C	Black	May 68 – Oct.68
Cortina Super saloon			
C132	Aqua – medium, C	Black	May 68 – Oct.68
Cortina Super saloon (Bench seats)			
C133	Aqua – medium, C	Black	May 68 – Oct.68

Trim code No.	Seat colour(s) and seat face material: (P = PVC, C = Cloth)	Floor covering colour	Dates used
Cortina Super saloon			
C134	Saddle, C	Black	May 68 – Oct.68
Cortina Super saloon (Bench seats)			
C135	Saddle, C	Black	May 68 – Oct.68
Cortina Super estate			
C136	Black, C	Black	May 68 – Oct.68
Cortina Super estate (Bench seats)			
C137	Black, C	Black	May 68 – Oct.68
Cortina Super estate			
C138	Ravenna Red, C	Black	May 68 – Oct.68
Cortina Super estate (Bench seats)			
C139	Ravenna Red, C	Black	May 68 – Oct.68
Cortina Super estate			
C140	Aqua – medium, C	Black	May 68 – Oct.68
Cortina Super estate (Bench seats)			
C141	Aqua – medium, C	Black	May 68 – Oct.68
Cortina Super estate			
C142	Saddle, C	Black	May 68 – Oct.68
Cortina Super estate (Bench seats)			
C143	Saddle, C	Black	May 68 – Oct.68
Cortina GT and Lotus saloon			
C144	Black, C	Black	May 68 – Oct.68
C145	Black, C	Black	May 68 – Oct.68
C146	Ravenna Red, C	Black	May 68 – Oct.68
C147	Ravenna Red, C	Black	May 68 – Oct.68
C148	Aqua – medium, C	Black	May 68 – Oct.68
C149	Aqua – medium, C	Black	May 68 – Oct.68
C150	Saddle, C	Black	May 69 – Oct.68
C151	Saddle, C	Black	May 68 – Oct.68
Cortina 1600E saloon			
C152	Black, C	Black	May 68 – Oct.68
C153	Ravenna Red, C	Black	May 68 – Oct.68
C154	Aqua – medium, C	Black	May 68 – Oct.68
C155	Saddle, C	Black	May 68 – Oct.68
Standard Cortina saloon			
D001	Black, P	Black	Oct.68 on
D002	Parchment, P	Black	Oct.68 on
Cortina De Luxe saloon			
D003	Black, P	Black	Oct.68 on
D004	Black, P	Black	Oct.68 on
D005	Black, P	Black	Oct.68 on
D006	Parchment, P	Black	Oct.68 on
D007	Parchment, P	Black	Oct.68 on
D008	Parchment, P	Black	Oct.68 on
D009	Cherry, P	Cherry – dark	Oct.68 on
D010	Cherry, P	Cherry – dark	Oct.68 on

Trim code No.	Seat colour(s) and seat face material: (P = PVC, C = Cloth)	Floor covering colour	Dates used
D011	Cherry, P	Cherry – dark	Oct.68 on
D012	Beechnut, P	Beechnut – dark	Oct.68 on
D013	Beechnut, P	Beechnut – dark	Oct.68 on
D014	Beechnut, P	Beechnut – dark	Oct.68 on
D015	Aqua, P	Aqua – deep	Oct.68 on
D016	Aqua, P	Aqua – deep	Oct.68 on
D017	Aqua, P	Aqua – deep	Oct.68 on
D018	Blue, P	Blue – deep	Oct.68 on
D019	Blue, P	Blue – deep	Oct.68 on
D020	Blue, P	Blue – deep	Oct.68 on

Cortina De Luxe saloon (Bench seats)

Trim code No.	Seat colour(s)	Floor covering colour	Dates used
D021	Black, P	Black	Oct.68 on
D022	Black, P	Black	Oct.68 on
D023	Parchment, P	Black	Oct.68 on
D024	Parchment, P	Black	Oct.68 on
D025	Cherry, P	Cherry – dark	Oct.68 on
D026	Cherry, P	Cherry – dark	Oct.68 on
D027	Beechnut, P	Beechnut – dark	Oct.68 on
D028	Beechnut, P	Beechnut – dark	Oct.68 on
D029	Aqua, P	Aqua – deep	Oct.68 on
D030	Aqua, P	Aqua – deep	Oct.68 on
D031	Blue, P	Blue – deep	Oct.68 on
D032	Blue, P	Blue – deep	Oct.68 on

Cortina De Luxe saloon

Trim code No.	Seat colour(s)	Floor covering colour	Dates used
D033	Black, C	Black	Oct.68 on
D034	Black, C	Black	Oct.68 on
D035	Black, C	Black	Oct.68 on
D036	Cherry, C	Cherry – dark	Oct.68 on
D037	Cherry, C	Cherry – dark	Oct.68 on
D038	Cherry, C	Cherry – dark	Oct.68 on
D039	Beechnut, C	Beechnut – dark	Oct.68 on
D040	Beechnut, C	Beechnut – dark	Oct.68 on
D041	Beechnut, C	Beechnut – dark	Oct.68 on
D042	Aqua, C	Aqua – deep	Oct.68 on
D043	Aqua, C	Aqua – deep	Oct.68 on
D044	Aqua, C	Aqua – deep	Oct.68 on
D045	Blue, C	Blue – deep	Oct.68 on
D046	Blue, C	Blue – deep	Oct.68 on
D047	Blue, C	Blue – deep	Oct.68 on

Cortina De Luxe saloon (Bench seats)

Trim code No.	Seat colour(s)	Floor covering colour	Dates used
D048	Black, C	Black	Oct.68 on
D049	Black, C	Black	Oct.68 on
D050	Cherry, C	Cherry – dark	Oct.68 on
D051	Cherry, C	Cherry – dark	Oct.68 on
D052	Beechnut, C	Beechnut – dark	Oct.68 on
D053	Beechnut, C	Beechnut – dark	Oct.68 on
D054	Aqua, C	Aqua – deep	Oct.68 on
D055	Aqua, C	Aqua – deep	Oct.68 on
D056	Blue, C	Blue – deep	Oct.68 on
D057	Blue, C	Blue – deep	Oct.68 on

Cortina De Luxe estate

Trim code No.	Seat colour(s)	Floor covering colour	Dates used
D058	Black, P	Black	Oct.68 on
D059	Black, P	Black	Oct.68 on
D060	Black, P	Black	Oct.68 on

Trim code No.	Seat colour(s) and seat face material: (P = PVC, C = Cloth)	Floor covering colour	Dates used
D061	Parchment, P	Black	Oct.68 on
D062	Parchment, P	Black	Oct.68 on
D063	Parchment/Black, P	Black	Oct.68 on
D064	Cherry, P	Cherry – dark	Oct.68 on
D065	Cherry, P	Cherry – dark	Oct.68 on
D066	Cherry, P	Cherry – dark	Oct.68 on
D067	Beechnut, P	Beechnut – Dark	Oct.68 on
D068	Beechnut, P	Beechnut – dark	Oct.68 on
D069	Beechnut, P	Beechnut – dark	Oct.68 on
D070	Aqua, P	Aqua – deep	Oct.68 on
D071	Aqua, P	Aqua – deep	Oct.68 on
D072	Aqua, P	Aqua – deep	Oct.68 on
D073	Blue, P	Blue – deep	Oct.68 on
D074	Blue, P	Blue – deep	Oct.68 on
D075	Blue, P	Blue – deep	Oct.68 on

Cortina De Luxe estate (Bench seats)

Trim code No.	Seat colour(s)	Floor covering colour	Dates used
D076	Black, P	Black	Oct.68 on
D077	Black, P	Black	Oct.68 on
D078	Parchment, P	Black	Oct.68 on
D079	Parchment, P	Black	Oct.68 on
D080	Cherry, P	Cherry – dark	Oct.68 on
D081	Cherry, P	Cherry – dark	Oct.68 on
D082	Beechnut, P	Beechnut – dark	Oct.68 on
D083	Beechnut, P	Beechnut – dark	Oct.68 on
D084	Aqua, P	Aqua – deep	Oct.68 on
D085	Aqua, P	Aqua – deep	Oct.68 on
D086	Blue, P	Blue – deep	Oct.68 on
D087	Blue, P	Blue – deep	Oct.68 on

Cortina De Luxe estate

Trim code No.	Seat colour(s)	Floor covering colour	Dates used
D088	Black, C	Black	Oct.68 on
D089	Black, C	Black	Oct.68 on
D090	Black, C	Black	Oct.68 on
D091	Cherry, C	Cherry – dark	Oct.68 on
D092	Cherry, C	Cherry – dark	Oct.68 on
D093	Cherry, C	Cherry – dark	Oct.68 on
D094	Beechnut, C	Beechnut – dark	Oct.68 on
D095	Beechnut, C	Beechnut – dark	Oct.68 on
D096	Beechnut, C	Beechnut – dark	Oct.68 on
D097	Aqua, C	Aqua – deep	Oct.68 on
D098	Aqua, C	Aqua – deep	Oct.68 on
D099	Aqua, C	Aqua – deep	Oct.68 on
D100	Blue, C	Blue – deep	Oct.68 on
D101	Blue, C	Blue – deep	Oct.68 on
D102	Blue, C	Blue – deep	Oct.68 on

Cortina De Luxe estate (Bench seats)

Trim code No.	Seat colour(s)	Floor covering colour	Dates used
D103	Black, C	Black	Oct.68 on
D104	Black, C	Black	Oct.68 on
D105	Cherry, C	Cherry – dark	Oct.68 on
D106	Cherry, C	Cherry – dark	Oct.68 on
D107	Beechnut, C	Beechnut – dark	Oct.68 on
D108	Beechnut, C	Beechnut – dark	Oct.68 on
D109	Aqua, C	Aqua – deep	Oct.68 on
D110	Aqua, C	Aqua – deep	Oct.68 on
D111	Blue, C	Blue – deep	Oct.68 on
D112	Blue, C	Blue – deep	Oct.68 on

Trim code No.	Seat colour(s) and seat face material: (P = PVC, C = Cloth)	Floor covering colour	Dates used
Cortina Super saloon			
D113	Black, P	Black	Oct.68 on
D114	Black, P	Black	Oct.68 on
D115	Parchment, P	Black	Oct.68 on
D116	Parchment, P	Black	Oct.68 on
D117	Cherry, P	Cherry – dark	Oct.68 on
D118	Cherry, P	Cherry – dark	Oct.68 on
D119	Beechnut, P	Beechnut – dark	Oct.68 on
D120	Beechnut, P	Beechnut – dark	Oct.68 on
D121	Aqua, P	Aqua – deep	Oct.68 on
D122	Aqua, P	Aqua – deep	Oct.68 on
D123	Blue, P	Blue – deep	Oct.68 on
D124	Blue, P	Blue – deep	Oct.68 on
Cortina Super saloon (Bench seats)			
D125	Black, P	Black	Oct.68 on
D126	Black, P	Black	Oct.68 on
D127	Parchment, P	Black	Oct.68 on
D128	Parchment, P	Black	Oct.68 on
D129	Cherry, P	Cherry – dark	Oct.68 on
D130	Cherry, P	Cherry – dark	Oct.68 on
D131	Beechnut, P	Beechnut – dark	Oct.68 on
D132	Beechnut, P	Beechnut – dark	Oct.68 on
D133	Aqua, P	Aqua – deep	Oct.68 on
D134	Aqua, P	Aqua – deep	Oct.68 on
D135	Blue, P	Blue – deep	Oct.68 on
D136	Blue, P	Blue – deep	Oct.68 on
Cortina Super saloon			
D137	Black, C	Black	Oct.68 on
D138	Black, C	Black	Oct.68 on
D139	Cherry, C	Cherry – dark	Oct.68 on
D140	Cherry, C	Cherry – dark	Oct.68 on
D141	Beechnut, C	Beechnut – dark	Oct.68 on
D142	Beechnut, C	Beechnut – dark	Oct.68 on
D143	Aqua C,	Aqua – deep	Oct.68 on
D144	Aqua, C	Aqua – deep	Oct.68 on
D145	Blue, C	Blue – deep	Oct.68 on
D146	Blue, C	Blue – deep	Oct.68 on
Cortina Super saloon (Bench seats)			
D147	Black, C	Black	Oct.68 on
D148	Black, C	Black	Oct.68 on
D149	Cherry, C	Cherry – dark	Oct.68 on
D150	Cherry, C	Cherry – dark	Oct.68 on
D151	Beechnut, C	Beechnut – dark	Oct.68 on
D152	Beechnut, C	Beechnut – dark	Oct.68 on
D153	Aqua, C	Aqua – deep	Oct.68 on
D154	Aqua, C	Aqua – deep	Oct.68 on
D155	Blue, C	Blue – deep	Oct.68 on
D156	Blue, C	Blue – deep	Oct.68 on
Cortina Super estate			
D157	Black, P	Black	Oct.68 on
D158	Black, P	Black	Oct.68 on
D159	Parchment, P	Black	Oct.68 on
D160	Parchment, P	Black	Oct.68 on

Trim code No.	Seat colour(s) and seat face material: (P = PVC, C = Cloth)	Floor covering colour	Dates used
D161	Cherry, P	Cherry – dark	Oct.68 on
D162	Cherry, P	Cherry – dark	Oct.68 on
D163	Beechnut, P	Beechnut – dark	Oct.68 on
D164	Beechnut, P	Beechnut – dark	Oct.68 on
D165	Aqua, P	Aqua – deep	Oct.68 on
D166	Aqua, P	Aqua – deep	Oct.68 on
D167	Blue, P	Blue – deep	Oct.68 on
D168	Blue, P	Blue – deep	Oct.68 on

Cortina Super estate (Bench seats)

D169	Black, P	Black	Oct.68 on
D170	Black, P	Black	Oct.68 on
D171	Parchment, P	Black	Oct.68 on
D172	Parchment, P	Black	Oct.68 on
D173	Cherry, P	Cherry – dark	Oct.68 on
D174	Cherry, P	Cherry – dark	Oct.68 on
D175	Beechnut, P	Beechnut – dark	Oct.68 on
D176	Beechnut, P	Beechnut – dark	Oct.68 on
D177	Aqua, P	Aqua – deep	Oct.68 on
D178	Aqua, P	Aqua – deep	Oct.68 on
D179	Blue, P	Blue – deep	Oct.68 on
D180	Blue, P	Blue – deep	Oct.68 on

Cortina Super estate

D181	Black, C	Black	Oct.68 on
D182	Black, C	Black	Oct.68 on
D183	Cherry, C	Cherry – dark	Oct.68 on
D184	Cherry, C	Cherry – dark	Oct.68 on
D185	Beechnut, C	Beechnut – dark	Oct.68 on
D186	Beechnut, C	Beechnut – dark	Oct.68 on
D187	Aqua, C	Aqua – deep	Oct.68 on
D188	Aqua, C	Aqua – deep	Oct.68 on
D189	Blue, C	Blue – deep	Oct.68 on
D190	Blue, C	Blue – deep	Oct.68 on

Cortina Super estate (Bench seats)

D191	Black, C	Black	Oct.68 on
D192	Black, C	Black	Oct.68 on
D193	Cherry, C	Cherry – dark	Oct.68 on
D194	Cherry, C	Cherry – dark	Oct.68 on
D195	Beechnut, C	Beechnut – dark	Oct.68 on
D196	Beechnut, C	Beechnut – dark	Oct.68 on
D197	Aqua, C	Aqua – deep	Oct.68 on
D198	Aqua, C	Aqua – deep	Oct.68 on
D199	Blue, C	Blue – deep	Oct.68 on
D200	Blue, C	Blue – deep	Oct.68 on

Cortina GT and Lotus

D201	Black, P	Black	Oct.68 on
D202	Black, P	Black	Oct.68 on
D203	Black, P	Black	Oct.68 on
D204	Parchment, P	Black	Oct.68 on
D205	Parchment, P	Black	Oct.68 on
D206	Parchment, P	Black	Oct.68 on
D207	Cherry, P	Cherry – dark	Oct.68 on
D208	Cherry, P	Cherry – dark	Oct.68 on
D209	Cherry, P	Cherry – dark	Oct.68 on

Trim code No.	Seat colour(s) and seat face material: (P = PVC, C = Cloth)	Floor covering colour	Dates used
D210	Beechnut, P	Beechnut – dark	Oct.68 on
D211	Beechnut, P	Beechnut – dark	Oct.68 on
D212	Beechnut, P	Beechnut – dark	Oct.68 on
D213	Aqua, P	Aqua – deep	Oct.68 on
D214	Aqua, P	Aqua – deep	Oct.68 on
D215	Aqua, P	Aqua – deep	Oct.68 on
D216	Blue, P	Blue – deep	Oct.68 on
D217	Blue, P	Blue – deep	Oct.68 on
D218	Blue, P	Blue – deep	Oct.68 on
D219	Black, C	Black	Oct.68 on
D220	Black, C	Black	Oct.68 on
D221	Black, C	Black	Oct.68 on
D222	Cherry, C	Cherry – dark	Oct.68 on
D223	Cherry, C	Cherry – dark	Oct.68 on
D224	Cherry, C	Cherry – dark	Oct.68 on
D225	Beechnut, C	Beechnut – dark	Oct.68 on
D226	Beechnut, C	Beechnut – dark	Oct.68 on
D227	Beechnut, C	Beechnut – dark	Oct.68 on
D228	Aqua, C	Aqua – deep	Oct.68 on
D229	Aqua, C	Aqua – deep	Oct.68 on
D230	Aqua, C	Aqua – deep	Oct.68 on
D231	Blue, C	Blue – deep	Oct.68 on
D232	Blue, C	Blue – deep	Oct.68 on
D233	Blue, C	Blue – deep	Oct.68 on

Cortina 1600E Saloon

Trim code No.	Seat colour(s)	Floor covering colour	Dates used
D234	Black, P	Black	Oct.68 on
D235	Black, P	Black	Oct.68 on
D236	Parchment, P	Black	Oct.68 on
D237	Parchment, P	Black	Oct.68 on
D238	Cherry, P	Cherry – dark	Oct.68 on
D239	Cherry, P	Cherry – dark	Oct.68 on
D240	Beechnut, P	Beechnut – dark	Oct.68 on
D241	Beechnut, P	Beechnut – dark	Oct.68 on
D242	Aqua, P	Aqua – deep	Oct.68 on
D243	Aqua, P	Aqua – deep	Oct.68 on
D244	Blue, P	Blue – deep	Oct.68 on
D245	Blue, P	Blue – deep	Oct.68 on
D246	Black, C	Black	Oct.68 on
D247	Black, C	Black	Oct.68 on
D248	Parchment, C	Black	Oct.68 on
D249	Parchment, C	Black	Oct.68 on
D250	Cherry, C	Cherry – dark	Oct.68 on
D251	Cherry, C	Cherry – dark	Oct.68 on
D252	Beechnut, C	Beechnut – dark	Oct.68 on
D253	Beechnut, C	Beechnut – dark	Oct.68 on
D254	Aqua, C	Aqua – deep	Oct.68 on
D255	Aqua, C	Aqua – deep	Oct.68 on
D256	Blue, C	Blue – deep	Oct.68 on
D257	Blue, C	Blue – deep	Oct.68 on

Standard Cortina Saloon

Trim code No.	Seat colour(s)	Floor covering colour	Dates used
D493	Black, P	Black	Jan.69 on
D494	Black, P	Black	Jan.69 on

Trim Code Numbers D629 – D696 were allocated but applied only to the Swedish market.

SVC Ref As for Mark I Cortinas.

Vehicle number

This consists of:

Two letters:

Country of origin and assembly plant – details as for Mark I Cortinas.

Two figures; Body type;

80	= 4 door Standard.
90	= 2 door Standard.
91	= 2 door Lotus.
92	= 2 door De Luxe.
93	= 4 door De Luxe.
94	= 2 door Super.
95	= 4 door Super.
96	= 2 door GT.
97	= 4 door GT and 1600E.
98	= Estate car De Luxe.
99	= Estate car Super.

Two letters:

Year and month of manufacture (or date of assembly abroad).

Please see table under Cortina Mark I section.

Five figures;

Vehicle Identification Number, unique to the vehicle.

Paint code

BA/AB	= Ermine White
BZ	= Spruce Green
CN	= Velvet Blue
CH	= Purbeck Grey
CJ	= Lagoon
CL	= Black Cherry

CM	= Alpine Green
CP	= Seafoam Blue
CU	= Dragoon Red
AQ	= Aubergine
BJ	= Anchor Blue
BN	= Red II 65
BV	= Beige 67
*A5	= Aquatic Jade
CG	= Light Blue
CR	= Light Green 67
*A2	= Silver Fox
*A3	= Blue Mink
*A6	= Saluki Bronze
*A8	= Light Orchid
*B4	= Amber Gold
*B5	= Fern Green
*	= Metallic Finish

Escort Mark I (Up to August, 1970)

Vehicle identification

A plate similar to that used on the Mark II Cortinas was fitted to the early Escorts, up to August 1970. Many of the codes used on the early Escorts differed from those used on the Cortinas. The codes applicable to the Escort are listed below;

Drive

R/1	= right hand drive
L/2	= left hand drive

Engine

B	= 1098cc, high compression.
C	= 1098cc, low compression.
R	= 1298cc, GT.
S	= 1298cc, high compression.
T	= 1298cc, low compression.

Trans. (i.e. gearbox)

1	= Floor change (manual).
7	= Automatic.

Axle (i.e. rear axle ratio)

A	= 3.777:1, Heavy duty
B	= 4.125:1, Heavy duty
C	= 4.444:1, Heavy duty
D	= 3.900:1, Heavy duty
2	= 3.900:1, Not heavy duty
4	= 4.125:1, Not heavy duty
5	= 4.444:1, Not heavy duty
9	= 3.777:1, Not heavy duty

Trim

The Escorts up to August, 1970 used trim code numbers similar to those used for the Cortinas, consisting of a letter, followed by a three figure number, denoting the colours of the seats and floor coverings. The application of the various trim combinations between models was rather complex, so, for clarity and ease of identification, the codes are listed in numerical order, with model designations shown as appropriate.

Trim code No.	Seat colour(s) and seat face material: (P = PVC, C = Cloth)	Floor covering colour	Dates used
Standard Escort saloon			
B864	Ravenna Red, P	Dark Red	Oct.67 – Sep.68
B865	Black, P	Black	Oct.67 – Sep.68
Escort De Luxe saloon			
B866	Ravenna Red, P	Dark Red	Oct.67 – Sep.68
B867	Aqua – medium, P	Dark Aqua	Oct.67 – Sep.68
B870	Black, P	Black	Oct.67 – Sep.68
B871	Ravenna Red, C	Dark Red	Oct.67 – Sep.68
B872	Aqua – medium, C	Dark Aqua	Oct.67 – Sep.68
B875	Black, C	Black	Oct.67 – Sep.68
Escort Super saloon			
B876	Ravenna Red, P	Dark Red	Oct.67 – Sep.68
B877	Aqua – medium, P	Dark Aqua	Oct.67 – Sep.68
B878	Saddle, P	Saddle	Oct.67 – Sep.68
B879	Black, P	Black	Oct.67 – Sep.68
B880	Ravenna Red, C	Dark Red	Oct.67 – Sep.68
B881	Aqua – medium, C	Dark Aqua	Oct.67 – Sep.68
B882	Saddle, C	Saddle	Oct.67 – Sep.68
B883	Black, C	Black	Oct.67 – Sep.68

Trim code No.	Seat colour(s) and seat face material: (P = PVC, C = Cloth)	Floor covering colour	Dates used
Escort GT saloon			
B884	Ravenna Red, P	Dark Red	Oct.67 – Sep.68
B885	Aqua – medium, P	Dark Aqua	Oct.67 – Sep.68
B886	Saddle, P	Saddle	Oct.67 – Sep.68
B887	Black, P	Black	Oct.67 – Sep.68
B888	Ravenna Red, C	Dark Red	Oct.67 – Sep.68
B889	Aqua – medium, C	Dark Aqua	Oct.67 – Sep.68
B890	Saddle, C	Saddle	Oct.67 – Sep.68
B891	Black, C	Black	Oct.67 – Sep.68
Escort De Luxe estate			
B951	Black, P	Black	Oct.67 – Sep.68
B952	Ravenna Red, P	Dark Red	Oct.67 – Sep.68
B953	Aqua – medium, P	Dark Aqua	Oct.67 – Sep.68
B954	Black, C	Black	Oct.67 – Sep.68
B955	Ravenna Red, C	Dark Red	Oct.67 – Sep.68
B956	Aqua/Aqua – medium, C	Dark Aqua	Oct.67 – Sep.68
8 cwt van			
B957	Black, P	Black	Feb.68 on
6 cwt van			
B958	Black, P	Black	Feb.68 on
Standard Escort saloon			
D366	Black, P	Black	Sep.68 – Aug.70
D367	Parchment, P	Black	Sep.68 – Aug.70
Escort De Luxe saloon			
D368	Black, P	Black	Sep.68 – Aug.70
D369	Parchment, P	Black	Sep.68 – Aug.70
D370	Cherry, P	Cherry – dark	Sep.68 – Aug.70
D371	Beechnut, P	Beechnut – dark	Sep.68 – Aug.70
D372	Aqua, P	Aqua – deep	Sep.68 – Aug.70
D373	Blue, P	Blue – deep	Sep.68 – Aug.70
D374	Black, C	Black	Sep.68 – Aug.70
D375	Cherry, C	Cherry – dark	Sep.68 – Aug.70
D376	Beechnut, C	Beechnut, dark	Sep.68 – Aug.70
D377	Aqua, C	Aqua – deep	Sep.68 – Aug.70
D378	Blue, C	Blue – deep	Sep.68 – Aug.70
Escort De Luxe estate			
D379	Black, P	Black	Sep.68 – Aug.70
D380	Parchment, P	Black	Sep.68 – Aug.70
D381	Cherry, P	Cherry – dark	Sep.68 – Aug.70
D382	Beechnut, P	Beechnut – dark	Sep.68 – Aug.70
D383	Aqua, P	Aqua – deep	Sep.68 – Aug.70
D384	Blue, P	Blue – deep	Sep.68 – Aug.70
D385	Black, C	Black	Sep.68 – Aug.70
B386	Cherry, C	Cherry – dark	Sep.68 – Aug.70
D387	Beechnut, C	Beechnut – dark	Sep.68 – Aug.70
D388	Aqua, C	Aqua – deep	Sep.68 – Aug.70
D389	Blue, C	Blue – deep	Sep.68 – Aug.70

Trim code No.	Seat colour(s) and seat face material: (P = PVC, C = Cloth)	Floor covering colour	Dates used
Escort Super saloon			
D390	Black, P	Black	Sep.68 – Aug.70
D391	Parchment, P	Black	Sep.68 – Aug.70
D392	Cherry, P	Cherry – dark	Sep.68 – Aug.70
D393	Beechnut, P	Beechnut – dark	Sep.68 – Aug.70
D394	Aqua, P	Aqua – deep	Sep.68 – Aug.70
D395	Blue, P	Blue – deep	Sep.68 – Aug.70
D396	Black, C	Black	Sep.68 – Aug.70
D397	Cherry, C	Cherry – dark	Sep.68 – Aug.70
D398	Beechnut, C	Beechnut – dark	Sep.68 – Aug.70
D399	Aqua, C	Aqua – deep	Sep.68 – Aug.70
D400	Blue, C	Blue – deep	Sep.68 – Aug.70
Escort GT			
D401	Black, P	Black	Sep.68 – Aug.70
D402	Parchment, P	Black	Sep.68 – Aug.70
D403	Cherry, P	Cherry, dark	Sep.68 – Aug.70
D404	Beechnut, P	Beechnut – dark	Sep.68 – Aug.70
D405	Aqua, P	Aqua – deep	Sep.68 – Aug.70
D406	Blue, P	Blue – deep	Sep.68 – Aug.70
D407	Black, C	Black	Sep.68 – Aug.70
D408	Cherry, C	Cherry – dark	Sep.68 – Aug.70
D409	Beechnut, C	Beechnut – dark	Sep.68 – Aug.70
D410	Aqua, C	Aqua – deep	Sep.68 – Aug.70
D411	Blue, C	Blue – deep	Sep.68 – Aug.70
Escort Super estate			
D482	Black, P	Black	Mar.69 – Aug.70
D483	Parchment, P	Black	Mar.69 – Aug.70
D484	Cherry, P	Cherry – dark	Mar.69 – Aug.70
D485	Beechnut, P	Beechnut – dark	Mar.69 – Aug.70
D486	Aqua, P	Aqua – deep	Mar.69 – Aug.70
D487	Blue, P	Blue – deep	Mar.69 – Aug.70
D488	Black, C	Black	Mar.69 – Aug.70
D489	Cherry, C	Cherry – dark	Mar.69 – Aug.70
D490	Beechnut, C	Beechnut – dark	Mar.69 – Aug.70
D491	Aqua, C	Aqua – deep	Mar.69 – Aug.70
D492	Blue, C	Blue – deep	Mar.69 – Aug.70

Trim code numbers D572 – D628 were allocated but applied only to the Swedish market.

SVC Ref.
As for Mark I and II Cortinas.

Vehicle number
This consists of:
Two letters:
First letter denotes country of origin;
B = Britain.
D = W. Germany.
Second letter denotes assembly plant;
Right hand drive;
A = Dagenham.
B = Halewood.

C = Langley.
D = Southampton.
Left-hand drive;
A = Cologne, W. Germany.
B = Genk, Belgium.

Two figures;
Body type;

40 = Standard saloon.
42 = De Luxe saloon.
43 = Estate car.
44 = Super saloon.
48 = GT.
49 = Twin Cam.

50 = 6 cwt. van.
51 = 8 cwt. van.
Two letters:
Year and month of manufacture (or date of assembly abroad).
Please see table under Cortina Mark I section.
Five figures;
Vehicle Identification Number, unique to the vehicle.

Paint code
A = Savoy Black or Ebony
M = Ambassador Blue
AZ = Imperial Maroon

AB/BA = Ermine White
BR = Goodwood Green
BS = Monaco Red
BT = Aqua Blue
BU = Platinum Grey
BX = Tuscan Yellow
BY = Glacier Blue
BZ = Spruce Green
CA = Sable
CB = Midnight Blue
CD = Lombard Grey
CF = Alcuda Blue
CG = Malibu Gold
CH = Purbeck Grey
CJ = Lagoon Blue
CL = Black Cherry
CM = Alpina Green
CN = Velvet Blue
CP = Seafoam Blue
CR = Blue Mink
CS = Saluki Bronze
CT = Venetian Gold
CU = Dragoon Red
CV = Silver Fox
CW = Anchor Blue

Escort Van identification plates carry, in addition, details of the maximum gross output of the engine (in bhp), and the engine speed in rpm at which this is obtainable, plus the wheelbase (W.B.) of the vehicle, in inches.

Escort Mark I, August, 1970 on, and Escort Mark II

The vehicle identification plate employed new codes, which can be decoded as follows, under the headings used on the plate:

Typ/type
Five letters:
First letter denotes country of origin;

B = England.
G = W. Germany.
Second letter denotes model;
A = Escort.
Third letter denotes body type;
T = 2 door saloon.
F = 4 door saloon.
D = Estate car.

Fourth letter denotes year;
K = 1970
L = 1971
M = 1972
N = 1973
P = 1974
R = 1975
S = 1976
T = 1977
U = 1978
W = 1979
A = 1980
Fifth letter denotes engine capacity;
G = 1098cc
J = 1298cc
L = 1599cc
One figure; denotes engine type;
1 = LC, ohv.
2 = HC, ohv.
3 = 2V (GT), ohv.

Version
Single letter; denotes appointment level;
S = 'Base'
D = 'Decor' (more fittings)
P = 'High Level'
E = 'Luxury'

Fahrgestell/Vehicle no.
(Some of the information given in this section of the plate duplicates that shown in the 'Typ/Type' section, but is given here in full, to avoid confusion):
Six letters;
First letter denotes country of origin;
B = England.
G = W. Germany.
Second letter denotes assembly plant;
B = Halewood.
S = Saarlouis (W. Germany).
Third letter denotes model;
A = Escort.
Fourth letter denotes body type:
T = 2 door saloon.
F = 4 door saloon.
D = Estate car.
Fifth letter denotes year of production;
(Please see complete table in Cortina Mark I section).
Sixth letter denotes month of production;
(Please see complete table in Cortina Mark I section).
Five figures; Vehicle Identification Number, unique to the vehicle.

Lenk/drive
1 = Left hand drive.
2 = Right hand drive.
Motor/engine
Denotes engine capacity and type, as indicated in 'Typ/Type' section of plate.
Getr/trans
Denotes gearbox type;
B = Manual, with remote gearchange.
D = Automatic.
Achse/axle
Denotes final drive ratio;
A = 3.545:1
B = 3.777:1
C = 3.889:1
D = 4.125:1
E = 4.444:1
N = 4.4111:1

Farbe/colour:
Single letter/figure; denotes paint colours. Note that many of the paint colours changed on a year by year basis.

B = Diamond White
C = Sahara Beige
D = Carnival Red
E = Olympic Blue
F = Purple Velvet
G = Royal Blue
H = Astral Silver
M = Modena Green
Q = Arizona Spring Gold
T = Daytona Yellow
V = Vista Orange
Y = Special Vehicle Order
1 = Miami Blue
3 = Aerosilver/Stardust
5 = Jade Green
7 = Copper Brown
Single figure; denotes model year;
5 = 1975
6 = 1976, etc
Polst/trim

Trim codes, August, 1970 to August, 1973:
These codes consist of two letters;
First letter, denoting colour;
A = Black
F = Marquis
H = Ruby
J = Tan
K = Parchment
M = Deep Aqua

N = Olive
Y = Non standard
Second letter, denoting material;
A, G, H, K or L = PVC
1, 7, 8 or 9 = Cloth

The trim codes you are most likely to encounter for vehicles from August, 1970 to August, 1972 are;
AA = Black, PVC
AI = Black, Cloth
FA = Blue – Marquis, PVC
FI = Blue – Marquis, Cloth
HI = Ruby – light, 71, Cloth
JA = Tan – light, 70, PVC
JI = Tan – light, 70, Cloth
KA = Parchment, PVC
KI = Parchment, Cloth
NA = Olive – light, 70, PVC
NI = Olive – light, 70, Cloth
YA = Non-standard, PVC
YI = Non-standard, Cloth

The trim codes you are most likely to encounter for vehicles from August, 1972 to August, 1973 are:
AA = Black, PVC
AI = Black, Cloth
FA = Blue – Marquis, 71, PVC
FI = Blue – Marquis, Cloth
HA = Ruby – light, 71, PVC
HI = Ruby – light, 71, Cloth
KA = Tan – light, 73, PVC
KI = Tan – light, 73, Cloth
YA = Non-standard
YI = Non-standard
(Note – the numbers 70, 71 and 73 refer to the year in which the colour was first used, where 70 = 1970, etc.).

Trim codes, August, 1973 onwards:
These consist of two letters:
First letter, denoting colour;
A = Black
B = Light Marquis, Tan, 79, or Bitter Chocolate/Tan stripe, for sports types.
C = Cloud, 74
E = Medium Blue, 74, or Light Marquis
F = Blue, 79, or Bitter Chocolate/Blue stripe, for sports types.
H = Red, or Bitter Chocolate/Red stripe, for sports types.
J = Chocolate, 76
K = Light Tan
L = Saddle Brown, 74
M = Green, 77
N = Orange, 77
P = Bitter Chocolate/Individual or Red stripe, for sports types.
S = Grey
W = Light Tan, 76
Y = Non-standard (special vehicle order)
Second letter, denoting material;
1, 4, 5, 7, 8 and 9 = Cloth
A, G and H = PVC/Vinyl
The trim codes you are most

likely to encounter for vehicles from August, 1973 to December, 1975 are:
LA = Saddle, PVC
LI = Saddle, Cloth
EA = Mid Blue, PVC
EI = Mid Blue, Cloth
KA = Light Tan, 73, PVC
KI = Light Tan, 73, Cloth
AA = Black, PVC
AI = Black, Cloth
YA = Non-standard, PVC
YI = Non-standard, Cloth

Other items
The BS AU48:1965 simply acknowledges the U.K. safety belt standard.
The remaining sections of the plate are normally found to be blank. They cover axle load, brakes and K.D. reference, and apply to certain export markets only.

6 Clubs and Specialists

When owning – and particularly when restoring – an 'old' car, it is helpful to belong to the 'one make' club or clubs catering for your particular vehicle. Not only then are you brought into contact with other owners of the same type of vehicle, which is enjoyable in itself, but you also gain a great deal of useful information about the car. This includes, of course, background information on the history of the particular model you own, the availability of spares, and so on. Most clubs publish their own newsletters or magazines, which are filled with articles of technical and general interest, and most also arrange get-togethers, rallies and so on.

Existing club members are usually only too willing to help you with information to enable you to overcome particular problems you may encounter as your restoration project proceeds. In addition you may also have the opportunity of looking closely at other members' cars, to see how they *should* look.

In most clubs there is a certain camaraderie, through sharing a common interest, and you will almost certainly make new friends among the other members, most of whom will be as enthusiastic as you are about your car.

As the cars get older, the availability of spares becomes increasingly important, and the appropriate club for your model is a good place to seek advice on where to get specific parts. Some clubs provide their own spares service, while others normally have an 'information' officer to deal with enquiries. You can save a great deal of time and money by approaching the club at the outset for such advice. Just a word of caution here, though – try to restrict your telephone calls to club officials to 'reasonable' hours. Most such officials take on club duties in addition to their normal daily routine activities – like going to work and looking after families – so, with a few exceptions, they probably won't be too pleased to be contacted at midnight about some elusive mechanical part!

Cortina Clubs

Cortina Mark I Owners' Club, Karen Clarke, Membership Secretary, 6, Hobson's Acre, Gunthorpe, Notts, NG14 7FF. Tel/Fax: 0115 966 3995. E-mail: membership@mk1cortina.com Website: www.mk1cortina.com

Cortina Mark 1 and Ford Owners' Club, Mrs. Linda Chambers, 149 Blue Hill Lane, Wortley, Leeds, LS12 4PD. Tel: 0113 2792973

Ford Cortina Mk II Owners' Club, Lesley Willis, 7, Underdown Road, Herne Bay, Kent, CT6 5BP. Tel: 01227 369114. Website: www.fordcortinamk2oc.co.uk

Ford Cortina 1600E Owners' Club (caters for all Mark II Cortinas), Dave Johnson, Membership Secretary, 16 Woodlands Close, Sarisbury Green, Nr. Southampton, Hampshire, SO31 7AQ.

Ford Cortina 1600E Enthusiasts' Club, Ian Gordan, 4 Harvard Close, Lewes, East Sussex, BN7 2EJ.

Ford Cortina Owners' Club, Stephen Schofield, 20, Abbot Drive, Bootle, Liverpool, L20 0AR. Tel: 0151 286 3725 (after 6pm). Website: www.cortina1to5.f9.co.uk

East Anglian Cortina Group, 11 Newgate Road, Tydd St. Giles, Nr. Wisbech, Cambs, PE13 5LH. Tel: 01945 870854.

Ford Cortina Club of Ireland, John Noel Cronin. Tel: 00353 22 47281.

Lotus Cortina Register, 64 The Queens Drive, Chorley Wood, Rickmansworth, Hertfordshire, WD3 2LT.

Escort Clubs

Sporting Escort Owners' Club (for all rear wheel drive Escorts), 30 Rowan Way, Thurston, Suffolk, IP31 3PU. E-mail: seoc1@aol.com Website: www.seoc.co.uk

AVO Owners' Club, 21 Carey, Hockley, Tamworth, Staffs, B77 5QB. Tel: 01827 707510.

Ford Escort 1300E Owners' Club, 44 Third Avenue, Chelmsford, Essex, CM1 4EY. Tel: 01245 261615. Website: www.1300eownersclub.co.uk

RS Mk II Escort Club
(includes Mexico, RS1800 and
RS2000 models), Phil Teear, 26A
Gloucester Avenue, Syston,
Leicester, LE7 2EL.

RS Owners' Club, P.O. Box
4044, Pangbourne, Berks, RG8
7XL. Tel: 0118 984 1583. Fax:
0118 984 2424.

General Ford Clubs

Pre-'67 Ford Owners' Club
(for Fords introduced before
1967), Alastair Cunninghame,
13 Drum Brae Gardens,
Edinburgh, EH12 8SY.
Tel: 0131 339 1179.

Specialists

Please note: *This list is not
exhaustive. Inclusion on this list
does not imply any
recommendation.*

Cars, spares and services

Aldridge Trimming, St. Marks
Road, Chapel Ash,
Wolverhampton, West Midlands,
WV3 0QH. Tel: 01902 710805.
Fax: 01902 427474.
(Interior trim components/
sets.)

Affordable Classics, Great
Yeldham, Essex. Tel: 01787
237887. Mobile: 07802 713484.
Website:
www.classicfordcars.co.uk
(Classic Fords of all types for
sale and bought.)

Auto Recycle. Tel: 01670
519299. Website: www.auto-
recycle.co.uk (New and used
components for pre-1985 Fords,
including Cortinas and Escorts;
old Fords wanted.)

Automec Equipment and
Parts Ltd., 36 Ballmoor,
Buckingham, Bucks, MK18 1RQ.
Tel: 01280 822818. Fax: 01280
823140. E-mail:
info@automec.co.uk. Website:
www.automec.co.uk (Silicone
brake fluid; copper brake pipe
sets.)

Steve Bilverstone, 2 Hendon
Avenue, Carbrooke, Thetford,
Norfolk, IP25 6JW. Tel: 01953
885439. (Wide range of unused
spares for classic Fords.)

Burlen Services, Frank
Hafmann, Unit 3, 502,
Wallisdown Road, Wallisdown,
Bournemouth, Dorset, BH11
8PT. Tel: 01202 532997. Fax:
01202 532993. (Carburettors,
fuel system spares and engine
management systems/parts.)

Classic Components. Tel:
01535 635829. (Unused genuine
Ford components for classic
models of the 1950s/60s/70s and
80s.)

Classic and Rally Spares,
Aberdeenshire, Scotland –
please see entry under our
'Performance/uprating' section.

Classic Ford Parts, Bracknell,
Berkshire. Tel/Fax: 01344
304064. Mobile: 07802 811566.
E-mail:
classicfordparts@hotmail.com
(Bodywork and mechanical
parts for older Fords.)

Collector's Car Parts, 43/45
Sipson Way, Sipson, West
Drayton, Middlesex, UB7 0DW.
Tel: 020 8897 3774. Fax: 020
8759 8288. E-mail:
collectorscarparts@breathemail.
net (Exhausts, suspension
components and wide ranges of
other parts.)

East Kent Trim Supplies,
Jubilee Road, Worth, near Deal,
Kent, CT14 0DT. Tel: 01304
611681. Fax: 01681 619936.
Website: www.classiccar-
trim.com (Screen rubber seals,

carpet sets, headlinings, etc. for
Cortinas, Escorts and other
models.)

The Escort Agency, South
West Wales. Tel/Fax: 01834
860929. Mobile: 07702 572857.
E-mail:
martin@theescortagency.net
Website:
www.theescortagency.net (New
and used spares, road, rally and
project cars for sale, etc.)

Escort Developments, Wales.
Tel: 01550 720812. Fax: 01550
721518. Mobile: 07971 220572.
(Escort dismantlers; used parts
and complete cars for sale.)

Escort Mk I and II Specialist,
RWD, County Durham. Tel:
07961 539557. (Escort
dismantler, also car sales.)

Ex-Pressed Steel Panels Ltd.,
Ickornshaw Mill, Cowling,
Keighley, West Yorkshire, BD22
0DB. Tel: 01535 632721. Fax:
01535 636977. E-mail:
enquiries@steelpanels.co.uk
Website: www.steelpanels.co.uk
(Wide range of top quality
reproduction body panels and
repair sections for all models
covered by this book.)

Ford Spares (Tendring), near
Colchester, Essex. Tel: 01255
830244. Fax: 01255 831480.
Website: www.ford-spares.co.uk
(Specialist Ford dismantler –
established 1960.)

GMS Capri Spares + Ford
Surplus Spares, Tel/Fax: 0191
3771718. (Various Ford parts,
including distributors, brake
master cylinders, and so on.)

Goldendays, The Grange,
Dereham Road, Easton,
Norwich, Norfolk, NR9 5EJ. Tel:
01603 881155. Fax: 01603
881095. E-mail:
goldendaysparts@aol.com (New
and used bodywork and
mechanical spares for Fords
from 1950 to 1980, including
Cortinas and Escorts.)

GTS Classic and Performance Fords. Tel: 0191 4607080. (New, used and re-manufactured parts for all Fords from 1960 to 1990; old Fords wanted.)

Holden Vintage and Classic, Linton Lane Trading Estate, Bromyard, Herefordshire, HR7 4QT. Tel: 01885 488000. Fax: 01885 488889. E-mail: sales@holden.co.uk Website: www.holden.co.uk/www.bygone-era.co.uk (Vast range of classic spares and accessories.)

Honeybourne Mouldings, Station Road, Alcester, Warks, B49 5EQ. Tel/Fax: 01789 762071 (Suppliers of glassfibre panels.)

LMC Hadrian Ltd., Quartermaster Road, West Wilts Trading Estate, Westbury, Wiltshire, BA13 4JT. Tel: 01373 865088 (order line). Fax: 01373 865464. (Wide range of top quality reproduction body panels/repair sections.)

Mark I Cortina Spares Unlimited, PO Box 6543, Loughborough, Leics, LE11 3WB. Tel/Fax: 01509 264550 (evenings). (Body panels – including reproduction front wings, running gear and drivetrain components.)

MGC Motors UK (Engineering). Tel: 01825 841363. Mobile: 07774 109658. E-mail: markgcarless@hotmail.com (Ford RS Mk I/II/III complete vehicles and parts bought and sold.)

Motor Vehicle Dismantlers Association, 33 Market Street, Lichfield, Staffs., WS13 6LA. Tel: 01543 254254. E-mail: mvdaofgb@aol.com Website: www.mvda.co.uk (Founded in 1943; official organisation representing motor vehicle dismantlers; names, addresses and telephone numbers available of members around the country.)

Newford Parts Centre, Abbey Mill, Abbey Village, Nr. Chorley, Lancashire, PR6 8DN. Tel: 01254 830343. Fax: 01254 830370. E-mail: Newfordpartscentre@btinternet.com Website: www.newfordparts.co.uk (Genuine obsolete Ford parts – late 1940s on, also engine, gearbox and steering box reconditioning services.)

Old Ford Auto Services, London Road, Binfield, Bracknell, Berkshire, RG42 4BS. Tel: 01344 422731. Fax: 01344 307196. E-mail: oldford62@aol.com (Escort Mk I/II mechanical components and 'poly' suspension bushes.)

Old Fords Never Die. Tel: 07770 882801. (Complete cars, dismantled Fords and unused, genuine parts for sale.)

PJG Graphics, Studio 1, Froanes Close, Millhill, Enderby, Leicester, LE9 5XL. Tel: 0116 284 9911. Fax: 0116 284 9922. Mobile; 07802 854 682. ('original spec.' graphics, stripes, etc. for Mark I and II Escorts and other models.)

SIP (Industrial Products) Ltd, Gelders Hall Road, Shepshed, Loughborough, Leics, LE12 9NH. Tel: 01509 500300. Fax: 01509 503154. E-mail: info@sip-group.com Website: www.sip-group.com (Manufacturer of welding and compressed air equipment for do-it-yourself and commercial use.)

Smith and Deakin Fibreglass, 75 Blackpole Trading Estate West, Worcester, WR3 8TJ. Tel: 01905 458886. Fax: 01905 458889. (Glass fibre front wings, bonnets and boot lids, also wide wheel arches, etc.)

Sparky's Capri Heaven. Tel: 0777 1598161. (Full array of used components for classic Fords, including Cortinas and Escorts; some rare items.)

Stonyford Sales. Tel/Fax: 01889 585676. Mobile: 07733 075490. (Wide variety of used components, including high performance items.)

Woolies (I and C Woolstenholmes Ltd), Whitley Way, Northfields Industrial Estate, Market Deeping, Peterborough, Cambs, PE6 8AR. Tel: 01778 347347. Fax: 01778 341847. E-mail: info@woolies-trim.co.uk Website: www.woolies-trim.co.uk (Full range of interior trim components/materials.)

Performance/uprating

Burton Power, 631 Eastern Avenue, Ilford, Essex, IG2 6PN. Tel: 020 8554 2281. Fax: 020 8554 4828. E-mail: sales@burtonpower.com Website: www.burtonpower.com (Performance engines/components, exhausts, transmission parts and so on.)

Classic and Rally Spares, Aberdeenshire, Scotland. Tel/Fax: 01771 622937. Mobile: 07714 332594/087116. (Cars, shells and projects for sale, also performance parts, genuine Ford body panels, new and used spares, etc.)

Classic Spotlights, Tel: 0845 1249741. Fax: 01285 869351. E-mail: Mail@PowerfulUK.com Website: www.PowerfulUK.com (traditional style auxiliary lamps.)

Competition Parts UK, Manor Farm, Collum Lane, Kewstoke, Weston-super-Mare, Somerset, BS22 9JL. Tel: 01934 522999. Fax: 01934 522512. Website: www.competitionpartsuk.co.uk (Broad range of performance parts, also cars and unfinished projects bought.)

Compomotive, 4/6 Wulfrun Industrial Estate, Stafford Road, Wolverhampton, WV10 6HG. Tel: 01902 311499. Fax: 01902 715213. E-mail: sales@comp.co.uk Website: www.comp.co.uk (Wide range of classic/performance road wheels.)

CTM Performance Cylinder Heads, 619 Eastern Avenue, Ilford, Essex, IG2 6PN. Tel: 0208 554 3534. Fax: 0208 518 1299. (Special cylinder heads.)

Cylinder Head Developments, 56 Sherwood Road, Aston Fields Industrial Estate, Bromsgrove, Worcestershire, B60 3DR. Tel/Fax: 01527 870472. Mobile: 07790 934302. E-mail: Enquiries@cylinderheaddevelopments.fsnet.co.uk

Bob Dowen Rally Services. Tel: 01633 838738. Mobile: 07074 838738. (Rally preparation of Group 4 Mk I/II Escorts and other models; spares too.)

DPL Engineering, Tel: 01494 484694/482278. Mobile: 07966 523194. (Engine machining, custom-made fuel tanks, parts for all Ford applications.)

Ford Escort Rally Car Specialists, Red Cross Garage, Knypersley, Biddulph, Stoke-on-Trent, Staffs, ST8 7AA. Tel: 01782 523664. Fax: 01782 518631. Mobile: 07771 856396. (Body shell and mechanical components for motor sport.)

Gartrac Motorsport Fabrication Specialists. Tel: 01428 682263/4. (Escort Mark I and II motor sport components.)

Ian Harwood Ltd., Capenhurst Lane, Whitby, Ellesmere Port, Cheshire, CH65 7AQ. Tel: 0151 339 2801. Fax: 0151 356 5008. (Competition body shells/parts, wheels, transmission components and so on.)

Historic Rallysport. Tel: 01267 233742. E-mail: mark@historicrallysport.co.uk (Suppliers of all components to build Escort RS1600s for motor sport.)

Janspeed Engineering Ltd., Castle Road, Salisbury, Wiltshire, SP1 3SQ. Tel: 01722 21833/4/5/6. (Manufacturers of performance manifolds and other tuning components.)

Leda Suspension, Unit 1, Park Drive Industrial Estate, Braintree, Essex, CM7 1AP. Tel: 01376 326531. Fax: 01376 326530. E-mail: UK@Leda.com (Performance suspension components and kits.)

Peter Lloyd Rallying, Kodak House, Abergarw Trading Estate, Brynmeynyn, Bridgend, Glamorgan, CF32 9LW. Tel: 01656 742777. Fax: 01656 725125. E-mail: peterlloyd2@aol.com Website: www.peterlloydrallying.co.uk (All manner of performance enhancing products, including suspension and transmission components, wheels, etc.)

Mad For It Performance Car Parts, The Old Mill, Doublebois Industrial Estate, Liskeard, Cornwall, PL14 6LD. Tel: 01579 320070 or 321735. Fax: 01579 321747. (Wide array of performance components, rolling shells, and so on.)

Northampton Motor Sport, Unit 14, Rothersthorpe Avenue, Northampton, NN4 8JH. Tel: 01604 766624. Fax: 01604 706334. Website: www.northamptonmotorsport.com (Rolling road tuning, carburettor reconditioning, race/rally preparation and servicing, and so on.)

Performance Wheels Ltd., Unit E, Merry Lees Industrial Estate, Merry Lees, Leicester, LE9 9FS. E-mail: sales@performwheels.co.uk Website: www.performwheels.co.uk and www.superlitewheels.com (Wide variety of sports road wheels.)

Polybush, Clywedog Road South, Wrexham Industrial Estate, Wrexham, LL13 9XS. Tel: 01978 664316. Fax: 01978 661190. E-mail: sales@polybush.co.uk Website: www.polybush.co.uk (Manufacturers of polyurethane suspension bushes.)

Powerstop. Tel: 01608 646837. Website: www.powerstop.co.uk (Performance brake pads/discs, also Sport brake fluid.)

Prepfab Motorsport Engineering, Bodyshell and component manufacturers, Newark-upon-Trent, Notts. Tel/Fax: 01777 228004. Mobile: 07831 678078. E-mail: helen@prepfab.com Website: www.prepfab.com (Tanks, cooling system components, tyres, wide arches and body panels, etc.)

Rallybits.com Motorsport Spares. Tel: 020 8943 1659. (New and used performance components.)

Rally Design, Units 8-10, North Quay, Upper Brents Industrial Estate, Faversham, Kent, ME13 7DZ. Tel: 01795 531871. Fax: 01795 530270. Website: www.raldes.co.uk (Upgraded running gear parts, 'poly' suspension bushes, special clutches and exhausts, etc.)

Rally Weld Fabrications. Tel/Fax: 01495 769778. Mobile: 07970 782375. (Wide range of Escort motorsport products; specialists in all alloy fabrication and welding.)

RallyXtreme. Tel: 01473 737555. Fax: 01473 737555. Mobile: 07808 588411. (Group4 RS1800 Escort for hire, also workshop facilities for customers to prepare their own rear-drive Escorts.)

Retrosport, Scotland. Tel: 01821 641010. (Body shells/components, complete vehicles, performance modifications, etc.)

Retro-UK, PO Box 100, Castleford, West Yorkshire, WF10 3YU. Tel: 01977 555553. Mobile: 07831 111471. Website: www.retro-uk.com (Rear-wheel-drive Escort fabricated parts, new and used components, models, re-trimming service, etc.)

Southern Carburettors and Injection, Unit 6, Nelson Trading Estate, Morden Road, Wimbledon, London, SW19 3BL. Tel: 0208 540 2723. Fax: 0208 540 0857. E-mail: sales@southerncarbs.co.uk (Performance fuel feed system components/units.)

Specialised Engines Ltd., 15 Curzon Drive, Grays, Essex, RM17 6BG. Tel: 01375 378606. E-mail: specialisedengines@talk21.com Website: www.specialisedengines.co.uk (Modified engines, gas-flowed cylinder heads and 'big for small' engine exchanges.)

Spectra Dynamics Ltd., Unit A1, Ffordd Derwen Industrial Estate, Rhyl, LL18 2YR. Tel: 01745 360070. Fax: 01745 360086. Website: www.Deflex.co.uk (Manufacturers of 'Deflex' performance polyurethane bushes, which have a lifetime guarantee.)

Speed Shack, 119 High Street, Yiewsley, West Drayton, Middlesex, UB7 7QL. Tel: 01895 449066. Website: www.speedshack.co.uk (New and used performance parts of all descriptions.)

Mike Stewart Performance Engineering, Unit 1, Muir Houses, The Grange, Errol, Perthshire, Scotland. Tel: 01821 642576. (Engine rebuilds and tuning; specialists in competition repairs and preparation, etc.)

Tubetorque Exhaust Specialists. Tel: 01625 511153. Fax: 01625 501900. E-mail: mark@tubetorque.co.uk Website: www.tubetorque.co.uk (Manifolds and systems in mild and stainless steel.)

Vulcan Engineering, 185 Uxbridge Road, Hanwell, London, W7 3TH. Tel: 020 8579 3202/2988. Fax: 020 8579 7390. E-mail: sales@vulcanengines.com Website: www.vulcanengines.com ('Maxiflow' performance engines and cylinder heads, full engine machining services, Weber carburettors/jetting, etc.)

West Wales Rally Spares, Station Yard, Pontwell, Llandysul, Carmarthenshire, SA44 4AR. Tel: 01559 363731. Mobile: 07074 363731. Fax: 01559 363308. E-mail: Gareth@wwrs.freeserve.co.uk (Rally components, wheels, running gear upgrades, etc.)

Chris Witor. Tel: 07000 787383 or 01749 678152. Fax: 07000 287432 or 01749 671404. Website: www.superflex.co.uk (Supplier of Superflex polyurethane suspension bushes.)

General

ASJ Classic Cars. Tel: 0115 970 5693. Mobile: 07867 621721. (Classic Fords for sale/purchased.)

The Busby Press, PO Box 213, Crawley, West Sussex, RH10 4YL. E-mail: media116@aol.com Website: www.plainandsimpleguide.com (Publishers of 'MIG Welding – The Plain and Simple Guide', an excellent, comprehensive and easy to understand book for beginners at the art of MIG welding, written by Chris Graham.)

Classic Reproductions, PO Box 2031, Coventry, CV7 7YJ. Tel/Fax: 024 7669 4019. (Reproduction decals, chassis plates, handbooks and workshop manuals, etc.)

Mike Davison, 107 Farnham Road, Newton Hall, Durham, DH1 5LN. Tel: 0191 384 4903. (Prints and T-shirts of Works Escorts, 1968-79.)

Midland Racing Models, Churchside Arcade, 20 Little Church Street, Rugby, Warks, CV21 3AW. Tel/Fax: 01788 552133 (after hours, 01788 815220). (Motor sport liveried models.)

Millingtons Models and Collectables, Tel/Fax: 01606 853710. E-mail: andy@millington64.freeserve.co.uk Website: www.motor-web.com/classic6 (Model cars, including Cortinas and Escorts.)

Rallyart, Llyshelyg, Llyn-y-fran Road, Llandysul, Carmarthenshire, SA44 4JW. Tel: 01559 363731. Fax: 01559 363308. E-mail: info@rallyartmotorsportprints.com Website: www.rallyartmotorsportprints.com (Prints of original Ford Escort rally car paintings; also other models covered.)